5 KEYSTONE PARISH EDITION

**SADLIER'S
Coming to Faith Program
Parish Annotated Guide**

COMING TO
GOD'S LIFE

Dr. Gerard F. Baumbach

Dr. Eleanor Ann Brownell

Joan B. Collins

Moya Gullage

Helen Hemmer, I. H. M.

Gloria Hutchinson

Dr. Norman F. Josaitis

Rev. Michael J. Lanning, O. F. M.

Dr. Marie Murphy

Karen Ryan

Joseph F. Sweeney

> The Ad Hoc Committee
> to Oversee the Use of the Catechism,
> National Conference of Catholic Bishops,
> has found this catechetical series to be
> in conformity with the
> *Catechism of the Catholic Church.*

Official Theological Consultant
   The Most Rev. Edward K. Braxton, Ph. D., S. T. D.

Scriptural Consultant
   Rev. Donald Senior, C. P., Ph. D., S. T. D.

Catechetical and Liturgical Consultants
   Dr. Gerard F. Baumbach
   Dr. Eleanor Ann Brownell

Pastoral Consultants
   Rev. Msgr. John F. Barry
   Rev. Virgilio P. Elizondo, Ph.D., S. T. D.

William H. Sadlier, Inc.
9 Pine Street
New York, New York 10005-1002
http://www.sadlier.com

Contents

Overview of the New Edition T6
For the Child, Family, and Parish T8
For the Catechist T10
Scope and Sequence for
Grades 3–6 .... T12
Detailed Scope and Sequence
for Grade 5 .... T14
Catechism of the Catholic Church T18
Catechist's Workshop T19
   Congratulations! You Are a Catechist .. T20
   The Learning-Teaching Process T22
   Text and Guide T24

Catechist's Workshop (cont.)
   Lesson Planning for Different
   Learning Styles T28
   How to Create a Catechetical
   Atmosphere T30
   Hints for Creative Catechesis T32
   How to Teach Thinking Skills
   for Discipleship T34
   Time Line: Shaping Our Catechetical
   Heritage over the Ages T35
   Catechist Resources T36
   Planning Guide T37

Called to Life

For the Catechist 7A
Overview of the Lesson
   Jesus the Good Shepherd
   Life in all its fullness

Faith Alive at Home and in the Parish 11

UNIT 1: JESUS CHRIST BLESSES OUR LIVES

1 Jesus Christ Reveals God

For the Catechist 13A
Overview of the Lesson
   Jesus Christ, human and divine
   God's love in our lives

Faith Alive at Home and in the Parish 17

2 Jesus Christ and the Kingdom of God

For the Catechist 19A
Overview of the Lesson
   The kingdom of God
   The good news of God's love

Faith Alive at Home and in the Parish 23

3 Jesus Christ Blesses Our Lives

For the Catechist 25A
Overview of the Lesson
   Jesus welcomed all people
   Jesus forgave and healed

Faith Alive at Home and in the Parish 29

4 The Church Carries on Jesus' Mission

For the Catechist 31A
Overview of the Lesson
   A welcoming and serving Church
   A healing and forgiving Church

Faith Alive at Home and in the Parish 35

5 The Sacraments and the Church

For the Catechist 37A
Overview of the Lesson
   Jesus, the sacrament of God
   Seven effective signs

Faith Alive at Home and in the Parish 41

6 Celebrating Reconciliation

For the Catechist 43A
Overview of the Lesson
   The good news of God's forgiveness
   Examining our conscience

Faith Alive at Home and in the Parish 47

7 Celebrating Eucharist

For the Catechist 49A
Overview of the Lesson
   Jesus, our Bread of Life
   Eucharist, meal and sacrifice

Faith Alive at Home and in the Parish 53

Unit 1 Review 55
Unit 1 Test 56

UNIT 2: SACRAMENTS OF INITIATION

8 Jesus Christ Brings Us Life

(Baptism)
For the Catechist 57A
Overview of the Lesson
　Reborn of water and the Holy Spirit
　Living our baptismal promises
Faith Alive at Home and in the Parish 61

9 Jesus Christ Strengthens Us

(Confirmation)
For the Catechist 63A
Overview of the Lesson
　Sealed with the Holy Spirit
　Pentecost; witnessing to our faith
Faith Alive at Home and in the Parish 67

10 Jesus Christ Feeds Us

(Eucharist)
For the Catechist 69A
Overview of the Lesson
　The Last Supper
　The real presence of Jesus
Faith Alive at Home and in the Parish 73

11 Our Church Celebrates the Eucharist

(The Mass)
For the Catechist 75A
Overview of the Lesson
　Liturgy of the Word
　Liturgy of the Eucharist
Faith Alive at Home and in the Parish 79

12 The Church Remembers

(Liturgical Year)
For the Catechist 81A
Overview of the Lesson
　Seasons of the Church year
　Feast days of Mary and the saints
Faith Alive at Home and in the Parish 85

13 Celebrating Advent

For the Catechist 87A
Overview of the Lesson
　Promise of a Savior
　Preparing for Jesus, our Savior
Faith Alive at Home and in the Parish 91

14 Celebrating Christmas

For the Catechist 93A
Overview of the Lesson
　Jesus, Savior of all people
　Jesus, one of us
Faith Alive at Home and in the Parish 97

Summary One Review 99
Summary One Test 101

Nihil Obstat
✠ Most Reverend George O. Wirz
Censor Librorum

Imprimatur
✠ Most Reverend William H. Bullock
Bishop of Madison
February 17, 1998

The *Nihil Obstat* and *Imprimatur* are official declarations that a book or pamphlet is free of doctrinal or moral error. No implication is contained therein that those who have granted the *Nihil Obstat* and *Imprimatur* agree with the contents, opinions, or statements expressed.

UNIT 3: SACRAMENTS OF HEALING AND SERVICE

15 Jesus Christ Forgives Us

(Reconciliation)
For the Catechist 103A
Overview of the Lesson
    Jesus' mission of forgiveness
    Celebrating God's forgiveness
Faith Alive at Home and in the Parish 107

16 Jesus Christ Helps Us in Sickness and Death

(Anointing of the Sick)
For the Catechist 109A
Overview of the Lesson
    Jesus' mission of healing
    Caring for the sick and dying
Faith Alive at Home and in the Parish 113

17 Jesus Christ Helps Us to Love

(Matrimony)
For the Catechist 115A
Overview of the Lesson
    Matrimony, a covenant of love
    Practicing unselfish love
Faith Alive at Home and in the Parish 119

18 Jesus Christ Calls Us to Serve

(Holy Orders)
For the Catechist 121A
Overview of the Lesson
    Jesus Christ gives us leaders
    Bishops, priests, and deacons
Faith Alive at Home and in the Parish 125

19 We Share Jesus Christ's Priesthood

(Ministry)
For the Catechist 127A
Overview of the Lesson
    The priesthood of the faithful
    Vocations in our Church
Faith Alive at Home and in the Parish 131

20 Celebrating Lent

For the Catechist 133A
Overview of the Lesson
    Jesus prepares for His ministry
    Lenten Practices
Faith Alive at Home and in the Parish 137

21 Celebrating Easter

For the Catechist 139A
Overview of the Lesson
    Jesus' final entry into Jerusalem
    Holy week and the Easter Triduum
Faith Alive at Home and in the Parish 143

Unit 3 Review 145
Unit 3 Test 146

UNIT 4: A COMMUNITY OF FAITH, HOPE, AND LOVE

22 Becoming a Catholic
(The Marks of the Church)
For the Catechist 147A
Overview of the Lesson
   One, holy, catholic, and apostolic
   Living the four marks of the Church
Faith Alive at Home and in the Parish 151

23 All People Are God's People
For the Catechist 153A
Overview of the Lesson
   Respecting other religions
   Working against prejudice
Faith Alive at Home and in the Parish 157

24 The Gift of Faith
For the Catechist 159A
Overview of the Lesson
   The virtue of faith
   The Apostles' Creed
Faith Alive at Home and in the Parish 163

25 God Fills Us with Hope
For the Catechist 165A
Overview of the Lesson
   The virtue of hope
   Mary, a sign of hope
Faith Alive at Home and in the Parish 169

26 The Gift of God's Love
For the Catechist 171A
Overview of the Lesson
   The virtue of love
   The Works of Mercy
Faith Alive at Home and in the Parish 175

27 Sacramentals
For the Catechist 177A
Overview of the Lesson
   Blessings and holy objects
   The Rosary
Faith Alive at Home and in the Parish 179

28 Celebrations for the Year
For the Catechist 181A
Overview of the Lesson
   Mass of the Holy Spirit
   A Way of the Cross
   We Honor Our Immaculate Mother

Summary Two Review 187
Summary Two Test 189

Day of Retreat 191
Sharing Our Faith as Catholics 197
Prayers and Practices 203
Glossary 209
Our Catholic Identity Section 213
Index 214
Answers to Reviews 217
Scripture References T38

Religion K–8

SCHOOL

Coming to Faith provides a rich, authentic, complete presentation of our Catholic faith for Grades K–6. **Faith and Witness** challenges adolescents with topic-specific courses of study. Each presentation fosters commitment to the teachings and tradition of our Catholic Church.

Sadlier is proud that the **KEYSTONE EDITION** has been found by the Ad Hoc Committee to Oversee the Use of the Catechism, National Conference of Catholic Bishops, to be **in conformity with the** *Catechism of the Catholic Church*.

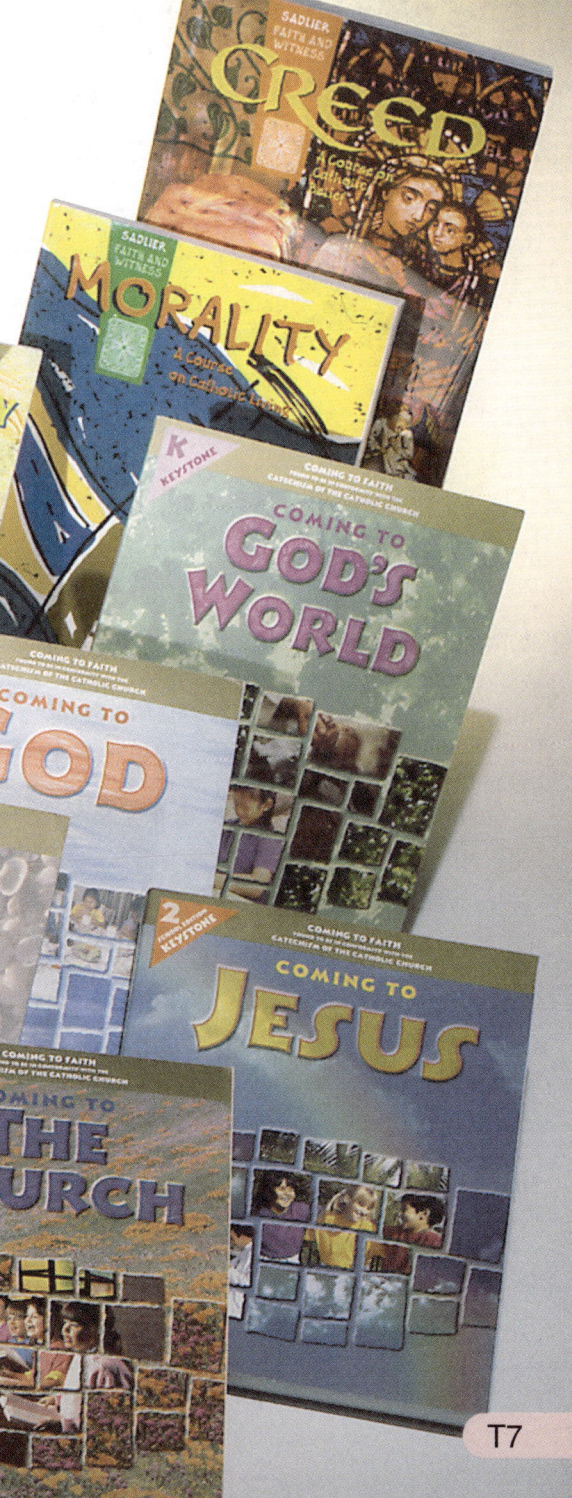

The Ad Hoc Committee to Oversee the Use of the Catechism, National Conference of Catholic Bishops, has found this catechetical series to be in conformity with the *Catechism of the Catholic Church.*

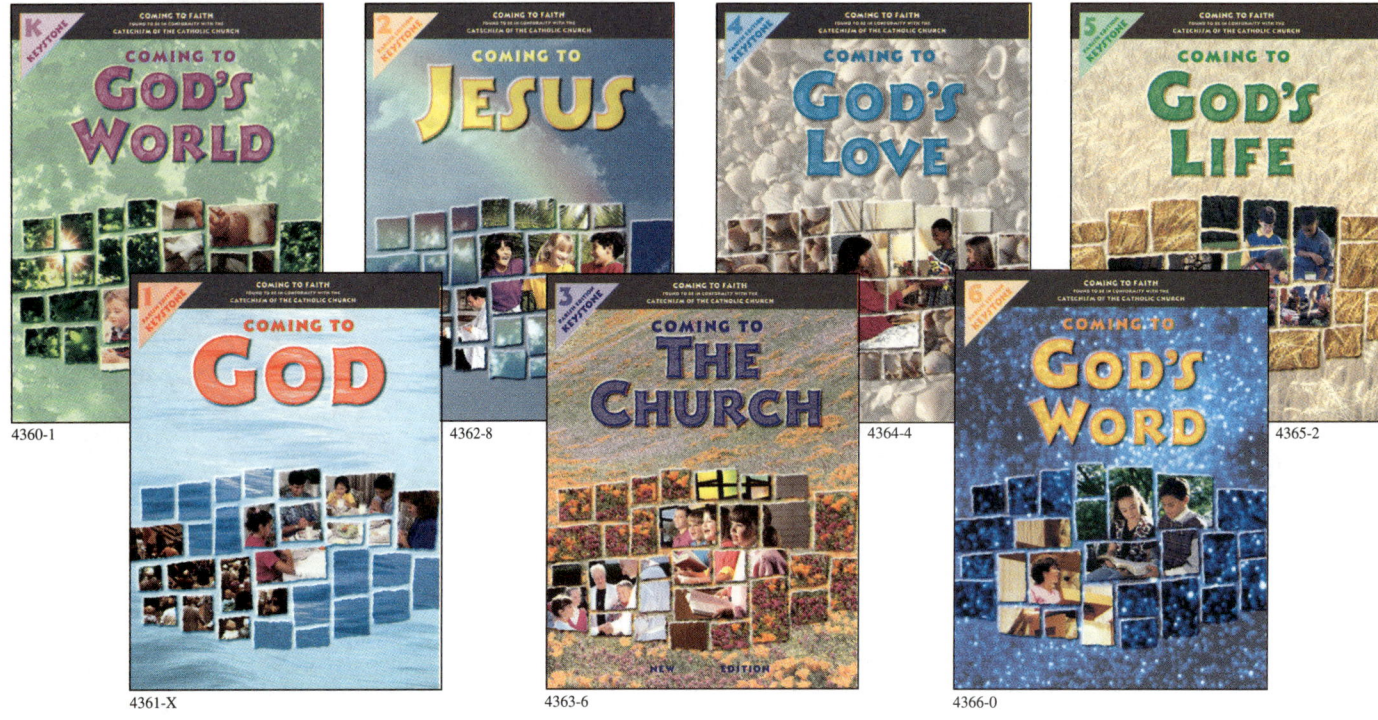

4360-1
4361-X
4362-8
4363-6
4364-4
4365-2
4366-0

Coming to Faith

The **KEYSTONE EDITION** of *Coming to Faith* initiates children into the heart and beauty of Catholic teaching. The treatment of the catechetical content is based on each of the four sections of the *Catechism of the Catholic Church*: the Creed, Sacraments, the Commandments, and Prayer, and is deeply rooted in Scripture. The curriculum of the *Coming to Faith Program* carefully blends child development with faith and moral development.

Each text contains numerous features that help turn the richness of our Catholic heritage into a lived faith. Beautiful **art** makes the text come alive and sparks the child's imagination. **Faith Words** in each chapter provide the child with an extensive vocabulary to develop **Catholic literacy. Our Catholic Identity** is a 16 page tear-out booklet that features Catholic customs, traditions, and heritage. Texts also contain **Catholic Belief Booklets: My Catholic Faith Book** (grades K–3) and **Sharing Our Faith as Catholics** (grades 4–6).

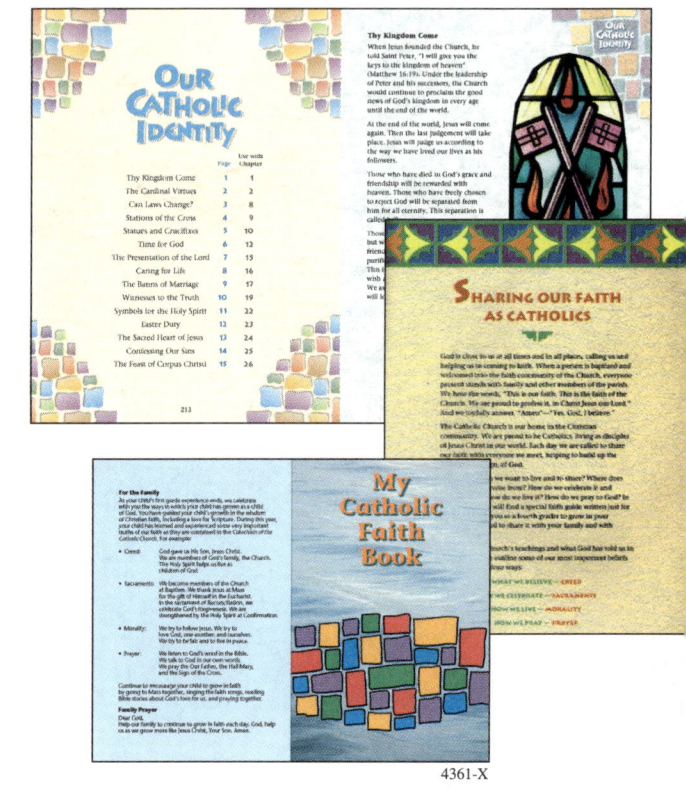

4361-X

T8

Liturgy Lessons are an important component of each text and are designed to enhance the child's understanding of the ebb and flow of the liturgical seasons and celebrations.

Sadlier strives for **Family involvement.** Every chapter concludes with **Faith Alive at Home and in the Parish.** These practical tear-out pages summarize the lesson for the parent, engage the family in creative activities, and encourage review of the chapter's content. A **Family Scripture Moment** also encourages the family to read and discuss a weekly Scripture passage that appears in each lesson.

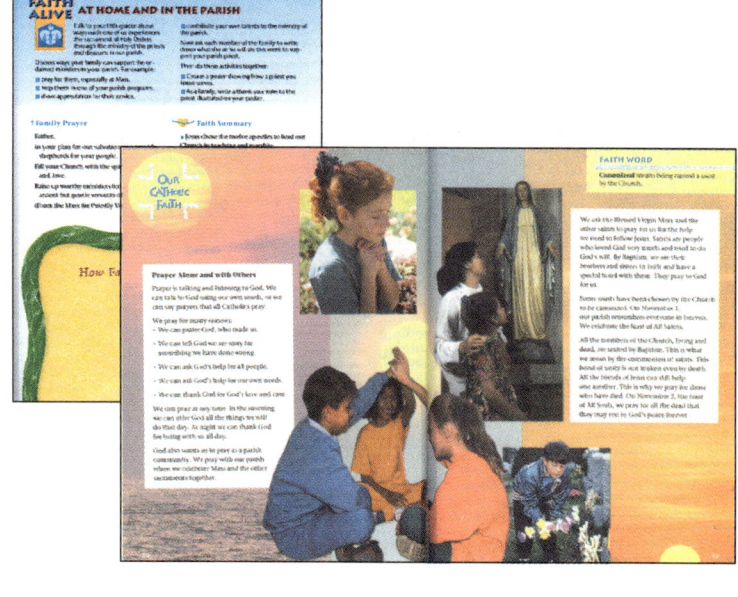

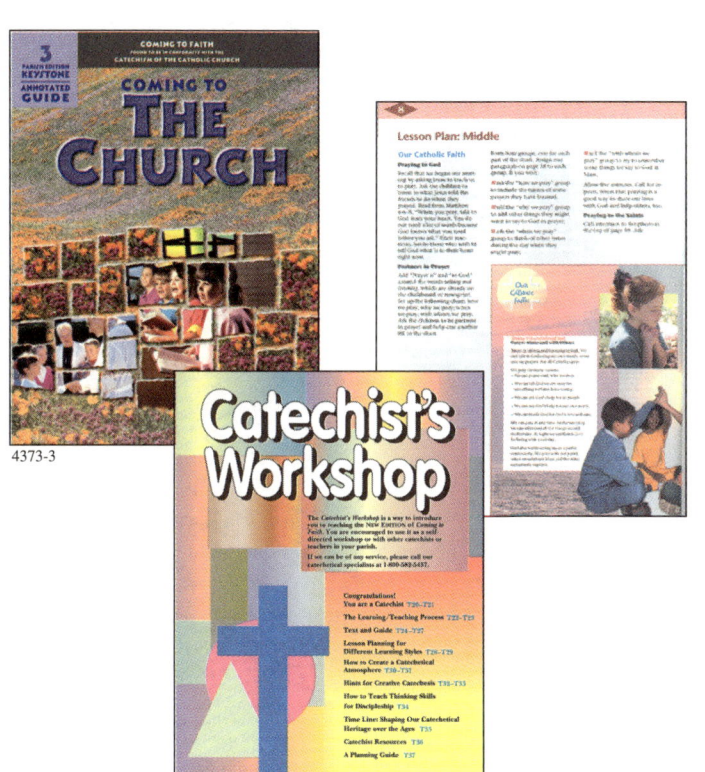

Catechist's Guides are clear, concise, and easy to use! One of the most useful features of the Guide is the **Catechist's Workshop,** a wonderful catechist training tool. Every lesson plan begins with **Adult Background**. **Liturgical** and **Justice and Peace Resources** are provided as well. **Wraparound Lesson Plans** feature clearly stated objectives and activities for each reduced child's page and are easy to follow. **Enrichment** and **Optional Activities** are provided, as well as **Special Needs Activities** that focus on visual, auditory, and tactile-motor needs. *Catechism of the Catholic Church* references occur in each chapter making this a useful and practical reference.

Enrichment Materials include **Activity Books** for each grade level. These provide creative activities that reinforce the theme of each lesson. Age-appropriate **Music** is available for grades K–4 in **cassettes.** A **Blackline Testing Program** is available for each grade level from 1–6, including chapter, unit, and cumulative tests. An **Assessment Program** containing quarterly assessments in standardized test format with a reproducible report for families is also available in paks of 20.

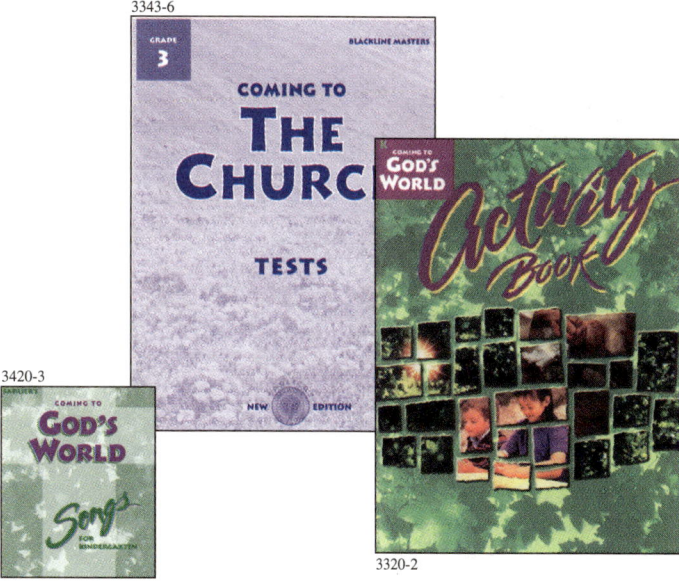

T9

Keystone Parish

> The Ad Hoc Committee to Oversee the Use of the Catechism, National Conference of Catholic Bishops, has found this catechetical series to be in conformity with the *Catechism of the Catholic Church*.

Faith and Witness

The **KEYSTONE EDITION** of the *Faith and Witness Program* is a series of **semester texts** that invites and challenges young people to become committed members of the faith community! It is a creative response to the needs of **adolescents** in the Catholic Church.

Each **semester text** provides a topic-specific course that involves adolescents as active and responsible partners in the learning process. Every lesson incorporates a **Forum Activity** that involves the young person immediately and interactively in the day's work. **Art** is the cornerstone of each session's opening **Prayer Activity**, as well as a powerful learning-teaching tool.

Abundant features focus on **Catholic identity** and **heritage**, **Catholic teachings**, **Scripture Updates**, and highlight **heroes of faith**.

A **Journal** is available for each semester title to furnish the adolescents with a directed reflection on their thoughts, dreams, and questions regarding the theme as it relates to their lives.

5652-5
5653-3

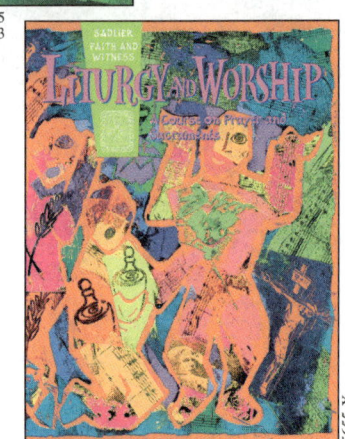

5655-X

5632-0

5654-1

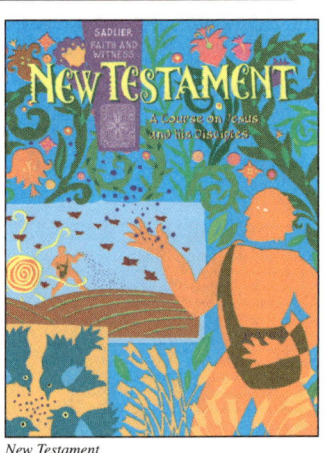

New Testament

5651-7

T10

Because support for the catechist is essential, an easy to use **Catechist's Guide** has been developed. Guides are arranged in a **Wraparound Format**. The activities for the session surround the corresponding text page. Every session begins with an **Adult Focus** for background. The **Teaching Resources Page** outlines everything necessary for the session's work. Three **Reproducible Masters** are incorporated into each session of the Guide. These include an **Activity Handout**, **Assessment Page**, and **Highlights for Home**.

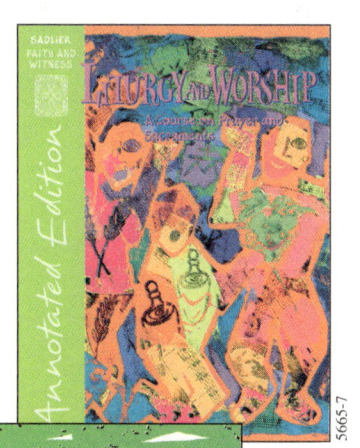

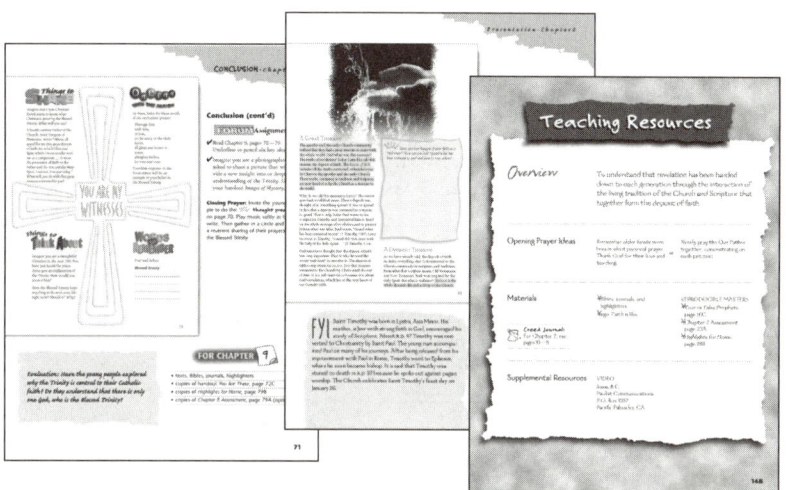

Additional resources include **Posters** featuring the beautiful art of selected chapter openers and **Blackline Master Test Books** which provide additional assessment for each of the semester texts.

Church History: A Course on the People of God is a 15-chapter resource text providing an age-appropriate introduction to the people, events, and movements in the story of our Church. **Prayer Celebrations for the Liturgical Year** provides adolescents with the opportunity to work together to plan their own prayer celebrations for different seasons of the liturgical year. **Parish Guides** are available for fifteen-chapter editions of **Morality** and **Creed,** should you choose the option of one year-long course of study.

T11

SCOPE & SEQUENCE
GRADES 3–6

- *Catechism of the Catholic Church* references for the Grade 5 text are on pages T14–T17.

GRADE	Doctrine	Prayer and Worship	Scripture
3			**Family Scripture Moment:** Gospel of Mark
Unit 1	**Jesus is our Friend;** Jesus' mission and teaching; the calling of the apostles; Jesus' death and resurrection; the Holy Spirit: Pentecost; the Church carries on Jesus' mission; the parish, a place of prayer and worship; *Reconciliation; Eucharist*	Being Jesus' disciple; prayer for help in following Jesus; prayer to the Holy Spirit; bringing about the kingdom of God; visit to the Blessed Sacrament; celebrating forgiveness; planning and celebrating the Mass	Isaiah 43:1 Mark 10:13–16 Matthew 4:18–20; 12:50; 25:40; 28:19, 20 John 13:34–35; 15:9–14 Luke 5:27–28 Acts 2:1–12, 33, 38, 42 1 Corinthians 12:12–27
Unit 2	**Our parish prays:** kinds of prayer, praying to Mary and the saints, praying for the dead; the sacraments; God's life and love in us: grace; sacraments of initiation, healing, and service; sacrament of Reconciliation; celebrating the Mass and the Eucharist; the parts of Mass; *Advent; Christmas*	Evening prayer; living sacrament; Absolution; **Our Father;** invitation to Mass; Sunday Mass; Advent prayer; Christmas celebration	Luke 2:1–20; 10:38–42; 15:11–32 Matthew 26:26–28 Psalm 95 Acts 2:42
Unit 3	**The Bible:** Old and New Testament; the Church passes on the good news; missionaries; the parish church community: pope, bishops, pastors, lay people, the family; vocations; justice and peace for all; the kingdom of God; parables; *Lent; Easter*	Praying with the Bible; sharing good news; vocations: working for God's kingdom; peacemakers; **Our Father;** Stations of the Cross; a Lenten prayer; Jesus' resurrection: an Easter Play	Matthew 6:10; 13:3–8; 33, 44; 22:1–14; 28:16–20 Acts 9:1–5; 11:3
Unit 4	**Marks of the Church:** one, holy, catholic, apostolic; Latin and Eastern Rites; ecumenical movement: Orthodox, Protestants, Judaism; Mary, Mother of the Church; members of the Church; *Prayer, the Saints*	**Apostles' Creed;** prayer for Church leaders; prayer for Christian unity; immaculate conception; prayer to Mary; making a "Faith Book"; **Hail Mary; Grace Before Meals; Act of Contrition; Glory to the Father;** prayers to the saints; prayer for vocation	John 11:41–42; 17:21; 19:26, 27 Matthew 16:18
GRADE 4			**Family Scripture Moment:** Paul's Letters
Unit 1	**Jesus preached the good news;** meaning of the kingdom of God; faith, hope, and love; Law of Love: new commandment; Church guided by the Holy Spirit; Beatitudes; Corporal and Spiritual Works of Mercy; *Reconciliation; Eucharist*	Working for the kingdom of God; living with faith, hope, and love; worship and service; prayer for Jesus' help in living the Beatitudes; Acts of Mercy; prayer for forgiveness; preparing a Mass	Luke 1:28, 31; 4:16–22; 5:1–11, 17–25; 10:27, 30–35; 22:19, 20 Isaiah 31:5; 43:1 Matthew 5:3–10; 6:26, 32–33; 13:44; 25:31–46; 28:20 John 14:26; Micah 6:8; Psalm 40:6–8
Unit 2	**Exodus story;** Ten Commandments: Law of Love; God's will: responsibility; sin: kinds of sin; First, Second, and Third Commandments: putting God first, respecting God's name, the Sabbath; *Advent;* the *Christmas* Season	Covenant with God; prayer for Jesus' help; prayer of petition; praising God's name; **Our Father:** worshipping God; **Angelus; Magnificat; Hail Mary;** *Advent* and *Christmas* prayer services	Exodus 3:14–15; 12:31—19:15; 20:1–17 Psalm 19:7–8 Luke 1:26–39, 46–50, 56; 4:1–12; 10:27 Matthew 2:1–16; 21:12–13 Philippians 2:9–11
Unit 3	**Fourth Commandment:** loving and honoring parents; Fifth Commandment: respecting and choosing life; original sin; Sixth and Ninth Commandments: being faithful to self and others; Seventh and Tenth Commandments: respecting property; Eighth Commandment: truthfulness; *Lent;* the *Easter Triduum*	Praying for our family; honoring life; prayer for faithfulness; sharing our gifts; prayer to speak the truth with love; *Lenten* celebration; *Easter* prayer	Luke 2:41–51 Exodus 20:12–17; Genesis 1:27 Mark 1:15; 10:6–9 John 8:31–32; 10:10; 12:24, 26; 14:6 Psalm 15:2–3 Matthew 16:24; 25:40
Unit 4	**The Holy Spirit:** gifts and guidance; the Laws of the Church; Spirit's help; forming and examining conscience; original sin; forgiveness; Reconciliation: individual and communal rites; Eucharist: the parts of the Mass; *patron saints; Mary and the Rosary*	**Come, Holy Spirit;** prayers to the Holy Spirit; help and guidance from the Church; examination of conscience; prayer for guidance; **Our Father;** celebrating Reconciliation: **Act of Contrition;** praying and participating in Mass; thanking Jesus; prayer service for the saints; mysteries of the rosary; **Hail Mary**	1 Corinthians 2:15; 12:4–5 Matthew 18:21–22 John 20:23 Luke 24:13–35

T12

GRADE	Doctrine	Prayer and Worship	Scripture
5			**Family Scripture Moment: Gospel of John**
Unit 1	**Jesus Christ blesses our lives:** Jesus is both human and divine; the incarnation; Jesus reveals God's love; He preaches the reign of God; He welcomed, forgave, and healed people; His Church carries on Jesus' mission through the sacraments; discipleship; We receive God's grace in the sacraments; *Reconciliation; Eucharist*	A prayer for the year; a prayer for followers of Jesus; prayer of Saint Francis; prayer service of forgiveness; celebrating Reconciliation, Eucharist	John 6:35; 10:7–15; 11:1–44; 13:34; 20:19–23 Matthew 6:9–14; 8:5–11, 23–27; 20:28; 22:34–40 1 John 4:8; Luke 7:18–22; 12:54–56; 23:34 Acts 2:1–13; 1 Corinthians 10:16–17; 11:24; 12:26; 2 Kings 4:1–7
Unit 2	**Sacraments of Initiation; Liturgical Year:** original sin, grace; we receive God's own life (grace) in Baptism; we are strengthened to give witness in Confirmation; we are fed with the Bread of Life in the Eucharist; we remember the story of faith during the Liturgical Year; *Advent; Christmas*	Prayer service for Baptism; prayer for the gifts of the Spirit, celebrating Advent; celebrating Christmas	John 6:35, 41–43, 47–53, 60, 66 Acts 1:7–14; 2:1–13 1 Corinthians 10:16–17; 11:23–25 Ecclesiastes 3:1, 4 Isaiah 9:2, 6, 7; 11:2; 61:1–2, 3 Luke 1:26–33; 2:6–16, 21–32
Unit 3	**Sacraments of Healing and Service:** Jesus forgives and brings peace; rites of Reconciliation; Jesus heals and comforts, Anointing of the Sick; Matrimony, a covenant of love; Holy Orders, a special call to ministry; the priesthood of the faithful; *Lent; Easter*	Prayer services for the sick, for married people, for ordained ministers, for vocations; celebrating Lent; celebrating Easter	Hosea 14:4, 8 James 5:14–15 Numbers 6:24–26 Mark 10:35–45; 11:1–11 Matthew 4:1–11; 28:19–20 John 21:17
Unit 4	**Faith, hope, and love:** the marks of the Church; respect for all people, other beliefs; the virtues of faith, hope, love; the works of mercy; *sacramentals; celebrations*	Prayer service on the marks of the Church; prayer for justice; **the Apostles' Creed;** prayer to be signs of hope; **Hail, Holy Queen;** the **rosary;** prayer of thanks for the presence of God; Mass of the Holy Spirit; Stations of the Cross; honoring Mary	Ephesians 2:20; 4:5–6 Leviticus 19:1–2 Mark 16:15 John 6:58, 60, 66–69 Matthew 14:31; 25:31–46 Romans 8:39 1 John 4:7–11
GRADE 6			**Family Scripture Moment: Prophets—Acts of the Apostles**
Unit 1	**The Bible:** revelation and guidance of the Spirit; books of the Bible; literary forms; faith; creation stories; symbols; grace, a sharing in the divine life; God's promise to Noah; our covenant with God in Jesus; *Reconciliation; Eucharist*	Asking a blessing; praising God's word; praying a Bible verse; a psalm of praise; meditation on mercy; celebrations of Reconciliation, Eucharist	1 Samuel 3:4–21 Genesis 1:1—2:4; 2:5–25; 3:1–24; 6:1—9:17 Isaiah 41:10; John 15:12; 20:23 Mark 5:34; 10:46–52; Exodus 6:7 Psalm 9:1; 16:2; 19:1–4; 63:1–3; 78:1–4
Unit 2	**The Covenant:** our ancestors' covenant with God; our covenant with God; Rebecca and Joseph; channels of grace; Moses, Passover; the Exodus; the Ten Commandments; Samson, Ruth; *Advent; Christmas*	Meditation on faithfulness, prayer to be channels of grace; prayer service on freedom; Commandments prayer service; celebrations for Advent, Christmas	Genesis 9:12–13; 12:1–3, 7; 15:5; 17:1–16; 22:1–18; 24:1–67; 25:27–34; 27:5–29; 37—50 Exodus 1—12; 12:37—15:21; 19:1–8 Judges 13—16; Ruth 1—4; Isaiah 9:2 Matthew 3:17
Unit 3	**Living by Faith:** Israel's golden age, Saul, David; Solomon; the prophets: Elijah, Hosea, Micah, Isaiah, Jeremiah, Ezekiel; the Exile and the return; *Lent; Easter*	Prayer of Micah; prayer service of prophets; prayer of Isaiah; prayer for second chances; celebrations for Lent, Easter	1 Samuel 8:1—15:10; 16:4—17:53 2 Samuel 5:6—6:19; 11:1—12:15 1 Kings 3:1–15; 17—18 2 Chronicles 5:2–14; Hosea 1:1—3:1; Isaiah 1:4, 17, 18; 2:8; 6:1–8; 42:1–4; 53 Romans 6:3–4
Unit 4	**The New Testament:** Jesus and His times; the ministry of Jesus; the disciples; Beatitudes; Bread of Life; the early Church, Paul; discipleship, the works of mercy, prayer; Mary and the saints; a *Mass for Peace; celebrating vocations*	Scripture meditation (Matthew 4:18–22); **Our Father; prayer of Saint Francis;** prayer service for vocations; prayer of inner stillness; celebrating the feasts of All Saints, All Souls; **Angelus; Litany of Our Lady**	Matthew 4:18–22; 5:3–10 Luke 1:38; 2:46; 4:18–21; 10:25–37 John 13:35; 15:12; 20:1–18 Mark 6:34–44 Acts 9:1–10 Jeremiah 1:4–5

SCOPE & SEQUENCE
GRADE 5

UNIT 1 — Jesus Christ Blesses Our Lives

Chapter	Our Life	Sharing Life	Our Catholic Faith	Coming to Faith	Practicing Faith
1. *Jesus Christ Reveals God*	I look at pictures that tell how God is with us today.	We share ways Jesus showed He was both human and divine.	**Incarnation** Stories from the gospels show us how Jesus knew all our human joys and sorrows, and was also God's own Son.	We explain in sentence completions how Jesus is both human and divine.	We pray together about how to respond in life the way Jesus did.

- Doctrinal Correlation to the *Catechism of the Catholic Church*: paragraph 464   *Our Catholic Identity*: Family Portraits of Jesus

2. *Jesus Christ and the Kingdom of God*	I explore good news and create some of my own.	We share ideas about what might be the best news of all.	**The Reign of God** Jesus announced the good news of the reign of God's life and love in the world.	We act out a gospel scene of the kingdom and give Jesus' response.	We share what it means to belong to God's reign; we pray the Our Father.

- Doctrinal Correlation to the *Catechism of the Catholic Church*: paragraph 526   *Our Catholic Identity*: Migrant Ministry; St. Teresa of Avila

3. *Jesus Christ Blesses Our Lives*	I talk about how I would resolve difficulties.	We share why and how we should heal separations.	**Jesus, Healer and Forgiver** Jesus taught that forgiveness heals the separation from God and others caused by sin.	We role-play situations involving healing and forgiveness.	We pray together and decide how we will be welcomers, healers, forgivers.

- Doctrinal Correlation to the *Catechism of the Catholic Church*: paragraphs 440, 547   *Our Catholic Identity*: Servants of the Lord

4. *The Church Carries On Jesus' Mission*	I learn something about Jesus' disciples.	We discuss ideas about difficulties in working together.	**The Church—Jesus' Mission** Like Jesus, the Church serves, heals, and forgives.	We share ways our parish serves, heals, and forgives, and how we can share in that work.	We decide on a group project to serve, welcome, or heal. We offer our gifts to Jesus.

- Doctrinal Correlation to the *Catechism of the Catholic Church*: paragraph 789   *Our Catholic Identity*: Parish Communities

5. *The Sacraments and the Church*	I think of ways I show people how I feel.	We discuss ways people give signs of caring; Jesus' signs.	**The Sacraments** Sacraments are effective signs through which Jesus Christ shares God's life and love with us.	We share how Jesus is a sign of God's love and how we can be signs of love, too.	We share a prayer service on the sacraments.

- Doctrinal Correlation to the *Catechism of the Catholic Church*: paragraph 1076

6. *Celebrating Reconciliation*	I learn about another culture's way of reconciling.	We share the best ways for us to show forgiveness.	**Sacrament of Reconciliation** We recall how to prepare for and celebrate Reconciliation.	We work together to make some "We can . . ." statements.	We celebrate a prayer service of forgiveness.

- Doctrinal Correlation to the *Catechism of the Catholic Church*: paragraphs 447, 448

7. *Celebrating Eucharist*	I read the story of Elisha from the Old Testament.	We imagine what special food we would ask for and recall the food Jesus gave us.	**The Mass** At Mass we celebrate the Eucharist in the Liturgy of the Word and the Liturgy of the Eucharist.	We recall what happens at Mass and express our thanks for the real presence of Jesus.	We plan a celebration of the Eucharist in which we will all take part.

- Doctrinal Correlation to the *Catechism of the Catholic Church*: paragraph 1346

The **Coming to Faith** program makes inclusive use of the four signs of catechesis as called for in the *National Catechetical Directory* (NCD): biblical, liturgical, ecclesial, and natural. In this Scope and Sequence, the signs are noted by these symbols:

Biblical which show how God is revealed in the Scriptures.

Liturgical which flow from the sacramental life of the Church.

Ecclesial which include doctrinal and creedal formulations.

Natural which are expressed in the environment, arts, science, and culture.

UNIT 2 — Sacraments of Initiation

	Chapter	Our Life	Sharing Life	Our Catholic Faith	Coming to Faith	Practicing Faith
8	Jesus Christ Brings Us Life (Baptism)	I finish a story about new life.	We discuss life as God's greatest gift to us.	**Baptism** At Baptism we are initiated into the Church, the body of Christ.	We work together to make a mural of the signs of Baptism.	We celebrate our Baptism in a prayer service.

• Doctrinal Correlation to the *Catechism of the Catholic Church*: paragraph 1213 *Our Catholic Identity*: Important Church Records

9	Jesus Christ Strengthens Us (Confirmation)	I read a story about the North American martyrs.	We discuss things that make it difficult to be a Christian.	**Confirmation** We are sealed with the gift of the Holy Spirit and strengthened to give witness.	We share ways to give witness to the faith.	We pray together for the gifts of the Holy Spirit.

• Doctrinal Correlation to the *Catechism of the Catholic Church*: paragraph 1285 *Our Catholic Identity*: Fruits of the Holy Spirit

10	Jesus Christ Feeds Us (Eucharist)	I explore a gospel story about Jesus the Bread of Life.	We discuss the hungry of the world and why Jesus called Himself the Bread of Life.	**Eucharist** The Eucharist is the sacrament of the Body and Blood of Christ.	We discuss how we would explain the Eucharist to someone who is not a Catholic.	We make a group plan about how and when we will share Jesus this week.

• Doctrinal Correlation to the *Catechism of the Catholic Church*: paragraph 1359 *Our Catholic Identity*: The Gifts of Bread and Wine

11	Our Church Celebrates the Eucharist (The Mass)	I read a story about someone who makes a difference.	We discuss people who have made a difference in our lives.	**The Mass** We learn more about the two major parts of the Mass.	We remember what happens during each part of the Mass.	We decide how we can live as the body of Christ in the world.

• Doctrinal Correlation to the *Catechism of the Catholic Church*: paragraph 1346 *Our Catholic Identity*: Communion Under Both Kinds

12	The Church Remembers (Liturgical Year)	I learn a scripture verse about how everything has a season.	We discuss the "seasons" that happen in our lives and how God is always with us.	**Liturgical Year** The seasons of the Church year remind us that we always live in the presence of God.	We plan how we would explain the Liturgical Year to a fourth grader.	We celebrate a prayer service together on the Liturgical Year.

• Doctrinal Correlation to the *Catechism of the Catholic Church*: paragraph 1171 *Our Catholic Identity*: Liturgical Colors; Liturgical Time

13	Celebrating Advent	I read a legend that tells me how I am to prepare for Jesus.	We share together ways Jesus comes into our lives.	**Advent** We follow Mary by serving others as we await Jesus' coming.	We recall Isaiah's prophecy of the Savior and plan how we will serve.	We celebrate an Advent prayer service.

• Doctrinal Correlation to the *Catechism of the Catholic Church*: paragraph 489

14	Celebrating Christmas	I read about *Las Posadas* and Mary and Joseph in Bethlehem.	We share Christmas customs; we tell what is most important about Christmas.	**Christmas** Jesus is the Light of the World. Jesus means "God saves."	We plan and have our own *Las Posadas*.	We dramatize the Christmas story.

• Doctrinal Correlation to the *Catechism of the Catholic Church*: paragraph 525

SCOPE & SEQUENCE
GRADE 5

UNIT 3 — Sacraments of Healing and Service

Chapter	Our Life	Sharing Life	Our Catholic Faith	Coming to Faith	Practicing Faith
15 *Jesus Christ Forgives Us (Reconciliation)*	I explore a story about grace.	We discuss what it means to be truly forgiven.	**Reconciliation** This is the sacrament in which we are forgiven by God and the Church for our sins.	We review the key ideas associated with Reconciliation.	We celebrate together a prayer service of forgiveness.

- Doctrinal Correlation to the *Catechism of the Catholic Church*: paragraph 1443 *Our Catholic Identity*: The Seal of Confession

16 *Jesus Christ Helps Us in Sickness and Death (Anointing of the Sick)*	I read a true story about healing.	We discuss how we would feel facing death.	**Anointing of the Sick** This sacrament brings God's special blessings to the sick, the elderly, the dying.	We act out together the celebration of the sacrament.	We decide how we will help someone who is sick; we pray together for all those who suffer.

- Doctrinal Correlation to the *Catechism of the Catholic Church*: paragraph 1514 *Our Catholic Identity*: Preparing for a Sick Call

17 *Jesus Christ Helps Us to Love (Matrimony)*	I think about what makes marriage work.	We discuss why it is sometimes difficult to keep promises.	**Matrimony** This sacrament is a powerful and effective sign of Christ's presence; it joins a man and woman together for life.	We describe what the wedding vows mean and why Matrimony is a sacrament of service.	We pray together for all married couples.

- Doctrinal Correlation to the *Catechism of the Catholic Church*: paragraph 1603 *Our Catholic Identity*: The Ministers of Marriage

18 *Jesus Christ Calls Us to Serve (Holy Orders)*	I explore ways priests serve.	We share how priests have served us.	**Holy Orders** Bishops, priests, and deacons are ordained in Holy Orders to serve the Church.	We imagine a day in the life of a priest.	We choose a way we can help the priests in our parish.

- Doctrinal Correlation to the *Catechism of the Catholic Church*: paragraph 1572 *Our Catholic Identity*: Permanent Deacons; A Daring Priest

19 *We Share Jesus Christ's Priesthood (Ministry)*	I learn how people in the Church serve others.	We discuss how our Baptism calls us to share Jesus' ministry.	**Christian Vocation** We each have a call to spread the good news of Christ. It is our vocation.	We explain what a vocation is and how we can use our gifts.	We work together to choose a way we will serve others this week.

- Doctrinal Correlation to the *Catechism of the Catholic Church*: paragraph 871

20 *Celebrating Lent*	I explore what material things mean to me.	We discuss what can be done about sharing the world's goods.	**Lent** Lent prepares us to enter more fully into the death and resurrection of Jesus.	We choose what we will do to be closer to Jesus during Lent.	We celebrate a Lenten prayer service.

- Doctrinal Correlation to the *Catechism of the Catholic Church*: paragraph 1164

21 *Celebrating Easter*	I read a true story about new life.	We share experiences of new life.	**Easter Triduum** The paschal mystery celebrates the events of Jesus' "passing" through suffering and death to new life.	We recall what we celebrate on each day of the Triduum and how we can take part.	We celebrate an Easter prayer service; we renew our baptismal promises.

- Doctrinal Correlation to the *Catechism of the Catholic Church*: paragraph 1165

UNIT 4 — Becoming a Community of Faith, Hope, and Love

Chapter	Our Life	Sharing Life	Our Catholic Faith	Coming to Faith	Practicing Faith
22 Becoming a Catholic (The Marks of the Church)	I think about what qualities a good team should have.	We discuss what marks or qualities the Church should have.	**Marks of the Church** The Church is one, holy, catholic, and apostolic.	We plan a TV spot telling how our parish lives the marks of the Church.	We pray and decide together on how we can live the marks.

- Doctrinal Correlation to the *Catechism of the Catholic Church*: paragraph 811

Chapter	Our Life	Sharing Life	Our Catholic Faith	Coming to Faith	Practicing Faith
23 All People Are God's People	I examine ideas about prejudice.	We share thoughts on prejudice and how God wants us to treat all people.	**Respect for Others** The Church teaches that we must treat all people and all religions with respect. We must work to overcome prejudice and racism.	We discuss how we can learn to live with others without prejudice.	We do a prayer activity to remind us that we are all God's people.

- Doctrinal Correlation to the *Catechism of the Catholic Church*: paragraph 839

Chapter	Our Life	Sharing Life	Our Catholic Faith	Coming to Faith	Practicing Faith
24 The Gift of Faith	I explore a gospel story about faith.	We share ideas and thoughts about what faith is.	**Virtue of Faith** Faith enables us to believe in God, to accept what God has revealed, and to live God's will. *Apostles Creed.*	We share what our faith means to us and what the Apostles' Creed teaches.	We express our faith in art and words.

- Doctrinal Correlation to the *Catechism of the Catholic Church*: paragraph 198   *Our Catholic Identity*: Saints Old and New

Chapter	Our Life	Sharing Life	Our Catholic Faith	Coming to Faith	Practicing Faith
25 God Fills Us with Hope	I read about Pope John Paul II and his message of hope to young people.	We share experiences of feeling hopeless and hope-filled.	**Virtue of Hope** Hope enables us to trust that God will always be with us.	We discuss situations in which the virtue of hope is needed.	We pray together that we will be people of hope and that we will share hope with others.

- Doctrinal Correlation to the *Catechism of the Catholic Church*: paragraph 1817   *Our Catholic Identity*: Paschal Candle; Alpha and Omega

Chapter	Our Life	Sharing Life	Our Catholic Faith	Coming to Faith	Practicing Faith
26 The Gift of God's Love	I read John's letter about what God's love is.	We discuss how Jesus expects us to love others.	**Virtue of Love** Love enables us to love God, our neighbor, and ourselves. *The Works of Mercy.*	We rewrite the Works of Mercy as action statements.	We plan a work of mercy that we will do as a group project.

- Doctrinal Correlation to the *Catechism of the Catholic Church*: paragraph 1823

Chapter	Our Life	Sharing Life	Our Catholic Faith	Coming to Faith	Practicing Faith
27 Sacramentals	I explore some ways our country honors people.	We share things in our parish church that helps us remember Jesus, Mary, and the Saints.	**Sacramentals** Sacramentals are blessings, actions, and objects that remind us of God, Jesus, Mary, and the saints.	We tell how sacramentals help us remember God's presence in our lives.	We explore how the lives of the saints can help us live as disciples of Jesus.

- Doctrinal Correlation to the *Catechism of the Catholic Church*: paragraph 1668

28 Celebrations for the Year	This Chapter does not follow the configuration of the others. It suggests three separate celebrations that can be used at different times during the year. There is a *Mass of the Holy Spirit*, *A Way of the Cross*, and a *Prayer Service Honoring Mary*.

- Doctrinal Correlation to the *Catechism of the Catholic Church*: paragraph 1674

The Catechism of the Catholic Church

What Is the Catechism?

After many years of intense work and preparation, the *Catechism of the Catholic Church* was officially promulgated by His Holiness, Pope John Paul II, in 1992, some thirty years after the beginning of the Second Vatican Council.

What is this catechism and why is it such a gift to our Church? A catechism is a faithful presentation of the truths of the Catholic Church. These include the teachings of Sacred Scripture, the Tradition of the Church, and the teachings of the magisterium of the Church. A catechism does not teach new doctrine but faithfully hands on the received doctrine of the Church. However, the content of a catechism is often presented in a new way to help answer the questions and issues raised in each age.

That is why we have been given this gift of the new *Catechism of the Catholic Church*, to pass on to the faithful in our day the authentic teaching of the Catholic Church and to help us answer in adult language the challenges that are ours at the end of the twentieth century and those that will come in the new millennium. The *Catechism* is not in a question-and-answer format, and does not address the kinds of methodologies available for handing on the faith to our children, young people, and adults. Rather, it concerns itself with the clear presentation of Catholic teaching on the truths of faith.

For Whom Is It Written?

The *Catechism of the Catholic Church* is addressed, first of all, to bishops, who are the principal teachers of our Catholic faith. It is also addressed to those who prepare catechetical materials, priests, catechists, and all those who wish to know what the Catholic Church believes. It is not intended to replace local catechisms or deny cultural differences throughout the world, but to help preserve the unity of faith and fidelity to the deposit of faith.

Sadlier's Involvement

For over 165 years, William H. Sadlier, Inc., has worked in service to the Catholic Church. We welcome the publication of the *Catechism of the Catholic Church* as a reference for the development of our future catechetical materials. We have always ensured that our books accurately reflect the authentic teachings of the Church. This new catechism, the first such major catechism in more than 400 years, provides us with an essential standard for the presentation of Church teaching. As we revise existing works and develop new materials for the generations to come, we will certainly look to the *Catechism of the Catholic Church* for guidance and inspiration.

The *Coming to Faith* Program meets the high standards set by this gift of the *Catechism* and the four pillars that provide its basic framework. Indeed, the *Catechism*'s fourfold emphasis on creed, sacraments, the moral life of the Christian, and prayer, rooted in and supported by the Scriptures, is an emphasis and structure with which we feel a particular compatibility. In addition, Sadlier's methodology and pedagogy have long supported and provided for the authentic presentation of Catholic doctrine, and will continue to do so in the future.

We are proud that we are co-publishers of the *Catechism of the Catholic Church* in the United States in both English and Spanish editions. May it be and remain a work of reference, resource, and renewal.

Easy Reference for the Catechist

To assist you in understanding the relation between the *Catechism of the Catholic Church* and the *Coming to Faith* Program, there are the following references in the program's annotated guides:

▶ In the **Scope and Sequence Chart**, a reference to the appropriate *Catechism* paragraph for each major chapter theme;

▶ For each lesson, a reference to the pertinent *Catechism* paragraph in the **For the Catechist—Spiritual and Catechetical Development** pages.

Catechist's Workshop

The *Catechist's Workshop* is a way to introduce you to teaching the *Coming to Faith* Program. You are encouraged to use it as a self-directed workshop or with other catechists or teachers in your parish.

If we can be of any service, please call our catechetical specialists at 1-800-582-5437.

**Congratulations!
You are a Catechist** T20–T21

The Learning/Teaching Process T22–T23

Text and Guide T24–T27

**Lesson Planning for
Different Learning Styles** T28–T29

**How to Create a Catechetical
Atmosphere** T30–T31

Hints for Creative Catechesis T32–T33

**How to Teach Thinking Skills
for Discipleship** T34

**Time Line: Shaping Our Catechetical
Heritage over the Ages** T35

Catechist Resources T36

A Planning Guide T37

T19

CATECHIST'S WORKSHOP

Congratulations! You Are a Catechist

The Church is responsible for continuing the mission of Jesus to proclaim and teach about the kingdom of God. Through its ministry, the Catholic Church invites people such as yourself to share in this responsibility.

You have been called to a very special ministry in the Church. You have been chosen to be a catechist, a minister of the word in your parish or school. Each time you gather to share the faith of the Church, you are proclaiming the good news that Jesus Christ is risen and present in our lives. Think:

● Why were you invited to be a catechist?

● What gifts or talents do you believe you bring to this ministry?

What Is Catechesis?

Through catechesis, we discover and learn the Christian message passed on by the community of faith. We are challenged as believers to justice, peace, and service as we are formed within the worshiping community. As Pope John Paul II reminds us in describing the early Church's catechetical efforts, catechesis is about "making disciples" (*Catechesi Tradendae*, 1).

Sharing the Light of Faith, the *National Catechetical Directory* (NCD), provides this comprehensive statement about catechesis: "Catechesis refers to efforts which help individuals and communities acquire and deepen Christian faith and identity through initiation rites, instruction, and formation in conscience. It includes both the message presented and the way in which it is presented" (NCD, 5).

What Role Do Parents Play in Catechesis?

It is within the family that faith is nurtured and grows. Parents have a vital role in their children's faith development. Indeed, families catechize by their attitudes, values, and beliefs. As a catechist you are called to assist families. As the NCD reminds us, "parents, catechists, and community all have roles in the catechesis of the young" (NCD, 181).

> *God promises you:*
> Before I formed you in the womb I knew you, before you were born I dedicated you....
> Have no fear before them....
> See, I place my words in your mouth!
>
> Jeremiah 1:5, 8, 9

What Do Catechists Do?

As a catechist your role is to lead young people to an understanding of their Catholic faith and to encourage them and their families to participate actively in the parish community.

As a catechist you promote important catechetical goals:

● *information*—religious concepts and content presented according to the age and readiness of your group

● *formation*—prayer and worship experiences that invite and engage the young believers to adhere to and deepen their faith

> Go, therefore, and make disciples of all nations....
>
> Matthew 28:19

● *instruction*—in Creed, the Scriptures, sacraments and ritual, Christian living and morality, and our common prayer heritage

Your *Catechist's Annotated Guide* will help you to prepare yourself by studying the teachings of our faith, by deepening your understanding of Catholic doctrine, and by becoming more familiar with the teachings of Scripture. It will also enable you to plan your lessons creatively so that you may present the good news of the Catholic faith with enthusiasm and confidence.

What Is Important When Teaching Fifth Graders?

You have been asked to help bring a group of children to understand and live their Catholic faith according to their age and readiness. It is neither necessary nor expected that the children will come to an adult understanding of the teachings of our faith. It is important, however, that each child begin to develop a relationship with God, that he or she learn to praise God and to experience God through prayer. This is the beginning of a lifelong experience with God.

Keep in mind that the experiences that the home provides can enrich the development of the child's religious imagination and the practice of her or his Catholic faith. For this reason, it is important to understand the child's background and to find ways to involve the family in the religious education of their child. Here are some things you can do:

◐ Invite families to participate in the children's special liturgies, projects, and celebrations.

◐ Involve families regularly through the *Faith Alive at Home and in the Parish* pages and family faith-sharing activities.

◐ Encourage family-parish activities and celebrations.

What Is Helpful to Know About Fifth Graders?

◐ Fifth graders are developing the ability to think abstractly. They are capable of formulating abstractions of concrete objects such as love, peace, and justice, which are so prominent in *Coming to God's Life*.

◐ Fifth graders have a keen sense of what is and what is not fair. They are, however, very much influenced by the values of their peer group. Parents and catechists need to work together to help the young people develop a correct moral sense of what is right and wrong by providing guidance and good example.

◐ Fifth graders are ready to assume certain responsibilities for their lives and their faith. *Coming to God's Life* will help your fifth graders to understand the truths of faith, to respond to them emotionally, and to practice them in their daily lives.

How Can You Help Your Fifth Graders Grow in Faith?

◐ Be alert to peer pressure in the group and its effect on the behavior of the young people. Praise individual positions and accomplishments.

◐ Teach personal responsibility by allowing the young people freedom to make personal choices. Provide guidance in their efforts at decision making.

◐ Teach justice by practicing justice within the group. Help the young people to see that treating others justly leads to peace.

CATECHIST'S WORKSHOP

THE LEARNING/TEACHING PROCESS

- Shared Christian Praxis is the learning/teaching process you will be using in the *Coming to Faith* Program.

- This process helps you to see the relationship between our life and our faith.

- The process begins with a focusing prayer.

- Shared Christian Praxis is made up of five movements, described briefly below.

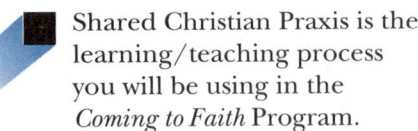

Movement One
Our Life

Invites the children to think about and name a personal or faith experience related to the theme of the lesson.

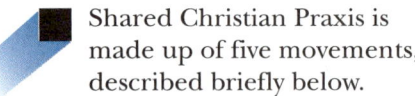

Movement Two
Sharing Life

Invites the children to critical reflection by using their memories, imaginations, and reasoning abilities. The children are encouraged to think, share, or talk with God, one another, and/or the catechist about the life or faith experiences named in *Our Life*.

Movement Three
Our Catholic Faith

Presents the Catholic Church's Story and Vision, which includes:

- Doctrine
- Scripture
- Tradition
- Liturgy
- Faith stories of our Catholic Church

Following the presentation of *Our Catholic Faith* comes an explanation of how we might apply it to our lives today.

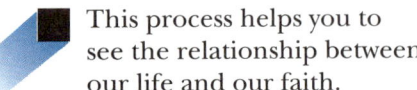

Movement Four
Coming to Faith

Offers questions and activities to help the children learn, understand, and relate our Catholic faith to their own lives.

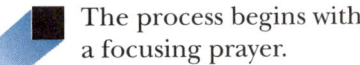

Movement Five
Practicing Faith

Challenges the children to decide how to live the Catholic faith today in their homes and parish.

FAITH ALIVE AT HOME AND IN THE PARISH

The *Faith Alive at Home and in the Parish* (FAAHP) pages are designed to help the family reinforce what the children have learned and to encourage them in the practice of their faith. These pages are filled with a variety of activities for the family, including the new *Family Scripture Moment*, which engage the family in partnership with the catechist and parish to bring the child to a knowledge of and lived response to faith.

Each lesson has a *Faith Summary* accompanied by a "Learn-by-Heart" symbol:  The symbol reminds you and/or the parent to help the child learn the *Faith Summary* by heart.

The *Review* on the back of this page gives the family and the catechist a way to determine the child's growth in faith.

A WAY TO LEARN AND TEACH THAT MAKES FAITH COME ALIVE

Overview of the Lesson

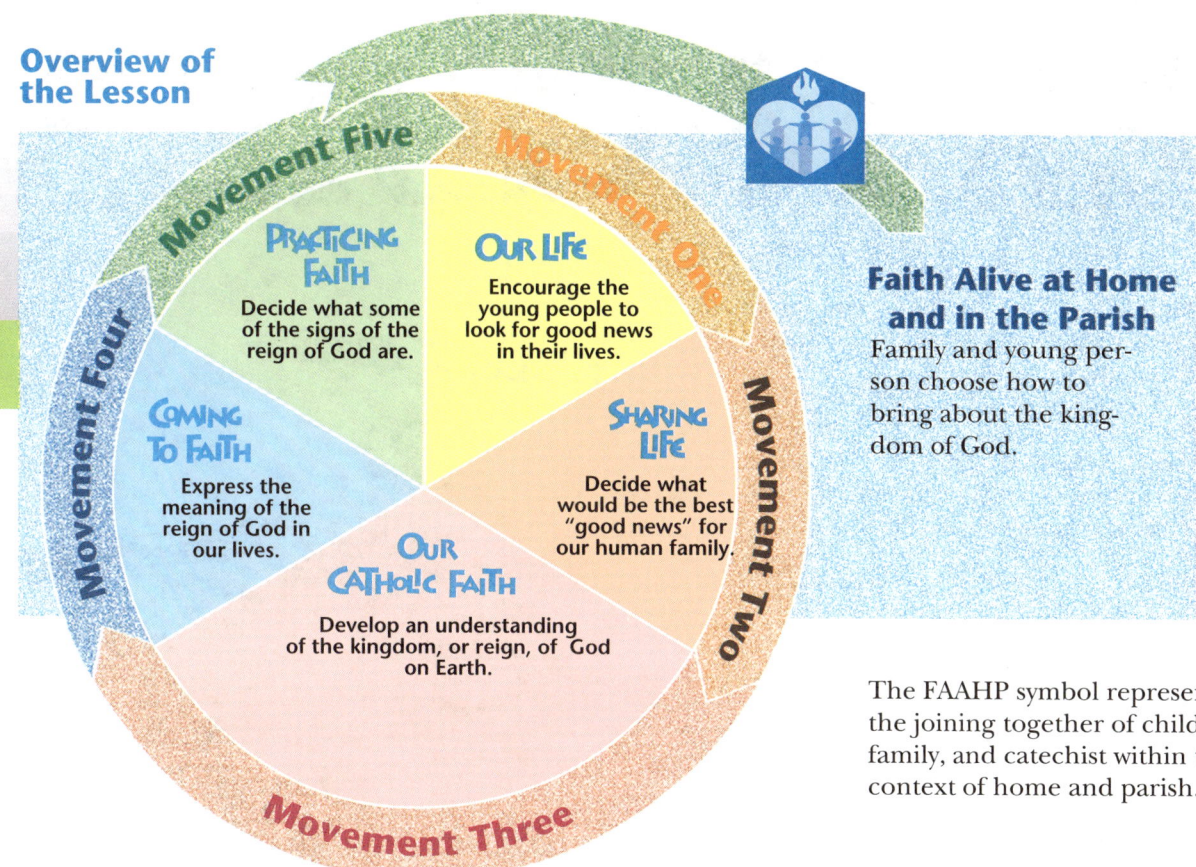

Faith Alive at Home and in the Parish
Family and young person choose how to bring about the kingdom of God.

The FAAHP symbol represents the joining together of child, family, and catechist within the context of home and parish.

How to Plan Your Lesson Time

In planning your lesson it is important to know how to use your time wisely. Each lesson has a *Beginning*, a *Middle,* and *End.* To help you determine how many minutes should be devoted to each part, recommended percentages are given here.

Using *Our Catholic Identity*

This new feature supplements 15 chapters and is found after page 213 as perforated pupil pages. The middle section of each designated lesson plan contains suggestions for the best use of these pages.

You may also use the *Our Catholic Identity* pages at any other appropriate time during the year. It is suggested that the children remove the section at the end of the year to use as a reminder of their Catholic heritage.

Beginning
25%_____ min.
FOCUSING PRAYER
Invite the child to prayer.

Movement One
OUR LIFE
Focus on and name a life or faith experience.

Movement Two
SHARING LIFE
Reflect on and talk about that experience.

Middle
50%_____ min.
Movement Three
OUR CATHOLIC FAITH
Learn the Story and Vision of our Catholic faith.

End
25%_____ min.
Movement Four
COMING TO FAITH
Understand and make the faith their own.

Movement Five
PRACTICING FAITH
Decide through prayer or action to live the faith.

Enrichment and Optional Activities
The *Enrichment* activities and optional activities may be used to extend the time period of your lesson.

FAAHP Pages
Reinforce learning and encourage the practice of a living faith both in the family and in the parish.

CATECHIST'S WORKSHOP

TEXT & GUIDE

Teaching the *Coming to Faith* Program

The text and guide are your most important resources. Familiarize yourself with both. They are designed to help you proclaim the good news, filled with confidence and enthusiasm.

Look at the cover of the children's text. The mosaic you see pictured represents major themes of our Catholic faith, as outlined in the Scope and Sequence.

Open the child's text to the *Table of Contents* (see pages T2–T5).

☾ Look at each unit and lesson title. Read the doctrinal summary statements below each lesson title and the corresponding FAAHP materials. Note whether there is an *Our Catholic Identity* reference.

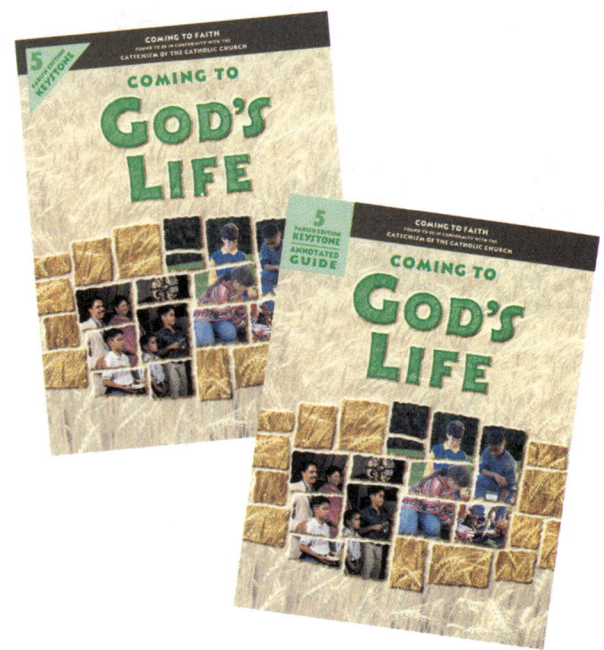

TEXT

Introductory Lesson

(See text pages 7–12.)

☾ The introductory lesson welcomes the children to the grade 5 program.

☾ Use this lesson to help the children get to know each other and to establish a sense of belonging.

Core Lessons

(See pages 13–42. Turn to Lesson 1 on text page 13.)

Each core lesson opens with a focusing prayer. The four teaching pages are structured according to the Shared Christian Praxis approach. Each lesson has:

☾ **A Beginning:** The beginning leads the children into the lesson theme through *Our Life* and *Sharing Life*.

☾ **A Middle:** *Our Catholic Faith* presents the important doctrines, Scripture, and teachings of our Catholic Church and their meaning for our lives. *Our Catholic Identity* pages enrich the child's understanding of Catholic traditions and practices.

☾ **An End:** The ending of each lesson, *Coming to Faith* and *Practicing Faith*, helps the children internalize and practice their faith in the home and in the parish.

Liturgy Lessons

(See text pages 43–48.)

Liturgy lessons appear at the end of each unit. Use these lessons at appropriate times during the year.

Review

(See text pages 55–56.)

Unit Review/Unit Test

A review and a test follow each unit in grades 1–6. Use them to help you and the families assess the progress of the children in internalizing the Catholic faith presented in the KEYSTONE EDITION of *Coming to Faith*.

In the kindergarten text, the activities on the FAAHP pages review the lesson content.

Faith Alive at Home and in the Parish (FAAHP)

(See text pages 17–18.)

Each lesson concludes with two FAAHP pages. These pages contain:

☾ *Family Faith Background*—updates families on the faith learned in each lesson;

☾ *Faith Summary*—contains key Church teaching to be learned by heart;

☾ *Family Activities*—a variety of activities to choose from to help families work together to deepen their faith;

☾ *Review*—an opportunity to recall key ideas presented in the lesson.

☾ *Family Scripture Moment*—special new feature for families to listen to, study, reflect on, and share God's word from the Bible.

CATECHIST'S WORKSHOP

Everything you need to prepare, plan, and present your lesson

End-of-Book Resources

☾ *Retreat Day* gives the young people the opportunity to journal, pray, and participate in activities.

☾ *Sharing Our Faith as Catholics* outlines foundations of Catholic faith: creed, sacraments, morality, prayer.

☾ The *Prayers and Practices* section is designed to help the young people learn important prayers and recall various Catholic practices.

☾ The *Glossary* defines religious words and terms.

☾ The *Sacrament of Reconciliation* describes the steps in celebrating the Individual Rite and the Communal Rite.

☾ *Our Catholic Identity* section is a supplement to fifteen of the class lessons. The content list on page 213 indicates the chapters suggested for their use.

Teaching Resources

(See page 7C.)

The page headed *Teaching Resources* contains important helps for you in the preparation of your lesson:

☾ *Overview of the Lesson,* which outlines the objective of each Shared Christian Praxis movement;

☾ *Teaching Hints,* which contain practical tips for teaching the lesson;

☾ *Faith Alive at Home and in the Parish,* which states the purpose of the FAAHP pages;

☾ *The Special-Needs Child,* which gives recommendations for helping children with visual, auditory, or motor-tactile needs;

☾ *Supplementary Resources,* which suggest optional materials to enrich your lesson, if time allows.

GUIDE

For the Catechist: Spiritual and Catechetical Development

(See pages 7A–7B.)

These pages, which are found at the beginning of every lesson:

☾ provide an opportunity to deepen your own spirituality by using the Shared Christian Praxis learning/teaching process yourself;

☾ provide theological and scriptural background and resources for your understanding of the lesson and for enriching the children's liturgical practices and justice/peace experiences;

☾ provide a reference to the *Catechism of the Catholic Church* for your knowledge of Catholic teaching.

You might wish to meet occasionally with two or three other catechists to prepare your lessons and share your own faith responses.

Lesson Plan Pages

(See text pages 7–12.)

Each lesson plan is designed to help you to teach the lesson found in the text according to the Shared Christian Praxis approach. In order to teach your lesson, remember these steps:

1 Know your *Objectives*—they contain the purpose of the lesson.

2 Prepare the *Focusing Prayer*—this will draw the children into the lesson theme through prayer.

3 Choose your learning activities—these activities are integral to the lesson and will involve the children in the actual learning process.

4 Gather your materials—they are listed after each activity.

5 Read the annotations—they are printed in red on reduced text pages. Use them to highlight specific points in the lesson.

6 Remember to *Evaluate Your Lesson*—this is an opportunity to assess the overall effect of the lesson.

7 Use your *Enrichment* activities—these may be used to deepen the content of the lesson.

8 Select *Optional Activities*—they can be used as creative ways of extending the lesson.

9 Look at the *Faith Alive at Home and in the Parish* pages—encourage the children to bring these pages home to their families or complete them while they are with you.

10 Notice whether the lesson calls for the use of a page from the new *Our Catholic Identity* Section found in the back of the book.

Reminder:

Before you begin teaching the program, read the children's text from cover to cover, and browse through your Parish Annotated Guide.

CATECHIST'S WORKSHOP

Lesson Planning for Different Learning Styles

Reflective Questions to Assist You in Presenting Your Lesson

Lesson Plan: Beginning

- Do you welcome the children and gain their full attention before you begin the lesson?
- Do you show by your actions and expression that you are happy to be with the children?
- Do you make a point of calling each child by name during the lesson?

Lesson Plan: Middle

- Do you sit with the children when you are telling a story?
- Do you move from child to child or group to group when they are involved in learning activities?
- Do you take time to encourage or help each child?
- Do you use different tones of voice when storytelling, reading scripture, asking questions, and giving directions?

Lesson Plan: End

- Do you give the children quiet time to think about what they have learned?
- Do you send the children forth to know and practice their faith?

Presenting the *Beginning*, *Middle*, and *End* of Your Lesson

Evaluating Your Lesson

A successful catechetical program includes regular opportunities for assessment. Assessment is both measurement and evaluation, as well as a means of enrichment.

Ways to Evaluate Learning

● Invite the children to respond orally to a variety of questions.

● Have the children recite the *Faith Summary* statements of each lesson. These are indicated by the "Learn-by-Heart" symbol on the FAAHP pages.

● Have the children retell the doctrinal stories orally, in a drawing, or by role-playing.

● Have the children act out Scripture stories.

● Use word games to evaluate the children's religious literacy.

● Use the *Faith Words* from the lessons to help develop a religious vocabulary.

● Have the children write a letter to someone telling about what they have learned.

● Use the reviews and tests provided at the end of each unit.

● Have the children make up their own questions and answers on the content of faith.

Ways to Evaluate Your Teaching

● Are you using the *Catechist Resource* pages to prepare yourself for each lesson?

● Are you choosing activities that engage the children?

● Are you using the *Evaluating Your Lesson* section to assess your teaching and the children's participation?

● Is prayer an integral part of each lesson?

Use this page to review the effectiveness of your lessons.

Congratulations, Catechist! You truly are a minister of the word!

CATECHIST'S WORKSHOP

How to Create a Catechetical Atmosphere

A catechetical atmosphere is created when children experience true Christian community in their families, their neighborhood, and their cultures. This community is formed through study, prayer, worship, and shared faith experiences. Here are its components:

KNOWING ABOUT THE FAMILIES AND NEIGHBORHOOD OF THE CHILDREN

From the very beginning of the child's life, the parents have been the primary catechists. You are a partner with the parents. The environment and practices in the home and neighborhood have had, and continue to have, a powerful influence on the faith development of the children in your group. To encourage and strengthen family involvement:

◆ Review the information your parish has given you regarding each child.

◆ Become familiar with where and with whom each child lives and who has legal custody of the child.

◆ Make sure you are aware of children who may be neglected or who come from homes that appear to be unhappy.

◆ Be mindful of and sensitive to the language spoken in the home and the religious affiliation of parent(s) or guardians.

◆ Be alert to the general health and well-being of the child.

◆ Be sensitive to the concerns of the local community.

You can, by your care and concern, guide the children to God's unconditional love. The experience of affirmation and support that you provide may indeed change a child's life.

Family Involvement

GETTING FAMILIES INVOLVED

It is essential to involve the family in the catechetical process. Regular family conversation about God and religion has a tremendous positive effect on a child's lifelong faith attitudes and practices.

Welcome the families at the beginning of the year. Explain the catechetical program and invite their participation.

◆ Introduce them to the children's text. The *Table of Content*s provides an excellent overview of what the children will be expected to learn about our Catholic faith over the course of the year.

◆ Explain how to use the *Faith Alive at Home and in the Parish* pages.

◆ Encourage a conversation about the *Faith Summary* statements. The symbol reminds families to help the children learn these by heart.

◆ Talk about the *Family Scripture Moment*, which is designed to encourage families to spend time each week using Scripture for study and prayer.

◆ Be attentive to ways in which you can express joy or sympathy to families of the children in your group when someone is born, is hospitalized, dies, celebrates a sacrament for the first time, or experiences some other special event.

INVOLVING CHILDREN AND FAMILIES IN PARISH LIFE

The parish is an integral part of the faith life of the child. It is within the parish that the child celebrates the major events of life from birth to death.

◆ Invite the children and families to attend Mass on Sunday.

◆ Invite the whole parish community to take part in the celebration of sacraments.

◆ Encourage families to pray for one another and all the members of the parish.

◆ Begin the practice of sending greeting cards to the elderly, to the sick, and to families of those who have died.

◆ Encourage families to participate at Mass by singing, proclaiming as a lector, and in bringing up the gifts.

DEVELOPING MULTICULTURAL AWARENESS

True Christian community takes place within the context of the cultural heritage and the identity of the children we teach.

◆ Be aware of and sensitive to ethnic and cultural diversity.

◆ Encourage the children to express their cultural uniqueness through art, music, dance, food, and dress.

◆ Send communications home in the languages of the families, if possible.

◆ Invite families to share their cultural symbols and food at celebrations.

Ways to Build a Compassionate Community

PERSONAL INTERACTION

A true catechetical atmosphere is rooted in the personal interaction of the catechist, the child, and the family. You can play a vital role in creating a compassionate community by treating each child as a child of God. You do this by:

◆ being hospitable; making sure each child feels welcomed, accepted, and safe;

◆ knowing and calling each child by name often;

◆ showing kindness, love, and forgiveness to each child;

◆ sharing your thoughts, beliefs, and hopes with the children; giving them the same opportunity;

◆ being aware of and sensitive to the feelings and emotions of each child.

How to Create a Comfortable Atmosphere for Learning and Teaching

COMFORTABLE ENVIRONMENT

A suitable and comfortable environment is important for your catechetical undertakings. Such an atmosphere promotes a heightened sense of respect for the parish's catechetical mission. To help children and families feel comfortable:

◆ enhance your lesson by arranging the physical environment in as comfortable a manner as possible;

◆ wherever possible, set aside a special place for prayer. A prayer corner may be created by covering a small table with a cloth and placing a Bible and candle on the table.

MAKING DISCIPLINE POSITIVE

The word *discipline* comes from the root word *disciple*. Discipline means not only correcting misbehavior but also forming attitudes and responses that lead to good behavior. To create and maintain good discipline:

◆ use positive affirmation; acknowledge the children and remember to praise and affirm good behavior;

◆ involve the children in setting a few rules that are easy to remember, and explain why they are for the benefit of all;

◆ provide activities to build self-esteem and help children to feel good about themselves;

◆ respect the children's thoughts and ideas, and expect them to do the same with their peers;

◆ provide activities that challenge the children to cooperate with one another;

◆ deal with children who act inappropriately in a way that will calm them; set aside a space ("time out") where they can think quietly about their actions and the consequences of them.

CATECHIST'S WORKSHOP

HINTS FOR CREATIVE CATECHESIS

Here are some creative ways to make your lessons come alive.

Knowing How to Ask Questions

 Ask direct, clear, and concise questions.

 Give the children time to think about their responses.

 Encourage the children to use their imaginations when responding to questions.

 Encourage a variety of thoughtful, imaginative responses.

Being a Good Storyteller

 Set the scene and identify the characters.

 Look at the children. Keeping eye contact adds to the story's excitement.

 Be dramatic in voice and gesture.

 Pause for dramatic effect or to ask questions.

 Encourage the children's participation in the story. Invite them to add to it or finish it.

 Whenever possible use text pictures to illustrate the story.

Using Silence

Children are very busy people. Silence can be both calming and enjoyable. Use short periods of silence (15–20 seconds):

 before and after prayer time;

 after asking a thought–provoking question;

 for "time out";

 as personal reflection time;

 as a transition between periods of high activity and quiet time.

T32

Memorization: Learning by Heart

Learning by heart enables children to know and recall their faith. Knowing their Catholic faith enables the children to live and practice faith.

 Singing, questioning, oral recitation, word games, and storytelling are all ways of helping children to memorize.

 Remember to help the children to understand their faith before they memorize it.

 Memorization is aided by the "Learn-by-Heart" *Faith Summaries* in every lesson.

Acting and Role-Playing

Acting out a story or scene is a natural and dramatic way for children to express themselves and learn.

 Invite the children to act out some of the stories in their text.

 Encourage the children to tell a story as other children act it out.

 Have the children role-play various situations to enter into the story and characters.

 Feel free yourself to act out or pantomime a particular story, inviting the children to provide the sound effects.

Music

Music unites cultures, languages, and customs and provides a common voice to praise God. Use music:

 to celebrate;

 to set a calm and prayerful tone;

 to reiterate the theme of the lesson;

 to relate lesson themes to contemporary songs, when appropriate;

 to encourage children to use dance to express themselves.

Photos/Illustrations

Photographs and illustrations are an integral part of each lesson.

 Point out and discuss the photos and illustrations on the text pages.

 Have the children use or refer to the art and/or photos on the text pages to retell stories.

 Have the children imagine themselves in the text pictures.

T33

CATECHIST'S WORKSHOP

HOW TO TEACH THINKING SKILLS FOR DISCIPLESHIP

TODAY'S WORLD DEMANDS "CRITICAL THINKERS." What does being a critical thinker mean to you?

As catechists, our goal is to help young people become disciples of Jesus Christ.

Disciples of Jesus Christ act as "critical thinkers." They apply the teachings of the Church as presented in Scripture and Tradition to the real world in which they live.

Here are a few suggestions to help the young people develop critical-thinking skills in your lessons.

✝ Pray about contemporary events with the children.

✝ Help the children to distinguish between unfavorable events and those that are examples of the presence of God with us.

✝ When telling Scripture or faith stories, encourage the children to recall events and apply the message to their own lives.

In the learning/teaching process of Shared Christian Praxis, children develop critical thinking. At all times encourage the children to think and act as Jesus did.

CATECHIST'S WORKSHOP

T>I>M>E>L>I>N>E
Shaping Our Catechetical Heritage over the Ages

From the beginning of Christianity, the followers of Jesus Christ have turned to important documents of the Church for guidance. Sources such as those cited here are a valuable part of our Catholic teaching, tradition, and history. No attempt is being made to present an exhaustive list, but rather to show the role that documents such as those listed have played in our catechetical heritage through the ages.

The Didache   1st Century
The *Didache*, or *Teaching of the Apostles*, included early Church instruction for those preparing for Baptism.

Early Catechisms   5th–14th Centuries
An important faith summary was written by Saint Augustine in the 5th century. Other faith summaries appeared in the 9th and 14th centuries.

The Roman Catechism   1566
The landmark *Roman Catechism*, called for by the Council of Trent, was written to help priests in teaching Catholic people after the Protestant Reformation. The *Roman Catechism* was the last major catechism of the Church until the *Catechism of the Catholic Church*, promulgated in 1992.

The Second Vatican Council   1962-1965
The Council documents urged and outlined renewal throughout all phases of Church life.

The General Catechetical Directory   1971
The Second Vatican Council called for a renewal of catechesis. In response, *the General Catechetical Directory* presented guidelines for catechesis in the Church.

To Teach as Jesus Did   1972
A pastoral message on Catholic education that promoted message, community, and service as three critical elements for Catholic education.

Basic Teachings for Catholic Religious Education   1973
Doctrinal principles to guide the faith formation of Catholic people.

On Evangelization in the Modern World   1975
A turning point in the Church's understanding of the relationship between culture and the faith message.

On Catechesis in Our Time   1979
Important apostolic exhortation of Pope John Paul II on catechesis for today. Especially significant for identifying the aim and purpose of catechesis.

Sharing the Light of Faith: National Catechetical Directory   1979
A key resource for catechesis on all levels and the many dimensions of catechetical ministry. A description of and guidelines for catechesis and catechetical planning in the United States.

The Challenge of Adolescent Catechesis   1986
Addresses the foundations and ministry of adolescent catechesis, indicates a framework for such catechesis, and incorporates leadership dimensions.

Rite of Christian Initiation of Adults   1988
Restored the catechumenate for initiation into the Church, with important implications for the entire process of conversion, liturgy, catechesis, and the faith community.

Adult Catechesis in the Christian Community   1990
Focuses on and promotes the importance of adult catechesis in the faith community.

Catechism of the Catholic Church   1992
A major catechism and reference resource for bishops, priests, catechetical leaders, publishers of catechetical materials, and Catholic people.

"Until we all attain to the unity of faith and knowledge of the Son of God. . . ."   **Ephesians 4:13**

CATECHIST'S WORKSHOP

Catechist Resources

INTERMEDIATE GRADES

BOOKS FOR THE CATECHIST

Catechism of the Catholic Church
New York: William H. Sadlier, 1992
(1-800-221-5175)

Donze, ASC, Mary Terese
Touching A Child's Heart: An Innovative, Encouraging Guide to Becoming a Good Storyteller
Indiana: Ave Maria Press, 1985 (219-287-2831)

Groome, Thomas H.,
Sharing Faith
San Francisco: HarperCollins, 1991 (1-800-328-1991)

Manternach, Janaan, with Pfeifer, Carl J.
A Practical Book for Prayerful Catechists–and the Children Pray
Indiana: Ave Maria Press, 1989

Hubbard, Most Rev. Howard J.
I Am Bread Broken: A Spirituality for the Catechist
New York: Crossroads, 1996
(1-800-395-0690)

PERIODICALS FOR THE CATECHIST

The following periodicals contain articles that respond to the practical and enrichment needs of catechists and religion teachers:

Catechist
Peter Li, Inc., Dayton, OH
(1-800-543-4383)

Religion Teacher's Journal
Twenty-Third Publications, Mystic, CT (1-800-321-0411)

The Catechist's Connection
The National Catholic Reporter Publishing Co., Inc.,
Kansas City, MO (1-800-444-8910)

BOOKS TO READ TO CHILDREN

Fox, Paula
One-Eyed Cat
New York: Bradbury, 1984
(1-800-323-9872)

Sweet Clara and the Freedom Quilt
Hopkinson, Deborah
New York: Dragonfly Books, Alfred A. Knopf, Inc., 1992
(1-800-858-5450)

DRAMAS, CRAFTS, ACTIVITIES FOR CHILDREN

Fogle, Jeanne S.
Teaching the Bible with Puppets
Connecticut: Twenty-Third Publications, 1989
(1-800-321-0411)

Mathson, Patricia
Creativities: 101 Creative Activities for Children to Celebrate God's Love, for Kindergarten through Sixth Grade
Indiana: Ave Maria Press, 1992

Satter, Leslie, illustrations
Nakano, Karen
Mary, Feasts, May Activities, Mother's Day: Practical Activities for Teachers and Parents to Supplement Religious Instructions Grades 4–6
California: Lucia Ross, 1992

Vos Wezeman, Phyllis
When Did We See You? Sixty Creative Activities to Help Fourth to Eighth Graders Recognize Jesus Today
Notre Dame, IN: Ave Maria Press 1994 (1-800-282-1865)

RETREATS FOR CHILDREN

Hakowski, Maryann
Growing with Jesus: Sixteen half-day, full-day and overnight retreats that help children celebrate and share the light of Christ
Indiana: Ave Maria Press, 1993

CATECHIST'S WORKSHOP

A PLANNING GUIDE

LESSON	PAGE	DATES
Called to Life	7A	_____

Unit 1 Jesus Christ Blesses Our Lives

1. Jesus Christ Reveals God . . . . **13A*** _____
2. Jesus Christ and the Kingdom of God. . . . . **19A*** _____
3. Jesus Christ Blesses Our Lives. . . . . **25A*** _____
4. The Church Carries on Jesus' Mission. . . . . **31A*** _____
5. The Sacraments and the Church . . . . **37A*** _____
6. Celebrating Reconciliation . . . . **43A** _____
7. Celebrating Eucharist . . . . **49A** _____
   Unit 1 Review/Test . . . . **55** _____

Unit 2 Sacraments of Initiation

8. Jesus Christ Brings Us Life (Baptism) . . . . **57A*** _____
9. Jesus Christ Strengthens Us (Confirmation) . . . . **63A*** _____
10. Jesus Christ Feeds Us (Eucharist) . . . . **69A*** _____
11. Our Church Celebrates the Eucharist (The Mass). . . . **75A*** _____
12. The Church Remembers (Liturgical Year) . . . . **81A*** _____
13. Celebrating Advent. . . . . **87A** _____
14. Celebrating Christmas . . . . **93A** _____
    Summary One Review/Test . . . . **99** _____

Unit 3 Sacraments of Healing and Service

15. Jesus Christ Forgives Us (Reconciliation). . . . . **103A*** _____
16. Jesus Christ Helps Us in Sickness and Death
    (Anointing of the Sick) . . . . **109A*** _____
17. Jesus Christ Helps Us to Love (Matrimony). . . . . **115A*** _____
18. Jesus Christ Calls Us to Serve (Holy Orders) . . . . **121A*** _____
19. We Share Jesus Christs Priesthood (Ministry) . . . . . . **127A** _____
20. Celebrating Lent. . . . . **133A** _____
21. Celebrating Easter. . . . . **139A** _____
    Unit 3 Review/Test . . . . **145** _____

Unit 4 A Community of Faith, Hope, and Love

22. Becoming a Catholic (The Marks of the Church). . . . **147A** _____
23. All People are God's People . . . . **153A** _____
24. The Gift of Faith. . . . . **159A*** _____
25. God Fills us with Hope . . . . **165A*** _____
26. The Gift of God's Love . . . . **171A** _____
27. Sacramentals . . . . **177A** _____
28. Celebrations for the Year. . . . . **183A** _____
    Summary Two Review/Test . . . . **187** _____
    Day of Treat . . . . **191** _____
    Sharing Our Faith as Catholics . . . . **197** _____
    Prayers and Practices . . . . **203** _____
    Glossary . . . . **209** _____

*Look for *Our Catholic Identity*, page 213.

Liturgical chapters (6, 7, 13, 14, 20, 21, 27, 28) may be used as scheduling needs demand.

CALLED TO LIFE

For the Catechist: Spiritual and Catechetical Development

Adult Background

Our Life

Kate had been voted "Most Likely to Succeed" in high school. She worked hard to become the prominent attorney others thought she would be. Along the way, she sacrificed many of life's simple joys. On her fortieth birthday, Kate felt dissatisfied. The advice of a teacher came back to her: "Our first duty in life is to be true to who we are in God's eyes."

Ask yourself:

■ How might this story end?

■ How am I like or unlike Kate?

Sharing Life

What is the primary goal of your life?

What does your faith have to do with that goal?

Our Catholic Faith

"Life" is one of the Bible's most frequently used words. Over and over again in both testaments, life in all its fullness is affirmed as God's desire for all people. In the beginning, God blew the "breath of life" into the nostrils of the first human being (based on Genesis 2:7). God provided everything the man and the woman might need to enjoy the gift of life.

God's gift always meant more than mere existence. It meant living in harmony with God's will so that we might both experience life's blessings and be a blessing to others. God says:

> I have today set before you life and prosperity, death and doom. . . . Choose life. . . .
> (From Deuteronomy 30:15,19)

Jesus, the Son of God, came into the world as the Word who was the source of eternal life for all who would believe in Him. He is the Good Shepherd who says to us: "I came so that they might have life and have it more abundantly" (John 10:10).

By His teaching and witness, Jesus calls each of us to become the saint God intends us to be.

In an address to the youth of America, Pope John Paul II urged each to recognize that he or she is "someone very special whom God loves and for whom Christ died." The Holy Father then added:

> This identity of ours determines the way we must live, the way we must act, the way we must view our mission in the world.
> ("Address to Youth," September 12, 1987, New Orleans)

When we live our identity as Christians, we discover the meaning of life in all its fullness.

Coming to Faith

What is life in all its fullness for you?

What hopes do you have for your faith life as you begin this school year?

Practicing Faith

How will you live in harmony with God's will for you?

How will you encourage your fifth graders to appreciate the life Jesus came to give them?

CATECHISM OF THE CATHOLIC CHURCH

The Theme of This Chapter Corresponds with Paragraph 754

LITURGICAL RESOURCES

The Bible is the Book of Life. Turn to it often with your fifth graders as a source of guidance and inspiration on whatever theme you are exploring. Write the following words on the chalkboard or newsprint. Have everyone read them silently and then proclaim them aloud together.

> . . . live in a manner worthy of the call you have received. (Ephesians 4:1)

Invite volunteers to tell what this word of God means to them.

JUSTICE AND PEACE RESOURCES

To live life to its fullest, we must choose life not only for ourselves but for all creation. We are called to stand firm against the antilife forces of violence and injustice of every kind.

Invite volunteers to role–play what it might mean to "choose life" when the following happens:

- people litter the street;
- family members argue heatedly;
- friends are glorifying war;
- prejudice is expressed at school.

7B

Teaching Resources

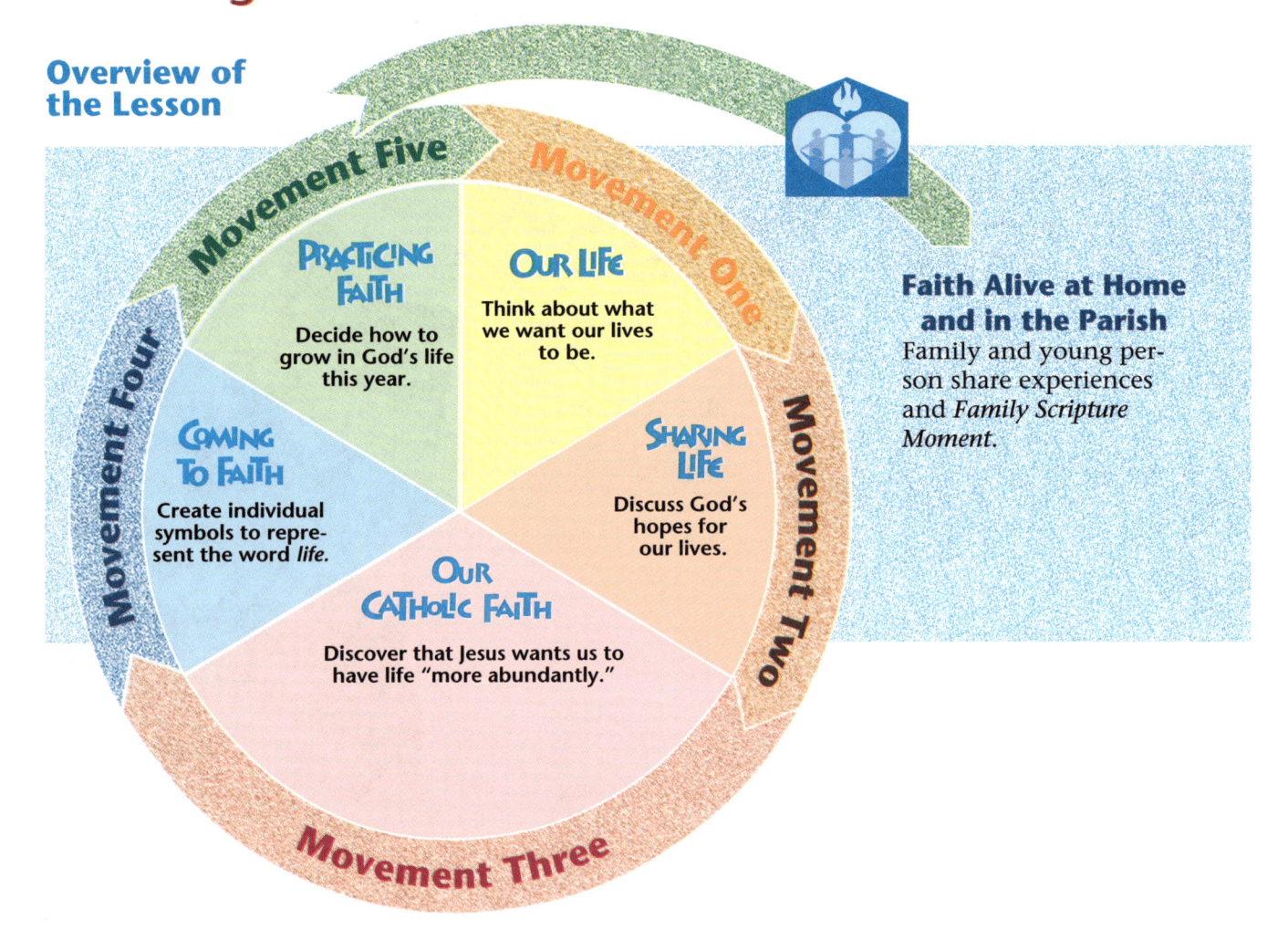

Overview of the Lesson

Movement One
- **Our Life**: Think about what we want our lives to be.

Movement Two
- **Sharing Life**: Discuss God's hopes for our lives.

Movement Three
- **Our Catholic Faith**: Discover that Jesus wants us to have life "more abundantly."

Movement Four
- **Coming To Faith**: Create individual symbols to represent the word *life*.

Movement Five
- **Practicing Faith**: Decide how to grow in God's life this year.

Faith Alive at Home and in the Parish
Family and young person share experiences and *Family Scripture Moment*.

Teaching Hints

This lesson seeks to focus the young people's thoughts on their futures—the kind of lives they will lead. As they read and react to the parable of the Good Shepherd, help them to discover what Jesus means by "life more abundantly." This concept is addressed as the fifth graders prepare this year to investigate how the Church's life-giving sacraments can lead them toward having "life more abundantly" about which Jesus spoke.

Special-Needs Child

Provide an atmosphere of acceptance in which everyone can feel special. Orient the visually impaired with a tour of the room, and if you ever rearrange things, be sure to inform these young people.

Visual Needs
■ preferential seating

Auditory Needs
■ headphones, recording of Scripture stories

Tactile–Motor Needs
■ peer helpers for writing projects

Supplemental Resources

NOTE: Resources listed throughout the guide were available at the time of publication but ongoing availability cannot be guaranteed.

Jesus the Storyteller (video) (from the *God's Story* series) Mass Media Ministries 2116 North Charles Street Baltimore, MD 21218 (1-800-828-8825)

NOTE: This edition of *Coming to Faith* uses the *New American Bible* for Scripture references.

Lesson Plan: Beginning

OBJECTIVES

To help the young people

- understand that Jesus brings "life more abundantly,"
- appreciate the help that the sacraments give;
- choose to grow in God's life this year.

Focusing Prayer

Welcome the young people and allow them time to greet old friends and meet new ones. Pass out the books and invite the fifth graders to open to the introductory lesson. Then pray together the prayer at the top of page 7.

Our Life

Read the first paragraph aloud and ask volunteers to respond to the questions. Distribute paper and pencils, then ask a volunteer to read the second paragraph. Allow time for the young people to write the descriptive words. Now read the last paragraph and have the young people make their lists.

Sharing Life

Ask a volunteer to read the first paragraph, then have the group form pairs. Tell the young people to read the rest of the section and follow the directions given.

If possible, take time for each pair to share its ideas with the group. Ask: "Does anyone see qualities in a young person not mentioned by his or her partner? How does each young person's hopes for his or her life match God's hopes?"

ENRICHMENT

Time Travel

Have the young people work in three or four groups. Provide each group with a sheet of newsprint or posterboard.

Invite the fifth graders to take an imaginary trip through time, to an everyday place 20 years in the future. Explain that they are to describe in writing and illustrate a day in their future lives. Each group's record should include a representation of how each person is fulfilling her or his hopes for the future.

Materials needed: newsprint or posterboard; crayons and/or markers

---

Called to Life

Jesus, we come to you as we begin this new year together. Help us to grow as your disciples.

Our Life

Have you ever thought about your future? What kind of life do you want to have? **Ask the students to close their eyes and "see" themselves in the future.** Take a few minutes now to write some key words that describe what your hopes are for your life.

Then write at least three qualities you have that will help you reach that goal. **Ask: What qualitites do the fifth-graders in the photos have that will help them in the future? Which ones do you have?**

Sharing Life

Join with a partner and share your ideas. Begin by making sure you know each other's name.

Listen carefully to each other. Maybe you can add to your partner's list of gifts and abilities. Sometimes people see gifts in us that we do not recognize in ourselves.

Then ask one another: What are God's hopes for your life? **Stress that God hopes we will use our gifts to love God, others, and ourselves.**

7

Lesson Plan: Middle

Our Catholic Faith

Life in Its Fullness

Read the first paragraph aloud, then ask a volunteer to read the parable and the question that follows it. Encourage the young people to speculate about why Jesus' listeners did not understand the parable.

Read the next paragraph aloud. Then invite the young people to read the following three paragraphs silently, and to draw a line under each sentence that tells something they will be doing this year. When everyone has finished, ask volunteers to read what they have underlined. Write the verbs on the chalkboard or newsprint to help the fifth graders understand that they will be taking

◆ ENRICHMENT ◆

A Modern Parable

Challenge the young people to write or illustrate a modern version of the parable of the Good Shepherd. Ask: "What might threaten Jesus' sheep today?" If the fifth graders have trouble coming up with ideas, suggest that things such as drugs, guns, and materialism all might harm Jesus' sheep. Encourage some young people to make cartoon strips to illustrate their ideas. Put all the stories, poems, and illustrations together in a booklet tied with colorful yarn and labeled *The Good Shepherd of the 90's*.

Materials needed: writing paper; pencils; construction paper; crayons or markers; hole puncher; colorful yarn

---

OUR CATHOLIC FAITH

Life in Its Fullness

Jesus once told this parable. His listeners did not understand it. Maybe you will.

"I am the gate for the sheep. . . . Whoever enters through me will be saved, ... A thief comes only to steal and . . . destroy; I came so that they might have life and have it more abundantly.

I am the good shepherd. A good shepherd lays down his life for the sheep. A hired man, who is not a shepherd . . . sees a wolf coming and leaves the sheep and runs away, and the wolf catches and scatters them. I am the good shepherd, and I know mine and mine know me."

Based on John 10:7–14

What does this parable say about Jesus' love for us?

Jesus, our Good Shepherd, wants us to have life. He was willing even to die that we might have fullness of life.

This year we will explore together the life that Jesus Christ came to give us. We will learn how this life can be nourished and grow through the life-giving sacraments of the Church.

We will share the life of faith among ourselves and find ways to reach out to others so they, too, may have life "more abundantly."

We will identify and fight against all those things that threaten Christ's life in us—the "thieves" and "wolves" of falsehood, abuse, violence, indifference, and irresponsibility.

Take a few minutes now to look through your new book *Coming to God's Life*. Share together what lesson you are most looking forward to studying this year.

Lesson Plan: Middle

action—exploring, learning, sharing, finding, identifying, and fighting "wolves."

Ask the young people to read the last paragraph in this section, then look through their books. Invite each one to tell which lesson she or he is most looking forward to studying and why.

Ask the young people to write a brief paragraph about what the parable of the Good Shepherd means to their lives. Invite them to repeat this short prayer after you:

Jesus, Good Shepherd, watch over me today; help me follow where You lead, and never go astray.

ENRICHMENT

A Special Invitation

Ask the young people to sit quietly as you read the invitation in Psalms 34:8–14. Invite each fifth grader to answer the invitation in the quiet of his or her heart. Then encourage them to illustrate how they felt as they listened to the psalm. Explain that they may write a short paragraph, story, or poem about the experience, or they may draw a picture. Display everyone's work on a bulletin board around a copy of the psalm.

Materials needed: Bible; paper; pencils; crayons or markers

Lesson Plan: End

Coming to Faith

Ask a volunteer to read the first paragraph and tell another volunteer to write down the ideas on the chalkboard or newsprint. Allow each young person to have a turn.

Then read the next paragraph with the group and have the young people draw their symbols. Let each fifth grader share her or his symbol with the group.

Have the young people silently read the last paragraph in this section. Ask them to suggest why someone's thoughts about life might change during the year.

Practicing Faith

Explain that at each meeting the young people will end with a group prayer. Direct their attention to the *Practicing Faith* section and read it together. Allow them a few moments to decide what they want to say, then form a prayer circle. After the prayer, let each young person know that he or she is an important part of the group, and that you are looking forward to seeing him or her next time.

Evaluating Your Lesson

■ Do the young people understand what Jesus wants for us?

■ Do they know that the sacraments nourish us?

■ Have they chosen ways to grow in God's life?

◆ Enrichment ◆

Bless the Year Ahead

Place a glass bowl filled with holy water on a prayer table that has been set with a special cloth, candle, flowers, and a Bible. Invite the young people to take turns using holy water to make the sign of the cross, while you extend your arms and pronounce this blessing:

May God bless you and encourage you.
May Jesus, the Good Shepherd, help you avoid the wolves that cross your path.
May the Holy Spirit guide you in growing in God's life.

Materials needed: glass bowl; holy water; setting for prayer table

Coming to Faith

Play a word association game. Take turns saying what words or pictures come to mind when you hear the word *life*. Have someone write the ideas on newsprint or the board as they are given.

Choose the word or picture that says best what life means to you. In the space above, create a personal symbol or logo that illustrates it.

During the year, you might want to look back occasionally at this page to see whether your thoughts about life have changed.

Practicing Faith

With your friends in a prayer circle, hold your *Coming to God's Life* book. Go around the circle, each one saying: "My name is …. This year I hope to grow in God's life by…." learning more about Jesus, helping others more, learning about the Church, etc.
† Close by praying the Our Father together.

Talk with your catechist about ways you and your family might use the "Faith Alive" pages together. You might especially want to do the Good Shepherd activity with a family member.

Optional Activities

Somewhere in Time (for use with page 7)

Invite the young people to write fictional diaries as if they had traveled forward in time and could see themselves as 30-year-olds. Remind the fifth graders that sometimes a person has plans for the future, but when she or he arrives there, life turns out to be different from the plans. Share the following example with the group:

Today's date: *If this time machine works, I'm off to the future. I'll be a famous rock star, I know, 'cause that's what I plan to be! I'll be rich and live in a big house. I can't wait!*

A date 10 years later: *I thought I just saw me on a college campus with a humongous pile of books . . . get real! Where's the guitar? Where's the music?*

A date 20 years later: *I work in a bookstore and I live in a small apartment. I wonder how this happened? Hey, look at that poster! I'm singing at a church fair to raise money for the homeless. Maybe it isn't what I planned, but I think I like this life!*

Materials needed: paper; pencils

Plan a Puppet Play (for use with pages 7–10)

Have the fifth graders work in small groups to plan a puppet show about the Good Shepherd parable. The young people might have one puppet to represent Jesus telling the parable, while other puppets represent a good shepherd, a bad shepherd, a wolf, and some sheep. Arrange for the group to perform the play for younger children. Have a narrator read the parable from the text before the group performs the puppet play. Your fifth graders might like to sing "Who's Afraid of the Big, Bad Wolf?" during the performance. Have the young people draw, color, cut out, and decorate the characters they need, then tape each one to a plastic drinking straw to make a stick puppet. A puppet stage can be formed from a table turned on its side; or let the young people make one from a large empty box.

Materials needed: Bible; white paper; pencils; scissors; crayons or markers; plastic straws; tape; scraps of colored construction paper, material and yarn for clothes and hair; large box (optional)

Sing Along (for use with page 7)

Invite the young people to sing along with you the following song, using the tune of "Who's Afraid of the Big, Bad Wolf?" Then encourage your fifth graders to write some more verses, especially if they plan to use the song in conjunction with the previously described puppet play that they will perform for the younger children. In that case, have the "flock" sing in sheep-like voices as they dance across the puppet stage!

Who's afraid of the big, bad, wolf? It's not me, no siree.
Why be afraid of a silly old wolf? Jesus watches me!
He keeps the big, bad, wolf away, every night, every day;
He's my Shepherd, I'm His lamb, and to Him I pray!

10A

FAITH ALIVE AT HOME AND IN THE PARISH

This year your son or daughter will explore what Jesus meant when he said that he had come to bring life—life in all its fullness. He or she will learn how as Catholics we are called to live a sacramental life, a life ever alert to a special awareness of God's presence in the ordinary things and events of life. This awareness is the basis of the seven sacraments that we celebrate as Catholics.

In the seven sacraments, the Church recalls and carries on the work of Jesus Christ in our world. Your child will learn how we are to become life-giving signs ourselves—signs of God's life by becoming people who welcome, forgive, heal, and serve others. You can participate in this process by talking with your child about these things and by growing with your child in God's life. Here are some ways *Coming to God's Life* can assist you.

■ Talk about each lesson together, including the pictures and artwork, if possible, since they are an essential part of the program. Encourage a conversation about the *Faith Summary* statements. The symbol reminds you to help your child learn the *Faith Summary* statements by heart. Remember that "learning by heart" includes, but means much more than, memorization. It means taking and making these convictions one's own, making them part of one's heart. You will support this "learning by heart" by talking about the *Faith Summary* statements with your fifth grader. Some you may repeat a number of times to commit to memory, but be sensitive about this; not everyone has equal facility with memorization. It is much more important that a person have them in his or her heart, rather than being able to repeat the statements exactly.

■ Invite your son or daughter to share with you any songs or experiences of prayer that have been learned or shared. Even before truths of our Catholic faith are fully understood, they can be appropriated through a favorite song or prayer.

■ Use the *Faith Alive at Home and in the Parish* pages (this is the first of them) to continue and to expand your child's catechesis through the experience of the community of faith in your family and in the parish family. There will be a variety of activities on these pages. Try to do at least one with your fifth grader.

The **Family Scripture Moment** is offered as a unique opportunity for the family to share faith by "breaking open" God's word in the Bible together. The "moment" can be as brief or as long as you wish. The following simple outline is one way to use this time together.

■ **Gather** together as a family. All can participate from the youngest to the oldest.
■ **Listen** to God's word as it is read, slowly and expressively, by a family member.
■ **Share** what you hear from the reading that touches your own life. Give time for each one to do this.
■ **Consider** the points suggested as a way to come to a deeper understanding of God's word.
■ **Reflect** on and then share any new understandings.
■ **Decide** as a family ways you will try to live God's word.

In this fifth-grade text, selected passages from the Gospel of John will be suggested for family faith sharing, prayer, and reflection.

Faith Summary

Learn by heart

Who is our Good Shepherd?
• Jesus Christ is our Good Shepherd.

What does Jesus bring us?
• Jesus came to bring us life—life in all its fullness.

The Good Shepherd

In the parable Jesus talks about the good shepherd who will give his life for the sheep. He also talks about "thieves" and "wolves" who bring death. What things in your life can you recognize as dangers to God's life in you? How can you protect yourself from these dangers?

Review

Take a few moments to go over the *Faith Summary* together. Ask your fifth grader to tell you the parable of the Good Shepherd. Encourage him or her to learn the summary by heart.

Play a word game with your family. Take turns finishing this sentence and explaining your choice.

Life is like...

© William H. Sadlier, Inc. All rights reserved.

FAMILY SCRIPTURE MOMENT

Gather and invite family members to recall their favorite teacher. Ask: What did you admire about this teacher? Then **Listen** as a family as Jesus invites us to "Come and see."

John was there again with two of his disciples, and as he watched Jesus walk by, he said, "Behold, the Lamb of God." The two disciples heard what he said and followed Jesus. Jesus turned and saw them following him and said to them, "What are you looking for?" They said to him, "Rabbi" (which . . . means Teacher), "where are you staying?" He said to them, "Come, and you will see." So they went . . . and they stayed with him that day.

John 1:35–39

Share what kind of teacher you think Jesus was and how he taught best.

Consider for family enrichment:

■ As John's Gospel begins, John the Baptist serves as a witness, identifying Jesus as the Lamb of God. Two of John's disciples immediately follow Jesus, giving him the honored title of "rabbi," or teacher.

■ By our sharing of God's word, we also accept Jesus' invitation and are ready to learn from him, our best teacher.

Reflect and **Decide** What do we as a family hope to learn from Jesus the teacher this year? As a family, how will we show that we follow Jesus this week?

12

1 JESUS CHRIST REVEALS GOD

For the Catechist: Spiritual and Catechetical Development

ADULT BACKGROUND

Our Life

When the writers of the gospel set out to compose their respective portraits of Jesus, they had no official documents to turn to. But they did have two valuable resources. The first was memory—for some, their own, and for others, that of the Christian community. The second resource was prayerful imagination, which enabled them, with the Spirit's guidance, to fit those memories together into a compelling pattern.

Suppose that a contemporary evangelist invited you to contribute—from your own experience—to a portrait of Jesus.

Ask yourself:

■ What memories (stories, anecdotes, events) of Jesus' presence in my life might I share?

■ What personal insights about the identity of Jesus would I offer?

Sharing Life

How does your life reflect your understanding of Jesus?

Who or what calls you to come to know Him better?

Our Catholic Faith

Why is the presence of Jesus so vitally important in our lives? Can we come to know God through the Bible and the wonders of the created world? If our knowledge of God were limited to the evidence of Scripture and nature alone, we would remain deprived of God's most complete self-revelation. We would be like children trying to assemble a jigsaw puzzle without the most critical pieces.

In the Old Testament, God promised to be with the Israelites through the Sinai Covenant. The prophets and inspired leaders (such as Abraham, Moses, Ruth, Deborah, Isaiah, and Jeremiah) served as transmitters of God's word to the people. Each contributed to the communal knowledge of God. Yet the knowledge remained clouded and incomplete.

The Israelites awaited a new and more profound covenant that would endure forever. With the birth of Jesus, that covenant was realized. John's Gospel puts it simply:

For God so loved the world that he gave his only Son, so that everyone who believes in him might not perish but might have eternal life. (John 3:16)

In the life, death, and resurrection of Jesus Christ, we come to know our God. Jesus' teaching and example challenge us to participate in the building up of God's kingdom of justice and peace. His prayer draws us into a more intimate relationship with God. His dying and rising opens up for us the way into God's presence.

Again, John's Gospel captures a most profound truth in a few simple words for us to cherish:

No one has ever seen God. The only Son, God, who is at the Father's side, has revealed him.
(John 1:18)

Coming to Faith

How does God's self-revelation in Jesus challenge who you are right now?

What have you learned about God from the Jesus you encounter in the sacraments?

Practicing Faith

How will you help your fifth graders to "see Jesus"?

CATECHISM OF THE CATHOLIC CHURCH

The Theme of This Chapter Corresponds with Paragraph 464

LITURGICAL RESOURCES

To come to God, we follow the Way. To see God, we look at Jesus. This is a profound truth that it may take a lifetime to absorb. Even the Twelve were slow to catch on! Share with your fifth graders John 14:1–9, "Jesus the Way to the Father." After reading it aloud, invite four young people to give a dramatic reading as Jesus, Thomas, Philip, and the narrator.

Repeat, "If you know me, then you will also know my Father" (John 14:7). Have volunteers describe what they think God must be like because of what they know about Jesus.

Pray together: Jesus, in You we see the Father. You are our Way. In the name of the Father, and of the Son, and of the Holy Spirit. Amen.

JUSTICE AND PEACE RESOURCES

Early in Luke's Gospel the connection between Jesus and social justice (as well as human rights) is made clear. Jesus applies these words of Isaiah to Himself:

"The Spirit of the Lord is upon me,
  because he has anointed me to bring glad tidings to the poor.
He has sent me to proclaim liberty to captives
  and recovery of sight to the blind,
  to let the oppressed go free...."
(Luke 4:18)

Choose a justice-seeking action to share with the fifth graders in a simple project. For instance, they might encourage one another to respect the rights of their brothers and sisters at home, or they might ask other family members to send brief letters or postcards on behalf of political prisoners to government leaders in various countries.

(Addresses are available from Amnesty International, P.O. Box 37137, Washington, DC 20013.)

1

Teaching Resources

Overview of the Lesson

Movement One — Our Life: Explore the meaning of God.

Movement Two — Sharing Life: Explain when and why we feel close to Jesus.

Movement Three — Our Catholic Faith: Learn Scripture stories that show that Jesus is both human and divine.

Movement Four — Coming to Faith: Deepen the understanding that Jesus is both human and divine.

Movement Five — Practicing Faith: Decide how to solve problems as Jesus would.

Faith Alive at Home and in the Parish: Family and young person decide how the family members can be more like Jesus.

FAITH WORD

A **disciple** is one who learns from and follows Jesus Christ.

Teaching Hints

This lesson focuses on Jesus, the greatest sign of God's love. The presentation calls for an atmosphere of warmth and mutual supportiveness that should be a natural part of every session throughout the year. At times, fifth graders need to be reminded that they can reveal God's love as Jesus did by caring for others around them. Encourage the young people to think of themselves as disciples as they begin another year of growing in God's love.

Special-Needs Child

Keep in mind that disabilities may make group activities physically demanding. Watch for signs of fatigue or frustration.

Visual Needs
- flash card with faith word in sandpaper
- enlargements of on-page activities

Auditory Needs
- headphones and recording of Scripture stories

Tactile–Motor Needs
- peer helpers to assist with activities

Supplemental Resources

The Rocky Road
Mass Media Ministries
2116 North Charles Street
Baltimore, MD 21218
(1-800-828-8825)

Our Friend Is Always with Us . . . Everywhere (video)
Mass Media Ministries
2116 North Charles Street
Baltimore, MD 21218
(1-800-828-8825)

Lesson Plan: Beginning

OBJECTIVES

To help the young people

■ understand that Jesus is both human and divine;

■ appreciate that Jesus' life showed us that "God is love";

■ recognize ways we can show God's love.

Focusing Prayer

Have the young people open their books to Lesson 1. Explain that today we will discuss how God is present in our lives. Then pray together the prayer at the top of page 13.

Our Life

Read the first paragraph and have several volunteers respond to the question. Then invite the young people to think about what God means to them. Ask volunteers to share their thoughts about God. See the annotation. You might also have the young people begin their faith journals. Explain that they will use the journals to write their thoughts, feelings, and responses to personal questions.

Sharing Life

Encourage the young people to tell about times when they felt close to Jesus. You may wish to share an experience of your own. Read the last paragraph and invite responses.

ENRICHMENT

Images of Jesus

Form small discussion groups. Allow members of each group to share favorite Scripture stories about Jesus. Then ask each group to choose one story and discuss what Jesus might be teaching us about God's love.

Encourage each group to describe how it would illustrate the story. The young people may want to use *Coming to God's Life* as a resource.

Materials needed: Coming to God's Life books

---

1 Jesus Christ Reveals God

Jesus, thank you for showing us that "God is love."

OUR LIFE

Someone once said that "a picture is worth a thousand words." See how well you can "read" the pictures on this page. What do they tell you about the ways God is with us in our world today? In our worship and prayer, in love of others, in sharing with others, etc.

What does God mean to you? Answers will vary.

SHARING LIFE Possible responses:
Help one another remember what you know about Jesus that shows Jesus rose from the dead; He healed the sick.

• He is divine—God's own Son;

• He is human—as we are. He laughed and cried; He got hungry and tired as we do.

Imagine some things that Jesus can teach you about yourself.

13

Lesson Plan: Middle

Our Catholic Faith

Faith Word

Write the word *disciple* on the chalkboard or on newsprint, or show it on a flash card. Have the young people say the word, and tell them to watch for it in today's lesson.

Jesus Is Human

Introduce this section by reading aloud the first paragraph. Then guide the silent reading of the second paragraph. Invite volunteers to name some of the ways that Jesus was like us. Then ask how Jesus was different and discuss responses.

Read aloud the next sentence to introduce the gospel story of Lazarus, Martha, and Mary. Have the group read the story silently, then choose four people to role-play the story. Invite the young people to imagine what they might have said, done, or felt if they had been with Martha and Mary when Jesus wept. Complete the reading of this section.

Jesus Is Divine

Have the young people read aloud the first paragraph under "Jesus Is Divine," emphasizing the meaning of *divine*. Have the group silently read the second paragraph. Show the flash card for *disciple*. Call attention to it in the *Faith Word* section, and ask a volunteer to read the definition.

◆ ENRICHMENT ◆

Tears of Concern

Help your fifth graders to compile a list of things that cause them concern, such as war, crime, child abuse, drug use, poverty, hunger, homelessness, broken homes, and so on. Then give each young person paper and markers with which to draw several large teardrops. Have them write one of their concerns on each tear, then cut out the tear. Glue the tears on a large sheet of newsprint around a central heading entitled, "We Weep for People Involved in . . ."

Materials needed: drawing paper; markers; scissors; glue; newsprint

---

Our Catholic Faith

Jesus Is Human

We first learned about Jesus as small children when someone told us the Christmas story. We know that Jesus was born in a stable at Bethlehem because there was no room for Mary and Joseph in the inn.

Stress the underlined text.

As we got older we learned from other gospel stories how much Jesus was like us. Jesus got tired. He felt thirsty and hungry. Jesus loved and obeyed his parents. He enjoyed doing things with his friends. He prayed and worshiped in the synagogue. Jesus was like us in every way except one—he never sinned. He was tempted, but he always said no to sin.

This story helps us to remember how human Jesus was.

Among Jesus' closest friends were a man named Lazarus and his two sisters, Martha and Mary.

One day Lazarus became sick and was dying. Martha and Mary sent for Jesus, but by the time Jesus arrived, Lazarus had died.

When Jesus saw Mary and Martha crying, he felt very sad and began to cry, too. He felt as we do when someone we love dies.

Based on John 11:1–44

Jesus also faced death as all people do. In his suffering and death, Jesus was truly one of us.

Jesus Is Divine

Jesus is one of us, but he is also the Son of God. This is what we mean when we say that Jesus is divine.

In the Creed at Mass, we say that Jesus is "one in Being with the Father." This means "Jesus is true God." Here is one of the stories from the gospels that tells how the disciples began to learn that Jesus was God's own Son.

One day Jesus was in a boat on the lake of Galilee with his disciples. Jesus was sleeping when a fierce storm suddenly started. The disciples were so scared that they woke Jesus, yelling, "Lord, save us! We are perishing!"

"Why are you terrified, O you of little faith?" Jesus answered. Then he got up and commanded the winds and the waves to stop, and there was a great calm. The disciples were amazed. Jesus had done something only God can do.

Based on Matthew 8:23–27

Like the disciples in the boat, we turn in prayer to Jesus for help. Because Jesus is really one of us, we know that he always understands how we feel. Because he is the Son of God, he can always help us.

Lesson Plan: Middle

Invite the group to do a dramatic reading of the gospel story with volunteers taking the parts of narrator, Jesus, and the disciples. At the end of the reading, ask, "What did the disciples realize when Jesus calmed the storm?" and discuss responses.

Read aloud the next paragraph, then ask volunteers to share experiences when they have asked for help in prayer.

Ask the fifth graders to read the last two paragraphs in this section to themselves. Then have the young people write in their faith journals one important way Jesus showed us that God is love.

Interpreting Pictures

Use the annotation to initiate a discussion about the illustration. Ask volunteers to tell what they would say to comfort friends who are sad. Write suggestions on the chalkboard or newsprint, then invite volunteers to act out the pictured scene with dialogue.

Our Catholic Identity

Use page 1 from the *Our Catholic Identity* section in the back of the book. Introduce the page by sharing with the students a picture of your family. Talk about family pictures they might have. Discuss how we often think pictures look "just like us" or "not at all like us."

Show various pictures of Jesus. Have the youngsters choose a favorite picture and explain why they like it. Encourage the students to take up the suggestion about making a personal visit to church, perhaps inviting a close family member to join them.

You may wish to use pages 5-6 in the activity book for *Coming to God's Life*.

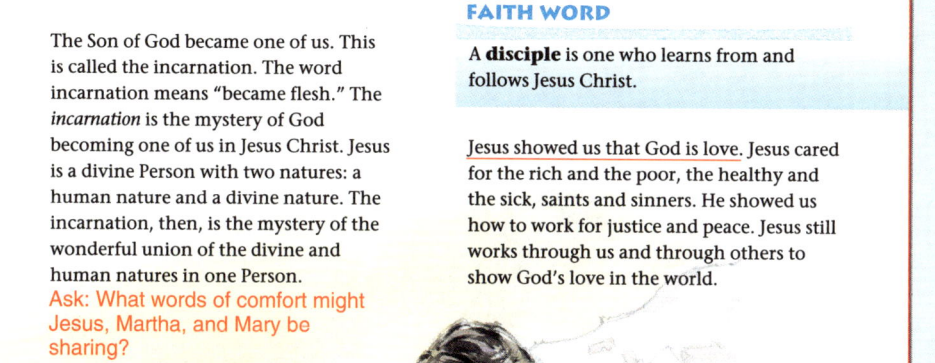

◆ ENRICHMENT ◆

Cast Your Cares

Give each young person a small strip of dry sponge. Ask them to close their eyes and tightly hold the sponge while they pray to Jesus about their fears, worries, or personal storms.

Have available a large tub or pan of water. Play music quietly as you invite the young people to place their sponges in the water and imagine Jesus calming their storms.

Materials needed: small strips of sponge; large tub or pan of water; music source

---

The Son of God became one of us. This is called the incarnation. The word incarnation means "became flesh." The *incarnation* is the mystery of God becoming one of us in Jesus Christ. Jesus is a divine Person with two natures: a human nature and a divine nature. The incarnation, then, is the mystery of the wonderful union of the divine and human natures in one Person.

Ask: What words of comfort might Jesus, Martha, and Mary be sharing?

FAITH WORD

A **disciple** is one who learns from and follows Jesus Christ.

Jesus showed us that God is love. Jesus cared for the rich and the poor, the healthy and the sick, saints and sinners. He showed us how to work for justice and peace. Jesus still works through us and through others to show God's love in the world.

1

Lesson Plan: End

Coming to Faith

Ask the first question under *Coming to Faith* and invite responses. Then ask the young people to write the endings for the four statements. Encourage volunteers to share their responses with the group.

Faith Summary

Use the annotations to review the *Faith Summary* on page 17. Discover whether the young people can express, in their own words, what they have learned.

Practicing Faith

Read aloud the first two sentences, and allow time for the young people to gather and to reflect on the presence of Jesus. Then read the remaining instructions. Proceed around the circle having the fifth graders share their responses. End the session with the closing prayer.

EVALUATING YOUR LESSON

■ Do the young people understand that Jesus is both human and divine?

■ Do they appreciate that Jesus revealed God's love in actions and words?

■ Have they chosen ways to show God's love?

◆ ENRICHMENT ◆

Vine and Branches

Read John 15:1–10 and allow a few moments of quiet reflection. Then give each young person a sheet of orange construction paper to make a pumpkin. Invite them to cut out their pumpkins and write their names on them. Twist a long strip of green crepe paper to resemble a pumpkin vine. Staple or tape the pumpkins to the vine. Display the vine in a prominent place.

Materials needed: orange construction paper; green crepe paper; tape or stapler; scissors

16

COMING TO FAITH

How would you explain to a friend that Jesus is both human and divine?

Complete the following sentences.

Because Jesus wept when his friend Lazarus died, I know that. . . Jesus is human.

Because Jesus calmed the storm at sea, I know that. . . Jesus is divine.

Because Jesus' love for us will never end, I know that God. . . loves and cares for us.

Because Jesus worked for justice and peace, we should. . . follow Jesus' example.

PRACTICING FAITH

Gather quietly in a circle. Imagine that Jesus is with you in the center of the circle. After a minute, read aloud each of the following situations. Take turns going to the center of the circle and responding to each situation the way you think Jesus would want. Encourage specific responses.

● I have a lot of trouble getting along with my brother or sister. Jesus says. . . .
● It really bothers me that I am not good at sports (or schoolwork). Jesus says. . . .
● Sometimes I feel sad and alone. Jesus says. . . .
● Some people think the best way to solve problems is through fighting. Jesus says. . . .
● I feel a friend has really betrayed me. Jesus says. . . .

† Pray together: Jesus, help us to be more like you. Help us to show God's love to others so that all will know that we are your disciples.

Talk with your catechist about ways you and your family can use the "Faith Alive" pages together. You might ask a family member to do the Incarnation activity with you.

16

Optional Activities

Talking to Jesus (for use with page 13)

Gather the young people around a statue or picture of Jesus. Form three groups and have them alternate praying the following:

Jesus, Son of God, be with us.

Jesus, Son of God, befriend us.

Jesus, Son of God, be in us.

Then have the entire group sing "Amen."

Materials needed: statue or picture of Jesus

Searching the Gospels (for use with page 14)

Using their Bibles, have the young people do a gospel search to find several stories that show how Jesus was human like us. List the stories on the chalkboard or newsprint. If time allows, ask volunteers to tell what human feelings Jesus showed in the stories they found and to make illustrations to show Jesus' humanity.

Materials needed: Bibles; drawing materials

Jesus—Human and Divine (for use with pages 14–16)

In the center of a large sheet of newsprint, paste a picture of Jesus. Write above it, "Jesus Is Human and Divine." Ask the young people to list ways that prove Jesus is human to the left of the picture and ways that prove He is divine to the right. Display the completed poster, then invite the young people to make up more statements, such as those in the *Coming to Faith* section, that prove Jesus' humanity and His divinity.

Materials needed: newsprint; glue; picture of Jesus; markers

Reporting on God's Love (for use with page 15)

Arrange the young people in small groups. Have each group write or role-play a news report. Tell them that the reports must illustrate that God works through people to show God's love in the world. Copy the following Scripture verses:

■ "Your every act should be done with love" (1 Corinthians 16:14).

■ "Love your enemies and do good to them" (Luke 6:35).

■ "Love does no evil to the neighbor" (Romans 13:10).

■ "[Love] is not rude; it does not seek its own interests" (1 Corinthians 13:5).

Ask each group to select one verse as the headline for its news report. Encourage the young people to be creative in developing their projects. Be sure to let each group read aloud or act out its report.

Showing God's Love to Others (for use with page 16)

Have the young people organize a "help" or "outreach" project in their parish or neighborhood. Encourage them to plan practical ways to reach out and help members of their families, the needy, the very young, and the elderly in the parish or neighborhood. From time to time, ask the young people to report on their activities.

FAITH ALIVE AT HOME AND IN THE PARISH

This lesson deepened your fifth grader's understanding that Jesus is both human and divine. That the divine nature and a human nature existed together in the one person of Jesus Christ is a central doctrine of the Christian faith. This doctrine that the Son of God took on a human nature gives us hope in God's overwhelming love for us.

Knowing that Jesus is one of us helps us to turn to him more readily and to try to live as he did. You can lead your son or daughter to an appreciation of God's love by providing an experience of a family trying to live as Jesus did.

Ask yourself:
- Do my daily actions show my family God's love for them?
- What will my family and I do this week to show we believe that God's love is present in each of us? in our friends? in the poor?

To help your fifth grader grow in his or her understanding that Jesus is like us and that we can imitate him, do the activity together.

† Family Prayer

O loving God, you showed your great love for us by sending your Son into the world. May we truly know and experience your love in our family. Help us to love one another as you love us. Amen.

Learn by heart Faith Summary

Is Jesus Christ both human and divine?
- Jesus Christ is both human and divine.

What did Jesus show us about God?
- Jesus showed us that "God is love" by the things he said and did.

How does God show God's love in the world?
- God works through us and others to show God's love in the world.

Describing the Incarnation

The Son of God became one of us. This is called the incarnation. The word *incarnation* means "became flesh." The incarnation is the mystery of God becoming one of us in Jesus Christ.

Describe:

one way Jesus was like us.

_____

_____

one way you will try to be like Jesus.

_____

_____

Review

Before doing this *Review*, have your fifth grader go over the *Faith Summary*. Encourage him or her to learn the first two statements by heart. The answers to numbers 1–4 appear on page 216. The response to number 5 will help you see how well your fifth grader understands that God's love is present in our lives. When the *Review* is completed, go over it together.

Circle the letter beside the correct answer.

1. In his suffering and death, Jesus showed us that he was truly
   a. weak.
   b. divine.
   c. human.
   d. none of the above

2. Jesus' miracles reveal that he is
   a. a magician.
   b. divine.
   c. human.
   d. none of the above

3. Jesus taught us that God
   a. is love.
   b. never forgives.
   c. has a white beard.
   d. is kind some of the time.

4. God loves and cares for
   a. the rich and poor.
   b. the healthy and sick.
   c. saints and sinners.
   d. all of the above.

5. How will you show you believe that God's love is present in your life?
   _____
   _____

FAMILY SCRIPTURE MOMENT

Gather and ask: Do we sometimes feel that we have lost our way in life? What do we do to get back on track? Then **Listen** as Jesus shows us the way.

"Do not let your hearts be troubled. You have faith in God; have faith also in me. In my Father's house there are many dwelling places. . . . And if I go and prepare a place for you, I will come back again and take you to myself, so that where I am you also may be. Where [I] am going you know the way." Thomas said to him, "Master, we do not know where you are going; how can we know the way?" Jesus said to him, "I am the way and the truth and the life. No one comes to the Father except through me."
John 14:1–6

Share what each person heard from Jesus in this reading.

Consider for family enrichment:

■ John's Gospel emphasizes the intimate relationship between Jesus the Son and God the Father. Jesus promises his disciples that he is the way to the Father.

■ By following Jesus, we will come to share in all he has prepared for us in heaven.

Reflect and **Decide** How can we as a family be more faithful to the way of Jesus? Pray together: Jesus, help us to follow you as the way, the truth, and the life.

2. Jesus Christ and the Kingdom of God

For the Catechist: Spiritual and Catechetical Development

ADULT BACKGROUND

Our Life

Choose any one of the following hypothetical situations and think about how it would represent good news to you:

- A woman or a minority candidate becomes President of the United States.
- Your parish becomes a leader in environmental justice issues.
- Capital punishment is abolished in the United States.

Add at least one description of an actual event or person that has represented good news in your life.

Ask yourself:

- In what ways am I good news to others?

Sharing Life

How do you think the Church communicates the good news today?

How does it sometimes fail to communicate the values of God's kingdom?

Our Catholic Faith

After His time of preparation in the desert, Jesus went into Galilee to preach the good news. "This is the time of fulfillment," he said. "The kingdom of God is at hand" (Mark 1:15). Throughout His ministry, Jesus identified Himself with the kingdom, which He preached with compelling zeal.

What is the kingdom or the reign of God that Jesus urges us to prepare for? This complex symbol is rich with meaning, but its primary definition refers to the realization of God's will for all creation.

The kingdom is both a process and a reality. Jesus announced that it had arrived and that everyone is invited to become a part of that kingdom. In the gospels we read that Jesus established the Church as the seed and the beginning of the kingdom. He entrusted to Peter the keys to the kingdom of heaven. (See Matthew 16:18-19)

Jesus spoke very often about the kingdom of God and how each of us contributes to its final perfection. In fact, Jesus told many parables to help people understand how important the kingdom is—a pearl of great price, a great treasure—and how we are to nurture the kingdom of God throughout our lives.

Coming to Faith

What signs of the kingdom of God do you recognize in your life right now?

Does the definition of God's kingdom invite you to change in any way?

Practicing Faith

What will you do this week to embody one of the values of the kingdom?

How will you communicate the meaning of the kingdom to your group?

CATECHISM OF THE CATHOLIC CHURCH

The Theme of This Chapter Corresponds with Paragraph 526

LITURGICAL RESOURCES

Reflecting on the Lord's Prayer, C.S. Lewis observed that whenever we pray "Thy kingdom come, Thy will be done," we are actually affirming our intention to help build the kingdom that very day.

Gather your group at the prayer table to pray or sing the Our Father. After praying, "Thy kingdom come, Thy will be done," pause for a few moments of silence. Invite each young person to complete the extemporaneous prayer line, "I will do your will today by _____." Then complete the prayer Jesus taught us.

JUSTICE AND PEACE RESOURCES

The kingdom of God must be promoted within the economic, political, and social structures of this world. Christians cannot simply separate themselves from the problems that surround them and await a better world at the end of time. Whenever we as a Church are perceived as an authentic community of faith, hope, love, and service, we are promoting the kingdom in our midst.

Invite the fifth graders to prepare a series of mini-reports on ways in which the Church (through its ministries and organizations) is promoting kingdom values in the home and in our society. Consider the role of Catholic education, health, and human relations services, as well as the work of groups like Pax Christi, Network, and Catholic Relief Services.

19B

Teaching Resources

Overview of the Lesson

Movement One — Our Life
Encourage the young people to look for good news in their lives.

Movement Two — Sharing Life
Decide what would be the best "good news" for our human family.

Movement Three — Our Catholic Faith
Develop an understanding of the kingdom, or reign, of God on Earth.

Movement Four — Coming To Faith
Express the meaning of the reign of God in our lives.

Movement Five — Practicing Faith
Decide what some of the signs of the reign of God are.

Faith Alive at Home and in the Parish
Family and young person choose how to bring about the kingdom of God.

FAITH WORD
The **kingdom**, or **reign, of God** is the saving power of God's life and love in the world.

Teaching Hints

This lesson offers you, the catechist, an excellent opportunity to witness to the reign of God. You may wish to spend a few minutes reflecting in private on the Scripture readings cited in this lesson. As catechist, you have been chosen to bring the good news to your young people, and the Spirit of the Lord is upon you. To share knowledge; to lovingly advise; to comfort the slow or troubled young person; and to be patient with the distracting ones—these are all ways you are living the reign of God, and God blesses you for it.

Special-Needs Child

When someone begins to speak, subtly direct the attention of any hearing-impaired young person toward the speaker.

Visual Needs
- tape recording of *Our Catholic Faith* section, including faith word and *Faith Summary*

Auditory Needs
- annotated questions on index cards

Tactile–Motor Needs
- peer tutors to record responses

Supplemental Resources

The Challenge of the Beatitudes (video)
Brown-ROA
2460 Kerper Blvd.
P.O. Box 539
Dubuque, IA 52004–0539
(1-800-922-7696)

The Touch of the Master's Hand
Mass Media Ministries
2116 North Charles Street
Baltimore, MD 21218
(1-800-828-8825)

19C

Lesson Plan: Beginning

OBJECTIVES

To help the young people

■ understand the good news of the reign of God;

■ appreciate that Jesus' life was the good news;

■ decide to live God's Law of Love.

Focusing Prayer

Have the young people open their books to Lesson 2. Remind them that previously we learned about Jesus' humanity and divinity. Explain that today's lesson is about Jesus and the kingdom, or reign, of God. Then pray together the prayer at the top of page 19.

Our Life

Remind the young people that sometimes news bulletins interrupt TV shows. Ask if such bulletins are usually good news or bad news. Then have three volunteers each read one of the good news bulletins in the section as if he or she were a newscaster. Read the last paragraph and invite responses. You also might ask the young people to write their good news in their faith journals.

Sharing Life

Read this section; then allow the young people to exchange ideas. Choose someone to list the ideas on the chalkboard or newsprint. You might also wish to choose a moderator for the discussion. When the "best" good news has been agreed upon, have the list maker place a large star next to it.

◆ ENRICHMENT ◆

Sharing Good News

Begin a modified version of the telephone game by reading aloud a recent "bad news" headline from your local newspaper and asking the young people to think of ways it could be changed to "good news." Then whisper one of the ways to the person on your right. Each person in turn is to pass the message to the person on her or his right. When the whispered message has been heard by everyone, ask the group to shout out the "good news."

---

2 Jesus Christ and the Kingdom of God

Jesus, help us to be messengers of your life to others—life in all its fullness.

OUR LIFE

Ask: How are the people in each bulletin sharing good news?

GOOD NEWS BULLETINS

Join us after 8 A.M. Mass. We need helpers to make sandwiches for our "special guests," the homeless.

Environment Guardians: Meet at 9 A.M. Saturday for beach and street cleanup. Bring plastic bags!

Thanks to all the fifth and sixth graders who visited the nursing home last week. Everyone wants you to come back!

Can you add a bulletin about something you have done or might do to bring good news to others?

SHARING LIFE

Share your ideas about what might be the very best "good news" our human family could hear.

Make a list of your ideas and try to come to agreement about the best "good news" of all. Talk about what you can do to make it happen.

19

Lesson Plan: Middle

Our Catholic Faith

Faith Word

Call attention to the *Faith Word* section. Emphasize that Jesus announced that God's kingdom had arrived and that everyone is invited to become part of that kingdom. Ask the children what they know about planting seeds. Recall that in the gospels we read that Jesus established the Church as the seed and the beginning of the kingdom, which will reach its final fulfillment in eternity.

The Kingdom of God

Have the young people read this section silently and then share their responses to any questions.

Ask volunteers to list on the chalkboard or newsprint ways in which Jesus preached and/or did something that spread the good news of God's love.

ENRICHMENT

Spread the News

Invite the fifth graders to write Haiku poems about Jesus' mission to spread the good news of God's love. Remind the young people that God loves them not because of what they can do but because of who they are—God's creations. They need not earn God's love; it is given freely by God. As an example of what they might write, read aloud the following poem to the group.

Build the reign of God,
Live the good news
  of God's love,
Share in the kingdom.

Materials needed: paper; pencils

Then invite the young people to speculate about what the people expected Jesus to answer when they asked whether He was the Messiah. Ask the fifth graders if they think the people understood Jesus' answer.

Living the Good News

Have a volunteer read aloud the opening paragraph in this section. Then ask the following questions to guide the reading: "What prevents us from living for God's reign?" and "How do we live for God's reign?" Invite volunteers to read aloud and to share their responses to questions.

Ask the young people what kinds of things would indicate that people are not living the good news. As they mention such things as prejudice and discrimination, help them understand how they could turn the bad news to good.

OUR CATHOLIC FAITH

Ask: What is Jesus telling His disciples?

Stress the underlined text.

The Kingdom of God

The best news we can hear is that God loves us and cares deeply about us—no matter what. God gave us Jesus to show us that God loves us and will always love us. This is the very best "good news" that Jesus came to share with us.

When Jesus was about thirty years old, he began his ministry of preaching the good news of God's love. He did this in word and action. He healed the sick. He helped the poor, fed the hungry, and forgave sinners. The people began to realize that Jesus was someone very special.

Just about the time Jesus began his work among the people, a prophet was telling everyone that the Messiah, or Savior, was coming soon. The prophet's name was John the Baptist.

One day some of John's followers came to see Jesus and asked whether he was the Promised One, the Messiah.

In response, Jesus pointed out the special things he was doing: "The blind regain their sight, the lame walk, lepers are cleansed, the deaf hear, the dead are raised, the poor have the good news proclaimed to them."

Based on Luke 7:18–22

Jesus was saying that his words and actions were the very things the Messiah, the Promised One of God, would say and do. Jesus Christ was the Messiah. He lived his whole life for the kingdom, or reign, of God.

Living the Good News

Jesus invites all people to live for the kingdom of God. In the Our Father Jesus taught us to pray "Your kingdom come, your will be done, on earth as in heaven"

Lesson Plan: Middle

Interpreting Pictures

Use the annotation to initiate a discussion about the large illustration on pages 20–21. Invite volunteers to take turns playing the parts of Jesus and John the Baptist as they suggest what the conversation might be. Also encourage discussing the smaller, round illustration on page 20 by asking the young people what they think Jesus and the disciples might be talking about. If the young people had been in the crowd, what questions would they have asked Jesus?

Our Catholic Identity

Use page 2 from the *Our Catholic Identity* section in the back of the book. Recall for the children that living for God's reign demands that we treat all people with love and respect. Call attention to the picture of migrant workers. Then have the youngsters discuss the question about their dreams for God's kingdom and tell how they might make their dreams come true. Explain that taking action is an important way to build the kingdom of God. Then talk about prayer as an equally important quiet way to help build the kingdom. Ask for comments on Saint Teresa's suggestions.

You may wish to use pages 7–8 in the activity book for *Coming to God's Life*.

FAITH WORD

The **kingdom**, or **reign**, **of God** is the saving power of God's life and love in the world.

Ask: What might Jesus and John the Baptist be saying to each other?

(Matthew 6:10). We are to share in Jesus' work of bringing about God's reign on earth by living as disciples of Jesus.

There are times when we do not live the good news of God's love. We fail to love others as we should. We fail to do the things that bring God's justice and peace. These things keep us from living for God's reign. Because of our sins, the reign of God is not yet complete.

There are many ways that we can live for God's reign. These include carrying an elderly person's bundles, cleaning up a messy room without being asked, or saying no to cheating. All these are ways of doing God's loving will for us.

We build the reign of God every time we try to be just, or treat others fairly, and work to be peacemakers. Living in God's reign also means helping everyone to know and share in God's life and love.

ENRICHMENT

A Message for the Future

Have available a large container that can be sealed tightly (metal, plastic, or glass). Tell the young people that this is their time capsule. Let the young people decorate a scroll-like paper and print on it: *May the power of God's life and love be with you.*

On the opposite side, have them write the date and the year, then ask each young person to sign his or her name. Invite the group to decorate the outside of the time capsule.

Get approval for an appropriate place where your group can bury the time capsule. Pray together for the people who might find the message in the future.

Materials needed: large, tightly sealable container; scroll of paper; crayons and markers

Lesson Plan: End

Coming to Faith

Read the paragraph with the group, then let the young people decide who will take which part as they act out the gospel scene. You may wish to allow the fifth graders to do the scene several times so that they can exchange parts.

Faith Summary

Ask a few volunteers to tell, in their own words, what they have learned.

Practicing Faith

Read the first paragraph, then have the young people work on their signs. Have the fifth graders show their ideas for being part of God's reign. As they pray the Our Father, ask the young people to stress the word *kingdom*.

EVALUATING YOUR LESSON

■ Do the young people know that the best news is the kingdom of God?

■ Do they appreciate that Jesus's life brought about the kingdom?

■ Have they chosen ways to live for the kingdom?

◆ ENRICHMENT ◆

Food for Thought

Collect nonperishable food items for the poor. Then invite the young people to work together to decorate large, paper grocery bags with good news messages about God's love.

Pack the food items into the decorated bags. Then ask your parish justice and peace coordinator or social concerns' chairperson to give the food to the needy.

Materials needed: large, paper grocery bags; food items; markers

Coming To Faith

Act out together the gospel scene on page 20 (Luke 7:18–23) where people ask Jesus whether he is the Messiah. Someone can be John the Baptist announcing that the Messiah, the Savior, is coming. Some can be the crowd asking Jesus, "Are you the Messiah?" "Are you the Savior?" "Are you the Promised One of God?" Choose someone to be Jesus and give his response.

Practicing Faith

Make some "signs of the reign of God." On the signs, write or draw or paste pictures that show how God's love is being lived in our world today.

Share together how you will be part of God's reign. Then pray the Our Father, repeating three times, "Your kingdom come, your will be done, on earth as in heaven."

Talk with your catechist about ways you and your family might use the "Faith Alive" pages together. Then share the prayer.

Optional Activities

Good News Pennants (for use with page 19)

Distribute markers and construction paper cut into pennant shapes. Invite the young people to write on their pennants the good news they personally would most like to hear. Have them display their pennants around the room. During the year, ask the young people to report to the group if their "good news" has come true.

Materials needed: construction-paper pennants; markers

Pass the Good News (for use with page 20)

Challenge the young people, working alone or with collaborators, to write poems or songs about good news for the young people of the world. Then invite them to share their work with the group. For example:

Listen, listen, what do you hear?
It's the best news you'll hear all year!
Jesus came to teach us how
We can live God's kingdom now!

A Kingdom Song (for use with page 21)

Invite a song leader or another musician to work with a group of volunteers to learn a "kingdom" song. Possibilities include "Seek Ye First," "The King of Glory," "Our God Reigns," or others from your parish hymnal. Have the volunteers explain the words and present their song to the group.

Materials needed: hymnals

A "Good News"-paper (for use with page 22)

Invite each young person to write a news article about something Jesus said or did as He taught people about God's reign. Attach the articles to a large sheet of newsprint and have the group write headlines or draw pictures to accompany the articles. Display the newspaper where others may read and enjoy it.

Materials needed: paper; pens or pencils; newsprint; crayons or markers

A Closing Prayer (for use with page 22)

Make copies of the following prayer for the young people or write it on the chalkboard or newsprint. Then ask the group to stand and pray together:

We believe in Jesus the Christ,
Who is our Savior.
He came into the world to tell the good news of God's love.
May His kingdom come!

22A

FAITH ALIVE AT HOME AND IN THE PARISH

In this lesson, your fifth grader continued to learn more about the reign of God. Although the kingdom has already come in Jesus, it is also a future reality that will only be completed at the end of time. As the Lord's Prayer teaches, it begins on earth and is completed in heaven. Jesus founded the Church to proclaim the good news of the kingdom of God. From its beginning, the Church contained the seed of the kingdom of God. (See Luke 12:32.) The Church is an instrument of the kingdom and helps us to live for it. Your son or daughter has learned that to live for the reign of God includes trying each day as hard as we can to love God, our neighbors, and ourselves. This includes living justly and being peacemakers. To help your family understand this, talk about the greatest of all the commandments, the Law of Love.

The Law of Love
"You shall love the Lord, your God with all your heart, with all your soul, and with all your mind. . . .You shall love your neighbor as you love yourself."
Matthew 22:34–40

Decide what you and your family will do to live the Law of Love so that you might help to bring about the reign of God. Then do the activity together.

✝ Family Prayer

As a family say the Our Father to pray for the kingdom of God. Close your eyes and imagine both what God wants the reign of God to be and how God wants you to live. (This kind of prayer is called meditation.)

Then pray aloud:
"Your kingdom come; your will be done on earth as in heaven."

Learn by heart — Faith Summary

What good news did Jesus announce?
● Jesus announced the good news of the kingdom, or reign, of God. The good news is that God loves us and will always love us.

What is the reign of God?
● The reign of God is the saving power of his life and love in the world.

What does Jesus call us to do?
● Jesus lived his whole life for the reign of God and calls us to do the same.

Living the Law of Love as a Family

We all like to be told how well we are doing. Write a congratulations card to someone in your family when you see the Law of Love in action.

Review

Before doing this *Review*, have your fifth grader go over the *Faith Summary*. Encourage him or her to learn the first two statements by heart. The answers to numbers 1–4 appear on page 216. The response to number 5 will show how well your fifth grader is learning to live for the reign of God. When the *Review* is completed, go over it together.

Circle the letter beside the correct answer.

1. Jesus announced the good news that
   a. he would conquer the Romans.
   b. God would make the apostles great rulers.
   c. God loves us.
   d. the Romans would leave Palestine.

2. Jesus pointed to his words and deeds to show that he was
   a. a foreigner.
   b. the Messiah.
   c. an Egyptian.
   d. a Palestinian.

3. Jesus came to
   a. bring about the reign of God.
   b. preach the good news.
   c. help us do God's loving will.
   d. all of these

4. We live for the reign of God by
   a. thinking only of ourselves.
   b. loving only those people who are kind to us.
   c. living the Law of Love.
   d. rejecting the poor.

5. How will you try to live for the reign of God this week?

_____
_____
_____

FAMILY SCRIPTURE MOMENT

Gather and recall times when family or friends have been seriously ill. Did you turn to God for help? Then **Listen** to a healing story from John's Gospel.

Now there is in Jerusalem at the Sheep [Gate] a pool . . . . One man was there who had been ill for thirty-eight years. When Jesus saw him lying there and knew that he had been ill for a long time, he said to him, "Do you want to be well?" The sick man answered him, "Sir, I have no one to put me into the pool . . . ; while I am on my way, someone else gets down there before me." Jesus said to him, "Rise, take up your mat, and walk." Immediately the man became well.

John 5:2–9

Share Imagine and discuss how Jesus felt and why he was prompted to heal this sick person.

Consider for family enrichment:

■ By healing the paralytic at a pool that had a reputation for its healing waters, Jesus gave a sign that the reign of God had come in him.

■ We, too, can turn to Jesus for healing and courage in times of illness and suffering.

Reflect and **Decide** How will we respond to people who are sick and disabled in our own family and in our parish?

3 Jesus Christ Blesses Our Lives

For the Catechist: Spiritual and Catechetical Development

Adult Background

Our Life

When its Director of Religious Education was publicly accused of wrongdoing and given a temporary leave of absence, the parish split apart. Supporters of the DRE were angry at those who had made the accusations. In their determination to defend her, they praised the DRE so highly that she could hardly recognize herself.

Those on the other side of the fence made no secret of their glee at the DRE's departure. They criticized her so vehemently that she could hardly recognize herself.

Ask yourself:

■ If I were the DRE, how might I handle this situation?

■ If I were a member of the above parish, what might I do?

Sharing Life

What kingdom values are being abused in this situation?

How do you think reconciliation is best achieved in a divided parish?

Our Catholic Faith

To know Jesus Christ is to recognize how central to God's identity are the healing ministries of hospitality, forgiveness, and reconciliation. Jesus consistently extended His friendship to the public sinner, the poor person, the outcast of society. He chose as His disciples ordinary fishermen, farmers, and homemakers. Among the Twelve was Matthew, who, as a tax collector, practiced a profession looked upon by the Jews with the same disdain as that accorded to prostitutes.

When the Pharisees inquired of Jesus why He associated with such an unsavory lot, He replied, "Those who are healthy do not need a physician, but the sick do. I have not come to call the righteous to repentance but sinners" (Luke 5:31-32).

Because sin can make an outcast of any one of us, forgiveness and reconciliation are essential to the Christian community. We recognize Jesus' presence among us not only in the sacraments of healing (Reconciliation and Anointing of the Sick), but in the ways we reach out to and "welcome home" those who have offended us. As a Church, we continue to carry out the reconciling mission of Jesus.

Paul's second letter to the Corinthians puts it this way:

> And all this is from God, who has reconciled us to himself through Christ and given us the ministry of reconciliation. (2 Corinthians 5:18)

Coming to Faith

How does your own image of Christ as welcomer and reconciler influence your relationships?

How might the Church be more effective in healing internal divisions?

Practicing Faith

How will you mirror Jesus the Reconciler for your fifth graders?

25A

CATECHISM OF THE CATHOLIC CHURCH

The Theme of This Chapter Corresponds with Paragraph 547

LITURGICAL RESOURCES

An inscription on the door of St. Stephen's in London reads in part:

> O God, make the door of this house wide enough to receive all who need human love and fellowship, narrow enough to shut out all envy, pride, and strife.

As members of the Catholic (universal) Church committed to the welcoming, healing, and reconciling mission of Jesus, we can profitably reflect on the meaning of this simple prayer.

Make a large poster on which this prayer is inscribed. Challenge the fifth graders to learn it by heart. Then invite them to apply the meaning of the prayer to:

- the door of their homes;
- the door of their classroom;
- the door of their parish church;
- the door of their hearts.

JUSTICE AND PEACE RESOURCES

In his World Day of Peace remarks to youth (delivered in 1979), Pope John Paul II observed:

> Young people, be builders of peace.... Follow the path suggested by your sense of free giving, of joy at being alive and of sharing. You like to utilize your fresh energies in meeting others fraternally without regard for frontiers... and in giving disinterested service to the countries with the least resources. You are the hope of peace.

Share these remarks with your group. Invite them to comment on why the pope believes that young people can be good peacemakers. Brainstorm ways in which the class might help to overcome barriers between any opposing groups or reach out in welcome to the youth from another culture.

3

Teaching Resources

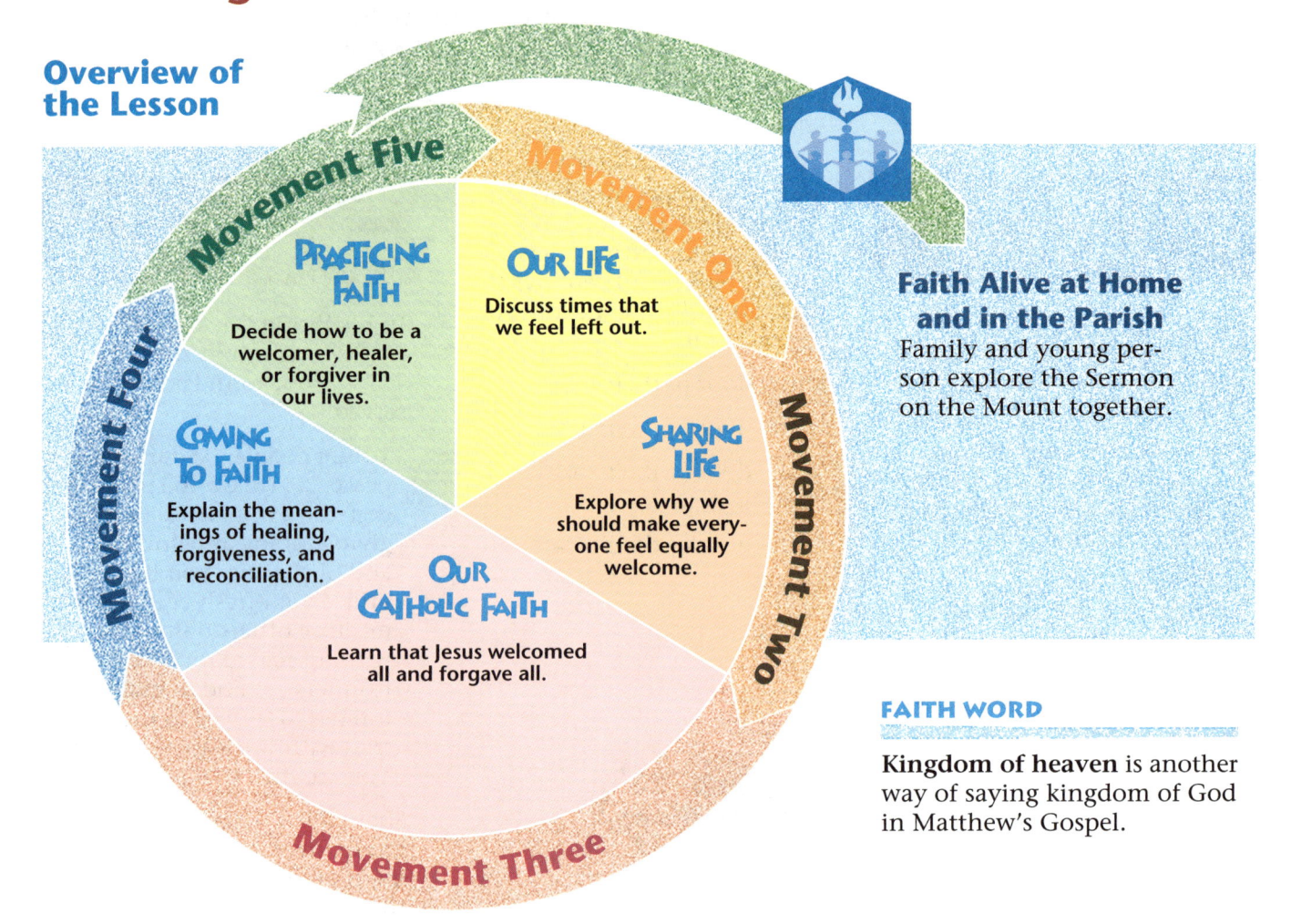

Overview of the Lesson

Movement One
Our Life
Discuss times that we feel left out.

Movement Two
Sharing Life
Explore why we should make everyone feel equally welcome.

Movement Three
Our Catholic Faith
Learn that Jesus welcomed all and forgave all.

Movement Four
Coming to Faith
Explain the meanings of healing, forgiveness, and reconciliation.

Movement Five
Practicing Faith
Decide how to be a welcomer, healer, or forgiver in our lives.

Faith Alive at Home and in the Parish
Family and young person explore the Sermon on the Mount together.

FAITH WORD
Kingdom of heaven is another way of saying kingdom of God in Matthew's Gospel.

Teaching Hints

This is an ideal time to enrich the young people's appreciation that Jesus reached out and welcomed all people. Often young people at this age are very peer-conscious and desire to be accepted in groups, sometimes at the risk of excluding others.

You, as catechist, can be a good role model by choosing as many young people as possible for parts in skits and role-playing activities. Be mindful of those who do not easily interact with others.

Special-Needs Child

Do not rush to help mainstreamed young people with motion disabilities. Ask if they need assistance.

Visual Needs
- large-print *Sharing Life* and *Coming to Faith* activities

Auditory Needs
- annotated questions written on the chalkboard or index cards

Tactile–Motor Needs
- peer to assist any writing

Supplemental Resources

Saint Francis of Assisi (video)
William H. Sadlier, Inc.
9 Pine Street
New York, NY 10005–1002
(1-800-221-5175)

A Time for Miracles
(Elizabeth Seton)
Vision Video
2030 Wentz Church Road
PO Box 540
Worcester, PA 19490
(1-800-523-0226)

25C

Lesson Plan: Beginning

OBJECTIVES

To help the young people

- understand that Jesus invites everyone to live for God's kingdom;
- appreciate the healing power of forgiveness;
- choose to offer healing and forgiveness to all.

Focusing Prayer

Invite the young people to open their books to Lesson 3. Explain that this lesson is about how Jesus blesses us with forgiveness. Pray together the prayer at the top of page 25.

Our Life

Introduce this section by telling the young people that it contains two short entries from someone's diary. Explain that the writer felt left out and upset.

Then read aloud the first three paragraphs, allowing time for the young people to fill in the ending. Discuss how the fifth graders would handle feeling left out.

Ask the young people to finish this section. Then ask volunteers to share their responses.

Sharing Life

Have the fifth graders share ideas about welcoming people and solving problems. Then ask the young people to write their suggestions in their faith journals.

ENRICHMENT

Filling in the Gaps

On a large sheet of newsprint, draw an outline of two mountain peaks with a deep valley between. Brainstorm with the entire group about feelings or actions that separate us from our parents or friends. Write these words in the gap on the drawing.

Then for each word or phrase you have written, ask the young people what could be done to close the gap.

As suggestions are given, color over the corresponding words. By the end of the activity, the entire space should be colored. Display the drawing in a prominent place.

Materials needed: large sheet of newsprint; markers or crayons

---

3 Jesus Christ Blesses Our Lives

Lord Jesus, make us instruments of your peace.

Our Life

Dana and Michael were helping their mother clean the attic. In the chest of drawers they found a diary. "That was mine," their mother laughed. "I kept that diary when I was about your age. You twins can look at it if you want."

They opened the diary to a page that said:
October 14: A bad day. Lisa, Carla, Anne, and I had planned to go shopping at the mall today. When I went to meet them, they had left without me. I feel....

Fill in how you think the diary entry might end. Have you ever felt left out? How did you handle it? Accept any reasonable responses.

Another entry in the diary said:
Mom and I had a real fight about what I wanted to wear to school. She's so out of it! But I know I upset her. I'll....

Complete the entry. What do you usually do to make up?

Sharing Life

Share together:
- why we should make people feel welcome and included in a group. Because this is the Law of Love
- how we can solve problems that separate us without hurting one another. Accept any reasonable responses.

25

Lesson Plan: Middle

Our Catholic Faith

Faith Word

Show a flash card for *kingdom of heaven*, or write the term on the chalkboard or newsprint. Call attention to the *Faith Word* section and have the group repeat the definition after you.

An Invitation to All

Use the annotations to guide the reading. Discuss the young people's responses to any questions.

Read the Scripture story to the group, or ask a few volunteers to read it reverently and dramatically. Be sure to take time for the young people to look over the illustration and discuss what is happening. Ask the fifth graders why they think the faith of the Roman officer amazed Jesus. Help them to understand that the officer was a Roman, not a Jew like most of Jesus' followers. Ask, "Why did the Roman say he was not worthy?"

Jesus, Healer and Forgiver

Emphasize that, by living in peace and justice, we help bring about God's reign.

Ask a volunteer to tell, in her or his own words, why *healing* and *forgiving* are synonymous in the context of today's lesson. Stress that forgiving others, and being forgiven by others, heals the spirit.

◆ ENRICHMENT ◆

Evening News

Invite the young people to pretend that they are news reporters assigned to follow Jesus in much the same way journalists follow and report on presidential candidates today. Have the fifth graders write copy covering the meeting between Jesus and the Roman officer. Remind the young people that good journalists tell the facts without prejudice. Tell them that the stories should include Jesus' amazement in the Roman's faith, the humility of the Roman officer, and the miraculous outcome of the story. Allow time for the young people to share their news stories.

Materials needed paper; pencils

26

Our Catholic Faith

Stress the underlined text.

An Invitation to All

Jesus chose disciples from among people left out by other people in society. His friends included women, tax collectors, poor people, and sinners. This may not seem strange to us, but in Jesus' time it was unusual.

Jesus was most interested in the people society ignored. He worked to change unjust or unfair attitudes and practices.

Here is a Bible story of Jesus reaching out to one of the Jewish people's greatest enemies, their Roman conquerors.

One day a Roman soldier said to Jesus, "Lord, my servant is lying at home paralyzed, suffering dreadfully."

Jesus immediately said, "I will come and cure him."

Surprised that Jesus would actually go to his house, the officer blurted out, "Lord, I am not worthy to have you enter under my roof; only say the word and my servant will be healed."

Amazed by this Roman's faith, Jesus turned to the people watching him and said, "I say to you, in no one in Israel have I found such faith. I say to you, many will come from the east and the west, and will recline . . . at the banquet in the kingdom of heaven."

Based on Matthew 8:5–11

By healing the Roman officer's servant, Jesus showed that all people are welcome in the reign of God.

26

Lesson Plan: Middle

Multicultural Awareness

Remind the group that just as Jesus forgives everyone's sins, so we, too, must forgive all those who have hurt us. Especially make the fifth graders aware of the unintended hurts that can arise from cultural misunderstandings.

Interpreting Pictures

Use the annotations to encourage discussion of the photos on page 27. Ask the young people why they think one girl is being excluded by the others. As the young people offer suggestions for resolving the problems of those in the photos, list the ideas on the chalkboard or newsprint. Invite the young people to tell about situations in which someone might feel excluded. Suggestions might include being left out when teams are chosen or not wearing what is popular. Allow group members time to brainstorm possible solutions for these situations.

Our Catholic Identity

Use page 3 from the *Our Catholic Identity* section in the back of the book. After reading the page, have the youngsters write a classified ad showing one way people their age might serve others. Examples: "Fifth grader available to teach younger children to ride a bike;" "Fifth grader in service to help students with class work." Have the students share their ads. You might all decide to post the ads on a church bulletin board.

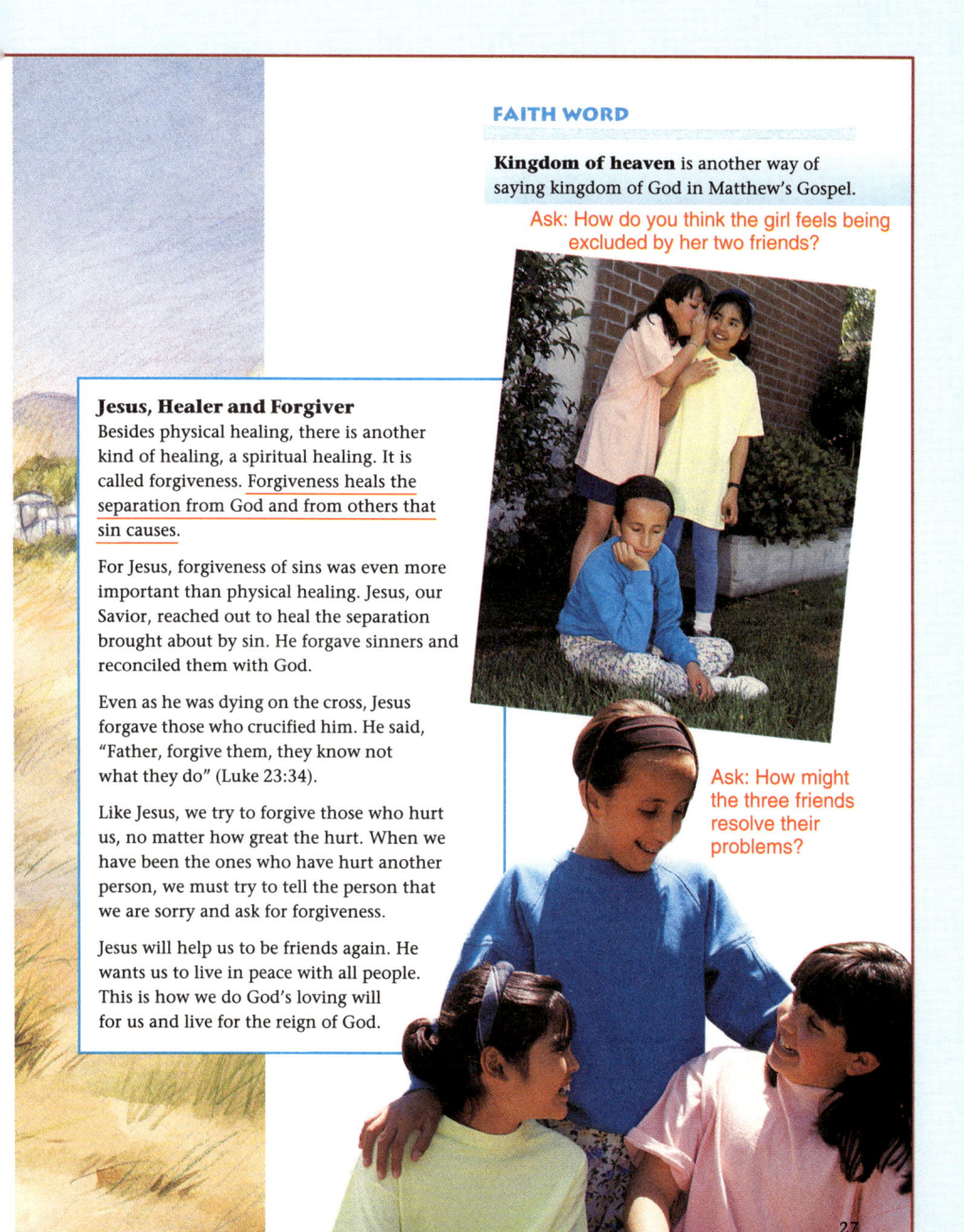

FAITH WORD

Kingdom of heaven is another way of saying kingdom of God in Matthew's Gospel.

Ask: How do you think the girl feels being excluded by her two friends?

Jesus, Healer and Forgiver

Besides physical healing, there is another kind of healing, a spiritual healing. It is called forgiveness. Forgiveness heals the separation from God and from others that sin causes.

For Jesus, forgiveness of sins was even more important than physical healing. Jesus, our Savior, reached out to heal the separation brought about by sin. He forgave sinners and reconciled them with God.

Even as he was dying on the cross, Jesus forgave those who crucified him. He said, "Father, forgive them, they know not what they do" (Luke 23:34).

Like Jesus, we try to forgive those who hurt us, no matter how great the hurt. When we have been the ones who have hurt another person, we must try to tell the person that we are sorry and ask for forgiveness.

Jesus will help us to be friends again. He wants us to live in peace with all people. This is how we do God's loving will for us and live for the reign of God.

Ask: How might the three friends resolve their problems?

ENRICHMENT

Coming Together

Have the young people work in four groups. Send each group to stand in one of the four corners of the room. Invite each group to walk to the center of the room as you read the last sentence of the quotation from Matthew 8.

Then ask the young people to form a circle. Pray together: Jesus, help us to welcome all people and to live in peace with them. Amen.

3

Lesson Plan: End

Coming to Faith

Read the first paragraph aloud. Then have the young people work in small groups to role-play the situations suggested on page 28. Allow time for the fifth graders to prepare and then act out the situations. Afterward review the ways in which the players resolved the situation. If time permits, allow each group to try one of the other situations to see if it can come up with other solutions.

Faith Summary

Ask several volunteers to tell, in their own words, what they have learned in this lesson.

Practicing Faith

As you read the first paragraph, help the group to understand that each of the words *(welcomer, healer, forgiver)* requires us to do something about our faith in and friendship with Jesus.

Read the remainder of the section, then invite the young people to follow the directions for making their strips. Gather in a prayer circle. Tell the fifth graders to keep their paper strips handy at home or school to remind them what they want to do during the week.

Materials needed: strips of paper 10" × 2"

◆ ENRICHMENT ◆

Bridges of Reconciliation

Give each young person a square piece of thick cardboard, push pins or dressmaker's pins, and thread, lightweight string, or yarn. Tell them to sketch an outline of a bridge, push pins in strategic places on the outline to form the frame of the suspension cables, then "string" the thread around the pins. Explain that just as a bridge joins two land masses, so forgiveness can join divided people and God.

Materials needed: cardboard; push pins; thread, string, or yarn

EVALUATING YOUR LESSON

■ Do the young people know that Jesus welcomed all to God's kingdom?

■ Do they appreciate how forgiveness heals?

■ Have they chosen ways to be healers and Bridges of Reconciliation?

Coming To Faith

Here are some role-playing situations to do with your friends to help you understand welcoming, healing, forgiveness, and reconciliation. Divide into groups and act out what might be said and done.

• Mike is coming back to school after a battle with cancer. He is anxious about it because he looks so different. His hair has not grown back yet and he is very thin. How will people react to him?

• Meg and Brittany have been arguing and fighting together. They say they hate each other. Friends decide to bring them together and try to solve the problem.

• A new boy has just joined your class. He seems to want to be by himself and be unfriendly.

If time allows, have more than one group act out each situation.

Talk with your catechist about ways you and your family can use the "Faith Alive" pages. Perhaps you can read together from the Bible the Sermon on the Mount and talk about some of the teachings of Jesus.

Practicing Faith

Take a strip of paper (10" x 2"). On one side write one of these words: welcomer, healer, or forgiver. On the back put one thing you will do this week to be the kind of person who lives for the reign of God.

†Now gather in a prayer circle. Quietly link your strip of paper with those of the people on either side. When the chain is complete, pray as follows:

• *The "welcomers" pray*: Jesus, your love and care went out to everyone. Help us to be welcomers in your name.

• *The "healers" pray*: Jesus, help us to be healers by speaking and acting kindly.

• *The "forgivers" pray*: Jesus, you forgave even those who put you to death. Teach us how to mend the things that separate us.

All hold the chain up high and pray the Prayer of Saint Francis (page 29).

Optional Activities

Feelings of Exclusion (for use with page 25)

Invite the young people to choose one of the following forms of communication to express their feelings about being welcomed or about being left out of a group:

- writing poetry or song lyrics;
- painting or sketching a picture;
- drawing a comic strip;
- preparing a pantomime or dance.

Allow time for the young people to share their creative work.

Materials needed: writing and drawing paper; pencils; paints; crayons, markers and/or colored pencils

Bible Stories of Healing (for use with page 26)

Arrange the young people into two groups. Have each group read and act out either Matthew 8:5–13 or Luke 5:17–26. The young people might enjoy performing the stories for younger children.

Materials needed: Bibles

A Parable About Forgiveness (for use with page 27)

Select four volunteers to portray Jesus, Peter, servant #1, and servant #2. Have the young people read the gospel parable about the unforgiving servant in Matthew 18:21–35 and prepare to mime it for the whole group. (If a young person knows how to sign, invite him or her to sign the parable as the others are miming it.) Afterwards, discuss how this parable teaches us to live as disciples of Jesus.

Materials needed: Bible

Forgiveness Collages (for use with page 28)

Invite the group to make collages about forgiveness, healing, and welcoming. Print one of these words at the top of each of three large sheets of newsprint. Distribute magazines, scissors, and glue. Have the young people cut out words and/or pictures associated with the three words, and paste each one under the proper heading. Display the finished collages in a prominent place.

Materials needed: large sheets of newsprint; magazines; scissors; glue

An Action Prayer Service (for use with page 28)

Ask the young people to think about how they can be more accepting of others. Have them respond in their faith journals. Ask volunteers to share what they have written.

Place several chairs around the prayer table. Have four or five young people come to the table as a reader proclaims:

"I say to you, many will come from the east and the west, and will recline... at the banquet in the kingdom of heaven" (Matthew 8:11).

Sing together the first verse of "They'll Know We Are Christians" while the rest of the group gathers around the table.

Materials needed: faith journals; hymn

28A

FAITH ALIVE

AT HOME AND IN THE PARISH

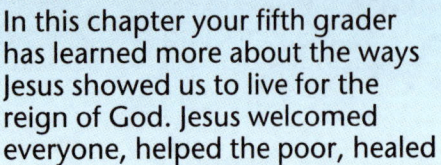

In this chapter your fifth grader has learned more about the ways Jesus showed us to live for the reign of God. Jesus welcomed everyone, helped the poor, healed the sick, and showed us how to forgive. To know Jesus Christ is to recognize how central to his identity are the ministries of hospitality, healing, forgiveness, and reconciliation. Jesus constantly extended his friendship to sinners, to the poor, to the outcasts. As Jesus' followers, we are called to continue his mission of healing and reconciliation.

The Sermon on the Mount contains a summary of many of Jesus' teachings about living for the reign of God. You may wish to read together part of the Sermon on the Mount (Matthew 5:1–7:29). Then do the activity with your son or daughter. In the space below write, draw, or paste one thing that Jesus taught in the Sermon on the Mount that you will try to do with your family before the next lesson.

† Family Prayer

Pray this prayer of Saint Francis after your evening meal.

Lord, make me an instrument of your peace:
 where there is hatred, let me sow love;
 where there is injury, pardon;
 where there is doubt, faith;
 where there is despair, hope;
 where there is darkness, light;
 where there is sadness, joy.
Grant that I may not so much seek
 to be consoled as to console,
 to be understood as to understand,
 to be loved as to love.

Learn by heart — Faith Summary

● Jesus invited everyone to live for the reign of God.
Whom did Jesus invite to live for the reign of God?

● Forgiveness heals the separation from God and from others that sin causes.
How does forgiveness heal us?

● Like Jesus, we try to forgive those who hurt us, no matter how great the hurt.
Whom should we try to forgive?

Living the Sermon on the Mount

Forgive • Love • Have Faith • Share

Review

Before doing this *Review*, have your fifth grader go over the *Faith Summary*. Encourage him or her to learn the second and third statements by heart. The answers to numbers 1–4 appear on page 216. The response to number 5 will show how well your fifth grader is trying to be fair and just to family and to others. When the *Review* is completed, go over it together.

Circle the letter beside the correct answer.

1. Jesus' healing of the Roman's servant showed that
   a. he was afraid of the Romans.
   b. faith is not important.
   c. all are welcome in God's reign.
   d. he obeyed the orders of the Romans.

2. Forgiveness heals the separation from God and others caused by
   a. friendship.
   b. sin.
   c. love.
   d. reconciliation.

3. Besides healing people's bodies, Jesus
   a. said they would never be sick again.
   b. reconciled them to God.
   c. forgave their sins.
   d. both b and c

4. Like Jesus, we try to forgive
   a. all those who hurt us.
   b. no one who hurts us.
   c. some of those who hurt us.
   d. only those who say "I'm sorry."

5. What will you do to be fair to another person this week?

   _____
   _____

FAMILY SCRIPTURE MOMENT

Gather and invite family members to recall times when friends turned away from them or refused their invitations and tell how they felt. Then **Listen** to Jesus at a time when many of his followers had found his teaching on the Bread of Life "too hard."

As a result of this, many [of] his disciples returned to their former way of life and no longer accompanied him. Jesus then said to the Twelve, "Do you also want to leave?" Simon Peter answered him, "Master, to whom shall we go? You have the words of eternal life. We have come to believe and are convinced that you are the Holy One of God."
John 6:66–69

Share Ask: What do you think of Peter's response? If you had been there, how would you have responded?

Consider for family enrichment:

■ After Jesus told the crowd that his own Body and Blood would be their source of everlasting life, many turned away from him. But the apostle Peter proclaimed the disciples' faith in Jesus.

■ Like Peter, we accept Jesus' invitation to remain with him and live for God's reign.

Reflect and **Decide** How might we extend Jesus' invitation to others—especially those who may feel left out of parish life?

4 THE CHURCH CARRIES ON JESUS' MISSION

For the Catechist: Spiritual and Catechetical Development

ADULT BACKGROUND

Our Life

It sounded like a simple project. The pastoral team at Holy Family would plan a dinner to honor all who serve in the parish. The list began with:

- liturgical ministers;
- religious educators and administrators;
- parish council members and members of other parish organizations;
- volunteers at parish suppers, fairs and other fund-raisers.

The team then took a deep breath and went on to add:

- those who visit the sick;
- those who serve in the soup kitchen;
- those who work for world peace.

"Let's face it," laughed Sister Pat. "We've only just begun!"

Ask yourself:

- What persons or categories would I add to this list?

Sharing Life

How do those who serve in your parish symbolize the body of Christ?

Our Catholic Faith

If the Church is to carry on the mission of Jesus, it must be seen as the living embodiment of both the Beatitudes and the Corporal and Spiritual Works of Mercy. The Sermon on the Mount and the description of the final judgment (Matthew 25:31–46) leave little doubt about the absolute necessity for compassionate care of those in need. To ignore the hungry or the stranger, the sick or the imprisoned, the homeless or the destitute, is to bypass Christ Himself. " 'I say to you, what you did not do for one of these least ones, you did not do for me' " (Matthew 25:45).

Our faith tells us that each of us is made in God's image and is loved by God. For this reason, we can judge no other person unworthy of our respect or care. We cannot dismiss the needs of others as no concern of ours.

In their 1986 pastoral letter, *Economic Justice for All,* the U.S. bishops wrote:

> Christian communities that commit themselves to solidarity with those suffering and to confrontation with those attitudes and ways of acting which institutionalize injustice, will themselves experience the power and presence of Christ.
> (Chapter 2, #55)

The bishops urged all faith communities to join "the quest for economic and social justice." Our ministry to a broken world requires us to act out of loving concern for all the temporal and spiritual needs of humanity. It requires us as the body of Christ to renew the face of the earth.

It is in such building actions that we as a Church help to renew the face of the earth in Jesus' name.

Coming to Faith

In what ways do you feel called to carry on the mission of Jesus Christ?

How might your parish commit itself in solidarity with those who suffer?

Practicing Faith

How will you choose to recognize the homeless or hungry Christ this week?

What will you do to inspire your group to care for the needs of others?

CATECHISM OF THE CATHOLIC CHURCH

The Theme of This Chapter Corresponds with Paragraph 789

LITURGICAL RESOURCES

Saint Paul's analogy of the body is a fruitful source of reflection for those who seek to build up the reign of God in solidarity with other believers.

As a body is one though it has many parts, and all the parts of the body, though many, are one body, so also Christ. (1 Corinthians 12:12)

Invite your fifth graders to envision themselves as the hands, feet, head, or heart of the body of Christ. Have them write a prayer in which they describe how they will serve as the different parts.

JUSTICE AND PEACE RESOURCES

In his December 30, 1987 encyclical, *On Social Concerns,* John Paul II points out that the goods of this world are "originally meant for all." The right to private property does not exempt Christians from the responsibility of sharing what they have with those who are in need.

Our concern for "the Lord's poor" must be translated into practical reforms. "Each local situation will show what reforms are most urgent and how they can be achieved" (VI, 43).

Invite a guest speaker who is engaged in helping the poor in the community. He or she might suggest ways in which the young people and their families can support or assist in this work.

31B

Teaching Resources

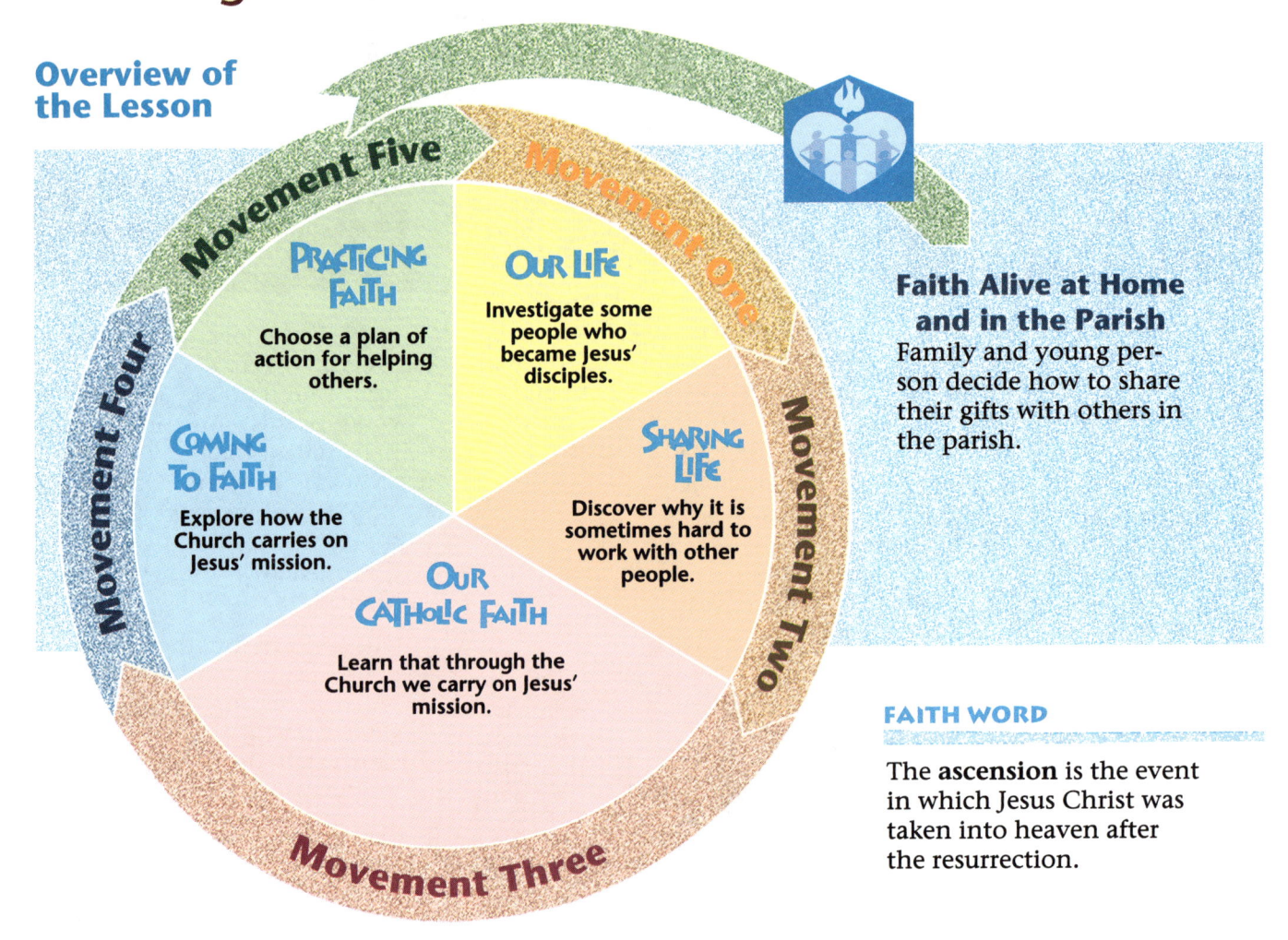

Overview of the Lesson

Movement One — **Our Life**: Investigate some people who became Jesus' disciples.

Movement Two — **Sharing Life**: Discover why it is sometimes hard to work with other people.

Movement Three — **Our Catholic Faith**: Learn that through the Church we carry on Jesus' mission.

Movement Four — **Coming To Faith**: Explore how the Church carries on Jesus' mission.

Movement Five — **Practicing Faith**: Choose a plan of action for helping others.

Faith Alive at Home and in the Parish
Family and young person decide how to share their gifts with others in the parish.

FAITH WORD

The **ascension** is the event in which Jesus Christ was taken into heaven after the resurrection.

Teaching Hints

This lesson focuses on the Church's role of carrying on the mission of Jesus. It is important that the young people understand that they, as members of the body of Christ, are carrying out this mission.

Help the young people to realize that they each have different talents to offer, and help them to feel enthusiastic about their part in this mission.

Special-Needs Child

It is best to assign only one task at a time to any mainstreamed young person.

Visual Needs
- flash card with sandpaper letters

Auditory Needs
- headphones and tape of *Our Catholic Faith* section and instrumental music

Tactile–Motor Needs
- partners for recording written responses

Supplemental Resources

Pentecost (video)
Ikonographics
P.O. Box 600
Croton–on–Hudson, NY 10520
(1-800-944-1505)

Peter and Paul
Vision Video
2030 Wentz Church Road
PO Box 540
Worcester, PA 19490
(1-800-523-0226)

31C

Lesson Plan: Beginning

OBJECTIVES

To help the young people

- know that each of us is part of Christ's body;
- appreciate that the Holy Spirit helps us to carry on Jesus' mission;
- decide to bring peace and justice to others.

Focusing Prayer

Have the young people open their books to Lesson 4. Explain that today we will learn how the Church carries on Jesus' mission. Pray together the prayer at the top of page 31.

Our Life

Invite the fifth graders to silently read this section. Then discuss the descriptions of the disciples. Ask the young people what they think about the flaws the disciples had. Remind the group that Jesus welcomed all kinds of people, and since the disciples were human, they were not perfect.

Ask volunteers to answer the questions at the end of the section and share their ideas with the group. You might also ask the young people to write their replies in their faith journals.

Sharing Life

Read this section aloud and encourage the young people to offer their ideas. Keep the discussion moving by asking questions such as: "What bothers you when you have to work with someone else?" and "Do you think that being enthusiastic or not-so-enthusiastic makes it harder for someone to work with others?" Tell the young people to give reasons for their responses.

ENRICHMENT

Disciple Spotlight

Encourage the young people to imagine themselves as casting directors for a movie about Jesus' disciples. Have them discuss who should play each disciple described on this page before reaching a consensus.

Also, ask each person to share what role he or she might like to play and why. If time permits, invite volunteers to act out chosen characters interacting with Jesus and/or each other.

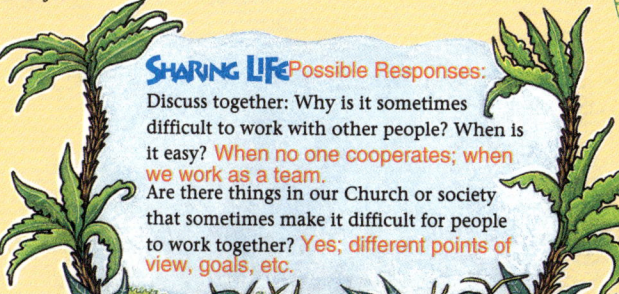

---

4 The Church Carries on Jesus' Mission

Jesus, help us to help one another bring about the reign of God.

Our Life

While Jesus was on earth, he had many disciples. Let's see how some of them might be described.

Peter—a rough, uneducated fisherman. He was good-hearted but often boastful. Jesus saw special qualities in Peter. He made Peter the leader.

Martha—sometimes worried too much about everyday cares. But she was one of the first disciples to recognize Jesus as the Messiah and Son of God.

Thomas—often called "Doubting" Thomas, because for him only "seeing was believing." He wouldn't accept Jesus' resurrection until he could actually touch him.

Mary Magdalene—described in the gospels as a helper of Jesus. With other women disciples, she stood at the foot of Jesus' cross and was one of the first to hear the good news of his resurrection.

These are just some of the disciples of Jesus. Why do you think they followed him?

How would you describe yourself as a disciple of Jesus?

Sharing Life Possible Responses:

Discuss together: Why is it sometimes difficult to work with other people? When is it easy? When no one cooperates; when we work as a team.

Are there things in our Church or society that sometimes make it difficult for people to work together? Yes; different points of view, goals, etc.

31

Lesson Plan: Middle

Our Catholic Faith

Write the word *ascension* on the chalkboard or newsprint, or show it on a flash card. Pronounce it and have the group repeat it. Explain that it refers to a special event celebrated each year by the Church.

The Church Welcomes

Have the young people turn to page 32. Set the scene for the Scripture story by reading aloud the first two sentences under "The Church Welcomes." Then dramatically read the story of the first Pentecost in the first paragraph.

Display the flash card for *ascension* and direct the group's attention to the *Faith Word* section. Have the group read the definition together. Then have the young people silently read the next four paragraphs. Discuss with the group the mission of the Church.

The Church Heals and Forgives

Read aloud "The Church Heals and Forgives" on page 32. Emphasize that the disciples healed and forgave in Jesus' name after His ascension.

The Church Serves

Ask a volunteer to read the next two paragraphs. Invite several young people to respond to the question: "How did the early Church serve as Jesus did?"

The Body of Christ

Have a volunteer read aloud the opening paragraph of "The Body of Christ." Then ask: "How are we the Body of Christ?" Invite the young people to share their responses.

ENRICHMENT

And the Winner Is...!

Have the young people design awards to give to classmates, family members, and others who serve people. Let the fifth graders share their designs, then have the group choose one to be used as a group award. This award will be bestowed upon any group member who uses his or her talents to benefit others. (Example: a group member who assists a special-needs classmate, or one who brings in material to share with the rest of the group.) Have multiple copies made.

Materials needed: paper; crayons, or markers

Our Catholic Faith

The Church Welcomes

Jesus knew his disciples would need help to build up his Church. He promised to send them the Holy Spirit. God the Holy Spirit is the third Person of the Blessed Trinity. After Jesus' ascension into heaven, the disciples were praying together with Mary. Suddenly they heard a strong wind. Then they saw what looked like tongues of fire settling over the heads of each one. They were filled with the Holy Spirit, as Jesus had promised. This happened on Pentecost, the day the Church celebrates the coming of the Holy Spirit.

The disciples, who were once afraid, were now full of courage. The Holy Spirit helped them to come out from behind locked doors and to preach the good news of Jesus to everyone.

Based on Acts 2:1–13

Stress the underlined text.
The disciples invited and welcomed all people into the community of Jesus' followers, the Church.

Today the mission of the Church is to teach Jesus' good news and way of life to all.

As Catholics we teach the good news when we welcome those who are pushed aside or treated unfairly by society. God the Holy Spirit, our Helper, gives us the courage to accept this responsibility to welcome and care for all, as Jesus did.

The Church Heals and Forgives

The Holy Spirit helped the disciples to carry on Jesus' mission of healing and forgiving. The New Testament has many stories about the disciples healing and caring for people's bodies, encouraging people to turn away from sin and be forgiven by God. They brought God's forgiveness and peace to all in Jesus' name.

The Church Serves

The first Christians never forgot that Jesus "did not come to be served but to serve" (Matthew 20:28). They also remembered his commandment, "As I have loved you, so you also should love one another" (John 13:34).

Jesus' disciples took special care of people in need, such as widows, orphans, and the poor. They knew that every baptized Christian was to take part in this work of justice and mercy.

Ask: What are some ways that Martha can help the poor boy?

Lesson Plan: Middle

Ask them to read with you the words of Saint Paul for added emphasis.

When you read the remaining paragraphs in this section, stress that as members of the Body of Christ, we all depend on each other. Have the group explain how we carry on the mission of Jesus.

Interpreting Pictures

Use the annotations to initiate discussion of the various illustrations on pages 32–33. Ask the young people for several suggestions about ways they might help the boy. Elicit from the fifth graders that they might feed him, tend his injured leg, ask him to sit down, help him understand what things he *is* able to do despite his disability, and so on. Peter might have several ways to help the hungry man. Write the young people's suggestions on the chalkboard or newsprint. Finally, talk about the last illustration, in which one young person is helping another, and how your group members might serve others.

Our Catholic Identity

Use page 4 from the *Our Catholic Identity* section in the back of the book. Display a picture of your parish church. Explain that since their Baptism each of the members of the group belong not only to their own family but also to their Church family. Try to instill in your students a sense of pride in belonging to the parish. Talk about the last paragraph and share what you know about the history of the parish.

You may wish to use pages 11–12 in the activity book for Coming to God's Life.

◆ Enrichment ◆

VIPs

On a long sheet of wide shelving paper, trace a large, paper-doll figure. Invite the young people to look through magazines and newspapers for pictures that illustrate people serving others.

Have the group decide which pictures to use for a collage to illustrate 1 Corinthians 12:26. Glue the chosen pictures onto the previously drawn figure. Then invite each young person to stand next to the figure as you say to him or her, "_____, you are a very important member of the body of Christ, the Church."

Materials needed: wide shelving paper; old magazines and newspapers; scissors; glue

FAITH WORD

The **ascension** is the event in which Jesus Christ was taken into heaven after the resurrection.

The Body of Christ

Today the Church carries on the mission that Jesus gave to his first disciples to heal and forgive. When the Church, by the power of the Holy Spirit, brings healing and forgiveness to one person in the name of Jesus, the whole Church shares in that joy.

Saint Paul said that we are all connected like the parts of a body. "If [one] part [of the body] suffers, all the parts suffer with it; if one part is honored, all the parts share its joy" (1 Corinthians 12:26). Jesus is the head of his body, the Church, and we are its members.

The Church continues to serve all people. Like Jesus, each member of the Church can give something to others. For example, we can give a special talent, a piece of clothing, or some food. The best gift we can give is the gift of ourselves and our time.

By Baptism we become members of Christ's body, the Church. As we work together, everyone's gifts are important. This means that each of us is a very important member of the body of Christ. Everyone has a part to play in carrying on the mission of Jesus. We must work together in this great mission. Ask: Can you think of one way to use a gift you have (friendliness, humor, helpfulness) today?

Ask: What are some ways that Peter can help the hungry man?

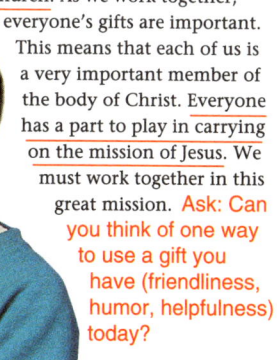

4

Lesson Plan: End

Coming to Faith

Read the first paragraph and ask the young people to write their descriptions in their faith journals. During the group discussion about your parish, you might wish to have a volunteer list the suggestions on the chalkboard or newsprint.

Allow each fifth grader to respond to the final question. Once again, ask a volunteer to jot down the ideas as they are given. Keep this to use in the *Practicing Faith* section.

Faith Summary

Use the annotations to review the *Faith Summary* on page 35. See if the young people can express, in their own words, what they have learned.

Practicing Faith

Slowly read the suggestions as the group reflects and decides which project it will undertake. Then have the young people read silently the questions that follow. Discuss the group's responses. Finally, gather the young people for prayer.

EVALUATING YOUR LESSON

- Do the young people understand that together we are the body of Christ?
- Do they appreciate how the Spirit helps us?
- Have they chosen ways to carry on Jesus' mission?

ENRICHMENT

Secret Prayer Pals

Provide strips of paper on which the young people will write their names. Collect the names in a box or other container.

Ask each person to draw out a name but not to share it with anyone.

Explain that each person should pray during the coming week for the person whose name he or she has chosen.

Materials needed: **strips of paper; box or other container**

COMING TO FAITH

Describe the ways in which the early Church carried on Jesus' mission.
Preaching, healing, forgiving, serving
Talk together about your parish. How does it:
- welcome?
- serve?
- heal?
- act justly?
- forgive?
- bring peace?

Choose one of the above. What can fifth graders do to help out?
Accept any reasonable responses for all of the above.

PRACTICING FAITH

Talk over these ideas about ways to serve your parish:
- welcome the newly baptized.
- form a "cleanup" group for the church and grounds.
- distribute or sort food and clothing for parish outreach.
- write a letter to a local newspaper about an issue of justice and peace.
- serve as ushers, gift bearers, or choir members at a parish liturgy.
- Other: _____

After you decide what your group will do, ask yourselves questions like these:
- Whom should we talk to in our parish?
- What adults do we need to help us?
- When will we do this service?

† Form a prayer circle. After a moment of quiet, pray together:

Jesus, we come to you with all our gifts and with our faults, too. We want to follow you as your disciples. Help us as we place ourselves at the service of others in your name. Amen.

Talk with your catechist about ways you and your family might use the "Faith Alive" pages together. Encourage a family member to become involved, if possible, in your service project and choose a time to pray the prayer together.

34

Optional Activities

Creating Comic Strips (for use with page 31)

Challenge the young people to make comic strips illustrating the consequences of refusing to work together in a family, a school, or a parish. Display the comic strips where the other religion groups or parishioners can enjoy them.

Materials needed: paper; pencils; crayons or markers

The Holy Spirit with Us (for use with page 32)

Ask the young people to think of times when they have experienced the Holy Spirit's presence—for example, when they were afraid and were given courage; when they were sad and felt comforted; when they felt like doing something wrong but were strengthened to do good. Ask the fifth graders to write about the experiences in their faith journals, or to draw on the experiences in writing true-life adventure stories.

Materials needed: faith journals; paper; pencils; crayons or markers

The Body of Christ (for use with page 33)

Distribute drawing paper and markers or colored pencils. Invite the young people to make symbolic drawings of the body of Christ as Paul describes it. Play quiet instrumental music while they work. Then collect and display the drawings.

Materials needed: drawing paper; markers or colored pencils

A Prayer Display (for use with page 34)

Have each of the words in the following prayer printed on a separate strip of construction paper:

Jesus, help us to work together as Your Church.

Distribute the strips to the group, and invite the young people to cooperate with one another in putting the "puzzle" together. Display the assembled prayer on posterboard or newsprint. Pray the prayer together and sing an "Amen."

Materials needed: construction paper strips; posterboard or newsprint; glue or tape

A Prayer of Petition (for use with page 34)

Gather at the prayer table, and have a young person take the part of the leader to read these petitions:

Leader: Jesus, help us to be a welcoming parish.
All: Hear us, Lord.
Leader: Jesus, help us to be a peacemaking parish.
All: Hear us, Lord.
Leader: Jesus, help us to be a healing parish.
All: Hear us, Lord. In the name of the Father, and of the Son, and of the Holy Spirit. Amen.

FAITH ALIVE

AT HOME AND IN THE PARISH

Your fifth grader has learned more about the way our Church began and how it continues Jesus' mission of welcoming, healing, forgiving, and serving today. A central theme of the Second Vatican Council is that, by Baptism, all of us are called to share in the mission and ministry of the Church—each according to his or her gifts.

You might ask yourself:

■ How do I help to carry on the mission of Jesus Christ?

If possible, read the first chapter of the Acts of the Apostles. Then choose a family project for all to work on together and to share their gifts as the early Christians did.

Help the Church come alive for your family. Ask your fifth grader to tell the story of how the Church began at Pentecost. Then have him or her do the following activity.

† Family Prayer

Pray this prayer that God may heal the sickness or poor health of a family member, or any separation caused by an argument.

Jesus Christ, our Savior and Messiah, send the Holy Spirit to help us bring forgiveness and healing to the people in our lives who need it. By doing this, may your body, the Church, grow and carry on your mission in the world. Amen.

Reporting the Pentecost Event

You are a reporter present at the first Pentecost. Write a headline for your eyewitness account for the *Jerusalem Journal*. Act out what happened.

Learn by heart Faith Summary

How does the Holy Spirit help the Church?
● The Holy Spirit helps the Church carry on the mission of Jesus to all people.

Who is the head of the Church? What are we?
● Jesus is the head of the Church, his body, and we are its members.

How does the Church carry on Jesus' work?
● Like Jesus, the Church serves people and brings them Jesus' healing and forgiveness.

Jerusalem Journal

Review

Before doing this *Review*, have your fifth grader go over the *Faith Summary*. Encourage your child to learn the three points by heart. The answers to numbers 1–4 appear on page 216. The response to number 5 will show how much your fifth grader wants to be involved in the mission of the Church. When the *Review* is completed, go over it together.

Circle the letter beside the correct answer.

1. The disciples received the Holy Spirit on
   a. Easter.
   b. Passover.
   c. Pentecost. (circled)
   d. Christmas.

2. Saint Paul compared the Church to
   a. a company.
   b. the body of Christ. (circled)
   c. a mustard seed.
   d. a storm at sea.

3. The Church is to serve
   a. some people.
   b. all people. (circled)
   c. only Catholics.
   d. only grown-ups.

4. Today the mission of the Church is to
   a. welcome all people.
   b. forgive and heal people.
   c. serve people.
   d. all of the above (circled)

5. How will you be part of the Church that welcomes, forgives, heals, and serves?

   _____
   _____
   _____

FAMILY SCRIPTURE MOMENT

Gather and invite family members to look at a picture of or draw a healthy tree or plant. Ask: What would happen to the branches if we cut them off? What would happen if we fed, watered and cared for the tree or plant? Then **Listen** as Jesus uses the image of the vine and the branches.

"I am the vine, you are the branches. Whoever remains in me and I in him will bear much fruit, because without me you can do nothing. Anyone who does not remain in me will be thrown out like a branch and wither. . . . If you remain in me and my words remain in you, ask for whatever you want and it will be done for you. By this is my Father glorified, that you bear much fruit and become my disciples."

John 15:5–8

Share what each one heard in this reading.

Consider for family enrichment:

■ Jesus uses the familiar image of the grapevine to express his unity with his disciples. The very life of Jesus is in us, just as the life of the vine is in each connected leaf.

■ We receive the very life of Jesus through the sacraments and remain in him by our prayer and service to others.

Reflect and **Decide** What good fruit might Jesus be calling us to produce? Link arms and pray: Jesus, keep us joined to you and to one another!

5 THE SACRAMENTS AND THE CHURCH

For the Catechist: Spiritual and Catechetical Development

Adult Background

Our Life

It was said of Saint Ignatius Loyola that the sight of a flower could send his heart soaring toward God. Reflect on how the following might affect you:

- touching a baby's hand;
- smelling fresh bread;
- hearing birds singing;
- looking at the sea;
- tasting plump grapes.

Ask yourself:

- What signs speak to me of God?

Sharing Life

In what ways do the sacraments connect with your daily life?

How do you want the sacraments to affect your daily life?

Our Catholic Faith

Saint Augustine called sacraments "signs of a sacred reality." He emphasized how God had chosen to communicate this sacred reality to us through the simple, earthy signs we employ in the sacraments, such as bread, wine, oil, and water.

Explaining the Church's traditional definition, Monika K. Hellwig says that the sacraments are "experiential happenings . . . that point to an elusive hidden reality of friendship with God . . . and have the power to bring about what they point to."

The foregoing definitions suggest that sacraments in the Catholic Church have a profound significance that seems to go beyond whatever words we may use to describe them. Like shared meals, embraces, and healing touches, they enrich and strengthen a loving relationship. The sacraments are, as Mircea Eliade has written, "doors to the sacred" through which we enter into communion with our God.

Although we most often use the term *sacrament* to signify the seven special liturgical signs of Baptism, Confirmation, Eucharist, Reconciliation, Anointing of the Sick, Matrimony, and Holy Orders—the Church, too, is itself a sacrament. Since the Second Vatican Council, the Church has been recognized as "the universal sacrament of salvation" and "the visible sacrament of . . . saving unity" (*Constitution on the Church in the Modern World*, 45, and *Dogmatic Constitution on the Church*, 9).

Finally, the greatest sacrament of all is Jesus Christ Himself, who is the effective sign of God's love present among us.

Coming to Faith

How might you describe the sacraments to one who has never heard of them?

What is your vision of the Church as a sacrament?

Practicing Faith

What will you do this week to experience one sacrament more profoundly?

How will you communicate the meaning of the sacraments to your group?

37A

CATECHISM OF THE CATHOLIC CHURCH

The Theme of This Chapter Corresponds with Paragraph 1076

LITURGICAL RESOURCES

Pope Leo the Great observed, "What was visible in the Lord has passed over into the sacraments." Each of the following gospel passages depicts Jesus in a sacramental action or encounter. Choose the one you find most appealing, and "enter into it" by picturing yourself as the person present in the encounter with Christ. Hear His voice and feel His presence. Reflect on your response to this sacramental moment.

- John 3:1–8 Jesus and Nicodemus
- John 6:53–59, 66–69 Jesus the Bread of Life
- Luke 8:43–48 the woman who touched Jesus' cloak

Share your chosen reflection with the fifth graders by guiding a meditation in which they, too, "enter into" the gospel story.

JUSTICE AND PEACE RESOURCES

To be a sacramental person is to share with others the nourishing, healing, renewing, and self-sacrificing presence of Jesus Christ. These sacramental actions lie at the very heart of justice and peacemaking. (Consider, for instance, the lives of Dorothy Day, Oscar Romero, Pope John XXIII.)

Invite fifth-grade volunteers to prepare for the classroom or church vestibule a gallery display of "Sacramental Persons." They may draw portraits of people such as Mother Teresa or Dr. Martin Luther King, Jr., and write brief descriptions of the ways in which these persons help others to encounter Christ in the world.

37B

Teaching Resources

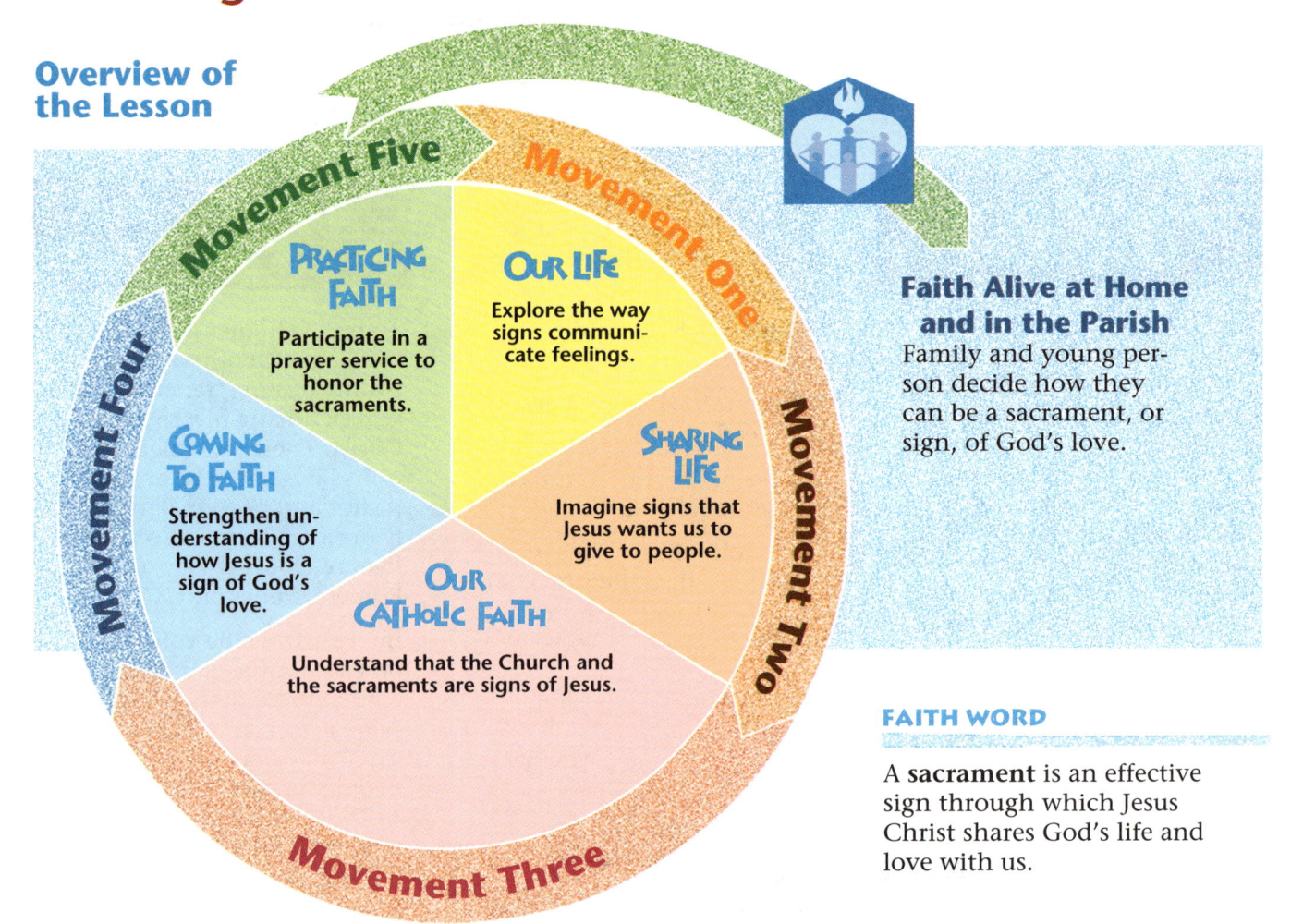

Overview of the Lesson

Movement One — Our Life
Explore the way signs communicate feelings.

Movement Two — Sharing Life
Imagine signs that Jesus wants us to give to people.

Movement Three — Our Catholic Faith
Understand that the Church and the sacraments are signs of Jesus.

Movement Four — Coming To Faith
Strengthen understanding of how Jesus is a sign of God's love.

Movement Five — Practicing Faith
Participate in a prayer service to honor the sacraments.

Faith Alive at Home and in the Parish
Family and young person decide how they can be a sacrament, or sign, of God's love.

FAITH WORD

A **sacrament** is an effective sign through which Jesus Christ shares God's life and love with us.

Teaching Hints

The objective of this lesson is to help the young people recognize that the Church celebrates the sacraments with God's people. The sacraments are signs of God's love in our lives. Be sure that the young people understand the significance of the sacraments in their everyday lives, and encourage them to respond to the Church's sacramental life frequently.

Special-Needs Child

When teaching the hearing-impaired, always face the children when addressing them.

Visual Needs
- magnifying glass for magazines and newspapers
- large-print sacrament chart

Auditory Needs
- headphones and tape of background music

Tactile–Motor Needs
- partner to assist with activities
- sacrament chart taped to desk

Supplemental Resources

We Celebrate Life in Christ (video)
Treehaus Communications
P.O. Box 249
Loveland, OH 45140
(1-800-638-4287)

Of Sacraments and Symbols series (video)
Teleketics
1229 S. Santee Street
Los Angeles, CA 90015

Lesson Plan: Beginning

OBJECTIVES

To help the young people

- know that there are many signs of God's love in our world;
- recognize the sacraments as special signs;
- decide to receive the sacraments more often.

Focusing Prayer

Explain that this lesson is about the seven sacraments. Ask the young people to open their books, then pray together the prayer at the top of page 37.

Our Life

Write the following on the chalkboard or on newsprint:

- I've got great news!
- I'm really sorry I hurt you.
- I'm worried about the test!

Call on volunteers to mime these statements for the group. Invite the others to identify the message. Then discuss how much we communicate through signs.

Explain that the stories in this section are about signs in our lives. Ask a volunteer to read the first paragraph. Use the questions following the story to initiate a discussion. Repeat the same procedure with the next story.

Sharing Life

Read the first paragraph and invite responses. Then read the next paragraph and ask the young people to write their thoughts in their faith journals.

ENRICHMENT

"Key Person" Plaques

Have the young people make "key person" plaques to present to someone in their lives who is like Kate's grandmother. Proceed as follows:
1) Protect the work surface with cardboard;
2) draw a picture of a key and tape it to an aluminum tray or pie plate;
3) use a small hammer and nail to punch out the design on the aluminum, and remove the paper;
4) make a card to explain the key symbolism: "You are a key person in my life."

Materials needed: cardboard; aluminum trays; hammers; nails; drawing paper; crayons; markers; tape or glue

---

5 The Sacraments and the Church

Jesus, we want to be signs of your love. May what we do tell others about you.

Our Life

Kate loves her grandmother. They talk to each other on the phone several times a week. Kate feels that she can tell her grandmother everything and her grandmother really listens! She doesn't criticize, but she gives Kate good advice. Kate loves the way her grandmother talks to her. "She treats me like a person," Kate says.
Possible responses:
How do Kate and her grandmother show each other love and respect?
They listen, share, and help each other.
How do you show respect to others?
I listen, share, and am polite.
Darryl was upset after soccer practice. "Coach Tate just doesn't like me," he complained to his friend Sam. "You're crazy," Sam replied. "Whatever made you come up with that idea? Has he told you that?"

"It's not what he says; it's how he acts," said Darryl. "He never puts me in the game. And he turns away when I come near him."

What signs made Darryl think the coach didn't like him?
He ignored Darryl.
Explain how actions can sometimes "speak louder than words."

What signs do you give people to let them know how you feel about them? I smile, show interest, and talk to them.

Sharing Life

People give us many signs of caring or not caring about us. Discuss together what some of these signs might be. You might want to list these under "family," "friends," "parish." Imagine some of the signs that Jesus wants us to give to other people. Choose some "caring signs" from the list above and act them out.

37

5

Lesson Plan: Middle

Our Catholic Faith

Signs of God's Love

Read the first paragraph and discuss the meaning of *sign*. Ask a volunteer to read the next two paragraphs. Ask if the fifth graders know of any other weather signs that sailors or farmers use, such as, "Red sky in the morning, sailors take warning; red sky at night, a sailor's delight."

As you read the next paragraph emphasize that Jesus is the perfect sign of God's love because He is God.

Show the flash card for *sacrament*. Have the young people locate the *Faith Word* section. Ask them to read the definition together. Then have the group complete the reading of the paragraphs in this section.

Seven Special Signs

Have volunteers read this section about the sacraments. Emphasize Jesus' action in us through the sacraments.

Call attention to "The Seven Sacraments" chart on page 39. Allow time for the young people to study the chart, then have them close their texts. Write on the chalkboard or on newsprint the headings: "Sacraments of Initiation," "Sacraments of Healing,"

ENRICHMENT

All Kinds of Symbols

Tell the young people that we often communicate by using different symbols. Explain that weather maps have symbols that represent different kinds of weather conditions. Remind the group that words are made up of letters that are symbols for sounds. Ask the fifth graders to name other kinds of symbols they know. Then have them work in small groups to design banners that show the symbols of God's love in their lives. Allow time for the young people to make their banners. Display the banners around the room.

Materials needed: craft or shelving paper; decorative materials; stencils for letters; markers

38

OUR CATHOLIC FAITH

Stress the underlined text.

Signs of God's Love

Signs of God's love are everywhere for us to see if we are willing to notice them. A *sign* is something visible that tells us about something invisible.

Jesus used many signs to show God's love. For example, he reminded farmers that they looked at signs in nature to predict the weather. He said, "When you see [a] cloud rising in the west, you say immediately that it is going to rain—and so it does. And when you notice that the wind is blowing from the south, you say that it is going to get hot—and so it is."

Jesus said we should look for signs of God's love just as we look for signs of the weather.

Based on Luke 12:54–56

We find the greatest signs of God's love in Jesus' words and actions. Jesus is the perfect sign of God to us. Saint Paul called Jesus "the image of the invisible God" (Colossians 1:15). Paul meant that in Jesus we meet the Son of God made flesh.

The Son of God became one of us and shared our everyday lives. Because Jesus is God, he is the perfect sign of God's love for all humankind. In Jesus we meet God. This is why we say that Jesus is the Sacrament of God to us.

A sacrament is the most effective kind of sign. It causes to happen the very thing for

Salvador Dali, The Last Supper, 1955

which it stands. Jesus is the greatest Sacrament of God because he is God with us.

Our Church is also a sign, or sacrament, of Jesus for us. We meet Jesus each time our Church welcomes, forgives, teaches, serves, and works for justice and peace.

But our Church is not always a perfect sign of Jesus Christ because it is made up of many imperfect people, including ourselves. As each of us becomes a better sign, the whole body of Christ, the Church, becomes a more effective sign, or sacrament, of Jesus.

Seven Special Signs

The seven sacraments—Baptism, Confirmation, Eucharist, Reconciliation, Anointing of the Sick, Matrimony, and Holy Orders—are effective signs of Jesus' presence with us.

These seven sacraments are called effective signs because they do more than ordinary signs. Through the power of the Holy Spirit,

38

Lesson Plan: Middle

"Sacraments of Service." Then have volunteers place each sacrament under the appropriate category. Ask other volunteers to mention one effect of each sacrament listed.

Interpreting Pictures

Direct the young people's attention to the illustration on pages 38–39. Explain that this is Salvador Dali's interpretation of the Last Supper. Show the group a traditional Last Supper picture, then have the fifth graders compare the styles and symbols in the two versions. Ask: "What are the similarities in both pictures? What are the differences? Which rendition do most of the young people like best? Help the fifth graders understand that each picture tries to illustrate the account of the Last Supper in its own unique way. As always, the appreciation of art is a matter of individual preference.

You may wish to use pages 13–14 in the activity book for *Coming to God's Life.*

FAITH WORD

A **sacrament** is an effective sign through which Jesus Christ shares God's life and love with us.

THE SEVEN SACRAMENTS

Baptism, Confirmation, and Eucharist
The Church carries on Jesus' mission of welcoming members into the body of Christ when we celebrate Baptism, Confirmation, and Eucharist. We call these the sacraments of initiation.

Reconciliation and Anointing of the Sick
The Church forgives and heals as Jesus did by celebrating Reconciliation and Anointing of the Sick. We call these the sacraments of healing.

Matrimony and Holy Orders
The Church serves others and is a special sign of God's love by celebrating and living the sacraments of Matrimony and Holy Orders. We call these the sacraments of service.

---

they actually bring about what they promise. The sacraments are the most effective signs of Jesus' presence with us.

In the sacraments, Jesus shares God's life with the Church by the power of the Holy Spirit. He calls us to respond by living as his disciples. In the seven sacraments, Jesus Christ, the Son of God, really and truly comes to us in our lives today.

God's life and love in us is called grace. *Grace is a sharing in the divine life, in God's very life and love.* We receive God's grace in the sacraments.

By celebrating the sacraments, the Church worships and praises God. In celebrating the sacraments, the Church becomes a powerful sign of Jesus' presence and God's reign in our world.

ENRICHMENT

Sharing Experience

Encourage the young people to share personal experiences in their sacramental lives. In particular, ask the fifth graders how they felt when they first celebrated Reconciliation, made their First Holy Communion, or watched the Baptism of a younger relative or friend. Invite them to write these feelings in their faith journals.

Lesson Plan: End

Coming to Faith

Read the *Coming to Faith* questions and have the young people respond either in their faith journals or orally. If oral response is used, ask a volunteer to list suggestions on the chalkboard or newsprint.

Faith Summary

Use the annotated questions to discover whether the young people can state, in their own words, the *Faith Summary* on page 41. Challenge those who can do so to memorize the statements printed in the text. Remember, however, that understanding is more important than rote repetition.

Practicing Faith

Allow the young people to form their own groups or you may wish to assign people to particular groups. Remind them that although the activity is fun, it is still a solemn ritual.

Evaluating Your Lesson

- Do the young people recognize the many signs of God's love?
- Do they know the seven sacraments?
- Have they decided to receive the sacraments more frequently?

Enrichment

A Dozen Ways

Brainstorm with the group ways that young people can be signs of God's love. Write the suggestions on the chalkboard or newsprint.

Give each young person an egg carton and twelve slips of paper. Tell them to choose a dozen loving ways from among those listed and write one on each slip of paper. Have them roll each slip and place it in a section of the carton. Tell them to take the cartons home, and then to choose one loving thing to do for each of the next twelve days. Also encourage the young people to decorate the lids and keep the cartons for future use.

Materials needed: egg cartons; slips of paper; crayons or markers

---

Coming To Faith Possible responses:

How is Jesus a sign, or sacrament, of God's love for you? **He makes God's love present in our lives.**
How can you be a sign of God's love to others today? **By trying to live as Jesus did**

Practicing Faith

Form seven small groups, one for each sacrament. As your group is named, step forward. At the end the groups should be in a single circle.

Leader: Baptism! (Group 1 steps forward.)
Group 1: We thank you, O Blessed Trinity, for the gift of new life with which you have blessed us.

Leader: Confirmation!
Group 2: We bless you, O Blessed Trinity, for the Holy Spirit, who strengthens us for service in your Church and in the world.

Leader: Eucharist!
Group 3: Our lives are nourished with the Body and Blood of Christ.

Leader: Reconciliation!
Group 4: Blessed are we, O Blessed Trinity, with your forgiveness and mercy and peace.

Leader: Anointing of the Sick!
Group 5: You bless us, O Blessed Trinity, with this healing sacrament. You comfort, console, and give us peace.

Leader: Holy Orders!
Group 6: Continue to bless your Church, O Blessed Trinity, with the gift of this sacrament of ministry and service.

Leader: Matrimony!
Group 7: Thank you, O Blessed Trinity, for this sacrament that blesses our lives with married love and families.

All: (stretching hands out to center of circle, palms down) For all these signs of your love and grace that bless our lives, thank you, God! Amen.

Talk with your catechist about ways you and your family might use the "Faith Alive" pages. You might want to use the blessing prayer at a meal during the week.

Optional Activities

God's Sign Language (for use with page 37)

Have the young people make a mural on a long piece of shelving paper using the theme "God's Sign Language." Assign small groups to make several different panels depicting the signs of God's love in nature, in the Church, in families, and in communities. Display the mural when completed.

Materials needed: shelving paper; markers; paint

Jesus, Sacrament of God (for use with page 38)

Invite the young people to brainstorm on the theme "Jesus Is the Sacrament of God to Us." Remind them that a sacrament is a sign. Encourage the young people to use their own ideas and experiences to explain the meaning of the theme. Allow quiet time for reflection before asking the fifth graders to write their thoughts in their faith journals. Invite volunteers to share their entries.

A Sacrament Mural (for use with page 39)

Have the young people use a large sheet of newsprint or shelving paper to make a mural on "The Seven Sacraments." Assign small groups to draw different panels for each of the sacraments of initiation, healing, and service. Hang this mural near your "Sign Language" mural as another example of God's signs.

Materials needed: newsprint or shelving paper; markers; paint

Sign Cards (for use with page 39)

Distribute index cards and have the young people prepare flash cards to review the lesson's key concepts and terms, such as *sacraments, signs, grace*. Let them quiz one another for recognition and understanding of the terms.

Materials needed: index cards

Meaning for Me (for use with page 40)

Gather the group around the prayer table where symbols of the sacraments are displayed (holy water, candles, Bible, chrism, host, wedding ring, stole). Invite each young person to complete statements such as, "Baptism is a sign of God's love for me because _____.

Materials needed: sacramental symbols

A Prayer of Thanks (for use with page 40)

Invite the young people to write prayers of thanks for each of the sacraments. Then gather around the prayer table and let the young people read their prayers. Read the following to the group as an example:

Jesus, we thank You for the Eucharist, which gives us the grace to live as the Body of Christ.

40A

FAITH ALIVE AT HOME AND IN THE PARISH

Your fifth grader has been introduced in a deeper way to the seven sacraments. She or he has been taught that Jesus is the perfect sign, or sacrament, of God and that the Church is the sacrament of Jesus. Each of us, as a member of the Church, is called to carry on Jesus' mission of welcoming, healing, forgiving, and serving. Here are some things your family can do to be signs of Jesus. Take some extra time to listen to your daughter or son. Share with each other the events of the day. Encourage surprise hugs among all family members. Say "I'm sorry" if you hurt one another. Encourage your fifth grader to do the activity below.

† Family Prayer

Leader: We thank you, O God, for the blessings of our lives.

All: For being welcomed into the Church, the body of Christ, at Baptism.
For being more closely united with one another through the Eucharist.
For being forgiven when we sin.

Leader: For all of these blessings we thank you, O God.

Signs of God's Love

Write on pieces of paper ways your family can be signs of God's love. Each day select one and read it aloud. Encourage one another to practice it. Write some of your ideas on cards, and make a wreath as shown below.

Learn by heart — Faith Summary

What is a sacrament?
- A sacrament is an effective sign through which Jesus Christ shares God's life and love with us.

What are the seven sacraments?
- There are seven sacraments: Baptism, Confirmation, Eucharist, Reconciliation, Anointing of the Sick, Matrimony, and Holy Orders.

What do we receive in the sacraments?
- We receive God's grace in the sacraments.

Review

Before doing this *Review*, have your fifth grader go over the *Faith Summary*. Encourage your child to learn the first and second statements by heart. The answers to numbers 1–4 appear on page 216. The response to number 5 will help you see how well your fifth grader is trying to be a sign of God's love. When the *Review* is completed, go over it together.

Circle the letter beside the correct answer.

1. Jesus is a sign of
   a. a pain-free future.
   (b.) God's love.
   c. fear.
   d. hopelessness.

2. The sacraments of initiation are
   a. Confirmation and Matrimony.
   b. Anointing, Eucharist, Baptism.
   (c.) Baptism, Confirmation, Eucharist.
   d. Reconciliation, Baptism, Eucharist.

3. The Church
   a. gives us the sacraments.
   b. carries on the mission of Jesus.
   c. works for God's reign.
   (d.) all of the above

4. God's life and love in us is called
   a. original sin.
   (b.) grace.
   c. sins.
   d. worship.

5. How will you be a sign of God's love to others this week?

   _____
   _____
   _____
   _____

FAMILY SCRIPTURE MOMENT

Gather and ask: What are some of the non-material things in life that we thirst for? Then **Listen** as Jesus leads us to find living water.

. . . Jesus stood up and exclaimed, "Let anyone who thirsts come to me and drink. Whoever believes in me, as scripture says:
   'Rivers of living water will flow from within him.'"
He said this in reference to the Spirit that those who came to believe in him were to receive. There was, of course, no Spirit yet, because Jesus had not yet been glorified.
John 7:37-39

Share what thirst in your life Jesus can satisfy and why.

Consider for family enrichment:

■ Jesus uses the Old Testament image of life-giving waters to prepare his disciples for the coming of the Holy Spirit after the resurrection.

■ Through the sacramental life of the Church, we can constantly drink the living water of the Holy Spirit.

Reflect and **Decide** What are the spiritual gifts for which we thirst, those that might transform us, our Church, and our world? How will we as a family bring our "thirst" and needs to Jesus?

© William H. Sadlier, Inc. All rights reserved.

42

6 CELEBRATING RECONCILIATION

CATECHISM OF THE CATHOLIC CHURCH

The Theme of This Chapter Corresponds with Paragraph 1448

For the Catechist: Spiritual and Catechetical Development

Our Life

Father Lawrence Jenco was held hostage in Lebanon for 18 months during the 1980s. When his terrible ordeal was over, he shared his story with many who wondered how he could forgive his captors. But Father Jenco observed that the need for forgiveness was not limited to the captors. The prisoners sometimes fought and argued among themselves. However, the priest said, "We always concluded the night by giving the handshake of peace."

Ask yourself:

■ What signs of forgiveness do I give?

Sharing Life

Why do we need to be reconciled?

Our Catholic Faith

The desire and ability to forgive is one of the greatest virtues parents and teachers can encourage in young people. Without this virtue, they cannot grow into the mature disciples and peacemakers that Jesus calls them to be.

We prepare our young people for the sacrament of Reconciliation by helping them to recognize their need for forgiveness, their call to live God's Law of Love, and their responsibility to be reconciled with God and others.

Coming to Faith

In what ways is Reconciliation a challenge and a consolation?

Practicing Faith

How will you practice forgiveness this week?

What will you do to inspire your group to be forgiving and reconciling?

Teaching Resources

Teaching Hints

Discuss with the young people the beauty of the sacrament of Reconciliation and the importance of sacramental absolution. The priest, who pronounces the words of absolution ("I absolve you. . ."), acts in the person of Christ. Through this sacrament we are restored to our baptismal innocence. Encourage the young people to take advantage of the sacrament of Reconciliation frequently.

Special-Needs Child

You may wish to have the following tools available for mainstreamed young people.

Visual Needs

■ peer helpers for picture study

■ dark, thick-lead pencils

Auditory Needs

■ audio tape and headphones for the prayer service

Tactile–Motor Needs

■ large, thick pencils, crayons, and markers

■ peer helpers for art projects

Supplemental Resources

Reconciliation: Closing the Gap (video)
Brown-ROA
2460 Kerper Blvd.
P.O. Box 539
Dubuque, IA 52004–0539
(1-800-922-7696)

Names of Sin (video)
St. Anthony Messenger/
Franciscan Communication
1615 Republic Street
Cincinnatti, OH 45210
(1-800-488-0488)
(1-800-989-3600)

43A

Lesson Plan: Beginning

OBJECTIVES

To help the young people

- understand our need for forgiveness;
- know that the Church forgives in Jesus' name;
- choose to celebrate a reconciliation service.

Focusing Prayer

Have the young people open their books to Lesson 6. Explain that this lesson is about forgiveness, then pray together the prayer at the top of page 43.

Our Life

A Harmonious People

Read aloud the information about the Masai in the first two paragraphs. Ask the questions that follow and invite the young people to respond. You may wish to have a volunteer list on the chalkboard or newsprint the ways that the young people show signs of forgiveness.

Sharing Life

Learning from the Masai

Invite responses to the question. Then allow the group to suggest ways in our culture that people show forgiveness. Have the young people write in their faith journals the one way they feel is most important.

---

6 Celebrating Reconciliation

Jesus, help us to forgive others as you forgive us.

OUR LIFE

In eastern Africa there is a fascinating tribe called the Masai. They are very tall, beautiful people who live gently and calmly in harmony with themselves and the natural world around them. This harmony is so important to the Masai that if one family offends another the whole tribe is upset. The whole tribe works to bring the separated families together so there can be peace and reconciliation.

The tribe members encourage the two families to prepare special foods, which they then bring to the center of the village. Everyone encourages them and cheers them on. The two families then exchange their food with each other and sit down to eat. This is the sign of forgiveness. The whole tribe then celebrates the return of peace and harmony.

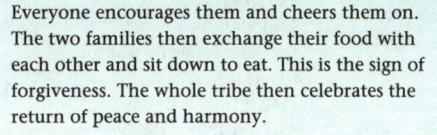

What do you think about the Masai sign of forgiveness? *Answers will vary.*

How do you show signs of forgiveness? *Encourage specific responses.*

SHARING LIFE

What can we learn from the Masai for our lives? *That harmony and reconciliation are important; how to make peace; etc.* Talk together about the best ways to show forgiveness in our culture. *Encourage specific responses.*

ENRICHMENT

Song of Peace

Invite the young people to write song verses for a peaceful, meditative classic tune. "Kumbayah" or "Michael, Row the Boat Ashore" are examples of songs that would be appropriate for the theme of peace and reconciliation.

Or teach the following words to the tune of "Kumbayah":

Jesus came and said,
"Peace be with you.
As the Father sent me,
I now send you."

Lesson Plan: Middle

Our Catholic Faith

Good News of Forgiveness

Ask volunteers to read aloud the first two paragraphs under "Good News of Forgiveness."

Emphasize God's great love as shown by God's readiness to always forgive us when we are sorry and ask for forgiveness.

Read aloud the next paragraph that introduces the gospel story, and have the group silently read the story. Then discuss with the young people what Jesus asked His disciples to do. Emphasize that Jesus gave His disciples the power to forgive sins in His name.

◆ ENRICHMENT ◆

Examination Cards

Invite the young people to copy the examination-of-conscience questions onto index cards that can be used when preparing to celebrate the sacrament of Reconciliation. You may wish to suggest that the fifth graders keep their cards tucked into their faith journals. Remind the young people to add any other questions to the list that they think would help them remember incidents that have taken place since their last confession. As the group works, play some appropriate music softly in the background to create a meditative mood.

Materials needed: index cards; pens or pencils; music

Our Catholic Faith

Good News of Forgiveness

God sent Jesus to show us that God is always waiting to forgive our sins, no matter how bad they are. Jesus taught us that God always forgives us when we are sorry for our sins and ask his forgiveness.

Jesus understood that living as his disciples and doing God's loving will are not always easy. He knew that his followers might sin and need God's forgiveness.

Here is a gospel story in which Jesus tells the disciples to forgive sins in his name.

Late the first Easter Sunday evening, Jesus' disciples were hiding in a locked room. They were afraid that the people who crucified Jesus would kill them, too.

Jesus came and said, "Peace be with you."

After looking at the wounds in Jesus' hands and side, they were amazed and filled with joy. They knew it was Jesus.

Jesus said to them again, "Peace be with you. As the Father has sent me, so I send you. Whose sins you forgive are forgiven them."

Based on John 20:19–23

Our Church Forgives

Today our Church continues Jesus' mission of forgiveness in the sacrament of Reconciliation. We prepare ourselves to celebrate Reconciliation by examining our conscience and by becoming aware of our sins.

We think about our sins or the things that showed we did not follow the way of Jesus. We are sorry for what we have done that is wrong. We remember that God is always ready to forgive us if we are sorry. We can think about the story of the prodigal son and his forgiving father (Luke 15:11–24).

When we examine our conscience, we may ask ourselves questions like these:

- Do I show that I love God?
- Does God come first in my life, or are other things more important to me?
- Have I used God's name with respect, or have I sometimes said God's name in anger?
- Do I take part in Mass on Sundays and on holy days of obligation, or have I missed Mass for no serious reason?
- Do I obey my parents or guardians or have I disobeyed them?
- Do I show that I love other people as I love myself?

Lesson Plan: Middle

Our Church Forgives

Ask: "How does our Church continue Jesus' mission of forgiveness?" and then have the young people silently read the first two paragraphs under "Our Church Forgives."

Introduce the examination of conscience on page 44 by reading the opening two lines. Then read aloud the questions slowly and reflectively. Allow time between each question for the young people to respond thoughtfully to themselves.

Invite a volunteer to read aloud the closing paragraph of this section. Then discuss the picture on page 45.

- Have I tried to act lovingly to others, or have I hurt anyone by my words or deeds?
- Have I shared my things with others, or have I been selfish or taken others' things without permission?
- Have I been truthful and fair, or have I lied and cheated?
- Have I cared about the poor, the hungry, and those who are oppressed?
- Do I try to be a peacemaker and treat everyone with justice?
- Do I try to live like Jesus?

After we have examined our conscience and are sorry for our sins, we are ready to continue with the celebration of the sacrament of Reconciliation.

Coming to Faith

Take a minute to look again at the examination of conscience. Then work in groups or with a partner to change each question into several "we can..." statements. For example:

Do I show that I love God? We can show we love God by being more patient with those who annoy us.

Share all your "we can..." statements with your group. If possible, these can be written on large paper, decorated, and displayed in the church vestibule or parish center.

◆ ENRICHMENT ◆

Disciple Diaries

Guide the young people's meditation on Jesus' words of peace on Easter Sunday evening. Then ask the young people to imagine that they are Jesus' disciples and to think about how they would answer the following questions: "Why are you hiding? How do you feel when you see and hear Jesus? How will you share Jesus' peace with others?"

Now invite the young people to write journal entries as if they were the disciples on that Sunday so long ago. Share the following example to get them started:

Sunday morning: The Lord is gone. We shall not see Him again. Tonight I shall meet with the others to talk about Him. We miss Him.

Sunday night, late: What I have to say some may doubt, but it's true. In a locked room, the Lord suddenly appeared out of nowhere!

Materials needed: journals

Lesson Plan: End

Coming to Faith

Saying, "We Can. . . ."

Read the text to the young people. Make sure the fifth graders understand what they are to do. If necessary, have a volunteer give another example to help anyone who is confused or unsure. Allow time for each group or pair to read its "We can . . ." statements to the others.

Practicing Faith

Select leaders, readers, actors, and hymns for the prayer service. Allow time for each participant to prepare for her or his role in the service. Briefly discuss the celebration with the young people, inviting them to spend some quiet time thinking about the things for which they want to ask forgiveness. Explain that this is a time for feeling better about ourselves, a time for beginning again to live as Jesus taught us. Use the annotation and the prayer service directions to guide the celebration.

Materials needed: music book; Bibles

EVALUATING YOUR LESSON

■ Do the young people understand that God always forgives?

■ Do they know that Jesus gave His disciples the power to forgive?

■ Have they celebrated a reconciliation service?

ENRICHMENT

Spread the Word

Have the young people repeat their prayer service to teach younger children about forgiveness. Arrange to have a younger group attend one of your sessions. Have your young people explain, in their own words, why it is important to forgive others and to receive forgiveness from others. Let your group celebrate its prayer service with one of the younger children standing beside each of the fifth graders so that everyone is included.

Practicing Faith

A Prayer Service of Forgiveness
Opening Hymn
Theme
We praise and give thanks for God's love and forgiveness.

Greeting
Leader: Jesus brings us God's forgiveness. May the peace and mercy of Jesus be with you.
All: And also with you.
Leader: Jesus, we have come to celebrate God's forgiveness. Hear us as we ask for your forgiveness and peace.
All: Amen.

First Reading
God is always ready to forgive us. A reading from the Book of Joel. (Read Joel 2:13.)

Responsorial Psalm
Leader: Teach me, O God, what you want me to do, and I will obey you faithfully.
All: Great is your love for us, O God.
Leader: You, O God, are a merciful and loving God, always patient, always kind, and always faithful. Turn to me and have mercy on me.
All: Great is your love for us, O God.

Gospel
The group may act out the gospel story about the prodigal son (Luke 15:11–24) or several readers may take different parts and read it together. Quiet instrumental recorded music may be helpful during the following reflection:

Examination of Conscience
A member of the group reads the examination of conscience questions on page 45. After each question is read, pause for quiet reflection. Then pray:

Leader: Jesus, forgive us our sins.
All: Lord, hear our prayer.

Leader: Jesus, help us to love one another.
All: Lord, have mercy on us.

Leader: Jesus, give us the courage to turn away from sin and to change our lives.
All: Lord, forgive us our sins.

Leader: Jesus, free us from our sins and lead us to the freedom enjoyed by your faithful disciples.
All: (Pray the Our Father together.)

A Prayer of Praise
Select a psalm as a prayer of praise, for example, Psalm 136:1–9 or Psalm 145:1–13.

Sign of Peace
Share with one another a greeting of peace.

Closing Hymn

Optional Activities

Picture of Forgiveness (for use with page 43)

Invite the young people to make a drawing of a modern-day prodigal son situation. Have them picture someone returning to a parent, teacher, or friend to ask forgiveness. Then invite the young people to share their drawings with the group and explain the stories behind them.

Materials needed: crayons or markers; paper

Forgiveness Fair (for use with page 44)

Invite the young people to express the feeling of peace and joy that God's forgiveness brings. They may express themselves through an essay, a poem, a drawing, or a song. Have the young people share their completed work with the group by holding a "Forgiveness Fair," during which essays and poems are read, songs and dances are performed, and drawings are displayed.

Materials needed: writing and drawing paper; pens; pencils; crayons and/or markers

An Evening Prayer (for use with page 44)

Invite the young people to relax, close their eyes, and silently repeat this prayer:

Lord Jesus, have mercy on me.

Close by praying the prayer of Saint Francis on page 29. Then sing an "Amen" or an "Alleluia." Encourage the young people to use this prayer exercise before going to bed each night.

On-Site Story (for use with page 46)

Challenge the young people to prepare an imaginary TV news show about the coming of the Holy Spirit on Pentecost. Let fifth graders play the parts of the news reporters, the disciples, and the neighbors from whom the press is getting reactions to the news that tongues of fire were seen in the area! Allow the young people to use their imaginations and any prior knowledge of tabloid news shows to help them make the show interesting and informative.

FAITH ALIVE AT HOME AND IN THE PARISH

This liturgical lesson provided your fifth grader with a further development of the meaning and grace of the sacrament of Reconciliation and a deepened awareness of the meaning of forgiveness. The ability and desire to forgive others and to ask forgiveness of others is one of the greatest virtues we can develop in our children. Forgiveness is a mature virtue, but it can be modeled and encouraged from your child's earliest years. When children witness and experience forgiveness in their homes, they more readily practice it themselves.

The first Christians, learning from their Hebrew roots in the Old Testament, came to realize that sins committed after Baptism are an offense to the whole community—that sin cuts us off from God's people. When they faced the problem of being reconciled for those sins, they might have remembered the Israelite Day of Atonement, on which the *whole people* approached God *as a people* to seek mercy. They surely remembered the parables and the example and words of Jesus and his ministry of forgiving sinners.

The sacrament of Reconciliation emphasizes the role of the Church community in our celebration of this sacrament. Since our sins are against one another and take from the holiness of the community, it is most fitting that our sacramental reconciliation with God should be through the ministry of the Church.

✝ Family Prayer: Forgiveness

Jesus, we come to celebrate your forgiveness. We do this by forgiving one another. Give us open hearts. Through your gift of forgiveness, bring our family harmony and peace. Help us to be your peacemakers in our world. Amen.

Learn by heart — Faith Summary

What is God always ready to do?
● God is always ready to forgive our sins.

What power did Jesus give His disciples?
● Jesus gave his disciples the power to forgive sins.

What is Reconciliation?
● Reconciliation is the sacrament in which we are forgiven by God through the ministry of the Church.

Share with your family how the Masai restored peace and harmony through a forgiveness rite. Talk about ways your family can share forgiveness. Describe these ideas below.

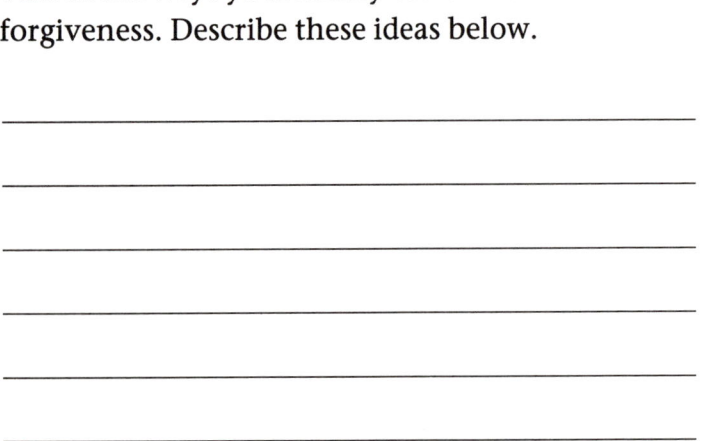

_____
_____
_____
_____
_____

Review

Go over the *Faith Summary* together and encourage your fifth grader to learn it by heart, especially the third statement. Then complete the *Review*. The answers to numbers 1–4 appear on page 216. The response to number 5 will indicate how well your son or daughter understands the rite of Reconciliation.

Fill in the circle next to the correct answer.

1. Jesus gave the apostles power to
   - ● forgive sins in his name.
   - ○ walk on water.
   - ○ ascend into heaven.

2. Jesus' mission of forgiveness continues in
   - ○ the Our Father.
   - ● the sacrament of Reconciliation
   - ○ the sacrament of Holy Orders.

3. Jesus always forgives us
   - ● when we are sorry.
   - ○ even when we are not sorry.
   - ○ whether we need it or not.

4. We prepare for Reconciliation by
   - ○ fasting for one hour.
   - ○ using holy water.
   - ● making an examination of conscience.

5. Tell what happens when you celebrate the sacrament of Reconciliation.

_____
_____
_____
_____

FAMILY SCRIPTURE MOMENT

Gather and ask: How do we feel when others accuse or blame us? Then **Listen** to this story of Jesus forgiving the woman caught in adultery.

They said to him, "Teacher, this woman was caught in the very act of committing adultery.... Moses commanded us to stone such women. So what do you say?"... Jesus ... said to them, "Let the one among you who is without sin be the first to throw a stone at her." And in response, they went away one by one.... Then Jesus ... said to her, "Woman, where are they? Has no one condemned you?" She replied, "No one, sir." Then Jesus said, "Neither do I condemn you. Go, [and] from now on do not sin any more."

John 8:4–7, 9–11

Share what you learn for your own life from this Scripture story.

Consider for family enrichment:

■ By refusing to condemn the woman, Jesus teaches his disciples to be merciful as God is merciful.

■ As disciples of Jesus we are called to grow rich in mercy, compassion, and understanding.

Reflect and **Decide** What are some of the ways we can help one another to avoid sin? Pray together: Lord Jesus, let us be peacemakers. Help us to recognize our own sins, rather than pointing a finger at others.

48

7 CELEBRATING EUCHARIST

CATECHISM OF THE CATHOLIC CHURCH

The Theme of This Chapter Corresponds with Paragraph 1346

For the Catechist: Spiritual and Catechetical Development

Our Life

A decorative plaque above the kitchen table read, "Christ, invisible guest at all our meals, come and eat with us." Whenever the family gathered for an evening meal, one of the parents or children would pray this invitation as a reminder of the unseen Guest among them. And at times when family members were scattered hither and yon, should one sit down for lunch alone, he or she would offer the prayer as a reminder that there was, in truth, a loving companion present.

Ask yourself:

■ How is Christ present at my table?

Sharing Life

■ What connections do you see between the Eucharist and your everyday meals?

Our Catholic Faith

Imagine the astonishment of the Israelites when Jesus, after feeding a huge crowd with a few loaves and fishes, told them:

"I am the living bread that came down from heaven; whoever eats this bread will live forever; and the bread that I will give is my flesh for the life of the world" (John 6:51).

Whenever we celebrate the Eucharist, we are nourished by this Living Bread. We are united not only with Jesus, but with all who share the "one loaf and the one cup." Having been fed for the journey, we go out into the world to communicate Christ's love to others. Our "invisible guest" remains present in the little churches of our families, where the Eucharist continues to feed us.

Coming to Faith

How might the Living Bread continue to nourish your family life?

Practicing Faith

How will you encourage your group to hunger for the "food that lasts forever"?

Teaching Resources

Teaching Hints

The young people will come to a deeper understanding of the Eucharist by planning a celebration of the Mass. It is important to allow them to be responsible for as much of the planning as possible. Be available to assist them. If it is not possible to celebrate the Eucharist together, plan a prayer service.

Encourage the young people to invite their families and friends to attend this liturgical celebration.

Special-Needs Child

You may wish to provide the following equipment and accommodations for mainstreamed young people.

Visual Needs

■ preferential seating

Auditory Needs

■ audio tape and headphones for the Bible story

Tactile–Motor Needs

■ large, thick markers and pencils

Supplemental Resources

The History and Meaning of the Eucharist (video)
Brown-ROA
2460 Kerper Blvd.
P.O. Box 539
Dubuque, IA 52004–0539
(1-800-922-7696)

49A

Lesson Plan: Beginning

OBJECTIVES

To help the young people

- understand the Eucharist as a sign of unity;
- know that the Eucharist is both a meal and a sacrifice;
- choose to celebrate the Eucharist.

Focusing Prayer

Remind the young people that the last lesson was about forgiveness and the sacrament of Reconciliation. Explain that today we focus on the Eucharist. Have the fifth graders open their books to Lesson 7, then pray together the prayer at the top of page 49.

Our Life

Elisha Helps a Widow

Introduce the *Our Life* story by explaining that it is about a poor woman who ran out of food.

Read aloud the introductory paragraph. Invite several volunteers to read the story of Elisha aloud. At the story's completion, invite several young people to write their responses to the concluding *Our Life* questions on newsprint or the chalkboard.

Sharing Life

Asking Elisha's Help

Invite the group to think about and share their responses to the questions. Encourage the young people to respond to the last question in their faith journals.

---

7 Celebrating Eucharist

Jesus, help us who share the Bread of Life to become one in mind and heart.

Our Life

In the Old Testament we read about a man named Elisha, who lived long ago. Elisha helped those who were sick or poor.

One time a woman explained to him that her husband had just died and that a man to whom her husband owed money had come to her demanding to be paid. The woman was very poor, and her family no longer even had food to eat. All that was left in her home was a small jar of olive oil.

Elisha instructed her to go home and borrow as many empty jars as she could. He told her to start pouring the olive oil from the small jar that she had into all the other jars her sons could bring to her.

Elisha smiled when the woman returned and told him that she had a house filled with jars of olive oil. He said to her, "Sell the oil to pay off your creditor; with what remains, you and your children can live."

Based on 2 Kings 4:1–7

What did you learn from this story? *God helps us through caring people; food is a sign of love and care.*
Who gives you what you need for life? *God, through the people who care for us and help us*

Sharing Life

Imagine you could ask Elisha for a certain food or drink that would never run out. What would you ask for? Why?
Accept all reasonable responses.
Did Jesus give us any special food?
Yes, the Eucharist
What is it? How does it help us? *It is the Body and Blood of Christ; it makes us one with Jesus and one another. It strengthens us to live as His disciples.*

49

ENRICHMENT

Act It Out

Invite the young people to act out the story of Elisha. Encourage everyone to take part in planning, producing, and putting on the plays. If the fifth graders want to use stick puppets, have them draw the characters and tape them to plastic drinking straws.

Materials needed: drawing paper; crayons or markers; tape; plastic straws

Lesson Plan: Middle

Our Catholic Faith

Food That Lasts Forever

Read aloud the first two paragraphs in this section and invite comments about the Christian family meal that we know as the Eucharist.

Have volunteers read aloud the next two paragraphs. Encourage the young people to share and discuss their responses to the material. Then invite a volunteer to read aloud Jesus' words, and challenge the group to memorize them.

One With Jesus and Others

Guide the silent reading of "One With Jesus and Others." Then encourage the young people to comment on the illustration.

ENRICHMENT

A Sign of Unity

Ask the fifth graders to draw and color four overlapping and interlocking rings, similar to the rings on the Olympic flag. Explain that this overlapping and interlocking might symbolize that our celebration of the Eucharist is the most powerful sign of our unity with Jesus and with one another. Then have the young people write one of the *four basic parts* of the Mass inside each circle.

Materials needed: white paper; crayons or markers

Our Catholic Faith

Food That Lasts Forever

The early Christians frequently shared the special meal Jesus gave us. They followed the instruction that Jesus gave to his disciples at the Last Supper, "Do this in remembrance of me" (1 Corinthians 11:24).

They came together to celebrate the Eucharist. They sang songs; remembered Jesus' teachings; and recalled his life, death, and resurrection. They took bread and wine and did what Jesus did at the Last Supper. Then they shared in the Body and Blood of Christ together.

Jesus himself is the Bread of Life, the food that we receive in the Eucharist. Jesus is really present with us in the Eucharist to nourish and strengthen us to live for the reign of God.

One time Jesus told the people, "I am the bread of life; whoever comes to me will never hunger, and whoever believes in me will never thirst" (John 6:35).

One with Jesus and Others

Celebrating the Eucharist together as the Church is the most powerful sign of our unity with Jesus Christ and with one another.

Teaching about the Eucharist as a sign of our unity with Jesus and one another, Saint Paul wrote:

"The cup of blessing that we bless, is it not a participation in the blood of Christ? The bread that we break, is it not a participation in the body of Christ? . . .we, though many, are one body, for we all partake of the one loaf."

1 Corinthians 10:16–17

We come together as the community of Jesus' followers to share in his life and love. In our eucharistic assembly, we unite ourselves with Jesus and the Church all over the world. We are the sign of Jesus' life and love in the world.

Our Thanksgiving Prayer

The Eucharist is both a meal and a sacrifice. At Mass we celebrate the Eucharist. It is the Christian community's greatest prayer of praise and thanksgiving to God.

In the *Introductory Rites* we prepare for our celebration. We remember that we are the community of Jesus' disciples.

The Scripture readings in the *Liturgy of the Word* recall how we are to live as the people of God, the body of Christ. We listen carefully, because God speaks to us through the Scripture readings. We learn how to live for the reign of God, as Jesus taught.

Lesson Plan: Middle

Our Thanksgiving Prayer

Read aloud the introductory paragraph under "Our Thanksgiving Prayer." Then write the terms *Introductory Rites, Liturgy of the Word, Liturgy of the Eucharist, and Concluding Rite* on the chalkboard or newsprint. Ask volunteers to explain, in their own words, what each term means. Tell the young people that the next few paragraphs will review the parts of the Mass.

Have several volunteers read aloud the next five paragraphs. Invite the young people to suggest relevant words for each part of the Mass. On the chalkboard or newsprint, write key action words that the young people have identified for each part of the Mass (for example: *prepare, listen, praise and thank, receive, live*).

Finally, ask the young people to write in their faith journals the four essential parts of the Mass and any key words that will help them relate to each part.

You may wish to use pages 17–18 in the activity book for *Coming to God's Life*.

In the *Liturgy of the Eucharist* we praise and thank God for Jesus, God's own Son. Jesus gave himself for us. We remember and celebrate his life, death, and resurrection. The priest offers this great sacrifice again in Christ's name. We give thanks that through Jesus we are made one again with God and one another.

The priest breaks the Bread because we who are many are one in the sharing of the one Bread. We receive the gift of Jesus, our Bread of Life, in Holy Communion. We give thanks to Jesus for coming to us.

We pray and receive God's blessing in the *Concluding Rite*. We go forth and try to show our family, our neighbors, and even strangers that we are the body of Christ in the world today. We try to live as disciples of Jesus.

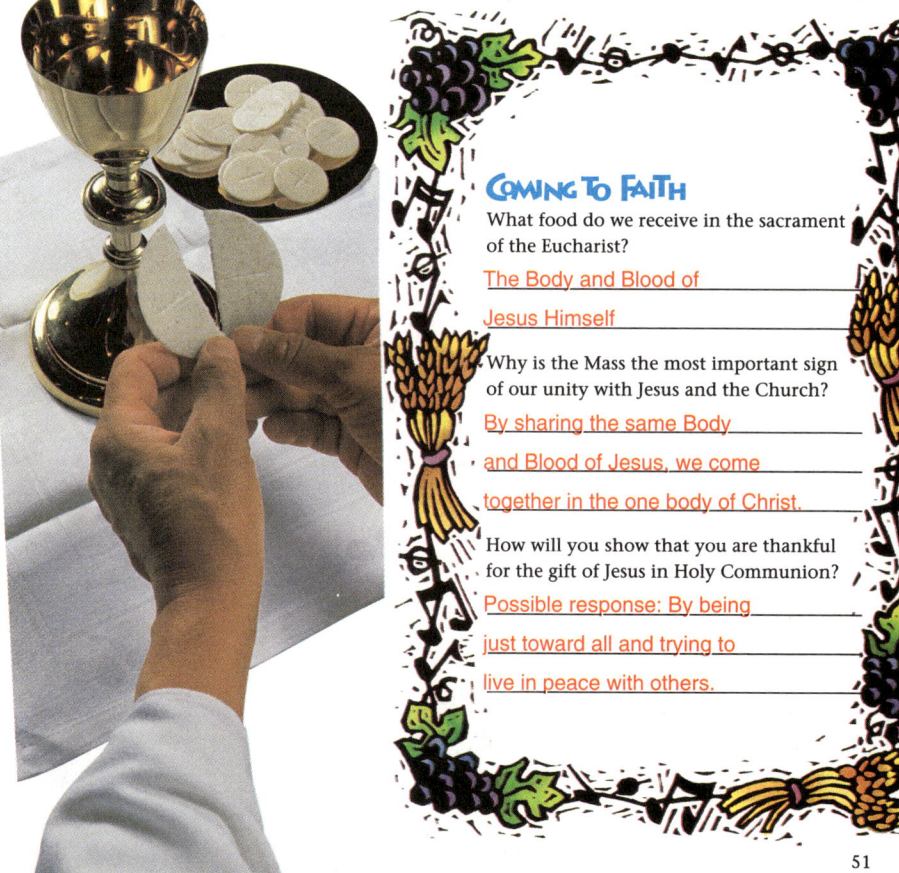

Coming to Faith

What food do we receive in the sacrament of the Eucharist?
The Body and Blood of Jesus Himself

Why is the Mass the most important sign of our unity with Jesus and the Church?
By sharing the same Body and Blood of Jesus, we come together in the one body of Christ.

How will you show that you are thankful for the gift of Jesus in Holy Communion?
Possible response: By being just toward all and trying to live in peace with others.

ENRICHMENT

Illustrating the Mass

Challenge the young people to make cartoon-like panels with simple pictures showing the step-by-step celebration of the Eucharist. Let them work independently, in pairs, or in small groups—whichever works best for them. Have the young people share their finished Mass strips with the group. Ask the group to choose one or two that are simple yet precise to share with children from a lower grade. Have the makers of those strips present the information to the younger children.

Materials needed: paper strips; pencils; crayons or markers

7

Lesson Plan: End

Coming to Faith

The Gift of Jesus

Invite the group's comments about the picture on page 51. Recall for the young people the two ways of receiving the Eucharist. Stress the importance of a reverent attitude.

Then ask each of the *Coming to Faith* questions. Allow time for the young people to write their responses. Encourage volunteers to share them with the group.

Faith Summary

Use the annotations to review the *Faith Summary* on page 53. Ask the young people to tell, in their own words, what they have learned in this lesson.

Practicing Faith

A Mass Celebration

Have missalettes available for each member of the group. You might read aloud the readings for the Mass of the day from a missalette or the Lectionary. Then have the group work together to plan other details for their celebration of the Eucharist. Use the annotated suggestions.

If possible, invite some guests to your group Mass or prayer service.

Evaluating Your Lesson

- Do the young people understand the Eucharist as a sign of unity?
- Do they know the parts of the sacrifice of the Mass?
- Have they chosen to plan a celebration?

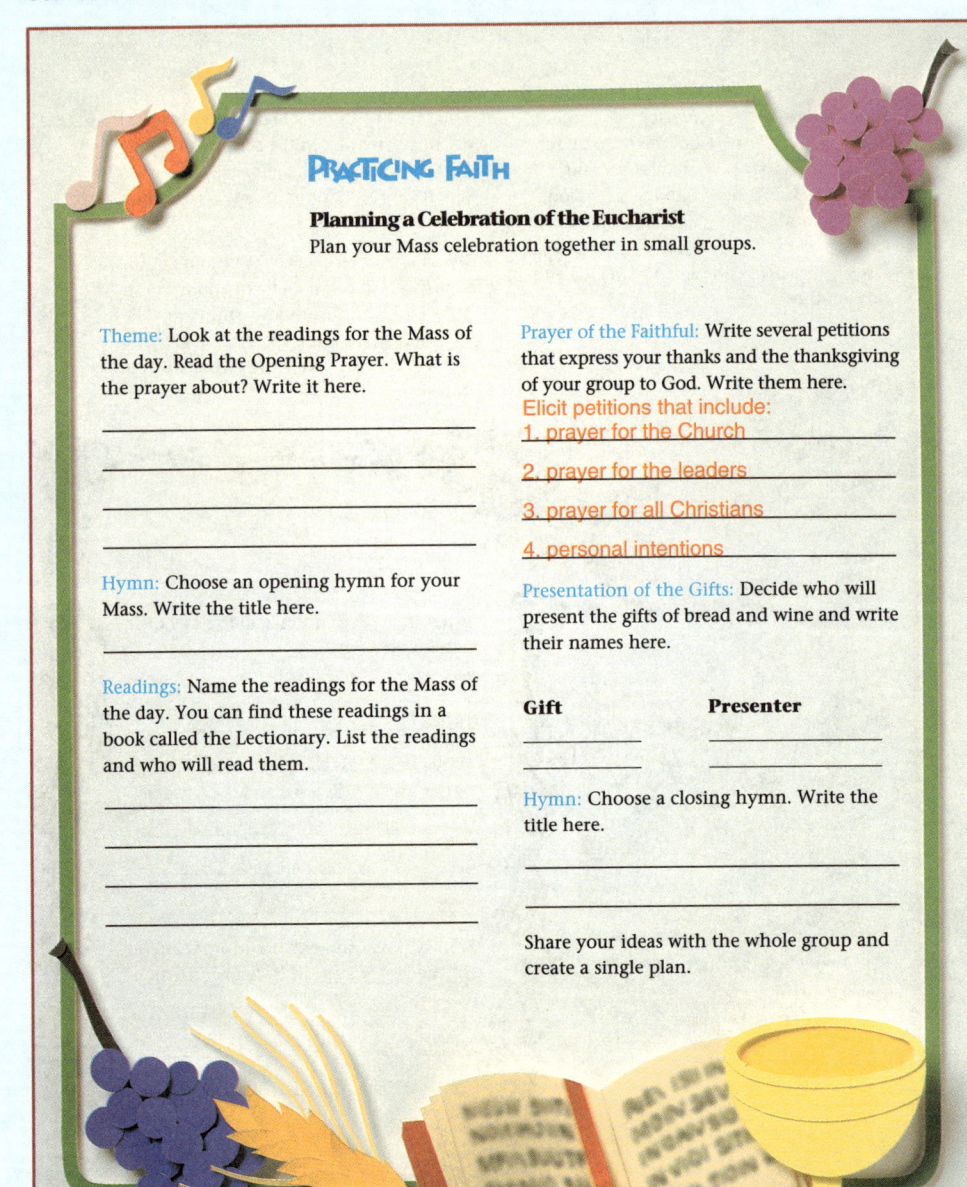

Enrichment

Announcing the Event

Invite the young people to write press releases about their celebration of the Eucharist. Remind them to include the who, what, where, when, and how. Allow the fifth graders to look through old newspapers to find reports of social, political, or religions events to see how the writer got a lot of information into a small space. Post some of the releases that the young people write to advertise the upcoming celebration.

Materials needed: paper; pencils or pens; newspapers

Practicing Faith

Planning a Celebration of the Eucharist

Plan your Mass celebration together in small groups.

Theme: Look at the readings for the Mass of the day. Read the Opening Prayer. What is the prayer about? Write it here.

_____
_____
_____

Hymn: Choose an opening hymn for your Mass. Write the title here.

_____

Readings: Name the readings for the Mass of the day. You can find these readings in a book called the Lectionary. List the readings and who will read them.

_____
_____
_____

Prayer of the Faithful: Write several petitions that express your thanks and the thanksgiving of your group to God. Write them here.
Elicit petitions that include:
1. prayer for the Church
2. prayer for the leaders
3. prayer for all Christians
4. personal intentions

Presentation of the Gifts: Decide who will present the gifts of bread and wine and write their names here.

Gift	Presenter
_____	_____

Hymn: Choose a closing hymn. Write the title here.

_____
_____

Share your ideas with the whole group and create a single plan.

52

Optional Activities

A Scripture Reading (for use with page 49)

From the Bible, read Acts 4:32, 34–35. Then invite the group to tell how the celebration of the Eucharist was a sign of unity for the early Christians. Also encourage the young people to draw pictures showing early Christians celebrating the Eucharist.

Materials needed: Bible, paper; crayons or markers

A Prayer for Unity (for use with page 50)

Gather at the prayer table, link arms, and pray together from 1 Corinthians 10:17: ". . . we, though many, are one body, for we all partake of the one loaf." Remind the young people that as Christians we are called to share what we have with others so that fewer people will be in need.

A Unity Display (for use with page 51)

Make a "We Are One in the Lord" display. Give each young person a long sheet of white shelving paper to make a full-length self-portrait to cut out. Ask a volunteer to sketch a large host and chalice on a sheet of paper, tape it to the wall or chalkboard, then place the portraits around the eucharistic symbols. Use the display as an integral part of your group celebration.

Materials needed: white shelving paper; pencils; crayons or markers; scissors; tape

You're on Candid Camera (for use with page 52)

Videotape your special group celebration of the Eucharist. Do the taping yourself, or let several volunteers take turns. Make sure everyone has a chance to be seen on tape. The young people will enjoy seeing a repeat performance, and you might even be able to have it shown on your local public access channel—if cable is available in your area.

Materials needed: video equipment

FAITH ALIVE: AT HOME AND IN THE PARISH

In this liturgical lesson the fifth graders are drawn into a deeper understanding of the Eucharist by planning a celebration of the Mass.

For Catholic Christians, the Eucharist is the spiritual meal in which we are fed by the Lord with his Body and Blood. During the celebration, we hear the word of God proclaimed in the readings. We respond with words of thanksgiving and praise. We are invited to share in the communal meal by the priest who offers the eucharist sacrifice in Christ's name.

In the Eucharist we become one with Jesus because we do this eucharistic action in memory of him. Being fed at the Lord's table means we have been nourished anew for the journey. We in turn need to feed others, share with others, and serve others in Jesus' name. Our Eucharist is our feast in order that we can fast with those who hunger and thirst after justice.

Your family might want to "go in peace" from the Eucharist to reach out to those who are physically hungry at a local shelter or soup kitchen. Or perhaps you might prepare a dinner for a neighbor who is disabled or housebound.

† Family Prayer

Jesus, you are the Bread of Life. If we come to you, we will never be hungry. If we believe in you, we will never be thirsty. Help us to respond to all the hungers and thirsts that we find in those we meet.

Make a prayer card for your table. Start a family custom: whenever you gather for a family meal a family member prays this prayer as a reminder of the unseen Guest among you.

Learn by heart — Faith Summary

What do we celebrate at Mass?
- At Mass we celebrate the Eucharist, our greatest prayer of thanksgiving and praise.

What do we do in the Liturgy of the Word?
- In the Liturgy of the Word we listen as God speaks to us in the readings.

What do we do in the Liturgy of the Eucharist?
- In the Liturgy of the Eucharist we praise and thank God for Jesus, whom we receive in Holy Communion.

Christ, invisible Guest at all our meals, come and be with us.

Review

Go over the *Faith Summary* with your fifth grader. Encourage him or her to learn it by heart. Then complete the Review. The answers to numbers 1–4 appear on page 216. The response to number 5 will help to indicate your fifth grader's understanding of the Eucharist. When the *Review* is completed, go over it together.

Circle the letter next to the correct answer.

1. Jesus said that whoever comes to him will
   a. sit at his right side.
   b. rule the world.
   c. never be hungry.

2. Paul said that all of us who share the Body of Christ
   a. are one.
   b. are teachers.
   c. are apostles.

3. In the Eucharist we come together as Jesus' followers to
   a. share in the life and love of Jesus.
   b. unite ourselves with Jesus and the Church.
   c. both a and b.

4. Circle the letter to show what does not belong to the Mass.
   a. Liturgy of the Word
   b. stations of the cross
   c. Liturgy of the Eucharist

5. Jesus said, "I am the Bread of Life." Explain what this means for your life.
   _____
   _____

FAMILY SCRIPTURE MOMENT

Gather and recall improvised meals for friends when there were more guests than expected. Ask: Why and how do we feed people when there may not be "enough food to go around"? Then **Listen** to the story of Jesus feeding a hungry crowd.

Jesus said, "Have the people recline." Now there was a great deal of grass in that place. So the men reclined, about five thousand in number. Then Jesus took the loaves, gave thanks, and distributed them to those who were reclining, and also as much of the fish as they wanted. When they had had their fill, he said to his disciples, "Gather the fragments left over, so that nothing will be wasted." So they collected them, and filled twelve wicker baskets with fragments. . . .
John 6:10-13

Share what you hear this gospel story saying for your life.

Consider for family enrichment:
■ By feeding the crowd with a few loaves and fishes, Jesus shows his concern for all who are hungry and gives a sign that he is the Bread of Life for all.
■ In the celebration of the Eucharist, we become signs of Jesus' love for a hungry world.

Reflect and **Decide** How might our parish feed those who hunger for bread? for the Bible? for dignity and self-esteem?

UNIT 1 • REVIEW

Ask: Who is Jesus Christ?
Jesus Christ Reveals God
Jesus Christ is truly human. Jesus was like us in every way except that he never sinned. Jesus Christ is also truly divine. Jesus is God's own Son. Jesus revealed by his words and deeds that "God is love" (1 John 4:8). Today, God works through us and other people to show God's love in the world.

Ask: How did Jesus announce the kingdom of God?
Jesus Christ and the Kingdom of God
Jesus showed by his words and actions that he was the Messiah. Jesus announced the good news of the kingdom, or reign, of God. The good news is that God loves us and will always be with us.

Jesus brought about the reign of God by his words and actions. Jesus showed us how to live for the reign of God by loving God, our neighbor, and ourselves.

Ask: How did Jesus show us how to live for God's kingdom?
Jesus Christ Blesses Our Lives
Jesus Christ invited everyone to live for the reign of God. Jesus forgave people their sins. By his words and actions Jesus lived his whole life helping and serving others. We live for the reign of God by following the example of Jesus.

Ask: How does the Church carry on the mission of Jesus?
The Church Carries on Jesus' Mission
After Jesus' ascension into heaven, the Holy Spirit came to Jesus' disciples and filled them with gifts to preach the good news to everyone. The Holy Spirit continues to help our Church to carry on the mission of Jesus to all people.

The Church welcomes all people to believe in Jesus and to follow him. The Church forgives and heals, as Jesus did. Every member of the Church is called to carry on Jesus' mission by serving others.

Ask: What is a sacrament? Name the seven sacraments.
The Sacraments and the Church
There are many signs of God's love in our everyday life. The Church is the sacrament of Jesus. The most effective signs of God's presence in our Church are the seven sacraments.

Baptism, Confirmation, and Eucharist are called sacraments of initiation. Through these sacraments the Church welcomes all people into the community of the Church.

Reconciliation and the Anointing of the Sick are sacraments of healing. Through these sacraments the Church brings us God's forgiveness when we sin, and strengthens us when we are sick.

Matrimony and Holy Orders are sacraments of service. Through these sacraments the Church continues Jesus' mission of service through married couples and through our ordained ministers: bishops, priests, and deacons.

UNIT 1 • TEST

Circle the answers.

1. Jesus was
- **a.** human.
- **b.** divine.
- **(c.)** both human and divine.
- **d.** an angel sent by God.

2. Jesus revealed to us that
- **a.** God cares about us.
- **b.** God is love.
- **c.** God forgives us.
- **(d.)** all of these

3. Jesus began his work by
- **a.** ascending into heaven.
- **(b.)** announcing the reign of God.
- **c.** dying on the cross.
- **d.** sending the Holy Spirit.

4. Jesus forgave sins to show that
- **(a.)** he was reconciling us with God.
- **b.** God forgives only some people.
- **c.** God only forgives some of our sins.
- **d.** we do not need to forgive others.

5. The most powerful signs of Jesus' presence in the Church are
- **a.** parish churches.
- **b.** priests.
- **(c.)** the seven sacraments.
- **d.** parents.

Possible responses:
Complete the following statements.

6. Baptism, Confirmation, and Eucharist are called sacraments of initiation because

through these sacraments the Church welcomes all into the

community of Christ.

7. Reconciliation and Anointing of the sick are called sacraments of healing because

these sacraments bring us God's healing and forgiveness.

8. Matrimony and Holy Orders are called sacraments of service because

these sacraments help us give loving service to the Church and to

all people.

Think and decide:

9. To me the reign of God means

living the Law of Love; doing God's will.

10. I will show that I live for God's reign by

treating others fairly.

Name _____

Your son or daughter has just completed Unit 1. Have him or her bring this paper to the catechist. It will help you and the catechist know better how to help your fifth grader grow in faith.

_____ He or she needs help with the part of the Review I have underlined.

_____ He or she understands what has been taught in this unit.

_____ I would like to speak with you. My phone number is _____.

Signature: _____ 56

8 JESUS CHRIST BRINGS US LIFE (BAPTISM)

For the Catechist: Spiritual and Catechetical Development

ADULT BACKGROUND

Our Life

It was initiation night for the entire Siguenza family. The new fire had been lit, the paschal candle was burning, and now it was time for Marta and Hestor, Michael and Rosie to be baptized.

Each of them was wearing white and a shy smile. As the celebrant called them each by name, they approached the baptismal font. In its saving waters they saw their own hopes reflected.

Ask yourself:

- What hopes do you have for the newly baptized in your family or parish?

Sharing Life

What symbols of Baptism are the most meaningful to you?

What messages do these symbols convey?

Our Catholic Faith

Saint Paul tells us that "We who were baptized into Christ Jesus were baptized into his death" (Romans 6:3). He reminds us that the sacrament of rebirth involves a dying and a rising. Baptism plunges us into the death of Christ. Yet, more importantly, it lifts us up into the fullness of His new life. In the waters of Baptism, we are:

- freed from original sin;
- given a share in the life of grace;
- made holy;
- made temples of the Holy Spirit;
- made members of the Church, the body of Christ.

Baptism initiates us into Christ's priestly, prophetic, and kingly roles, which require us to live for and to proclaim God's kingdom. Through this sacrament of initiation, we are called to minister to our sisters and brothers in the community of faith, and to be "other Christs" in the world.

Baptismal catechesis focuses on God's redemptive love embodied in the life, death, and resurrection of Jesus. By His sacrifice, we are saved from sin and death. By His Spirit, we are empowered to worship and commissioned to serve. By His rising, we are raised to the fullness of life.

Saint Paul puts it this way:

> We were indeed buried with him through baptism into death, so that, just as Christ was raised from the dead by the glory of the Father, we too might live in newness of life (Romans 6:4).

Whenever new members of our Church are baptized in our midst, we are called to welcome them with joy, pray for them with sincerity, and share their hopes for a new life in Christ.

Coming to Faith

How does Baptism challenge you to be "dead to sin but alive for God?"

Why do we sometimes fail to experience the new life given to us at our Baptism?

Practicing Faith

What will you do this week to fulfill your priestly, prophetic, or kingly role?

How will you strengthen your fifth graders' appreciation of Baptism?

CATECHISM OF THE CATHOLIC CHURCH

The Theme of This Chapter Corresponds with Paragraph 1213

LITURGICAL RESOURCES

In the rite of Baptism, the celebrant invites someone from the family, such as a parent, to present the newly baptized with the light of Christ. Addressing the baptized, the celebrant says:

> You have been enlightened by Christ. Walk always as a child of light and keep the flame of faith alive in your heart. When the Lord comes, may you go out to meet him with all the saints in the heavenly kingdom.

You might choose to celebrate a ceremony of light in which each young person is presented with an unlit candle and the words above are proclaimed to him or her. Conclude by singing to the melody of "Michael, Row the Boat Ashore" these words:

> You are Christ's child of light, alleluia.
>
> You are holy in His sight, alleluia.

Be sure to point out to your group that it is preferred that Baptism be celebrated during a Mass. The parish community is an important sign of the union of the believing assembly with the family of the one(s) being baptized.

JUSTICE AND PEACE RESOURCES

Most families experience the Baptism of an infant as a time of joyful celebration. A baptismal gown is purchased for the baby, who will be the center of attention. Relatives and friends are invited to a party or a reception after the liturgy. The event is preserved on videotape or for the family photograph album.

However, for some families with special needs, these signs of celebration cannot be taken for granted. Consider these possibilities:

- low-income families or unemployed parents;
- single parents (unwed, widowed, or divorced);
- newcomers who have few friends or relatives in the area.

Discuss with your pastor how the fifth graders might contribute to a baptismal celebration for someone with special needs. For instance, they might raise money for a baptismal gown or help prepare a reception in the parish hall.

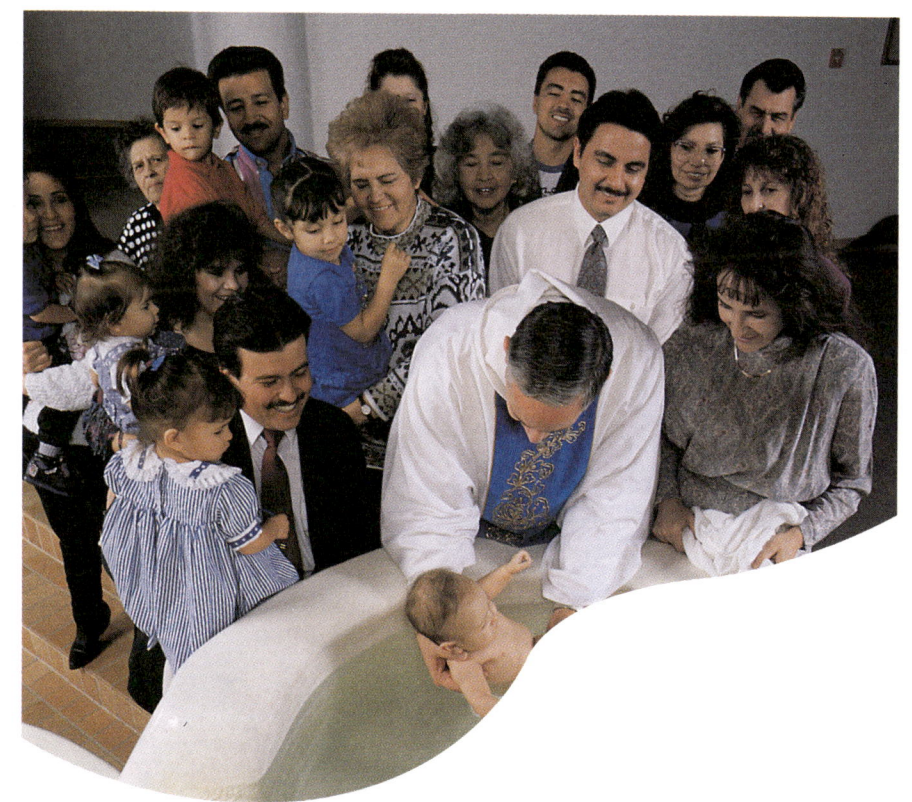

57B

8

Teaching Resources

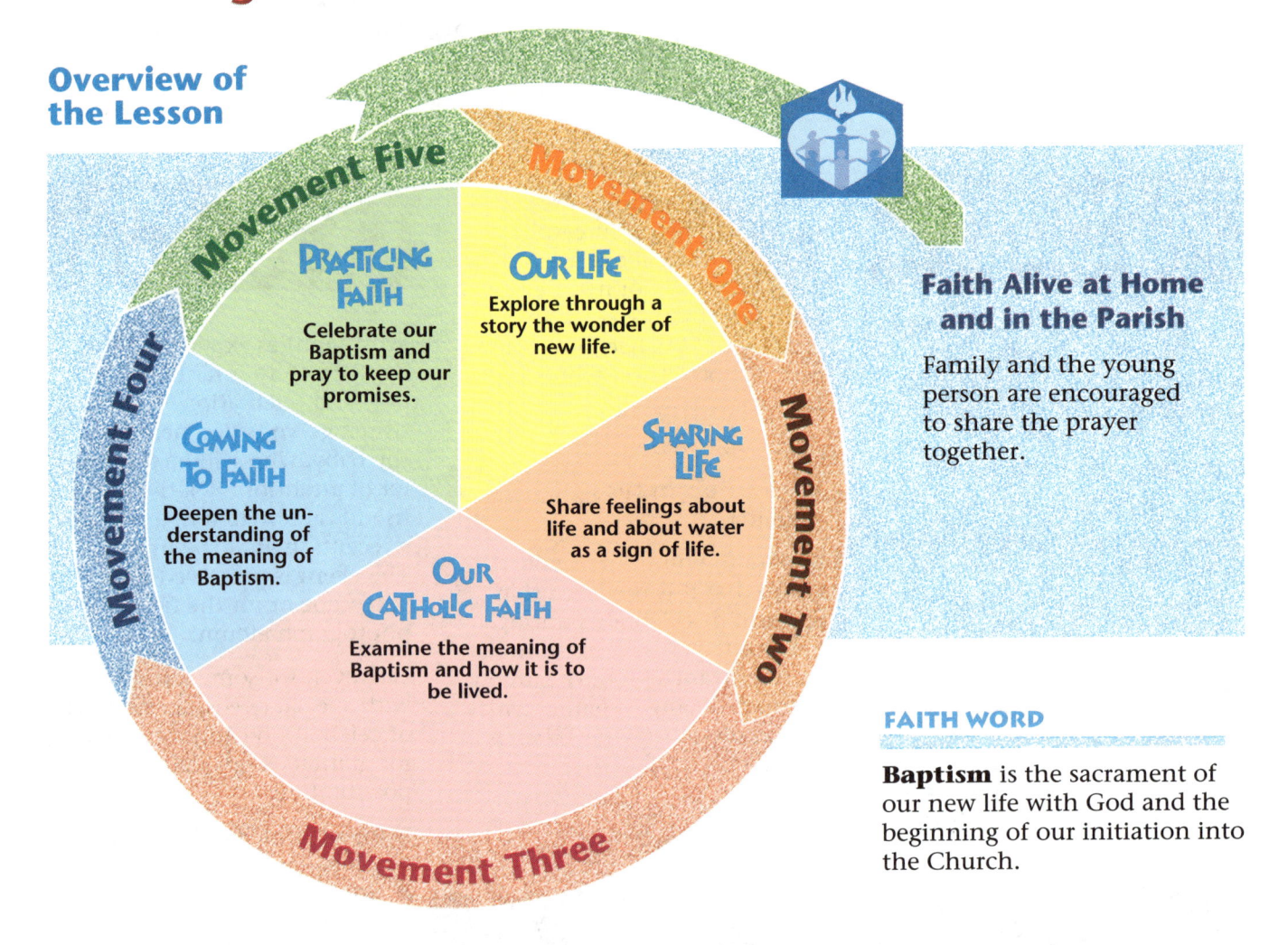

Overview of the Lesson

Movement One — Our Life: Explore through a story the wonder of new life.

Movement Two — Sharing Life: Share feelings about life and about water as a sign of life.

Movement Three — Our Catholic Faith: Examine the meaning of Baptism and how it is to be lived.

Movement Four — Coming To Faith: Deepen the understanding of the meaning of Baptism.

Movement Five — Practicing Faith: Celebrate our Baptism and pray to keep our promises.

Faith Alive at Home and in the Parish

Family and the young person are encouraged to share the prayer together.

FAITH WORD

Baptism is the sacrament of our new life with God and the beginning of our initiation into the Church.

Teaching Hints

This lesson will be enhanced if the young people can attend a parish baptismal celebration (at a liturgy, if possible). This would be a good time to make arrangements for a priest or deacon to be invited to speak to the group about Baptism.

Ask the young people to find out about their own Baptisms and, if possible, to bring baptismal photos to share with the group.

Special-Needs Child

Make it possible for any vision- or hearing-impaired young person to be seated close to any demonstration.

Visual Needs
■ enlargement of on-page activity

Auditory Needs
■ tape recordings

Tactile–Motor Needs
■ peers to help with written responses

Supplemental Resources

Baptism (video)
(from *Sacraments—Loving Actions of the Church* series)
Ikonographics
P.O. Box 600
Croton-on-Hudson, NY 10520

Baptism: Sacrament of Belonging
St. Anthony Messenger/
Franciscan Communication
1615 Republic Street
Cincinnatti, OH 45210
(1-800-488-0488)
(1-800-989-3600)

Lesson Plan: Beginning

Objectives

To help the young people

- know the sacrament of Baptism;
- understand the rite and the symbols of Baptism;
- recognize the baptized person's responsibilities.

Focusing Prayer

Play soft music and place some fresh flowers next to the open Bible, if possible. Gather the group quietly and pray together the prayer at the top of page 57.

Our Life

A Gift of Life

Invite the young people to recall times in their lives (or in the lives of others they know about) when there was a shortage or a total lack of water. Ask questions such as, "How does a lack of water affect one's daily living?"

Now explain the activity on page 57 and give the group time to read the story and write the ending. Invite volunteers to share their endings. Point out that sometimes we take life for granted and do not really see its signs all around us—and in us. Invite responses to the two questions in this section.

Sharing Life

God's Greatest Gift to Us

Encourage the young people to share their responses to the first direction and list them on the chalkboard or newsprint. Continue the discussion with the next question. Then discuss why water is an appropriate symbol for Baptism.

◆ Enrichment ◆

Life Expressions

Have the young people choose one of the following ways to express how they feel about the gift of life:

- write a poem or a song;
- write a short story;
- draw a comic strip;
- make a collage.

Materials needed: writing and drawing paper; markers; pencils; magazines; scissors; glue

---

8 Jesus Christ Brings Us Life
(Baptism)

Come, Holy Spirit, help us be signs of your life to others.

Our Life

Finish the story.

Angie went out on the tractor with her father as he plowed the field. She breathed in the wonderful smell of the earth as it was turned over to receive the new seed. In the spring days that followed, the gentle rains and warm sunshine made it a perfect growing season. Then one morning Angie saw the first green shoots of wheat covering the field. She ran out into the fields. Stooping down, she touched the new wheat shoots and whispered, **Possible response: "New life! How wonderful!   "**
Ask: What would you have said?
What does life mean to you? **Answers will vary.**

Each of us has dreams about our life. What are some of your dreams about life for yourself? for others? for our world? **Share some of your dreams with the group.**

Sharing Life

Discuss together. **We can grow, learn, love God and others.**
Give some reasons why you believe that life is God's greatest gift to us. **Use it well, in love of God, self, others.**
What do you imagine God wants us to do with the gift of life? **Water is necessary for life and growth.**
Come up with some good reasons why you think water is used as a sign of new life in the sacrament of Baptism. **of plants, animals**

57

57

Lesson Plan: Middle

Our Catholic Faith

Faith Word

Write the word *Baptism* on the chalkboard or show it on a flash card. Have the group pronounce the word and ask the young people to listen for it in the lesson.

Members of the Church

Introduce "Baptism, a Sacrament of Initiation" on page 58 by leading the young people in a brief discussion of the responsibilities of belonging to a group. Have a volunteer read aloud the first two paragraphs. Ask, "What happens in Baptism?"

New Life Through Baptism

Have the young people locate the *Faith Word* at the top of page 59. Read the definition aloud, and have the group repeat it. Ask the young people if they are beginning to see the connection between Baptism and new life.

Place a bowl of water, a small container representing oil, a white cloth, and a candle on a table. Ask for volunteers to act as the priest and the person to be baptized. As you read aloud the rest of this section, tell the volunteers to act out the rite of Baptism.

Ask the young people to explain the meaning of the oil, the white garment, and the candle. Have them underline the answers in their textbooks.

Materials needed: bowl; water; small container; white cloth; candle

We Live Our New Life

Read aloud the first two paragraphs under "Living Our Baptism." Then ask, "Who can help us to live our Baptism?" Seek a number of responses and compile a list of helpers.

Have individuals read each of the signs of living our Baptism. Encourage the young people to live these signs more faithfully now that they are aware of them.

◆ ENRICHMENT ◆

Water, Water Everywhere

Discuss with the young people the need for water in our lives: without it, life could not exist. Help the fifth graders list the many uses of water—for drinking, cooking, washing, gardening, farming, recreation, and for Baptism. Then invite them to write their thoughts about water in poems, raps, and songs.

Materials needed: paper; pencils

Our Catholic Faith

Stress the underlined text.

Baptism, A Sacrament of Initiation

When we are born, we become members of families. Then there is another important family that we are invited to join—the Church. By Baptism we join, or begin our initiation into, the Church, the body of Christ. We are freed from the power of original sin and become children of God.

By Baptism we are united with Jesus in his death and resurrection. We die to sin and rise to new life as Jesus did. Baptism enables us to live as God's own people. Baptism seals us with an indelible spiritual mark of our belonging to Christ. It is the mark of our salvation. That is why Baptism can never be repeated.

Many parishes celebrate Baptism during a Sunday Mass. This reminds all present of their own Baptism and of their responsibility to help new members to live their faith.

During the celebration of Baptism a priest or deacon blesses the water that will be used as a sign of rebirth. The celebrant prays, "We ask you, Father, with your Son to send the Holy Spirit upon the water of this font. May all who are buried with Christ in the death of baptism rise also with him to newness of life."

The priest or deacon pours the water on the heads of the people being baptized, or immerses them, saying, "(*Name*), I baptize you in the name of the Father, and of the Son, and of the Holy Spirit." The water and these words are the signs of the sacrament of Baptism.

At this moment they are reborn of water and the Holy Spirit. They receive new life. They are reborn into the divine life of God's grace, become members of the Church, the body of Christ, and receive the responsibility to live for God's reign.

The newly baptized are next anointed with holy oil, as Christ was anointed priest, prophet, and king. This shows that they share in Jesus' work of bringing about God's justice and peace.

The newly baptized are also given a white garment and a candle. The white garment shows that they have put on the new life of the risen Christ. A candle, lit from the Easter candle, is held. This is a sign that the baptized are to keep the light of Christ burning brightly by following Jesus Christ always.

Living Our Baptism

Most of us were probably very young when we were baptized. At that time our parents and godparents promised to help us live our new life as Christians. When we are old enough, we must also make this choice and renew our baptismal promises for ourselves.

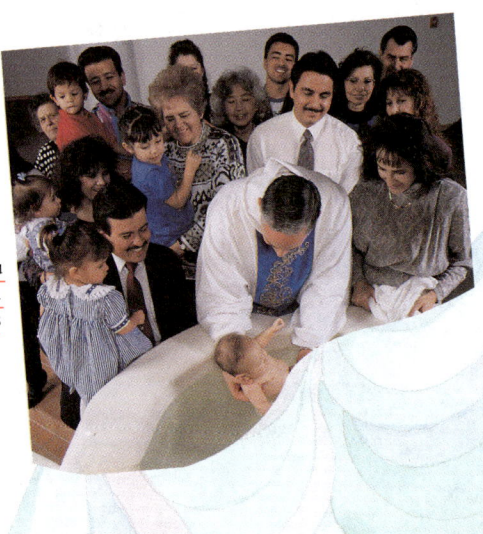

Lesson Plan: Middle

Priest, Prophet, and King

Invite a volunteer to read aloud the final paragraph. Explain that in the Old Testament, priests, prophets, and kings were anointed as a sign of their special roles among the people. Emphasize that Jesus is our great Priest, Prophet, and King.

Interpreting Pictures

Draw the young people's attention to the photographs in this section. Invite several volunteers to describe what is happening in the photograph on page 58. Ask if any fifth graders have attended a Baptism. Then ask, "Was the baby put into the water or was water poured over the infant's head?" Encourage those who have seen babies baptized to share their knowledge of the celebration with the group.

Ask the young people to study the photograph on page 59, then ask how the people in the photograph are living their baptismal promises.

Our Catholic Identity

Use page 5 from the *Our Catholic Identity* section in the back of the book. If time permits have each each student draw a self portrait on a sheet of paper. Underneath the picture, have each child print the following:

My name is
_____.

I became a child of God at
_____ Church.

My godparents are _____
_____.

Tell the young people to fill in the information they know and add the rest after speaking with their families.

You might wish to use pages 19–20 in the activity book for *Coming to God's Life.*

No one can live our Baptism for us. We receive God's grace and the support of others. We have the Holy Spirit to help us live our new life as disciples of Jesus. Our parents, friends, and the whole Christian community give us support. But we must choose now to live the way of Jesus.

Here are some signs that show you are trying to keep your baptismal promises:

• On waking, you thank God for another day and ask God to help you live the new life of Baptism.

• You decide who in your family needs a laugh, a hug, or a little help. You give it.

• You try to help those in need and to be a peacemaker between angry friends.

• You cooperate with your catechist so that you learn and grow in living your Catholic faith.

FAITH WORD

Baptism is the sacrament of our new life with God and the beginning of our initiation into the Church.

• On your way to and from school and on weekends, you see whether there are people in your neighborhood you can help.

• In your family or parish, you help teach younger children their prayers.

• You celebrate the sacrament of Reconciliation regularly. You listen carefully as the priest advises you how to live each day well.

• With your family, you take part in Mass on Sunday or Saturday evening. If they do not go, you try to go to Mass with others and ask God to help and bless your family.

• Each night you thank God for the day. You ask God to help you to become a peacemaker and to be fair and loving to all.

Priest, Prophet, King

Jesus was a priest, a prophet, and a king. He was a priest by offering his life to God, a prophet by calling us to do God's loving will, and a king by showing us how to let God reign in our lives.

◆ **ENRICHMENT** ◆

A Hands-On Approach

Invite the pastor to demonstrate and explain the rite of Baptism in the parish church. Let the young people see and touch and ask questions about the baptismal font, the oils, and the paschal candle.

8

Lesson Plan: End

Coming to Faith

Signs of New Life

This is designed as a group activity. Help the young people collaborate to create a simple expression of Baptism. Make the result a part of your closing prayer.

Faith Summary

Use the annotations to review the *Faith Summary* on page 61. See if the young people can express, in their own words, what they have learned.

Practicing Faith

Celebrating Our Baptism

Gather the young people around the objects that were part of the rite. If possible, light the candle and lead the group in prayer. At the end, bless the young people with holy water.

Materials needed: holy water

EVALUATING YOUR LESSON

- Do the young people know what Baptism is?

- Do they understand the meaning of its rites and symbols?

- Have they decided to live as baptized people?

ENRICHMENT

Taking Action

Invite the young people to act out what they, as baptized persons, should do if:

- they see a younger child being picked on;

- their brothers, sisters, or friends are arguing angrily;

- they see starving children on television.

Coming To Faith

Work together to create a collage or a mural of the signs of Baptism. Call it "Signs of New Life." Illustrate with drawings or pictures of water, a candle, a white garment, and holy oil. Then explain briefly what each signifies. This can be given as a gift to the catechumens (see below).

Practicing Faith

Talk together about ways your group might be of service to people in your parish preparing for Baptism. If possible, invite your pastor to discuss with you ways you might contribute. Examples: prayer cards of love and encouragement; a Baptism banner; names of candidates could be drawn for "Silent Prayer Partners."

† Then gather together to celebrate your Baptism.

Leader: Through Baptism we have become your beloved sons and daughters.
All: Blessed be God.

Leader: We have been born again of water and the Holy Spirit.
All: Blessed be God.

Leader: Help us to be faithful disciples of Jesus Christ and his witnesses.
All: Blessed be God.

End your prayer by making the sign of the cross together.

Talk with your catechist about ways you and your family might use the "Faith Alive" pages together. Invite your family to talk about ways of being signs of new life to others this week. Close this lesson by praying the baptismal blessing with your catechist and friends.

Optional Activities

Describing Water (for use with page 57)

Challenge the young people to tell how they would describe water to an alien from a waterless planet. Make sure the young people include why water is so important and enjoyable to human beings and why it can also be destructive. Have the young people illustrate their descriptions of water.

Materials needed: drawing paper; crayons and/or markers

New Life Collage (for use with page 57)

Distribute magazines, scissors, construction paper, and glue, and have the group create New Life collages. Suggest that the young people find pictures of new babies, budding plants, baptismal symbols, newborn pets, fresh flowers, water, and so on.

Materials needed: magazines; scissors; construction paper; glue

Sign of Baptism (for use with page 59)

Form the young people into groups. Invite them to role-play the "signs" given on page 59 that show they are trying to keep their baptismal promises.

Celebrating Baptism (for use with page 59)

Show slides, a filmstrip, or a videotape on the theme of Baptism. You may wish to invite a priest or deacon to describe to the group his own participation in a recent celebration of Baptism.

Materials needed: visual resource

Key Words (for use with page 60)

To help the young people internalize some key concepts of this lesson, put the following words on the chalkboard or newsprint: *white garments, cross, candle, water,* and *oil.* Ask them to explain how each word tells something about the sacrament of Baptism. List their responses under the appropriate words.

Role-playing a Gospel Story (for use with page 60)

Select volunteers to role-play or read dramatically the following gospel story about Jesus and Nicodemus:

Narrator: A Jewish leader named Nicodemus had heard many wonderful stories about all the things Jesus did for others. He wanted to talk to Jesus, but he was afraid because of what the other Jewish leaders might think. Finally, he got up enough courage to come to Jesus at night under the cover of darkness.

Nicodemus: "No one can do these signs that you are doing unless God is with him."
Jesus: "No one can enter the kingdom of God without being born of water and Spirit."
(Based on John 3:1-21)

Challenge the young people to explain what Baptism means to them, using this gospel story.

Faith Alive AT HOME AND IN THE PARISH

To help your fifth grader to appreciate better the sacrament of Baptism talked about in this lesson, tell the story of her or his own Baptism. Talk about what it means to live one's baptismal promises. By our Baptism we are called to holiness of life and active participation in the mission of the Church. Share how sacramental celebration should be a time of joy and celebration for the whole parish family.

You can make use of the many opportunities that arise to deepen the Christian life begun at Baptism. Each celebration of the Eucharist and of Reconciliation brings us into contact with the mystery of Christ's death and resurrection. All the sacraments are means to develop the life begun at Baptism.

Make a list of things your family will do this week to be a sign to others that by Baptism each of us has been freed from the power of original sin and empowered to do God's will. Write what you will do this week to show you are water, or new life, to someone.

† Family Prayer

Play recorded music that will help your family reflect upon water as a source of life. Ask each family member to think prayerfully about her or his Baptism. Then, two at a time, go to a prayer table on which some holy water and a large copy of this blessing have been placed. Take turns blessing one another. Make the sign of the cross on one another's forehead while saying,

"May God the Holy Spirit help you to fulfill the promises of your Baptism."

Learn by heart Faith Summary

What happens to us in Baptism?

• We receive new life at Baptism when we are reborn of water and the Holy Spirit.

Into what does Baptism initiate us?

• At Baptism we are initiated into, or begin to become members of the Church, the body of Christ.

What does Baptism call us to do?

• Our Baptism calls us to decide to live for the reign of God.

Bringing New Life to Others

Review

Go over the *Faith Summary* together. Encourage your fifth grader to learn it by heart, especially the first two statements. Then have him or her do the *Review*. The answers to numbers 1–4 appear on page 216. The response to number 5 will help you to see how well your fifth grader is growing in living the promises made at Baptism. When the *Review* is completed, go over it together.

Circle the letter beside the correct answer.

1. The most important sign of Baptism is
   a. oil.
   b. water.
   c. a white garment.
   d. a candle.

2. At Baptism we are initiated into, or become members of,
   a. our family.
   b. the body of Christ.
   c. our country.
   d. our neighborhood.

3. The Christian community, the Church,
   a. welcomes us as members.
   b. uses the sign of water in Baptism.
   c. is the body of Christ.
   d. all of these

4. We can live our Baptism by
   a. trying to live our Christian faith.
   b. avoiding people who need help.
   c. ignoring those who hurt us.
   d. not taking part in Mass.

5. In what way will you carry on the work of Jesus Christ in the world?

   _____
   _____
   _____

FAMILY SCRIPTURE MOMENT

Gather and ask: What experiences have we had that made us feel new or renewed? Then **Listen** as Jesus reveals a surprising truth.

Now there was a Pharisee named Nicodemus, a ruler of the Jews. He came to Jesus at night and said to him, "Rabbi, we know that you are a teacher who has come from God. . . . Jesus answered and said to him, ". . . no one can see the kingdom of God without being born from above." Nicodemus said to him, "How can a person once grown old be born again? Surely he cannot reenter his mother's womb and be born again, can he?" Jesus answered, ". . . no one can enter the kingdom of God without being born of water and Spirit. What is born of flesh is flesh, and what is born of spirit is spirit."
John 3:1–6

Share what each one understands by the phrase "being born again of water and the Spirit."

Consider for family enrichment:
■ Although Nicodemus was a deeply religious person, he did not understand that Jesus' disciples had to be born "from above," or from the Spirit.
■ By our Baptism, we have been born "of water and the Spirit" and have received a share in God's own life. We have become members of the Church, the body of Christ.

Reflect and **Decide** Invite family members to picture themselves at the moment of their Baptism. Ask: How will we show that we have been born of the Holy Spirit?

9 Jesus Christ Strengthens Us
(Confirmation)

For the Catechist: Spiritual and Catechetical Development

ADULT BACKGROUND

Our Life

Just as an unfinished painting is missing some paint that would make it complete, the person in each example below is missing something that would make her or him complete and whole. Consider what that something might be:

- An adult Catholic who believes that social justice and peace causes have "nothing to do with religion";
- A teen who is ashamed to let his friends know that he goes to church;
- A twelve-year-old who makes fun of poor people;
- A Catholic who obeys the laws of the Church but does not live gospel values.

Ask yourself:

- What are these people missing?
- What motivates me as a Catholic?

Sharing Life

How can Confirmation make a difference in our lives?

How do you think young people should be prepared for Confirmation?

Our Catholic Faith

Because of its varied historical development, Confirmation today may be the least understood or appreciated of the sacraments. In the early Church, it was celebrated together with its sister sacraments of initiation: Baptism and Eucharist. In the Middle Ages, it was separated from Baptism. However, it was closely related to Eucharist by Pope Saint Pius X early in the twentieth century.

Through the restoration of the catechumenate, those involved in the Rite of Christian Initiation of Adults have experienced the "intimate relationship" of the three sacraments celebrated together. It is no doubt easier for these Catholics to appreciate how they are reborn in Baptism, strengthened in Confirmation, and nourished by the Eucharist.

However, all Catholics, at whatever age they celebrate the sacrament, should be enabled to understand its particular significance.

By our Confirmation, we are strengthened in our baptismal call to holiness and gospel witness. We are empowered to proclaim Christ to a world that cries out for His love, justice, and peace. We are confirmed as Spirit-gifted disciples who, like Peter at the first Pentecost, invite others to conversion and discipleship.

The age at which a young person is prepared for this empowering sacrament varies among the dioceses of the United States. Catechesis generally includes a commitment to Church or community service, emphasizing the more mature faith life that Confirmation initiates.

Through the laying on of hands and anointing, the Holy Spirit "confirms" or strengthens us as baptized members of the Church. The gift of the Spirit is ours, and the Spirit frees us to live as disciples of Christ. We are called to a new level of witnessing to the good news and promoting the kingdom.

Coming to Faith

How does your life provide evidence of your Confirmation?

How might your parish call confirmation candidates to service?

Practicing Faith

How will you help your group to appreciate the value of Confirmation?

Catechism of the Catholic Church

The Theme of This Chapter Corresponds with Paragraph 1285

Liturgical Resources

In the rite of Confirmation the celebrant prays for the candidates in these words:

> All-powerful God, Father of our Lord Jesus Christ, by water and the Holy Spirit you freed your sons and daughters from sin and gave them new life. Send your Holy Spirit upon them to be their Helper and Guide. Give them the spirit of wisdom and understanding, the spirit of right judgment and courage, the spirit of knowledge and reverence. Fill them with the spirit of wonder and awe in your presence.

This "Promise of the Holy Spirit" might be shared with the fifth graders as a meditation on how Confirmation is intended to change their lives.

In response to the "Promise" the group could be asked to do one of the following:

- Write a prayer to the Holy Spirit for the courage to speak out on justice and peace issues.

- Make a poster illustrating how popular songs, TV shows, or movies encourage us to use the Spirit's gifts.

Justice and Peace Resources

Pax Christi, the international Catholic peace organization, has invited adult Christians to take a one-year "vow of nonviolence" to signify their refusal to countenance violence in the nuclear age. The vow is based on the Sermon on the Mount, in which Jesus exclaims:

> "Blessed are the peacemakers, for they will be called children of God" (Matthew 5:9).

Those who take the vow try to live the example of Jesus by carrying out specific acts of nonviolence. Among these are persevering in nonviolence of tongue; living simply so as not to deprive others of the means to live; and working to abolish war from the face of the earth.

Although fifth graders are not mature enough to take such a vow, they might be asked to brainstorm ways of practicing nonviolence in their daily lives. Examples might include refusing to argue with a brother or sister; not asking for more material goods than they need; using humor to defuse possible violence at school; writing peace letters to world leaders.

9

Teaching Resources

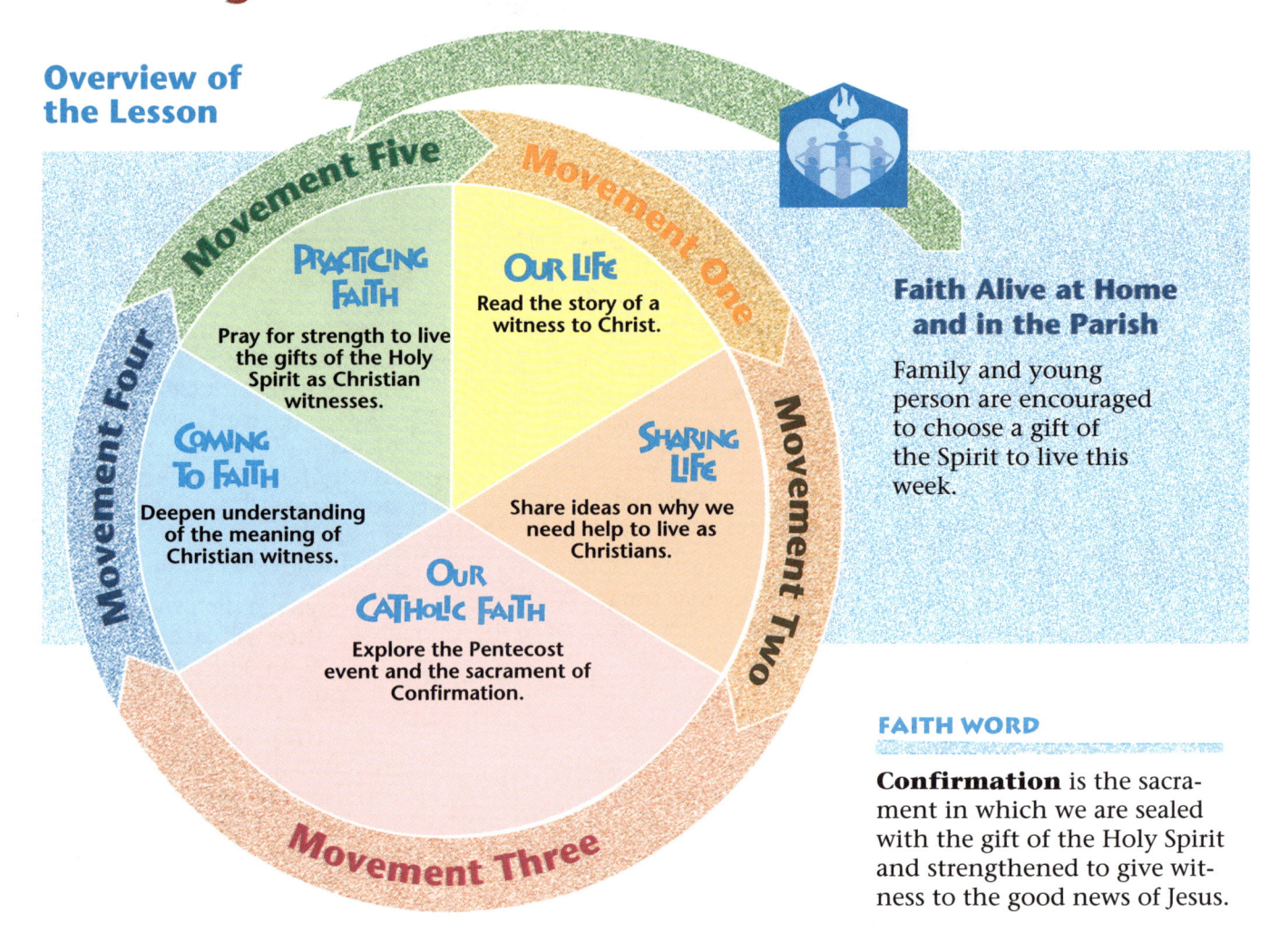

Overview of the Lesson

Movement One — Our Life: Read the story of a witness to Christ.

Movement Two — Sharing Life: Share ideas on why we need help to live as Christians.

Movement Three — Our Catholic Faith: Explore the Pentecost event and the sacrament of Confirmation.

Movement Four — Coming To Faith: Deepen understanding of the meaning of Christian witness.

Movement Five — Practicing Faith: Pray for strength to live the gifts of the Holy Spirit as Christian witnesses.

Faith Alive at Home and in the Parish

Family and young person are encouraged to choose a gift of the Spirit to live this week.

FAITH WORD

Confirmation is the sacrament in which we are sealed with the gift of the Holy Spirit and strengthened to give witness to the good news of Jesus.

Teaching Hints

The young people have already received the Holy Spirit in Baptism. Through this lesson they can come to appreciate that in Confirmation the Holy Spirit will enable them to become strong witnesses of Jesus.

Fifth graders desire to be of service and to participate in extracurricular projects in the parish and community. Such participation encourages them to call upon the Holy Spirit and prepare for the future reception of the sacrament of Confirmation.

Special-Needs Child

For the physically limited young person, the emphasis on the gift of spiritual strength in Confirmation should be especially comforting.

Visual Needs
- large, colored cut-out letters of *Faith Word*

Auditory Needs
- earphones and recording of hymn
- use of gestures for emphasis

Tactile–Motor Needs
- peer helper for activities

Supplemental Resources

Confirmation—Faith Alive (video)
Twenty-Third Publications
P.O. Box 180
Mystic, CT 06355
(1-800-321-0411)

Confirmation: It's Your Choice (video)
Liguori Video Resources
One Liguori Drive
Liguori, MO 63057–9999
(1-800-325-9521)

Lesson Plan: Beginning

Objectives

To help the young people

- know the definition of Confirmation;
- understand what it means to be a Christian witness;
- choose ways to witness to the faith.

Focusing Prayer

Gather the young people quietly and ask them to think for a minute about Jesus and their Catholic faith. Elicit from them that it might take courage to give witness to their faith. Then pray together the prayer on page 63.

Our Life

The North American Martyrs

Explain that missionaries are people who go all over the world to share the good news of Jesus Christ. They are witnesses to the faith. Sometimes people are killed for being a witness to Christ. When this happens, they are called martyrs.

Now have the group read the story of Isaac Jogues on page 63. Encourage several young people to share their responses.

Sharing Life

Our Need of the Holy Spirit

Have the young people think about and discuss the *Sharing Life* questions. You may wish to have them answer the last question in their faith journals.

Suggest ways the young people might become better witnesses—by speaking out against violence, by being honest and fair in all circumstances, by celebrating their faith openly and trying to share it with others.

Enrichment

A Martyr's Story

Have the young people prepare and give a dramatization of the story of Isaac Jogues and the Hurons. Tell the group to imagine what Father Jogues might have said to the Hurons about Jesus.

---

9 Jesus Christ Strengthens Us
(Confirmation)

Come, Holy Spirit, strengthen us to be Christ's witnesses.

Our Life

The early missionaries to North America faced many dangers. One day in 1642 Father Isaac Jogues was ambushed by the Iroquois, the enemies of the Hurons, and tortured as a hostage for one year.

Instead of returning home after being ransomed, Father Jogues assumed the role of a peacemaker between the Hurons and the Iroquois. Once again, he was taken hostage. This time he and seven other French missionaries were killed.

In 1930 the Church canonized these martyrs as saints. They are called the North American Martyrs. The word *martyr* means witness.

Why do you think Father Jogues stayed in North America? **To help make peace**

Tell some of the ways that you give witness to your Christian faith today. Who helps you? **Answers will vary.**

Sharing Life

Talk together about the following questions. **Encourage specific answers.**

What are some of the things that make it difficult for you to be a Christian? **Seeming "different" at times, living the Law of Love, etc.**

What in our society makes it difficult for anyone to be a good Christian? **Society values money, power, possessions, etc. above goodness.**

How do you imagine you could be a better witness to your Christian faith? **By being kind and fair to others, learning more about my religion, etc.**

63

Lesson Plan: Middle

Our Catholic Faith

God Sends the Holy Spirit

Read aloud the first two sentences under "Sending of the Holy Spirit" on page 64. Then have several young people read aloud the next four paragraphs about the coming of the Holy Spirit.

Stress how the disciples were different after the coming of the Holy Spirit by asking, "How did the Holy Spirit help the disciples?" and "Why do you think the Holy Spirit made such a difference in them?"

Then ask what we call the day the Holy Spirit came to the disciples. Have the young people read the last paragraph to find the answer.

We Receive the Holy Spirit

Invite the group to read silently the first paragraph under "Confirmation, a Sacrament of Initiation." Have the young people identify the invisible mark we receive when we are confirmed. Then have them read the next two paragraphs. Ask, "What are we called to do as confirmed Catholics?"

Remind the young people that, at their Baptisms, their parents and godparents made their baptismal promises for them. But now, in Confirmation, the fifth graders are all old enough to make their own statements of faith.

The Rite of Confirmation

Ask for volunteers to play the roles of the bishop and the person being confirmed. As you read the words of the rite on page 65, have the volunteers act out what is happening.

If possible, show the group some chrism, the oil of Confirmation. Explain that oil is a symbol of strength and

---

OUR CATHOLIC FAITH

Sending of the Holy Spirit

It is not always easy to be a witness to our faith. We need God's special help.

At the Last Supper on the night before he died, Jesus knew that his disciples would be afraid and feel lost without him. Jesus tried to give them courage by promising, "I will ask the Father, and he will give you another Advocate to be with you always."
John 14:16

After Jesus ascended into heaven, His disciples became frightened and locked themselves in an upper room. They were afraid of being found and arrested.

Ten days later, while they were still huddled there, God the Holy Spirit came. Each disciple was blessed with the fullness of the Holy Spirit and received the gifts that we receive in the sacrament of Confirmation. Jesus had kept his promise to send the Holy Spirit.

Stress the underlined text.

Our Church calls this day <u>Pentecost. On that day God the Holy Spirit came upon the first Christian disciples. They now had the courage to invite others to believe in and to follow Jesus.</u>
Based on Acts 1:7–14; 2:1–13

Confirmation, A Sacrament of Initiation

<u>In Confirmation we receive the sign, or seal, of the Holy Spirit.</u> This seal is not visible, but it marks us as followers and witnesses of Christ.

When we were baptized, we began our initiation into the Church. <u>Confirmation is one more step in this initiation into the body of Christ. Now we are called to give public witness to the good news to our family, our neighbors, and even strangers.</u> We are sealed with the Gift of the Holy Spirit and strengthened to live out our baptismal promises. Like Baptism, Confirmation imprints on the soul an indelible spiritual mark and so, like Baptism it can never be repeated.

When we are confirmed, we may choose another name in addition to the one we

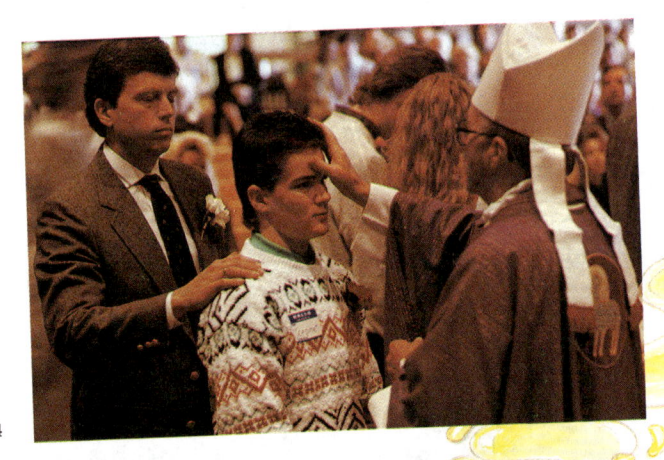

Lesson Plan: Middle

healing. Then ask why oil is an appropriate symbol for this sacrament.

Have the group complete the reading of this section. Allow time for all to learn the faith word, *Confirmation,* by heart. Then ask any who have received Confirmation or have been present at one to share their memories of the event.

You may wish to use pages 21–22 in the activity book for *Coming to God's Life.*

Our Catholic Identity

Use page 6 from the *Our Catholic Identity* section in the back of the book. Have the class examine the drawing. Explain that a dove is a symbol of peace and love; for this reason it is often used to represent the Holy Spirit. Ask why they think the virtues mentioned are called fruits of the Holy Spirit. Lead the students to see that a good fruit is a sign that a tree is healthy and has within it the nourishment it needs to produce good fruit. Point out that when we see the virtues of the Holy Spirit in a person's life, we know that the Holy Spirit is within that person, nourishing her or his life. Give examples of how you have seen some of the virtues lived out by others.

FAITH WORD

Confirmation is the sacrament in which we are sealed with the Gift of the Holy Spirit and are strengthened to give witness to the good news of Jesus.

---

were given at Baptism. We may select the name of a saint whose life we have read about and whom we admire.

Confirmation is celebrated during Mass with a bishop or his representative presiding. A high point of the celebration of Confirmation is the "laying on of hands." The bishop extends his hands over those to be confirmed, praying to God the Father,

"Send your Holy Spirit upon them to be their Helper and Guide.
Give them the spirit of wisdom and understanding,
the spirit of right judgment and courage,
the spirit of knowledge and reverence.

Fill them with the spirit of wonder and awe in your presence."

Then the bishop dips his thumb into blessed oil, called holy chrism. He makes the sign of the cross on their foreheads and anoints them, saying,

"*(Name),* be sealed with the Gift of the Holy Spirit."

This anointing is the most important sign of the sacrament of Confirmation.

Confirmation helps us to practice our faith openly and bravely, no matter who makes fun of us or how difficult it may be.

The Holy Spirit helps us so that other people will see the good news of Jesus alive in us. They will know by our actions that God loves every human being.

When we live our Confirmation, we become witnesses to the reign of God in the world today.

65

ENRICHMENT

Gospel Singing

Several of the young people who enjoy music might be invited a week in advance to plan a special presentation of the song "You Are the Light of the World" from the *Godspell* album. If possible, a dancing teacher or cheerleading coach might help them to learn a few basic movements that fit both the melody and the lyrics of this gospel song.

Another possibility would be to have your young people form three or four parallel rows with their arms over one another's shoulders. Then, as they sing "This little light of mine, I'm gonna let it shine," each row should sway in an opposing direction to the next.

Materials needed: song lyrics

Lesson Plan: End

Coming to Faith

Sharing Our Faith

Go over the *Coming to Faith* activity on page 66 and discuss each of the four points. Encourage the young people to share their thoughts.

Faith Summary

Use the annotations to review the *Faith Summary* on page 67. See if the young people can express, in their own words, what they have learned.

Practicing Faith

A Prayer for Witnesses

Remind the group of the gifts of the Spirit that are given to us in Confirmation. Go over the response and the hymn so that all can participate easily.

Then gather the group for the closing prayer.

Evaluating Your Lesson

■ Do the young people know what Confirmation means?

■ Do they understand what it calls us to do?

■ Have they decided how they will give witness to their faith?

Enrichment

"Gift" Cards

Have the young people work with partners to make Holy Spirit "gift" cards. Tell the young people to fold small sheets of red or white construction paper to make cards. Decorate the front of the cards with a Spirit symbol. Then each young person should write her or his partner's name on the inside with the following statement:
(Name), I believe the Holy Spirit has given you the special gift of _____ because _____
_____.

Suggest that the young people take the cards home to share with their families, and that they try to further develop their gifts.

Materials needed: red or white construction paper; crayons or markers

66

Coming to Faith

After your Confirmation, what would you tell others about: **Encourage specific responses.**

- the promises Jesus gave his disciples
- the coming of the Holy Spirit
- the important signs used at Confirmation
- how you can be a better Christian witness to others **Possible response: by being kind and just to others**

✝ Practicing Faith

Gather in a circle and pray together.

All: Come, Holy Spirit, be our Helper and Guide. (Repeat after each petition.) (All hold out arms to center of circle, palms down as seven people read.)

1. Give us Your gift of wisdom so we may know the right thing to do. (All)

2. Give us your gift of understanding so our faith will be real and deep. (All)

3. Give us your gift of right judgment so that we may help others in their faith. (All)

4. Give us your gift of courage so we may practice what we believe with courage. (All)

5. Give us your gift of knowledge so that we may desire to learn all we can about our faith. (All)

6. Give us your gift of reverence so that we may be people of prayer and worship. (All)

7. Give us your gift of wonder and awe so that we may treat all people and all creation with respect and wonder. (All)

Close by singing "Come, Holy Spirit."

Talk with your catechist about ways you and your family might use the "Faith Alive" pages. You might especially want to pray together the prayer to the Holy Spirit.

66

Optional Activities

Witnessing to God's Reign (for use with page 63)

Have the young people imagine that their religion group has been challenged to give witness to our Catholic faith. Have them work in pairs or small groups to decide on one way they can best give witness to our Catholic faith.

A Dramatization (for use with page 64)

Have volunteers act out the Pentecost story, dramatizing the change that came over the disciples at the descent of the Holy Spirit. Have one student read Acts 2:1-4 from the Scriptures, while others pantomime the story. If a young person knows how to sign, invite her or him to sign the story as it is being read.

A Debate (for use with page 65)

Plan a debate on the topic "Confirmation Candidates Should (or Should Not) Have to Serve Others." Explain that most Confirmation programs require completion of a service project—such as doing dishes at a soup kitchen, visiting the sick, or cleaning an elderly person's yard—before a person can be confirmed. Select young people to debate the topic. Have the group suggest other worthwhile service projects.

A Game (for use with page 65)

Have the young people form two teams. Have the first team prepare slips of paper with important statements from the lesson. Then have the second team make up a question that addresses each statement.

Materials needed: slips of paper; pencils

Christian Witnesses (for use with page 66)

Invite a recently confirmed young person to tell the group how he or she is trying to be an active witness to his or her Christian faith.

A Prayer to the Holy Spirit (for use with page 66)

Have the group make a "Spirit" banner to hang above the prayer table. Gather the young people at the table, and pray together the following prayer:

> Holy Spirit, come to us. Make us daring witnesses to our faith. Be the Light that guides us. Amen.

Materials needed: strip of shelving paper; crayons or markers

66A

FAITH ALIVE AT HOME AND IN THE PARISH

In this lesson your fifth grader has learned more about the sacrament of Confirmation. In this sacrament the baptized are sealed with the Gift of the Holy Spirit. "Like Baptism, which it completes, Confirmation is given only once, for it too imprints on the soul an indelible spiritual mark, the 'character,' which is the sign that Jesus Christ has marked a Christian with the seal of his Spirit. . .(*Catechism*, 1304). The Holy Spirit helps us live our faith by giving us special gifts and fruits. (See the chart below.)

Gifts of the Spirit

Choose one gift of the Holy Spirit. Discuss how you and your family will live it this week.

Fruits of the Spirit

The fruits of the Holy Spirit are the good results people can see in us when we use the gifts of the Holy Spirit. These fruits are *love, joy, peace, patience, kindness, goodness, faithfulness, humility,* and *self-control*.

✝ Family Prayer to the Holy Spirit

Holy Spirit, we thank you for your gifts. We ask your guidance for our family and parish. (Place hands on each family member.)

Faith Summary

What is Confirmation?

• Confirmation is the sacrament in which we are sealed with the Gift of the Holy Spirit and strengthened to give witness to the good news of Jesus Christ.

What does the Holy Spirit do for us in Confirmation?

• In Confirmation the Holy Spirit fills us with the gifts that we need to live our Christian faith.

How do we live our Confirmation?

• We live our Confirmation when we become witnesses to the reign of God in the world.

Gift	Helps us to
wisdom	know the right things to do.
understanding	explain our faith and know how to make good decisions.
right judgment	guide others in their faith because we live our own.
courage	practice courageously the faith we believe.
knowledge	learn about our Catholic faith from the Bible and from the Catholic tradition.
reverence	live the good news willingly and pray for ourselves and others.
wonder and awe	show respect for God, God's people, and God's world.

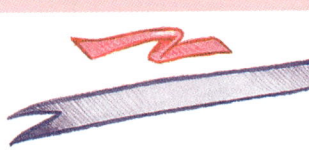

Review

Go over the *Faith Summary* together and encourage your fifth grader to learn it by heart, especially the first statement. Then have him or her do the *Review*. The answers to numbers 1–4 appear on page 216. The response to number 5 will help you to see how well your fifth grader understands our responsibility to live as witnesses to Jesus' mission. When the *Review* is completed, go over it together.

Circle the letter beside the correct answer.

1. At Confirmation we receive
   a. the gift of new life.
   b. freedom from original sin.
   c. the power to forgive sins.
   d. the fullness of the Holy Spirit.

2. The person who leads the Confirmation celebration is
   a. the bishop or his representative.
   b. the priest.
   c. our parents.
   d. the disciples.

3. The sign, or seal, of the Holy Spirit
   a. is visible.
   b. lasts only for the Confirmation ceremony.
   c. marks us forever as followers of Christ.
   d. is the bishop.

4. At Confirmation we accept the responsibility to
   a. live our baptismal promises.
   b. practice our faith openly.
   c. become witnesses to the reign of God.
   d. all of these

5. How will you give witness as a Christian this week?

   _____
   _____
   _____

FAMILY SCRIPTURE MOMENT

Gather and have family members recall times when they wanted to speak up about what they believe, but did not do so. Then **Listen** to an important message about the Holy Spirit.

"But when he comes, the Spirit of truth, he will guide you to all truth. He will not speak on his own, but he will speak what he hears, and will declare to you the things that are coming. He will glorify me, because he will take from what is mine and declare it to you. Everything that the Father has is mine; for this reason I told you that he will take from what is mine and declare it to you."

John 16:13-15

Share Ask: What kind of witnesses to our faith would we like to be? How can the Holy Spirit help us?

Consider for family enrichment:
■ At the Last Supper, Jesus promises that the Spirit will give him glory by enabling the disciples to know and live the truth.
■ At Confirmation we receive the Spirit's gifts that enable us to become witnesses to the good news of Jesus.

Reflect and **Decide** How do we need to grow as disciples who speak up about Jesus? When will our family pray for the help of the Holy Spirit?

10 JESUS CHRIST FEEDS US (Eucharist)

For the Catechist: Spiritual and Catechetical Development

ADULT BACKGROUND

Our Life

Saint Teresa of Avila is said to have remarked, "God can be found among the pots and pans." Practical mystic that she was, Teresa had plenty of experience in the kitchen as well as in the dining room. She would have recognized them as sacred spaces in which the Bread of Life made Himself at home.

Ask yourself:

■ How have I experienced kitchens and dining rooms as sacred spaces?

Sharing Life

How do certain meals enable people to be truly present to one another?

In what ways do you see the Eucharist as a sacrificial meal?

Our Catholic Faith

Although Jesus performed many miracles during the course of His public ministry, only one miracle appears in all four Gospels. The feeding of the five thousand is recorded in Matthew 14:13–21; Mark 6:30–44; Luke 9:10–17; and John 6:1–14. The evangelists may well have intended that we see in this story a sign of the Eucharist.

Whenever we hear the gospel account of the multiplication of the loaves and the fishes, we are inclined to focus on the miraculous way in which Jesus managed to feed the five thousand. We may be tempted to skip lightly over what is most important.

John's Gospel reminds us that, when Jesus spoke to the people about this miracle, He told them, "Do not work for food that perishes but for the food that endures for eternal life" (John 6:27). This is the Eucharist, the Living Bread, the Bread of Life.

Catholics believe in the real presence. This means that Jesus Christ, Body and Blood, soul and divinity, is really present under the appearances of bread and wine. This is more than commemoration, more than simple remembrance, more than just a community meal of shared fellowship. It is the reenactment, the saving mystery, of the passion and death of our Lord Jesus Christ. This is the mystery of faith that we proclaim.

When we receive Holy Communion, we believe that the Bread of Life becomes our spiritual food and nourishment. Our Catholic life could not survive without it. Through the Eucharist, Jesus becomes part of us and we become part of Him. He promises us that He will live in unity with us, just as He lives in unity with the Father. We will live in Him and He in us.

As the third sacrament of initiation, Eucharist fully joins us to the body of Christ. It joins us in the one sacrifice of Jesus by which we offer ourselves with Him to God. Finally, it joins us as members of the faith community who share the eucharistic meal, giving thanks and praise as the one body. Together, we anticipate the great feast of God's kingdom to which all are invited.

Coming to Faith

How can you deepen your love of Christ, who is really present in the Eucharist?

How can you share your faith in Him with those who truly hunger?

Practicing Faith

In what ways will you encourage your fifth graders to value the real presence of Jesus in the Eucharist?

CATECHISM OF THE CATHOLIC CHURCH

The Theme of This Chapter Corresponds with Paragraph 1359

LITURGICAL RESOURCES

One way to share a reflection on Eucharist and world hunger with your group is to plan a dramatization of "Jesus feeds five thousand" from Mark 6:30–44. Begin by telling the gospel story, then have the young people read it from the Scriptures, looking for clues about what Jesus expects of us. Ask the young people to volunteer to portray Jesus and several disciples. Have some other volunteers play people in the crowd who are willing to share their picnic lunches with the rest of the class, or "the crowd." Conclude the dramatization with a song such as "Take and Eat" by Michael Joncas.

JUSTICE AND PEACE RESOURCES

Bread for the World is an organization that actively works for governmental policy changes to reduce world hunger. The organization clearly links Christian faith with action against hunger. It educates people to use their "gift of citizenship" to help the hungry.

You might choose to share literature from Bread for the World with your group, and invite the young people to pass it on to their parents.

Write to:

Bread for the World,
1100 Wayne Avenue, Suite 1000
Silver Spring, MD 20910

Or you might have several young people prepare reports on Bread for the World, Oxfam, and other groups that help feed the hungry.

Teaching Resources

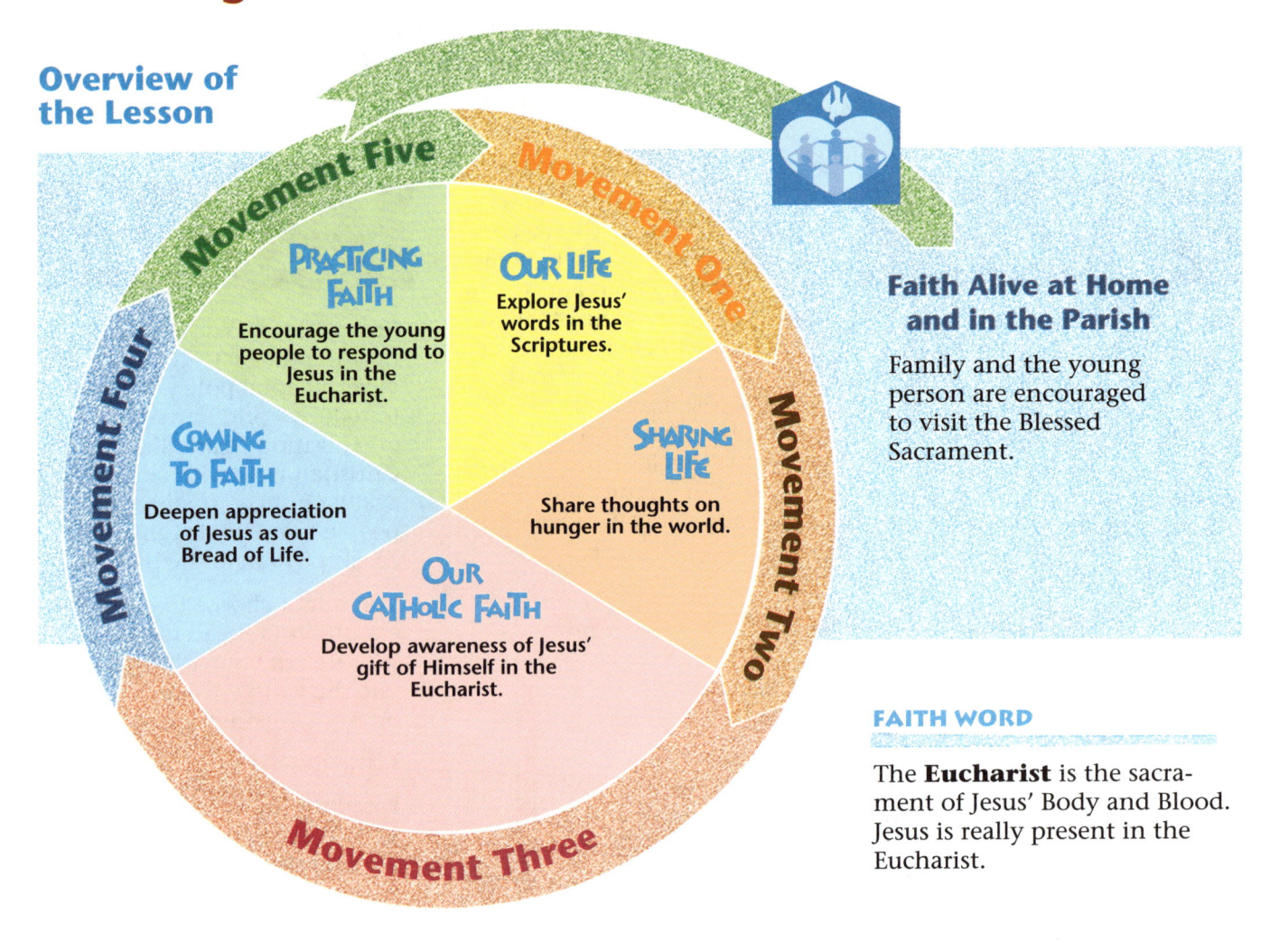

Overview of the Lesson

Movement One — Our Life: Explore Jesus' words in the Scriptures.

Movement Two — Sharing Life: Share thoughts on hunger in the world.

Movement Three — Our Catholic Faith: Develop awareness of Jesus' gift of Himself in the Eucharist.

Movement Four — Coming To Faith: Deepen appreciation of Jesus as our Bread of Life.

Movement Five — Practicing Faith: Encourage the young people to respond to Jesus in the Eucharist.

Faith Alive at Home and in the Parish

Family and the young person are encouraged to visit the Blessed Sacrament.

FAITH WORD

The **Eucharist** is the sacrament of Jesus' Body and Blood. Jesus is really present in the Eucharist.

Teaching Hints

In this lesson the connections between our daily bread, or food, and the Eucharist, in which Jesus gives Himself as our Bread of Life, should be clearly presented to the young people. The young people should be encouraged to receive Jesus in the Eucharist frequently. They should also be encouraged to respond to the hungry of the world.

Special-Needs Child

Assign a companion for any mainstreamed child who is absent frequently. The companion can help the young person catch up with the group.

Visual Needs
- enlargements of on-page activities

Auditory Needs
- earphones and recording for musical background

Tactile–Motor Needs
- large markers for print activities

Supplemental Resources

Eucharist (video)
(from *Sacraments—Loving Actions of the Church* series)
Ikonographics
P.O. Box 600
Croton-on-Hudson, NY 10520
(1-800-944-1505)

A Eucharist Parable (video)
St. Anthony Messenger/
Franciscan Communication
1615 Republic Street
Cincinnatti, OH 45210
(1-800-488-0488)
(1-800-989-3600)

Lesson Plan: Beginning

Objectives

To help the young people

- know the definition and meaning of Eucharist;
- appreciate that Jesus is our Bread of Life;
- choose to respond to Jesus in the Eucharist.

Focusing Prayer

If possible, place a Bible with wheat and grapes or a loaf of uncut bread on a table. Gather the young people and quietly pray together the prayer on page 69.

Materials needed: Bible; food items

Our Life

The Bread of Life

Read aloud the Scripture account, and then have the group do it again as a dramatic reading with volunteers acting as narrator, Jesus, and the crowd.

Ask the young people for their reactions to the Scripture reading.

Sharing Life

Invite the young people to respond individually to the first question. Then have them work in small groups to discuss the other two questions before sharing responses with the whole group.

---

10 Jesus Christ Feeds Us
(Eucharist)

Jesus, Living Bread, fill us with your life.

Our Life

Once the people asked Jesus what miracle he would do so that they might believe in him. Jesus said, "I am the bread of life; whoever comes to me will never hunger, and whoever believes in me will never thirst." John 6:35

The people started grumbling. They said, "Is this not Jesus, the son of Joseph?" John 6:42

Jesus answered, "I am the living bread that came down from heaven; whoever eats this bread will live forever; and the bread that I will give is my flesh for the life of the world." John 6:51

Then many of his disciples who were listening said, "This saying is hard; who can accept it?" John 6:60

As a result of this many of his followers turned away and walked with him no more.

What do you hear Jesus saying in this Scripture story?

Sharing Life

Why do you think Jesus compared himself to bread? Bread is necessary for human life and can be shared with all.
Discuss together: Why are there so many hungry people in our world? Poverty, wars, famines—all contribute to hunger.
What do you think Jesus wants us to do for people who are hungry? Share our food with them

Enrichment

Feeling the Hunger

Invite someone who ministers to the hungry to give the fifth graders some insights into how hunger affects people.

Challenge the young people to work together to plan something that will show their concern for those who are hungry. For instance, they might plan a food drive to restock a parish or community food pantry.

10

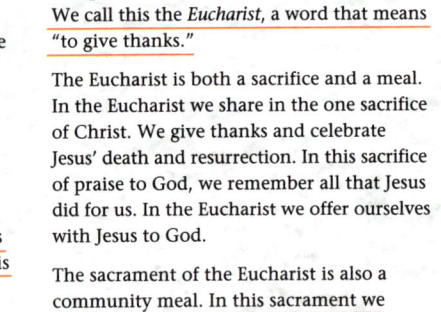

Lesson Plan: Middle

Our Catholic Faith

Sharing a Meal

Read aloud the first paragraph of "The Eucharist, A Sacrament of Initiation" on page 70. Invite volunteers to tell about meals they have shared to celebrate special events.

The Last Supper

Have the young people silently read the next two paragraphs. Then ask, "What did Jesus give us at the Last Supper?" Have them underline the answer in their textbooks.

Now have the young people imagine that they are the disciples at the Last Supper. Read aloud Jesus' words and actions as described by Saint Paul in 1 Corinthians. Encourage volunteers to share how they think the disciples must have felt.

Read aloud the remaining paragraphs of this section. Have the young people note the *Faith Word* on page 71 and ask them to learn it by heart. Then have them go back over the paragraphs they have just read to find the answers to these questions: "What do we do in the Eucharist?" and "What do we remember in the Eucharist?" The young people should be able to identify ways we participate, such as:

- We give thanks.
- We offer ourselves.
- We receive Jesus' gift of Himself.

And things we remember, such as:

- Jesus' great love in sacrificing Himself for us.
- Jesus' death, resurrection, and presence with us now.

We Give Thanks

Ask: "What does our participation in Mass signify?" before reading aloud the first two paragraphs in this section. Encourage the young people to share their responses with the group.

Stress the underlined text.

Our Catholic Faith

The Eucharist, A Sacrament of Initiation

Sometimes we share a meal not only because we are hungry, but also because we are celebrating a special event like Thanksgiving or a birthday.

At Passover the Jewish people celebrate an important meal to remember that God brought them from slavery in Egypt to freedom in the Promised Land. During Passover, on the night before he died, Jesus ate a very special meal with his friends. This meal is called the Last Supper.

At this Last Supper Jesus gave us the gift of himself, his own Body and Blood. Jesus' disciples never forgot this meal. This is what happened.

"The Lord Jesus, on the night he was handed over, took bread, and, after he had given thanks, broke it and said, 'This is my body that is for you. Do this in remembrance of me.' In the same way also the cup, after supper, saying 'This cup is the new covenant in my blood. Do this, as often as you drink it, in remembrance of me.'"
1 Corinthians 11:23–25

At the Last Supper Jesus gave thanks to God. Ordinary bread and wine became his own Body and Blood. Then Jesus asked his disciples to do the same in memory of him. We call this the *Eucharist*, a word that means "to give thanks."

The Eucharist is both a sacrifice and a meal. In the Eucharist we share in the one sacrifice of Christ. We give thanks and celebrate Jesus' death and resurrection. In this sacrifice of praise to God, we remember all that Jesus did for us. In the Eucharist we offer ourselves with Jesus to God.

The sacrament of the Eucharist is also a community meal. In this sacrament we receive the gift of Jesus, who gave himself to

70

Lesson Plan: Middle

Read aloud the opening sentences in the third paragraph. Then invite volunteers each to read one of the ways we can share Jesus, our Bread of Life. Allow the group to comment on these suggestions.

Ask questions to initiate a discussion of the illustration on these two pages. For example, "What is happening? Who are the people with Jesus? How do you think they felt at the moment when Jesus broke the bread and requested that they do this in memory of Him?"

Multicultural Awareness

Help the fifth graders to make the connection between Jesus feeding us and we, in turn, feeding the world. Explain to the group that Jesus is the Bread of Life that nourishes us. Encourage them to share Jesus and nourish others by welcoming newcomers or being kind to someone excluded by others.

You may wish to use pages 23–24 in the activity book for *Coming to God's Life*.

Our Catholic Identity

Use page 7 from the *Our Catholic Identity* section in the back of the book. If possible, have cruets with wine and water and some unconsecrated hosts (large and small). Let the youngsters examine these things. Demonstrate how the large eucharistic bread can be broken into parts. Have the students respond to the question by giving examples of how they can offer themselves to God in their family, at school, in their neighborhood. Explain that they can be "bread" for others by nourishing the spirits of those who are lonely, or sick, or neglected.

---

us as our food. Jesus is really present in the Eucharist. Sharing in the Eucharist makes us one with God and with one another in the Church, the body of Christ.

We assemble as Jesus' community of disciples to celebrate the Eucharist at Mass. We remember that Jesus loved us so much that he sacrificed himself for us and died on the cross to save us from our sins. Through the Eucharist we become a living sacrifice of praise.

We remember that Jesus rose from the dead and now remains with us in the Eucharist. We give thanks to Jesus for the gift of himself by living as his disciples.

FAITH WORD

The **Eucharist** is the sacrament of Jesus' Body and Blood. Jesus is really present in the Eucharist.

Thanking God for Jesus

At Mass our gifts of bread and wine become the Body and Blood of Christ. This happens through the power of the Holy Spirit. Jesus is really present under the appearances of bread and wine.

Our participation in Mass is a sign of our full initiation into the Church, the body of Christ. The Eucharist nourishes us to give thanks to God by living as God's own people. In Holy Communion we receive Jesus himself. He is our Bread of Life. We can also visit our parish church and pray to Jesus, who is present in the Blessed Sacrament.

Saint Augustine once said, "Because we receive the Body of Christ in Holy Communion, we must live as the body of Christ in the world." We can share Jesus, our Bread of Life, by:

- caring for the hungry by organizing food collections in our parish.
- sharing Jesus' joy by visiting a lonely or elderly person.
- welcoming a newcomer into our group or neighborhood.
  - being kind to someone whom others treat badly.
  - being careful not to waste food or drink when many other people are so hungry.
    - being kind and patient with our family and friends.

ENRICHMENT

Feeding Everyone

Invite the young people to close their eyes and picture their favorite food. Ask them to consider carefully how the food looks, smells, and tastes, and how they feel when they are eating it.

Ask them to imagine how they would feel if they could never again eat this favorite food. Invite them to thank God for this and all the other food they have eaten without thinking much about what it means to be well fed. Offer the following prayer for increased awareness of the gift of our food:

Jesus, teach us to appreciate the food You have given us. Help us to eat gratefully, and may we pray, and do all we can, for children all over the world whose plates are empty. Amen.

10

Lesson Plan: End

Coming to Faith

Reflecting on the Eucharist

Explain the *Coming to Faith* activity on page 72. Have two young people decipher the message on the chalkboard or newsprint while the others complete it in their texts. Invite the group to read the message together.

Allow time for the young people to discuss how they would explain the Eucharist to someone who knows nothing about it.

Faith Summary

Use the annotations to review the *Faith Summary* on page 73. See if the young people can express, in their own words, what they have learned.

Practicing Faith

Jesus, Really Present

Have the young people develop their plan to show their belief in the real presence of Jesus in the Eucharist by using one of the suggestions in their text or coming up with their own ideas. Then encourage them to commit themselves to carrying out the plan.

Close by praying the *Family Prayer* on page 73.

EVALUATING YOUR LESSON

- Do the young people know the meaning of Eucharist?
- Do they understand that Jesus is our Bread of Life?
- Have they chosen how they will respond to Jesus in the Eucharist?

ENRICHMENT

A Eucharistic Messenger

Invite a Eucharistic minister to talk to the young people. Ask him or her to share what it is like to bring the Eucharist to a sick or elderly person. The minister might also explain about *Viaticum*— Eucharist given to the dying. Encourage questions from the group, especially about how one becomes a Eucharistic minister.

72

TIHSEIBNRME
EAMDOORFYL
OIFFMEE

I AM

COMING TO FAITH

Decode the message from Jesus about the Eucharist. Beginning with the first letter in the lines of letters, circle every other letter to find the message. Then write the message.

THE BREAD OF LIFE

Discuss together the best way to explain the sacrament of the Eucharist to a young person who is not a Catholic. Volunteers may want to act out this scene.

PRACTICING FAITH

How can you show that you *really* believe that Jesus is present in the Eucharist? Remember, belief is expressed in action. Some ideas are listed on page 71. Your group might come up with your own. Make a group plan about how and when you will share Jesus, our Bread of Life, this week. Write your plan.

Close by praying the prayer on page 73.

Talk with your catechist about ways you and your family might use the "Faith Alive" pages. You might especially want to invite a family member to make a visit to the Blessed Sacrament.

72

Optional Activities

A Group Project (for use with page 69)

Brainstorm possible group projects that the fifth graders might undertake to respond, as concerned followers of Jesus, to the plight of the hungry. List the ideas on the chalkboard or newsprint.

A Eucharist Poster (for use with page 70)

Challenge the young people to create posters illustrating the theme "This Is My Body." Invite them to consider the ways in which we are all the body of Christ, as well as the ways in which the Eucharist makes us one.

Materials needed: sheets of posterboard; crayons; markers

The Eucharist (for use with page 71)

Have the young people write short essays on "Why I Love the Eucharist" or "What the Eucharist Means to Me." The essays may be used as short meditations with a quiet musical background.

A Flash-Card Quiz (for use with page 72)

Prepare a set of flash cards inscribed with the annotated questions from the *Faith Summary* on page 73. Invite one young person to use these questions to conduct a brief oral quiz of the other group members.

Dramatizing Scripture (for use with page 72)

Select volunteers for the parts of narrator, Jesus, Philip, Peter, and the boy, and have them present a dramatic reading of the following gospel story based on John 6:2–14:

Narrator: "One day almost five thousand people followed Jesus to hear His words. As the day went on, they became very hungry. Jesus knew how hungry they were. He was very concerned because they were far from the markets and had no food."
Jesus: "Philip, where can we buy enough food to feed all these people?"
Philip: "It would take two hundred days of work to make enough money to feed so many people!"
Peter: "There is a boy who has five loaves of barley bread and two fish. But that is certainly not enough for all these people!"
Jesus: "Make the people sit down, and have the boy come to Me."
Narrator: "Jesus took the bread and fish from the boy. He looked up to heaven and thanked God."
Jesus: (to His disciples) Pass the food out to all the people.
Narrator: All five thousand had enough to eat.
Jesus: (to His disciples) Gather the pieces that are left over; let us not waste a bit.
Narrator: The disciples went through the crowd and collected enough bread and fish to fill twelve baskets. Everyone was amazed.

Invite the young people to reflect on the gospel story and to imagine that they were present in the crowd. Have them respond in their faith journals to the following questions:

■ How did you feel when you received your bread and fish?

■ What did you say to Jesus?

■ What will you say to Jesus the next time you receive the Eucharist?

FAITH ALIVE AT HOME AND IN THE PARISH

This lesson on the Eucharist is an opportunity for your family to renew the central place this wonderful sacrament has in our Catholic faith. Saint Thomas Aquinas called the Eucharist "the sacrament of sacraments"—the greatest sacrament of all! Read with your family the words of Jesus in which he describes himself as the Bread of Life (John 6:35–61). Discuss what the words of Jesus from this story might mean for your family today.

The Blessed Sacrament is another name for the Eucharist. After Mass, the Blessed Sacrament is usually kept, or reserved, in the tabernacle in a special place in the church. This is done so that Holy Communion may be brought to the sick of our parish, and so that we may worship Jesus truly present in the Blessed Sacrament.

To deepen your love and the love of your family for the gift of the Eucharist, make a visit together this week to Jesus in the Blessed Sacrament.

† Family Prayer

Jesus, be with us and with our
  parish family.
Remind us to share our lives
  as bread for others;
help us to share our joys
  as wine for others.

Learn by heart Faith Summary

What is the Eucharist?
- The Eucharist is the sacrament of the Body and Blood of Christ.

What food does Jesus give us?
- Jesus is the Bread of Life. The food that Jesus gives us is his own Body and Blood.

How do we respond to the gift of the Eucharist?
- We respond to the gift of the Eucharist by living for the reign of God.

Blessed Sacrament

What will you share with Jesus during your family's visit to the Blessed Sacrament? Write it as a prayer.

Review

Go over the *Faith Summary* together and encourage your fifth grader to learn it by heart, especially the first two statements. Then have him or her do the *Review*. The answers to numbers 1–4 appear on page 216. The response to number 5 will show how well your fifth grader is growing in his or her love for the Eucharist. When the *Review* is completed, go over it together.

Circle the letter beside the correct answer.

1. Jesus celebrated the first Eucharist
   a. after his death.
   b. by himself.
   c. for himself.
   d. during a feast of Passover.

2. When we receive the Eucharist,
   a. we eat Jesus' Body and drink his Blood.
   b. we receive only bread and wine.
   c. we always celebrate alone.
   d. we do not need to receive it again.

3. The word *Eucharist* means
   a. "Last Supper."
   b. "bread and wine."
   c. "to give thanks."
   d. "blessed be God."

4. We receive Jesus himself, as our Bread of Life, in
   a. Baptism.
   b. Holy Communion.
   c. Confirmation.
   d. the Last Supper.

5. What one thing will you do this week to show that you are thankful for the Eucharist?

_____
_____
_____
_____

FAMILY SCRIPTURE MOMENT

Gather and ask: What does food do for us? What "foods" nourish our spirits? Then **Listen** as a family to the words of Jesus.

So Jesus said to them, "Amen, amen, I say to you, it was not Moses who gave the bread from heaven; my Father gives you the true bread from heaven. For the bread of God is that which comes down from heaven and gives life to the world."

So they said to him, "Sir, give us this bread always." Jesus said to them, "I am the bread of life; whoever comes to me will never hunger, and whoever believes in me will never thirst. . . . I will not reject anyone who comes to me."
John 6:32–35, 37

Share what each one heard Jesus saying.

Consider for family enrichment:

■ Jesus tells the crowd that the real bread from heaven is not the manna God provided for Moses and the people who wandered in the desert. Jesus himself is the Bread of Life sent by God.

■ We can bring all our spiritual hungers to the Eucharist and are nourished by the real presence of Christ.

Reflect and **Decide** What might we do as a family to increase our appreciation for the Eucharist and to live it this week?

11 Our Church Celebrates the Eucharist (The Mass)

For the Catechist: Spiritual and Catechetical Development

ADULT BACKGROUND

Our Life

Recalling the example of our ancestors in the faith, Saint Paul reminds us that "we are surrounded by so great a cloud of witnesses" (Hebrews 12:1). For each of us, that crowd includes not only our favorite canonized saints but many others (parents, priests, teachers, mentors). Their word and witness continue to refresh us when we turn to them in memory and in prayer.

Ask yourself:

■ Who are my faith witnesses?

■ How do they continue to influence me?

Sharing Life

In what ways do you share the impact your faith witnesses have had on you?

How do your memories of Jesus affect the way you experience the Mass?

Our Catholic Faith

"Do this in memory of Me." Whenever we gather to celebrate the liturgy, we respond to the eucharistic invitation of Jesus. In the Liturgy of the Word, we remember the merciful love of Jesus and our need to be forgiven. Through the proclamation of the gospel and the other New Testament readings, we recall the stories of Jesus and of the early Christian community. By reflecting prayerfully on what we have heard, we gradually absorb the example of those who have gone before us to integrate God's word into the fabric of our daily lives.

Both preachers and hearers are encouraged by the Church to spend time familiarizing themselves with each weekend's Scripture readings before celebrating the liturgy. For as Saint Jerome reminds us, "Ignorance of the Scriptures is ignorance of Christ."

In the Liturgy of the Eucharist, we celebrate the memorial of Christ's giving of Himself at the Last Supper. His words and actions are repeated by the celebrant who, through the power of the Holy Spirit, consecrates the bread and wine so that the community may be fed by the Body and Blood of Christ.

At the anamnesis ("calling to mind again"), we remember the passion, death, and resurrection of the Lord. As Eucharistic Prayer IV puts it, we "celebrate this memorial of our redemption" and anticipate Christ's coming in glory.

In the Lord's Prayer, the Sign of Peace, and in Communion itself, our integration into the Body of Christ is strengthened and renewed. We "go in peace to love and serve the Lord" who has invited us to do all of this in memory of Him.

Coming to Faith

Does this reflection call you to any new appreciation of the real presence of Christ in the Eucharist?

What is your vision of a faith community that truly lives the Eucharist?

Practicing Faith

What will you do this week as a direct response to "Do this in memory of Me"?

How will you help your group to integrate the Liturgy of the Word into their lives?

CATECHISM OF THE CATHOLIC CHURCH

The Theme of This Chapter Corresponds with Paragraph 1346

LITURGICAL RESOURCES

The Liturgy of the Eucharist also invites us to remember all members of the body of Christ, past and present. Prepare a "Remembering Prayer" worksheet for the fifth graders. For instance, duplicate these lines from Eucharistic Prayer III:

Father, hear the prayer of the family you have gathered here before you.

(Here insert blanks on which the young people may write the names of those with whom they attend Mass.)

In mercy and love unite all your children wherever they may be.

(Insert blanks for absent friends and relatives.)

Welcome into your kingdom . . . all who have left this world in your friendship.

(Insert blanks for names of those who have died.)

JUSTICE AND PEACE RESOURCES

How do we remember those who are not with us at the liturgical celebration but who seek the Lord "with a sincere heart"?

Here are a few suggestions to be discussed with the fifth graders as possible group projects:

■ Contact a eucharistic minister who serves nursing-home patients or parishioners confined to their homes. Arrange to go with the minister to visit and to present handmade gifts to the sick.

■ Contact the pastor or the parish council to find the names of any inactive parish families with young children who might welcome a visit from a small group of fifth graders. The group could share Bible stories or a lesson from their religion texts with the host family's children.

11 Teaching Resources

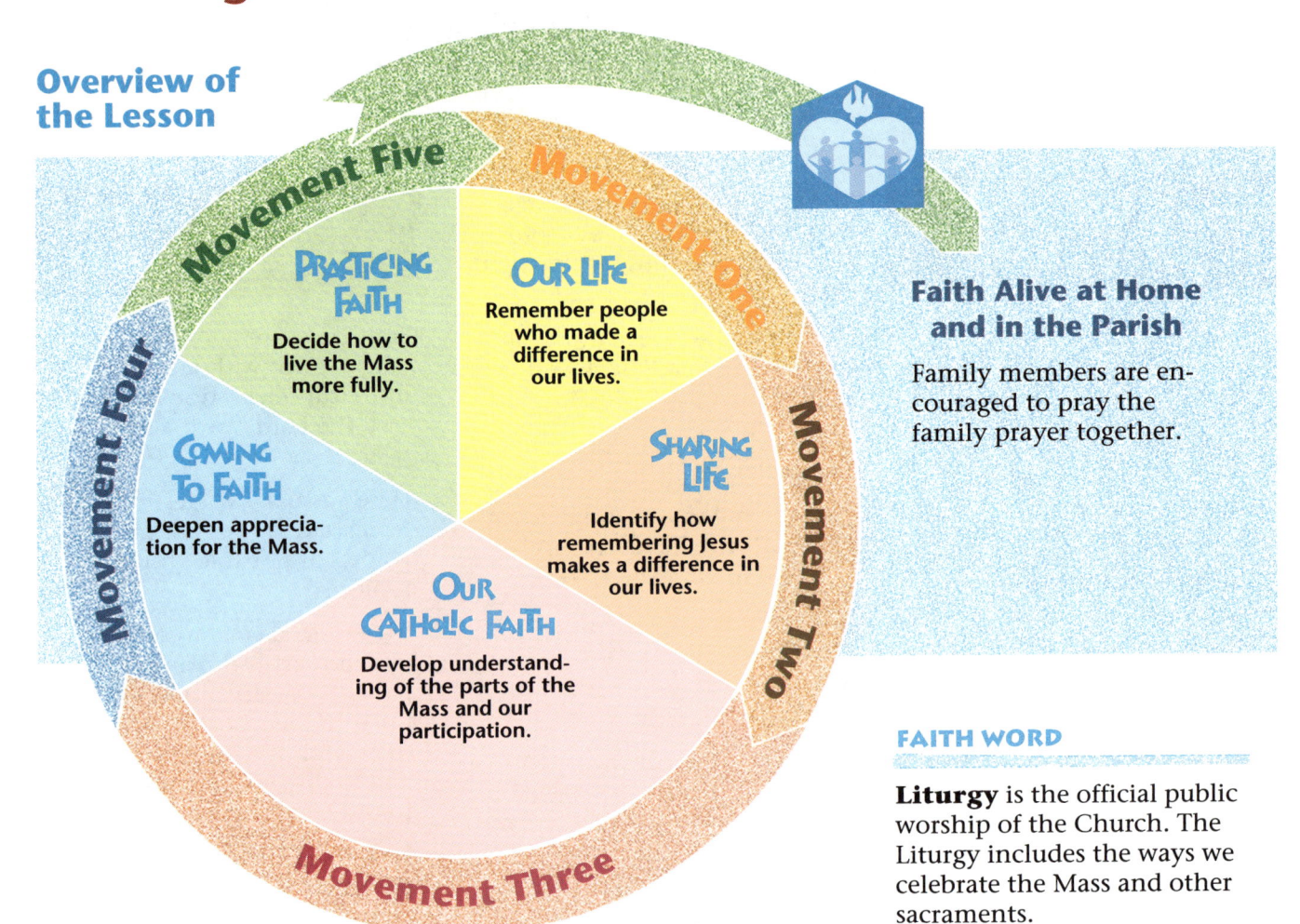

Overview of the Lesson

Movement One — Our Life: Remember people who made a difference in our lives.

Movement Two — Sharing Life: Identify how remembering Jesus makes a difference in our lives.

Movement Three — Our Catholic Faith: Develop understanding of the parts of the Mass and our participation.

Movement Four — Coming to Faith: Deepen appreciation for the Mass.

Movement Five — Practicing Faith: Decide how to live the Mass more fully.

Faith Alive at Home and in the Parish

Family members are encouraged to pray the family prayer together.

FAITH WORD

Liturgy is the official public worship of the Church. The Liturgy includes the ways we celebrate the Mass and other sacraments.

Teaching Hints

Before beginning this lesson, you may want to invite a priest or deacon to speak to the group about the Mass. If time and circumstances permit, a visit to the Church and sacristy would also be appropriate at this time. The priest or deacon might display and describe the books, vestments, and sacred vessels used at Mass.

This is also an excellent opportunity to plan a group Mass. The young people should be involved as much as possible in the planning.

Special-Needs Child

Encourage mainstreamed young people to sit close to the altar at Mass so that they can see, hear, and participate more easily.

Visual Needs
- preferential seating
- large-print *Coming to Faith* chart

Auditory Needs
- clear directions and use of gestures

Tactile–Motor Needs
- large markers for writing and art activities

Supplemental Resources

Let Us Pray (video)
William H. Sadlier, Inc.
9 Pine Street
New York, NY 10005–1002
(1-800-221-5175)

Understanding the Mass for Children (video)
The Liturgical Press
St. John's Abbey
Collegeville, MN 56321

75C

Lesson Plan: Beginning

OBJECTIVES

To help the young people

■ know what happens at Mass;

■ understand the meaning of the Mass;

■ decide to share more fully in the Mass.

Focusing Prayer

Gather the young people quietly. When all are settled, pray together the prayer at the top of page 75.

Our Life

Saying Good-bye

Introduce the *Our Life* story by asking the young people if they have ever given or been to a farewell party. Have the group look at the illustration as you read aloud the three paragraphs. Then invite the young people to discuss and respond to the questions.

Sharing Life

Remembering Loved Ones

Involve as many young people as possible in the *Sharing Life* discussion.

You might ask the young people to respond to the last two questions in their faith journals. You might also wish to share with the group how remembering Jesus makes a difference in your own life.

---

11 Our Church Celebrates the Eucharist
(The Mass)

Lamb of God, you take away the sins of the world, grant us peace.

Our Life

The parish is having a big farewell party for Mr. Sandro. He has been a catechist in the parish for five years, and now he is leaving to work as a lay missionary in Central America.

The fifth graders are sad. Mr. Sandro has been their catechist for two years. He has also been their friend. Two years is a long time. They wonder whether he will forget them.

Mr. Sandro says goodbye. He tells them that sharing faith with them was wonderful for him. He says, "I'll always remember you—each one of you!"

Is there someone who has been a special person in your life? Who? How?
Accept individual responses.
How would you say goodbye to that person? (1)
How would you remember that person? (2)
(1) Give a gift, have a party, etc.
(2) Phone calls, letters, etc.

Sharing Life

Discuss together.

Do you have memories of someone important to you to whom you had to say goodbye?
Encourage specific responses, but be sensitive to those who may not wish to share.
Tell how the memory of that person makes a difference in your life. *Answers will vary.*
How does remembering Jesus make a difference in your life now? *I am not alone. I know Jesus loves me. Jesus always helps me.*
What do you think is the best way to remember Jesus? *By participating in the Eucharist, by praying, by living the Law of Love*

ENRICHMENT

Something to Remember Me By

Ask the young people to imagine they were going to be moving away. Ask the fifth graders what each would want to give to closest friends to help them remember him or her. Some suggested answers include a photo, a favorite book, an address and phone number. Have each young person write a short paragraph telling what he or she would give and what he or she would want friends to give in return to remember them by. Help the young people see the correlation with Jesus and what He left us to remember Him by.

11

Lesson Plan: Middle

Our Catholic Faith

We Celebrate Together

Have volunteers read aloud the three paragraphs under "Celebrating Mass" on page 76. Stress that the Mass is our Catholic family celebration of thanksgiving for all of God's gifts—particularly God's greatest gift to us, Jesus Himself.

Put the word liturgy on the chalkboard or show it on a flash card. Stress that liturgy is the public prayer of the Church. It includes the ways we celebrate the Mass and other sacraments.

God Speaks to Us

Pose the question, "What happens during the Liturgy of the Word?" to introduce the reading of this section. Invite several volunteers to read this section to find the answer.

We Offer and Receive Gifts

Have the young people silently read the first two paragraphs under the "Liturgy of the Eucharist" on pages 76–77. Ask, "How does the Liturgy of the Eucharist begin?" Discuss responses, and begin to list the important parts of the Liturgy of the Eucharist on the chalkboard or newsprint.

Read aloud the next two paragraphs slowly and reverently. Ask, "What happens to the bread and wine?" Invite a young person to read the next paragraph aloud. Seek and discuss responses to the question. Emphasize that the bread and wine become Jesus' own Body and Blood.

Continue this section by having the young people silently read the remaining paragraphs up to the Concluding Rite. Invite volunteers to complete the list of the important parts of the Liturgy of the Eucharist. Ask, "What do we mean when we say 'Amen'?" Have the young people respond and then underline the answer in

ENRICHMENT

A Marker of Praise

Ask the fifth graders to make bookmarks as reminders of the parts of the Mass. Have each young person choose one part from either the Liturgy of the Word or the Liturgy of the Eucharist, then illustrate it with a symbol and a few key words. For example, a Eucharistic Prayer bookmark might feature someone singing and the words, "Holy, holy, holy, Lord."

Materials needed: construction paper strips, $2\frac{1}{2}" \times 6"$; markers

---

OUR CATHOLIC FAITH

Stress the underlined text.

Celebrating Mass

The Mass is our celebration of the Eucharist. Every Sunday or Saturday evening, the Catholic community gathers together as a worshiping assembly. We do this to remember the life, death, and resurrection of Jesus. At Mass we praise and honor God.

The two major parts of the Mass are the Liturgy of the Word and the Liturgy of the Eucharist.

In the Introductory Rites we begin our Mass with an opening song and greeting. We ask God and one another for forgiveness in the Penitential Rite. Then we praise God and pray for the strength to live for God's reign.

Liturgy of the Word

God speaks to us in the Liturgy of the Word. Selections from the Old and New Testaments are read aloud from the Bible by the reader, deacon, or priest.

The Responsorial Psalm follows the first reading. Praying this psalm response helps us to make a connection between our lives and the Old Testament reading.

The first New Testament reading is from one of the Letters, also called Epistles, or from the Acts of the Apostles or the Book of Revelation.

We prepare for the gospel proclamation by standing and singing the Alleluia. *Alleluia* is a Hebrew word meaning "praise to God."

The deacon or priest then proclaims the good news of Jesus from one of the four gospels: Matthew, Mark, Luke, or John.

After the gospel the priest or deacon gives a homily, or sermon, about the readings. This helps us to live God's word in our world today. After the homily we profess our common faith by saying the Creed together.

The Liturgy of the Word concludes with the Prayer of the Faithful. We pray for our own needs, the needs of others, the needs of the Church, and the needs of the whole world.

Liturgy of the Eucharist

The Liturgy of the Eucharist begins with the Preparation of the Gifts. Members of the assembly bring our gifts of bread and wine to the altar. These gifts are signs that we are returning to God the gift of our lives. They are also signs of our efforts to care for one another and all of God's creation. The priest prepares and offers the bread and wine to God.

Lesson Plan: Middle

their textbooks. Then together sing an "Amen," using a melody familiar to the group.

Ask: What must we do to receive Communion worthily?

Now have the group read aloud the final two paragraphs. Ask for responses to the question, "What does the Concluding Rite call us to do?"

Interpreting Pictures

Take time to talk about the photographs and illustrations on these two pages. First ask a volunteer to explain what is happening in the photo on page 76. Then ask, "At what times during the Mass do we stand?" Discuss what the priest is doing in the photo on page 77. Remind the young people that by the power of the Holy Spirit and through the words and actions of the priest, the bread and wine became the Body and Blood of Christ.

Have a volunteer explain the artist's use of wheat stalks, bread, and grapes. Ask for suggestions of other symbols that might be used to illustrate information about the Eucharist.

Our Catholic Identity

Use page 8 from the *Our Catholic Identity* section in the back of the book. Go over the words of consecration. Emphasize Jesus' complete presence under both forms – bread and wine. Talk with the children of the importance of receiving Holy Communion with reverence. Practice receiving Holy Communion with the youngsters, using unconsecrated hosts and grape juice.

You may want to use pages 25–26 in the activity book for *Coming to God's Life*.

ENRICHMENT

Special Clothing

Introduce the group to the vestments the priest wears at Mass. Show them an alb, a stole, and a chasuble. If possible, take the group to the parish sacristy, where your pastor can show the young people each vestment and how it is worn.

Materials needed: priest's vestments

We stand as the priest invites us to join in the Eucharistic Prayer. This is our Church's great prayer of praise and thanks to God for all creation and for our salvation. We respond with the "Holy, holy, holy, Lord" prayer.

Then the priest says and does what Jesus did at the Last Supper. Taking the bread, the priest prays, "Take this, all of you, and eat it: this is my body which will be given up for you."

Taking the chalice, he continues, "Take this, all of you, and drink from it: this is the cup of my blood, the blood of the new and everlasting covenant. It will be shed for you and for all so that sins may be forgiven. Do this in memory of me."

Through the power of the Holy Spirit and the words and actions of the priest, the bread and wine become Jesus' own Body and Blood. We call this the consecration.

FAITH WORD

Liturgy is the official public worship of the Church. The Liturgy includes the ways we celebrate the Mass and other sacraments.

After proclaiming the mystery of faith and the Great Amen, we prepare for Holy Communion by saying or singing the Our Father. We pray for God's forgiveness and then share a sign of peace with those around us.

While praying the Lamb of God prayer, the priest breaks the consecrated Host. This is a sign that we share in the one Bread of Life.

The priest receives Holy Communion. The members of the community next share Jesus' Body and Blood. We may receive the Host in our hand or on our tongue. We may also be invited to receive Communion from the chalice.

The priest or eucharistic minister says to us, "The body of Christ," and if we receive from the chalice, "The blood of Christ." We respond "Amen." Our Amen means that we believe Jesus is really present with us in the Eucharist and in our lives.

In the Concluding Rite the priest blesses us. He or the deacon sends us forth, and says, "Go in peace to love and serve the Lord."

Through the Mass, we receive the grace to live as true members of the Church, the body of Christ. We are nourished to be the sacrament of God's reign in the world.

To receive Communion worthily, we must be in the state of grace. A person who has committed a mortal sin must receive absolution in the sacrament of Reconciliation before going to Communion.

11

Lesson Plan: End

Coming to Faith

Reflecting on the Mass

Ask for responses to the opening statement. Allow time for the young people to think about and discuss their responses with the group. Then explain the activity and have the young people complete it. Invite volunteers to share their answers.

Faith Summary

Use the annotations to review the *Faith Summary* on page 79. See if the young people can express, in their own words, what they have learned.

Practicing Faith

Ask the young people to discuss and come to a consensus on ways they will try to live as the body of Christ in the world. Encourage them to be practical and to start with themselves, their families, and their parish.

Close by praying the prayer of Saint Francis on page 205.

EVALUATING YOUR LESSON

■ Do the young people know what happens at Mass?

■ Do they understand what the Mass means?

■ Have they decided how they will live the Mass?

◆ ENRICHMENT ◆

Joining in Prayer

Invite the young people to gather quietly and listen to a recording of "Lamb of God" from a Mass. (A beautiful one is the "Cordero de Dios" from *Misa Criolla*.)

Then have them stand in a circle and pray:

Leader: Through Him,
All: Through Jesus,
Leader: with Him,
All: with Jesus,
Leader: in the unity of the Holy Spirit, all glory and honor is yours, almighty Father,
All: forever and ever. Amen.

Materials needed: "Lamb of God" recording; record or cassette player

78

Coming To Faith

Explain why the Mass is the greatest celebration for God's people.

Put a "W" for the parts of the Mass in the Liturgy of the Word. Put an "E" for the parts of the Mass in the Liturgy of the Eucharist. Then number each part in the order in which it occurs.

Letter	Number	
E	8	Sign of Peace
W	2	Gospel
E	5	"This is my body."
E	6	"This is the cup of my blood."
W	3	Homily/Sermon
W	1	Epistle/Letter
E	4	Consecration
E	7	Lord's Prayer

Practicing Faith

Talk together about ways you can live as the body of Christ in the world. For example:

● serve, be a helper, in your parish
● find ways to help the poor, the homeless
● be aware of and respond to injustices
● be peacemakers at home, in your parish, in your neighborhood

Plan what your group will try to do this week. Then pray the prayer of Saint Francis together (page 205).

Talk with your catechist about ways you and your family might use the "Faith Alive" pages. You might plan to go to Mass together as a family this week.

78

Optional Activities

A Remembrance Prayer (for use with page 75)

Distribute paper or fabric shapes (stars, circles, triangles, crosses) and felt-tip markers. Invite the young people to think of one person who remains a part of their lives even though he or she has gone away. Have them inscribe that person's name in decorative print on the paper or fabric.

Play an appropriate recording (such as "You Are Ever a Part of Our Lives," by Weston Priory) as the young people walk to the prayer table. Encourage them to offer silent prayers for the persons they have chosen, and then to attach their name shapes (with straight pins) to a cloth covering the table.

Materials needed: fabric or paper shapes; markers; straight pins; music

Word-Portraits (for use with page 75)

Challenge the young people to create word portraits of people who have made a difference in their lives and who now remain with them only in memory. Encourage them to consider relatives, friends, neighbors, teachers, or priests who have had a strong influence on them. Remind them to pray for these persons and to follow their good examples.

Materials needed: writing paper; pens or pencils

A Guest Speaker (for use with page 76)

Invite a priest, deacon, pastoral associate, or liturgical commission member to speak briefly to the fifth graders about how the Mass makes a difference in his or her life. The guest might also respond to questions about how parish liturgies are planned and how young people might become more involved.

A Prayer Reflection (for use with page 77)

Invite the young people to relax, close their eyes, and prayerfully consider this question:

> When I leave the church after Mass, do I remember (in my heart and in my actions) that Jesus is relying on me to make His love real for others?

After a few minutes of silent reflection, have them write a brief response in their faith journals.

Materials needed: faith journals; pencils

Mass Portraits (for use with page 78)

Invite the young people to imagine and draw full-length portraits of themselves participating in the Mass as one of the following: priest or deacon, eucharistic minister, lector, altar server, minister of hospitality, or member of the congregation. Display the drawings around the room.

Materials needed: drawing paper; markers and/or crayons

FAITH ALIVE AT HOME AND IN THE PARISH

In this lesson your fifth grader has learned in more detail about the actual celebration of the Mass. The Mass is our greatest celebration and sign that we are the body of Christ in the world. Saint Paul wrote that we all share in the Body and Blood of Christ. "Because the loaf of bread is one, we, though many, are one body, for we all partake of the one loaf."

1 Corinthians 10:17

The laws of the Church require Catholics to participate in the Mass on Sunday or Saturday evening and on certain other holy days of obligation. This is a serious responsibility. Sometimes, however, our participation can become routine and thoughtless. Talk together as a family about what you will do to share more fully and responsively in the Mass. Be sure to discuss the reasons for worshiping together that go far beyond the level of obligation. Focus on the privilege of coming together as a community of faith to praise and thank God.

✝ Family Prayer

Pray this prayer each morning.

Jesus, help us to know what you want us to do for others today.

Learn by heart — Faith Summary

What are the two major parts of the Mass?
- The two major parts of the Mass are the Liturgy of the Word and the Liturgy of the Eucharist.

What do we do during the Liturgy of the Word?
- During the Liturgy of the Word, we listen to God's word from the Bible.

What happens during the Liturgy of the Eucharist?
- During the Liturgy of the Eucharist, our gifts of bread and wine become the Body and Blood of Christ.

Remember our call to live the Eucharist by loving and serving the Lord all week long.

Before Mass we will...
_____
_____

We will "live" the Mass by...
_____
_____

During Mass we will...
_____
_____

Review

Go over the *Faith Summary* together and encourage your fifth grader to learn it by heart, especially the first statement. Then have him or her do the *Review*. The answers to numbers 1–4 appear on page 216. The response to number 5 will help you to see how well your fifth grader is growing in appreciation of the Mass as our Church's greatest prayer. When the *Review* is completed, go over it together.

Circle the letter beside the correct answer.

1. The celebration of the Eucharist is
   a. the rosary.
   b. the Lord's prayer.
   c. the Mass.
   d. the Gospel.

2. At Mass we hear God's word read from the Bible during the
   a. Introductory Rites.
   b. Liturgy of the Word.
   c. Liturgy of the Eucharist.
   d. Concluding Rite.

3. The central part of the Liturgy of the Eucharist is
   a. the Eucharistic Prayer.
   b. the Our Father.
   c. the "Holy, holy, holy, Lord" prayer.
   d. the "Lamb of God" prayer.

4. At Mass the bread and wine become Jesus' own Body and Blood during the
   a. Liturgy of the Word.
   b. Holy Communion.
   c. Lord's Prayer.
   d. Eucharistic Prayer.

5. What will you thank God for at Mass next Sunday or Saturday evening?

_____
_____
_____

FAMILY SCRIPTURE MOMENT

Gather and ask: what does it mean for us to worship God? Then **Listen** as a family.

A woman of Samaria came to draw water. Jesus said to her, "Give me a drink." The Samaritan woman said to him, "How can you, a Jew, ask me, a Samaritan woman, for a drink?" Jesus answered and said to her, "Everyone who drinks this water will be thirsty again; but whoever drinks the water I shall give will never thirst; the water I shall give will become in him a spring of water welling up to eternal life."
John 4:7, 9, 13–14

Share what each person hears Jesus saying in this conversation with the Samaritan woman.

Consider for family enrichment:
■ By sharing the truth about himself as the source of life-giving water, Jesus reveals that in him all people can offer true worship to God.
■ At Mass we worship and give thanks to the Father, through the Son, in the Holy Spirit. It is our true worship "in Spirit and truth."

Reflect and **Decide** How can our worship influence our daily lives? Pray: Loving Father, by the power of the Holy Spirit, who sanctifies us, and with your Son, who redeems us, we worship you and give you thanks.

12 THE CHURCH REMEMBERS
(LITURGICAL YEAR)

For the Catechist: Spiritual and Catechetical Development

ADULT BACKGROUND

Our Life

Those Catholics who remember the "solemn high Mass" of the pre-Vatican II Church may recall the opening words of every sung gospel: "In illo tempore." The Latin phrase means "at that time." Its effect on the community at worship was to merge "that time" when Jesus walked among His disciples and "this time" when we gather to celebrate His presence with us.

Ask yourself:

- In what ways is my present enriched by my past?

- What seasonal rituals enable me to merge "that time" with "this time"?

Sharing Life

How do your seasonal rituals encourage you to "have reverence for God"?

What childhood memories of rituals from the liturgical year have helped to form your present spirituality?

Our Catholic Faith

The inherent appeal to our hearts and minds of the Church's liturgical year proves itself anew in every season. As Catholics, our identities are strongly influenced by the rituals (traditional and contemporary) that we celebrate at Advent and Christmas, Lent and Easter. Our calendars offer us a wealth of feast days on which to remember and rejoice in the life of Christ, as well as in the lives of Mary and the saints.

Within each year's cycle, the Church "unfolds the whole mystery of Christ, not only from His incarnation and birth until His ascension, but also as reflected in the day of Pentecost, and the expectation of a blessed, hoped-for return of the Lord" (*Constitution on the Sacred Liturgy,* 102).

With special love, the Church honors Mary on particular feasts such as the Annunciation and the Assumption because she was inseparably involved in the saving work of her Son. Although we may no longer celebrate some Marian devotions that have little or no authentic theological content, we are, as Carlo Carretto observes in *Blessed Are You Who Believed*, "starting again from the beginning with Mary . . . because in the Church, which is a living body and a living reality, everything is continuous."

We honor the martyrs and all the saints as reflections of Christ and witnesses to God's marvelous grace working through them for the fulfillment of the kingdom. Among the saints' days that have particular significance for us are:

- Saints Peter and Paul, Apostles (June 29);

- Birth of John the Baptist (June 24);

- Joseph, Husband of Mary (March 19);

- Mary Magdalene (July 22).

Time is God's gift to us and we keep it holy by entering wholeheartedly into the Church's celebration of the liturgical year.

Coming to Faith

How will you enter more deeply into a particular liturgical season?

What does it mean to keep time holy?

Practicing Faith

What will you do this week to live the Church's year in some special way?

How will you communicate the appeal of the liturgical year to your group?

CATECHISM OF THE CATHOLIC CHURCH

The Theme of This Chapter Corresponds with Paragraph 1171

LITURGICAL RESOURCES

Invite the group to work together to make a liturgical-year chart large enough to hang in the classroom. Have them draw a circle in the center of a large sheet of paper and divide the circle into the different periods of time that make up the Church year: Advent; Christmas; Ordinary Time (part 1); Lent; the Easter Triduum; Easter; Ordinary Time (part 2). Give prominence to the Easter Triduum and the Easter Season. Decorate each segment with seasonal symbols.

Have the young people mark the date on which each season begins during the present school year. When a season begins, have one or more volunteers explain the significance of that particular season.

JUSTICE AND PEACE RESOURCES

Have the young people work in several small groups to brainstorm specific justice and peace projects appropriate to the liturgical seasons. For example:

■ Advent—What can we do to further the cause of world peace?

■ Christmas—How can we help to "un-commercialize" Christmas?

■ Lent—What sacrifices can we make in order to feed the hungry?

■ Easter—How can we help refugees to enjoy a new life of freedom and peace in our country?

Teaching Resources

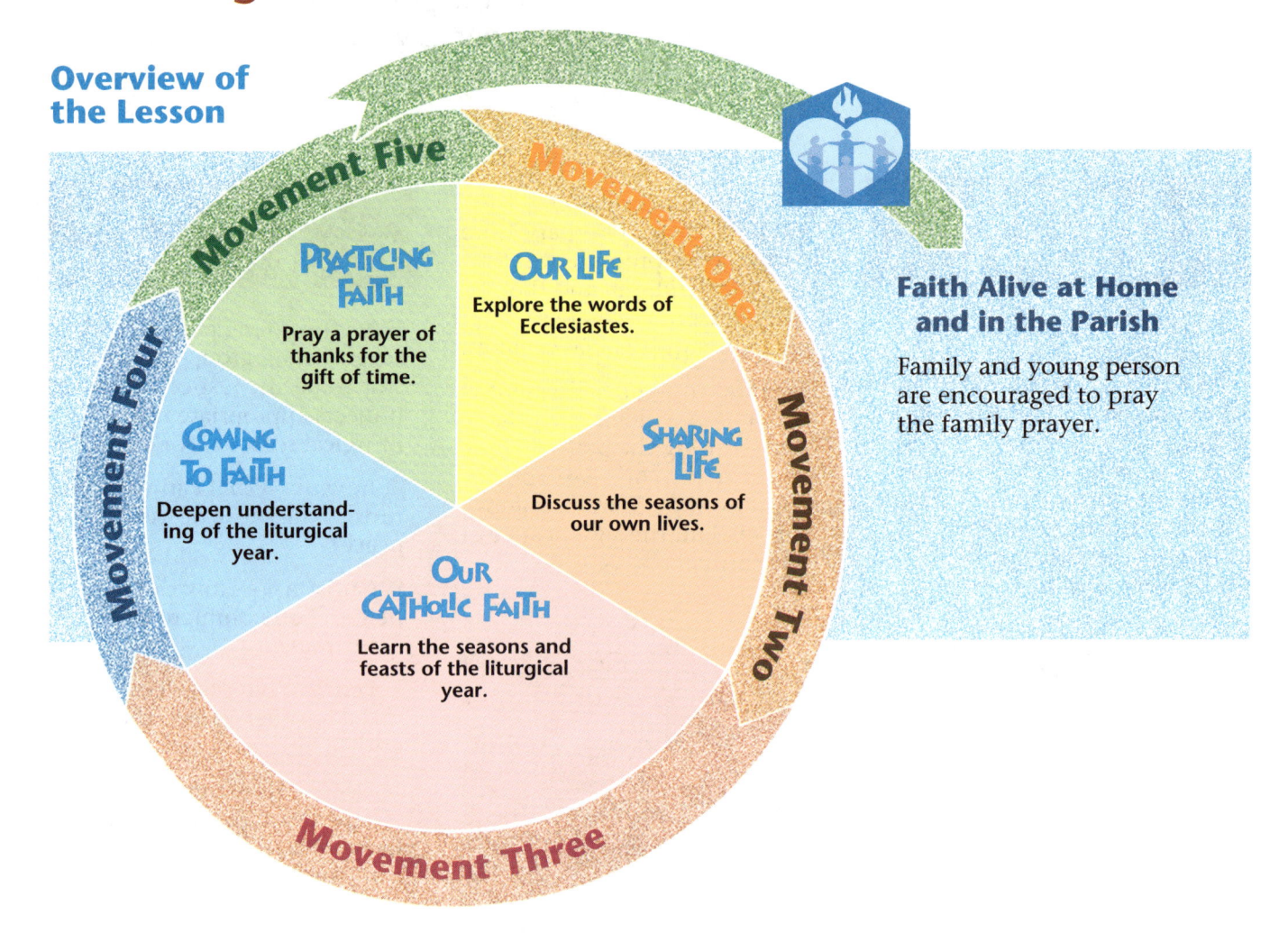

Overview of the Lesson

Movement One — Our Life: Explore the words of Ecclesiastes.

Movement Two — Sharing Life: Discuss the seasons of our own lives.

Movement Three — Our Catholic Faith: Learn the seasons and feasts of the liturgical year.

Movement Four — Coming to Faith: Deepen understanding of the liturgical year.

Movement Five — Practicing Faith: Pray a prayer of thanks for the gift of time.

Faith Alive at Home and in the Parish

Family and young person are encouraged to pray the family prayer.

Teaching Hints

This lesson focuses on the ways that the Church celebrates throughout the liturgical year. Encourage the young people to appreciate the seasons and special times in their lives, and help them to understand that the Church has seasons of celebration, too.

Music, art, prayer, and reflection relating to the liturgical year provide effective ways of reminding the young people that God is with us always.

Special-Needs Child

When involved in motion activities, you need to be aware of those who need assistance or a moderation of movement.

Visual Needs
- preferential seating

Auditory Needs
- eye contact, gestures for emphasis

Tactile–Motor Needs
- peer helpers to record responses

Supplemental Resources

To Everything There Is a Season (video)
Oblate Media and Communications
1944 Innerbelt Business Center Dr.
St. Louis, MO 63114

Prepare and Celebrate (videostrip)
Brown-ROA
2460 Kerper Blvd.
P.O. Box 539
Dubuque, IA 52004–0539
(1-800-922-7696)

Lesson Plan: Beginning

Objectives

To help the young people

- know the seasons of the liturgical year;
- understand some of the feasts of the year;
- decide how to celebrate the liturgical year in a meaningful way.

Focusing Prayer
Gather the young people in quiet and pray together the prayer at the top of page 81.

Our Life

Seasons and Times

Read aloud this section on page 81. Ask the young people what they think the words from Ecclesiastes mean. If possible, display pictures showing different seasons of the year. Then have the young people share their responses to the questions.

Materials needed: seasonal pictures

Sharing Life

Times of Our Lives

If possible, show the young people photographs of people in times of joy or sorrow, and in times of growing and of "harvesting" in their lives. Now invite the fifth graders to share their thoughts about the seasons in human lives and what we do during those times. Encourage the group to recognize God's presence at all times.

Materials needed: photographs of people

---

12 The Church Remembers
(Liturgical Year)

Thank you, God, for the gift of time. Help us to use it in your service.

Our Life

A wise teacher in the Old Testament once wrote:

There is a season for everything, a time for everything under heaven:
a time for being born,
a time for dying,
a time for planting,
a time for harvesting,
a time for tears,
a time for laughter,
a time for grieving,
a time for dancing.

Based on Ecclesiastes 3:1, 4

You may want to review one of the reasons for the seasonal change (the earth's revolution around the sun) to compare to the Church seasons which revolve around Jesus.

These words tell us that there is a season, a time, for everything. Talk about your favorite time of the year.
Answers may vary
How is each time different and special?
Encourage specific responses.
How does each season prepare us, and the world, for the next season? *Spring (new life), summer (growth), autumn (fullness, harvest) winter (death)*

Sharing Life

Are there "seasons," times of change, in our human lives? *Yes, we experience a similar cycle all through life.*
Discuss why we have times for planting and harvesting, for tears and for laughter, for grieving and for rejoicing. *Growth takes time. Different experiences of life*
At what time is God with us? How? *Always—in the Eucharist, in prayer, in love of others*

81

Enrichment

A Visual Experience

If possible, show the film *To Everything There Is a Season*. It is a meditative experience and one that will help the young people understand the words of Ecclesiastes in a visual way.

Materials needed: see *Supplemental Resources*

Lesson Plan: Middle

Our Catholic Faith

Seasons of the Church Year

Ask the annotated question to guide the silent reading of "The Liturgical Year" on page 82. Seek and discuss responses to the question. Point out that, like the calendar year, the Church year is marked by seasons. Advent, Christmas, Lent, the Easter Triduum, Easter, and Ordinary Time make up the liturgical year.

The Liturgical Seasons

As you introduce the liturgical seasons, point out on the twelve-month calendar when that season is celebrated. Explain that the dates for some seasons change each year.

Invite volunteers to read aloud the paragraphs under "Advent Season" and "Christmas Season." Discuss what we remember and celebrate during these seasons.

Have the young people silently read the "Lenten Season" section. Encourage volunteers to share their responses. Write the words *fast* and *abstain* on the chalkboard or newsprint, and have the group explain their meanings.

Have the young people silently read the paragraph under "Easter Triduum" on page 82. Invite volunteers to explain the Easter Triduum in their own words. Encourage the young people to explain the significance of each event of the Triduum.

Enrichment

Celebrating the Liturgical Year

Have the young people work together to make a large circular calendar divided into the seasons of the liturgical year. Then ask each fifth grader to choose a saint (perhaps his or her patron saint), find out when that saint's feast day is celebrated, and then write the saint's name and date of celebration on the calendar.

Materials needed: posterboard; markers; pencils; books about the saints

82

Our Catholic Faith

Ask: What does the liturgical year help us to remember?

The Liturgical Year
Our Church has seasons that make up our liturgical year to remind us of Jesus' life, death, and resurrection. These seasons help us to remember that all time is a holy time to be lived in the presence of God.

Advent Season
The liturgical year begins with the four weeks of the Advent season, immediately before Christmas. During this time, we remember that the Jewish people waited and hoped for a Messiah. We wait and hope for the coming of Jesus at Christmas and at the end of time.

Christmas Season
The Christmas season celebrates the birth of Jesus and the announcement to the world that he is the Messiah promised by God.

Ask: What do we prepare for during Lent?

Lenten Season
The season of Lent is a time of preparation for Easter and for the renewal of our Baptism. Lent begins on Ash Wednesday and lasts for forty days. It is a time to remember the words of Jesus, "The kingdom of God is at hand. Repent, and believe in the gospel" (Mark 1:15).

Catholics for centuries have prepared for Easter in special ways during Lent. Adults *fast*, or eat less and do without snacks between meals, on Ash Wednesday and Good Friday.

Those fourteen or older *abstain*, or do not eat meat, on Ash Wednesday and the Fridays of Lent. We do without things so that we can have more to share with the poor.

Passion, or Palm, Sunday is the last Sunday of Lent and the first day of Holy Week.

Easter Triduum
The Easter Triduum, or "three days," is the most important time of the entire Church year. It begins with the Mass of the Lord's Supper on Holy Thursday evening and continues through Good Friday and the Easter Vigil on Holy Saturday. It concludes with Evening Prayer on Easter Sunday. During these three days we remember the Last Supper and Jesus' gift of himself in the Eucharist. We recall his passion and death on the cross. We celebrate his resurrection.

Annunciazione, Domenica Ghirlandaio, (15th century)

82

Lesson Plan: Middle

Have volunteers read aloud the "Easter Season" section. Discuss the important days and events we remember and celebrate during this season. Ask the young people to discuss the pictures on these pages. Then invite them to read silently the "Ordinary Time" section. Emphasize that the liturgical seasons help us to remember that God is always present with us.

Celebrating Feast Days

Invite volunteers to read aloud the "Feast Days" section. Point out that the Church has named Mary as Patroness of the United States under her title of the Immaculate Conception. We celebrate that feast—recognizing Mary's being born free from original sin—on December 8. Share with the young people that we celebrate the following feast days of Mary each year:

- Birthday of Mary—September 8
- Immaculate Conception—December 8
- Our Lady of Guadalupe—December 12
- The Annunciation—March 25
- The Assumption—August 15

Our Catholic Identity

Use page 10 from the *Our Catholic Identity* section in the back of the book. Allow time for the youngsters to share their favorite Church season. Invite them to make a poster illustrating when the Church year begins and ends, and how the liturgical day goes from early evening to the evening of the next day.

You may wish to use pages 27–28 in the activity book for *Coming to God's Life*.

Easter Season
On Easter Sunday, the greatest feast of the liturgical year, we celebrate Jesus' resurrection and our new life with God. The Easter season continues for fifty days until Pentecost Sunday.

On Pentecost we remember the day the Holy Spirit came to Jesus' first disciples. We recall that without the Holy Spirit we could not live as God's people.

Ordinary Time
The weeks of the year that are not part of the seasons of Advent, Christmas, Lent, the Triduum, or Easter are known as Ordinary Time. The Church reminds us that God is always with us and present in our lives, no matter what the time.

Feast Days
Many feast days are celebrated during the liturgical year. The chart shows some of the feast days on which we remember the lives of Jesus, Mary, and the saints.

Advent Season
Immaculate Conception, December 8
Our Lady of Guadalupe, December 12

Christmas Season
Christmas, December 25
Mary, Mother of God, January 1
Epiphany

Ordinary Time
Presentation of the Lord, February 2

Lenten Season
Ash Wednesday
Joseph, Husband of Mary, March 19
Annunciation, March 25
Passion, or Palm, Sunday

Easter Triduum
Passion, death, and resurrection of the Lord

Easter Season
Easter
Ascension
Pentecost

Ordinary Time
Assumption, August 15
Birth of Mary, September 8
All Saints, November 1
All Souls, November 2
Christ the King

ENRICHMENT

Honoring Our Lady

Have the young people make a large, illustrated calendar marking the feasts of Our Lady. Tell the group to write a special prayer to Mary for each feast. Have the calendar on display in your room.

Materials needed: large sheet of posterboard or newsprint; crayons and markers

83

12

Lesson Plan: End

Coming to Faith

Remembering the Liturgical Year

Have volunteers take turns telling how they would explain the liturgical year to a fourth grader.

Then have the young people work in groups to come up with a key word for each season. Have the groups share their thoughts.

Faith Summary

Use the annotations to review the *Faith Summary* on page 85. See if the young people can express, in their own words, what they have learned.

Practicing Faith

The Gift of Time

Before the prayer service, go over the response that follows each prayer. Also ask the young people to have in mind what they would pray to do in each season. Assign readers for each prayer. Then gather the group for the prayer service.

Evaluating Your Lesson

■ Do the young people know the seasons of the liturgical year?

■ Do they understand some of its key feasts?

■ Have they decided ways to celebrate liturgical feasts?

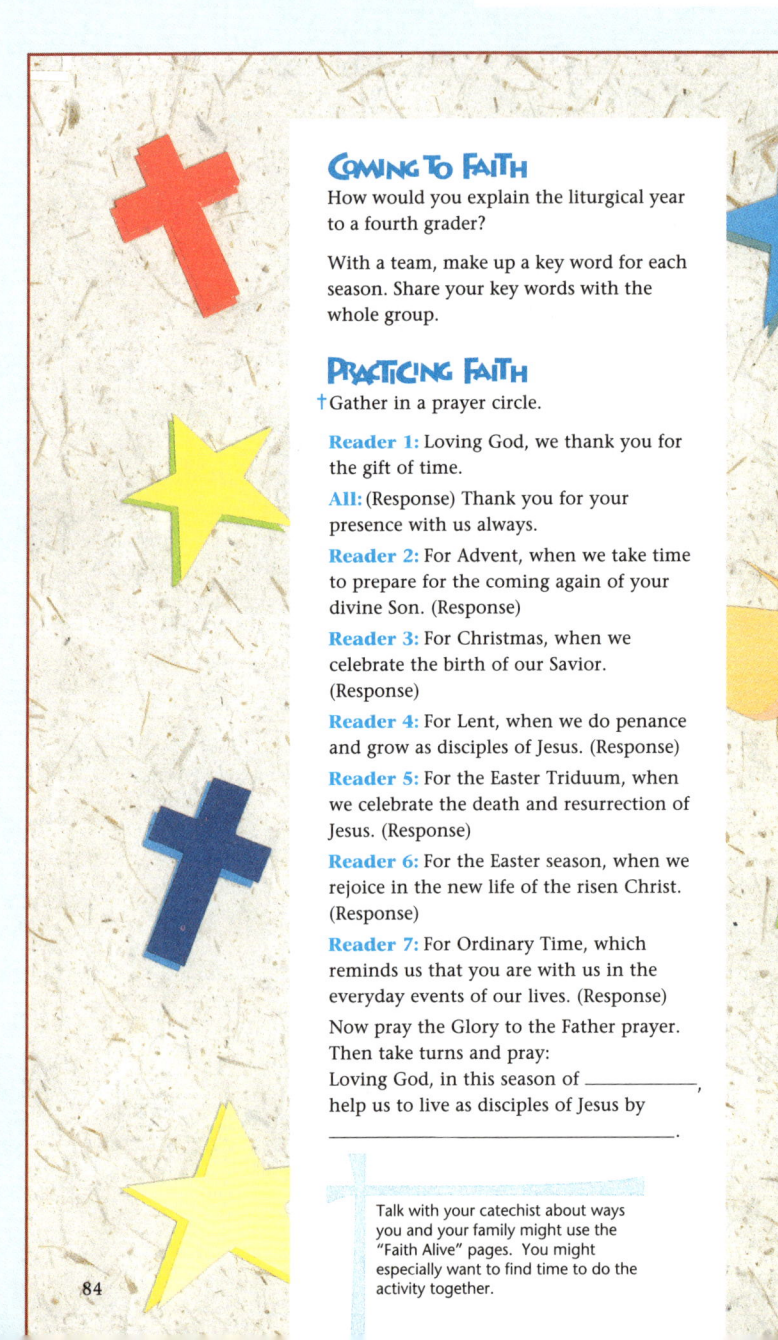

Enrichment

Dramatizing Scripture

To extend the closing prayer, you might want to have the young people do a dramatic reading of the passage from Ecclesiastes on page 81.

Observe a moment of silence and resting in God's presence. Then close by reading the opening prayer again: "Thank You, God, for the gift of time. Help us to use it in Your service. Amen."

Coming To Faith

How would you explain the liturgical year to a fourth grader?

With a team, make up a key word for each season. Share your key words with the whole group.

Practicing Faith

†Gather in a prayer circle.

Reader 1: Loving God, we thank you for the gift of time.

All: (Response) Thank you for your presence with us always.

Reader 2: For Advent, when we take time to prepare for the coming again of your divine Son. (Response)

Reader 3: For Christmas, when we celebrate the birth of our Savior. (Response)

Reader 4: For Lent, when we do penance and grow as disciples of Jesus. (Response)

Reader 5: For the Easter Triduum, when we celebrate the death and resurrection of Jesus. (Response)

Reader 6: For the Easter season, when we rejoice in the new life of the risen Christ. (Response)

Reader 7: For Ordinary Time, which reminds us that you are with us in the everyday events of our lives. (Response)

Now pray the Glory to the Father prayer. Then take turns and pray:
Loving God, in this season of _____, help us to live as disciples of Jesus by _____.

Talk with your catechist about ways you and your family might use the "Faith Alive" pages. You might especially want to find time to do the activity together.

Optional Activities

Singing About God's Presence (for use with page 83)

Gather the young people at the prayer table. To emphasize that all the times of our lives are holy if we live them in God's presence, sing "Day by Day" (from the *Godspell* album) or "This Day God Gives Me" (by James Quinn, S.J.).

Materials needed: song lyrics

Honoring Mary (for use with page 83)

Display on the prayer table a picture or statue of Mary. Invite six young people to present a real or artificial flower to Mary, our Mother, as each title is read from the litany below. Select a prayer leader, and ask everyone to respond to each petition with "We honor you, Mary."

- Our Lady of the Immaculate Conception
- Our Lady of Guadalupe
- Mary, our Mother
- Our Lady of the Annunciation
- Our Lady of the Assumption
- Mary, Mother of God

Materials needed: picture or statue of Mary; flowers

Remembering the Seasons (for use with page 84)

Write on the chalkboard or newsprint the headings: Advent, Christmas, Lent, and Easter. Ask the young people to share words or phrases that can be used to describe each of these liturgical seasons. List their responses under the appropriate heading.

Remembering Feasts (for use with page 84)

Have the young people work in small groups with one person acting as the leader. As the leader names a liturgical season, group members should name the feasts celebrated during that season and tell something about those feasts.

84A

FAITH ALIVE AT HOME AND IN THE PARISH

By celebrating the Church's liturgical year, we encounter the story of our faith over and over again. Jesus' life, death, and resurrection is the heart of the story. The stories of Mary and the other saints give us many examples of the way to live each day as disciples of Jesus Christ. The liturgical year reminds us that all time is sacred and is permeated with the presence of God.

Our identity as Catholics is strongly influenced by the rituals we celebrate in our parish and home during Advent, Christmas, Lent, and Easter. We have a wealth of feast days on which to celebrate the life of Christ and the lives of Mary and the other saints. Some Catholics, remembering Good Friday, keep the custom of not eating meat on Fridays throughout the year. All of these experiences can enrich our spiritual lives by drawing us each year into the cycle of our common faith story.

Do the activity below to help your fifth grader appreciate the liturgical year. Then pray the family prayer together.

† Family Prayer

Leader: Let us praise the Lord of days and seasons and years, saying: Glory to God in the highest!

Family: And peace to God's people on earth!

Our lives are made of days and nights, of seasons and years, for we are a part of our universe. We mark ends, and we make beginnings, and we praise God for the grace and mercy that fills our days. Amen.

The Liturgical Seasons

Make a five-sided diagram like this one to illustrate the liturgical seasons.

Learn by heart Faith Summary

What are the liturgical seasons of the Church year?
• The liturgical seasons of the Church year are Advent, Christmas, Lent, the Easter Triduum, Easter, and Ordinary Time.

Whom do we honor during the liturgical year besides Jesus?
• During the liturgical year we also honor and pray to Mary and the other saints.

Of what does the liturgical year remind us?
• The liturgical year reminds us that we always live in the presence of God.

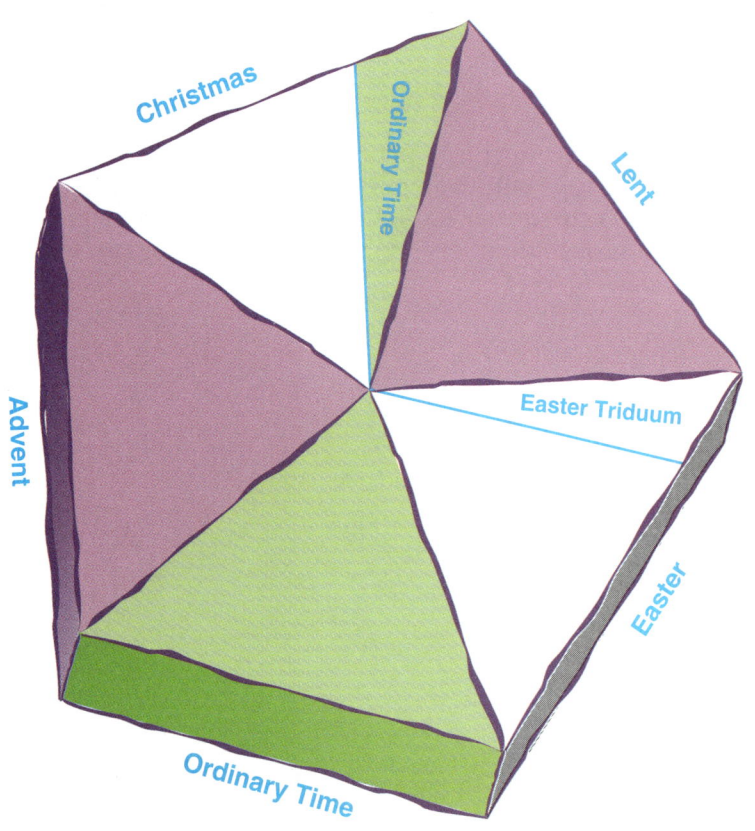

85

Review

Go over the *Faith Summary* together and encourage your fifth grader to learn it by heart, especially the first statement. Then have him or her do the *Review*. The answers to numbers 1–4 appear on page 216. The response to number 5 will show you how well your fifth grader understands the different liturgical seasons of the Church year. When the *Review* is completed, go over it together.

Circle the letter beside the correct answer.

1. The liturgical year begins with the season of
   a. **Advent.** *(circled)*
   b. Christmas.
   c. Lent.
   d. Easter.

2. Which is NOT a liturgical season?
   a. Advent
   b. Ordinary Time
   c. Easter Season
   d. **feast of the Immaculate Conception** *(circled)*

3. The most important time in the Church year is
   a. Ordinary Time.
   b. **the Easter Triduum.** *(circled)*
   c. Lent.
   d. Christmas.

4. The season of the liturgical year during which we prepare for Easter is
   a. Advent.
   b. Christmas.
   c. **Lent.** *(circled)*
   d. Ordinary Time.

5. What will you do to celebrate the present liturgical season?

   _____
   _____
   _____
   _____

FAMILY SCRIPTURE MOMENT

Gather and ask: What everyday clues have we observed that God is present in our lives? Then **Listen** as Jesus prays for his disciples at the Last Supper.

..."Father, the hour has come. Give glory to your son, so that your son may glorify you. I revealed your name to those whom you gave me out of the world. They belonged to you, and you gave them to me, and they have kept your word. . . . the words you gave to me I have given to them, and they accepted them and truly understood that I came from you, and they have believed that you sent me. . . . Holy Father, keep them in your name . . . so that they may be one just as we are."
John 17:1, 6, 8, 11

Share Ask: What is Jesus' message for us? What is Jesus' prayer for us?

Consider for family enrichment:

■ Jesus expresses his love for his friends by praying that they will experience the same loving unity he enjoys with the Father.

■ Jesus always intercedes for us that we may one day inherit the kingdom. Surely, Jesus' prayer is answered.

Reflect and **Decide** How does living in harmony with the Church year help us to be one with God and one another? What will we as a family do to celebrate the present liturgical season?

86

13 CELEBRATING THE ADVENT SEASON

CATECHISM OF THE CATHOLIC CHURCH

The Theme of This Chapter Corresponds with Paragraph 489

For the Catechist: Spiritual and Catechetical Development

Our Life

Don was stunned when he looked at the calendar. "I can't believe it!" he said. "Advent starts next Sunday. I hope I find time to appreciate it this year." Marla agreed. But she shared with Don her one Advent resolution for the new year. "I'm going to practice waiting patiently wherever I go," she observed.

Ask yourself:

■ In what situations do I need to be a more patient "waiter"?

Sharing Life

How might Advent be a fruitful time to practice creative waiting?

Our Catholic Faith

In announcing the future birth of the Savior, the prophet Isaiah proclaimed:

> You have brought them abundant joy and great rejoicing,
> As they rejoice before you as at the harvest,...
> (Isaiah 9:2)

Advent is a season of rejoicing at the coming of Christ—into the world at the Nativity, into our lives, and His future coming in glory. It is a time to reflect on the identity of the Promised One, who was recognized by His words that uplifted the poor, healed the sick, and liberated the oppressed.

When we serve others in these same ways, we enable them to experience the joy of His coming.

Coming to Faith

What Advent resolutions do you feel called to make?

Practicing Faith

What will you do to encourage your group to share and give joy to others?

Teaching Resources

Teaching Hints

Advent is a time to slow down and provide for the young people an atmosphere conducive to reflective waiting. Encourage them to try to carry this waiting spirit into their homes and share it with their families.

The presence of the Advent wreath and praying around it will help the group recall how Israel waited in hope for the coming of the Savior.

Special-Needs Child

Remember not to expect less from the mainstreamed child. Give assistance where needed but demand and expect results.

Visual Needs

■ large-print prayer so young person can be a reader

Auditory Needs

■ headphones and recorded music

Tactile–Motor Needs

■ peer assistant for play

Supplemental Resources

Awaited Messiah (video)
(from *Jesus of Nazareth*)
Vision Video
2030 Wentz Church Road
PO Box 540
Worcester, PA 19490
(1-800-523-0226)

Preparing for Christmas I (video)
Preparing for Christmas II (video)
St. Anthony Messenger/
Franciscan Communication
1615 Republic Street
Cincinnatti, OH 45210
(1-800-488-0488)
(1-800-989-3600)

Lesson Plan: Beginning

OBJECTIVES

To help the young people

- know the promise of the prophet;
- understand what it means to prepare for Jesus' coming;
- choose acts of generosity and service.

Focusing Prayer

Begin today's lesson by praying together the opening words of the Hail Mary on page 87.

Our Life

A Story About Waiting

Invite the young people to do a dramatic reading of the old legend. It might be done twice with different casts.

Then ask them to think of a meaning this story might have for our own lives.

Sharing Life

How Jesus Comes Today

Now have the group discuss the ways Jesus comes to us, how we can recognize Him, and how we might prepare for His coming.

---

13 Celebrating Advent

Hail Mary, full of grace, the Lord is with you.

Our Life

Here is an old legend that might have something true to say to us today.

Once long ago three children were playing in their garden. A messenger came along the road. "The king will pass this way today," he announced. The children were so excited. "Perhaps the king will stop by our garden! Let's make it beautiful!" So the children worked to make their garden beautiful, and they made sure they had fruit and bread and cool drinks. Then they waited... and waited...and waited.

It was almost sunset when an old man stopped at their garden wall. "What a beautiful garden," he said. "It looks so shady and cool. May I come in and rest awhile?"

The children did not know what to do. They were waiting for the king! But then—the poor man looked so tired and hungry. "Come in," they said and they had him sit in the shade and they brought him food and drink. Then they told him that they had worked to make everything ready for the king. But the king hadn't come. They were so disappointed.

Suddenly a lovely light shone around the man. He wasn't old or shabby anymore. He was handsome. He smiled at the children. "Your king *did* pass today," he said, "and you welcomed him."

Share what you learned from this story for your own life.

Sharing Life

Discuss together: what are the ways that Jesus comes into our lives today?

How can we recognize him?

Talk about ways we might get ready for his coming.

87

ENRICHMENT

An Advent Story

The opening story lends itself to dramatization. Perhaps the fifth graders might want to develop it into a play to be presented to other religion groups as part of the Advent preparation. The play might be entitled *The Coming of the King*.

At the end of the play, tell the fifth graders to ask the other young people what they think the play means.

Materials needed: **props for play**

Lesson Plan: Middle

Our Catholic Faith

Waiting for a Savior

Before reading, explain to the group that prophets were people who made God's actions well known to the people. Tell them that Isaiah was a great prophet. Have the group read the paragraphs on page 88 to find out Isaiah's message to the people of Israel.

List on the chalkboard or newsprint Isaiah's prophecies:

- The Savior would be born of a young woman. She would call Him *Immanuel*, which means "God with us."
- The Savior would rule the people wisely.
- The Savior would be a descendant of David.
- The Savior would be "Wonderful Counselor, Mighty God, Prince of Peace."
- He would help the poor, heal the sick, and free the oppressed.

ENRICHMENT

Looking for Jesus

Let the fifth graders make Advent calendars for young children. Make the calendars with window flaps to open and reveal surprises. On a sheet of construction paper, the young people should draw the same number of box shapes as there are days left until Christmas. In each box have them draw a Christmas symbol or write a note, such as "Jesus, I await You." Then ask the young people to tape a second sheet of paper over the top edge of the first. Next, tell them to draw seasonal pictures and cut three sides of a window flap over each box underneath. Finally, have them tape the other edges so that only the seasonal picture shows. Choose a time during which the group may share these calendars with younger children.

Materials needed: construction paper; markers; tape; scissors

---

OUR CATHOLIC FAITH

Stress the underlined text.

Waiting for a Savior

Hundreds of years before Jesus was born, a prophet named Isaiah told the Israelites many things about the promised Savior, or Messiah, for whom they were waiting. Isaiah said that the Savior would be born of a young woman who would name him Immanuel. *Immanuel* means "God with us."

Isaiah said that the Savior would rule the people of Israel wisely. Isaiah wrote:
   The spirit of the LORD shall rest upon him:
      a spirit of wisdom and of understanding,. . .
   a spirit of knowledge and of fear of the LORD (Isaiah 11:2).

Isaiah also described the Savior as a descendant of David, who was Israel's best loved king. The Messiah would be the great champion of justice who would rule as David's successor, basing his power on right and justice from now until the end of time.

Isaiah also said that the child born to be their Savior would be called "Wonder-Counselor, God-Hero, Father-Forever, Prince of Peace."

Like Isaiah, the other writers of the Bible often compared sin to darkness. At the time of Isaiah, many Israelites had turned away from God and were living in the darkness of sin. Isaiah compared the coming of the Savior to the breaking forth of light in darkness. The prophet said that the people who walked in darkness had seen a great light. They lived in a land of shadows but now light was shining on them. (Based on Isaiah 9:1–7)

Isaiah also told the Israelites that they could recognize the Savior by his works. The Savior

Lesson Plan: Middle

The Coming of the Savior

Ask, "How was the Savior's coming told to Mary?" Have the young people read this section to find the answer. Ask for suggestions as to how we prepare in Advent for Jesus' coming.

Have a volunteer list the responses on the chalkboard or newsprint. Encourage the fifth graders to think of specific suggestions applicable to their world.

You may wish to use pages 29–30 in the activity book for *Coming to God's Life*.

---

would help the poor, heal the sick, and free the oppressed. (Based on Isaiah 61:1–2)

The Coming of the Savior

Israel waited in hope for the coming of the promised Savior.

Many years after Isaiah, the angel Gabriel was sent to the Virgin Mary in the town of Nazareth in Galilee. The angel told her, "Behold, you will conceive in your womb and bear a son. . . . He will be great and will be called Son of the Most High, and the Lord God will give him the throne of David his father" (Based on Luke 1:26–33).

During Advent we remember the words of Isaiah and think about what they mean for us today. We prepare for the feast of Christmas and for Jesus' coming again. We believe that Jesus Christ is Immanuel, "God with us," and the Light of the World. As disciples of Jesus, we must bring his light to the world.

During Advent we prepare ourselves to bring the good news of Jesus to the poor. We try even harder to help care for the sick. We try to do what we can to stop injustice, discrimination, and oppression of any kind. We remember to be peacemakers.

Coming to Faith

Tell what you think Isaiah meant when he said our Savior would be:

- Immanuel
- a wise and just ruler
- a light shining in darkness
- one sent to bring good news

Maybe your group would like to bring in gifts of canned food or games for the children of your parish who are in need. Plan what you will do and make it a part of your Advent celebration.

◆ ENRICHMENT ◆

A Vocal Invitation

Write the word *Maranatha* on the chalkboard and explain that it means "Come, our Lord!" Form two groups. Have one group sing "Maranatha" (using the melody of the first two words of "Silent Night"), with the other group responding "Come, our Lord!" using the same melody. Repeat several times and close by ringing bells.

Materials needed: bells

89

Lesson Plan: End

Coming to Faith

What Isaiah Meant

Encourage the young people to talk about possible meanings for Isaiah's prophecies about the Savior.

Encourage your group toward acts of generosity and service. Work with them to organize a drive to collect food and games for needy families in the parish. Your parish Saint Vincent de Paul Society or other service organization would welcome your contributions.

Faith Summary

Use the annotations to review the *Faith Summary* on page 91. See if the young people can express, in their own words, what they have learned.

Practicing Faith

A Prayer Service

This prayer service should be held at a later session after the fifth graders have collected their gifts for the needy.

Before the prayer, go over the hymn and the responses. Assign a leader and a reader.

Gather the young people around an Advent wreath or an open Bible and have the prayer service.

Materials needed: Advent wreath or Bible

Evaluating Your Lesson

- Do the young people know how the Savior's coming was foretold?
- Do they understand how we should prepare for Jesus' coming?
- Have they performed acts of service?

Practicing Faith
An Advent Celebration

All sing:
O come, O come, Emmanuel,
And ransom captive Israel
That mourns in lonely exile here
Until the Son of God appear.
Rejoice! Rejoice, O Israel,
To you shall come Emmanuel!

Reading: (From Isaiah 61:1,3)

I am filled with the Lord's spirit.
God has chosen me and sent me
To bring good news to the poor,
To heal the brokenhearted,
To announce release to captives
And freedom to those in prison...
To give those who mourn
Joy and gladness instead of grief.

Leader: Let's pause now and think about these words of Isaiah. How can we bring Jesus' good news to the poor? healing to the brokenhearted? How can we bring freedom to those held captive by sin? How can we bring God's joy to others? (Silent reflection)

Leader: Jesus, we believe that you are Immanuel, God with us, our promised Savior.

All: Help us to live as your disciples in the world today.

Leader: Jesus, you are the Light of the World.

All: Help us to live as your disciples in the world today.

Leader: Jesus, you are the one sent by God to announce the good news.

All: Help us to live as your disciples in the world today.

Leader: Jesus, you are the Son of God.

All: Help us to live as Your disciples in the world today.

Leader: Jesus, you are the Savior, who has come to free us. Help us to bring good news to the poor, to heal the broken-hearted, and to bring freedom to all.

Presentation of Gifts

Walking in procession, all carry gifts for needy children and place them on a prayer table or near an Advent wreath.

All stand and sing:

O come now Wisdom from on high
Who orders all things mightily,
To us the path of knowledge show
And teach us in your ways to go.
Rejoice! Rejoice! O Israel
To you shall come Emmanuel!

Talk with your catechist about ways you and your family might use the "Faith Alive" pages. You might make the Angelus your family prayer for Advent.

Optional Activities

Preparing for Christmas (for use with page 87)

Ask the young people to complete the following statement in their faith journals:

> During Advent, I will prepare myself for the feast of Christmas by....

After a few minutes, ask volunteers to share what they have written.

Getting Ready for Jesus (for use with page 88)

Invite the young people to respond to the following question in their faith journals:

> If you knew for sure that Jesus was coming to your house next Sunday, how would you get ready for His arrival?

Have a few volunteers share their responses.

Jesus, Light of the World (for use with page 89)

Brainstorm with the group about the signs that show us that Jesus, the Light of the World, is with us today. Have the young people list these on the chalkboard or newsprint.

An Advent Prayer (for use with page 89)

Gather around an Advent wreath. Briefly recall the significance of the Advent wreath. Then sing "O Come, O Come, Emmanuel" or any other appropriate Advent hymn.

Materials needed: Advent wreath

Designing Advent Cards (for use with page 89)

Distribute drawing paper and markers or crayons. Challenge the young people to design Advent cards that are similar to Christmas cards. If appropriate, explain that you will collect the cards and randomly distribute them the next time the group meets. Otherwise, invite volunteers to share their completed cards with one another.

Materials needed: drawing paper; markers and/or crayons

FAITH ALIVE AT HOME AND IN THE PARISH

This Advent lesson introduced the Old Testament prophecies that promised the Savior, the Messiah—the one who would be a wise and just ruler, a light shining in the darkness, the bringer of good news, Immanuel (which means "God with us"). These are the great messianic prophecies fulfilled in Jesus.

Advent is a season to prepare again for the coming of God's Son into the world and into our lives, and for his future coming in glory. It is a time to reflect on our Savior, who gives hope to the poor, heals the sick, and liberates the oppressed. As a family, ask yourselves: how can we share the spirit of Advent with those in need in our parish or elsewhere?

† Family Prayer from the Angelus

The angel of the Lord declared to Mary,
and she conceived by the Holy Spirit.
Hail Mary....

Behold the handmaid of the Lord,
be it done to me according to your word.
Hail Mary....

And the Word was made flesh
and dwelled among us.
Hail Mary....

(See page 205 for the complete prayer.)

Learn by heart Faith Summary

What did the prophet Isaiah foretell?
- The prophet Isaiah foretold the coming of the Savior as One who would be Immanuel—"God with us."

Why was the angel Gabriel sent to Mary?
- Years later the angel Gabriel was sent to Mary to ask her to be the mother of the Savior.

How do we prepare for Christmas during advent?
- During Advent we prepare for Christmas by trying to serve the needs of others.

Random Acts of Kindness

On slips of paper have family members write ideas for "random acts of kindness" that can be done for one another and for others outside the family. Talk this over with your family. Collect their suggestions and write them below before putting them on slips. Then each one chooses a slip each week and tries to do what is suggested.

_____

_____

Review

Go over the *Faith Summary* together and encourage your fifth grader to learn it by heart, especially the third point. Then have him or her do the *Review*. The answers to numbers 1–4 appear on page 216. The response to number 5 will show your child's deepening understanding of Advent.

Fill in the blanks.

1. The prophet Isaiah said the Messiah would be called __Immanuel__, which means "God with us."

2. God sent the angel Gabriel to ask Mary to be the __Mother of the Savior__.

3. Isaiah compared the coming of the Savior to the breaking forth of __light__ in darkness.

4. Isaiah said the Savior would be a __wise and just__ ruler.

5. Tell one important way you can, as a follower of Jesus, be a "light" for the world.

_____
_____
_____
_____

FAMILY SCRIPTURE MOMENT

Gather and have each person name or describe someone in whom they have "seen Jesus" (or some quality of Jesus). Then **Listen** to an Advent messenger.

This is the testimony of John. When the Jews from Jerusalem sent priests and Levites [to him] to ask him, "Who are you?" he admitted and did not deny it . . . "I am not the Messiah." He said:
 "I am 'the voice of one crying out in the desert,
 "Make straight the way of the Lord,"' as Isaiah the prophet said . . . .

The next day he saw Jesus coming toward him and said, "Behold, the Lamb of God, who takes away the sin of the world."
John 1:19–20, 23, 29

Share how each one can point others to Jesus.

Consider for family enrichment:
■ By his fasting and prayer, John the Baptist prepared himself to recognize and proclaim the Messiah to the world.
■ By our Advent prayer and ministry, we make a path for the Lord in our lives. We look forward to the celebration of Christmas and to the second coming of Christ at the end of time.

Reflect and **Decide** What will we do as a family to be Advent messengers?

14 CELEBRATING CHRISTMAS

CATECHISM OF THE CATHOLIC CHURCH

The Theme of This Chapter Corresponds with Paragraph 525

For the Catechist: Spiritual and Catechetical Development

Our Life

It was Rokuro's idea and everyone loved it. "Let's put together a manger scene that everyone can contribute to. Each of us can make a figure that represents the country we or our ancestors came from. That will show that Jesus belongs to all people."

Ask yourself:

■ What Christmas customs have I "inherited" from my ancestors?

Sharing Life

How might you communicate the message that Jesus came to save all people?

Our Catholic Faith

When Joseph needed reassurance about the conception of Mary's child, an angel appeared to him in a dream and told him not to be afraid. "For it is through the holy Spirit that this child has been conceived in her," the angel said. "She will bear a son and you are to name him Jesus, because he will save his people from their sins" (Matthew 1:20-21).

From Christmas Eve through the feast of the Baptism of the Lord, the Church celebrates the Christmas season. We rejoice at the birth of Jesus, who saves us from our sins and gives light to the world.

The infancy narratives of Matthew and Luke contain our cherished stories of the Holy Family. In them we find once again the meaning and message of Christmas.

Coming to Faith

What values do the Christmas gospel stories challenge us to live?

Practicing Faith

How will you help your group to recognize that Jesus belongs to all people?

Teaching Resources

Teaching Hints

Plan a discussion of the group's celebrations of Christmas. This is a time of rich symbolism. Encourage the young people to share their families' Christmas customs with the group.

Christmas is also a time of giving—one of the season's greatest customs. Suggest that the young people give not only material presents, but also intangible gifts such as friendship to others.

Special-Needs Child

Make it possible for any mainstreamed fifth grader to participate in the Christmas activities.

Visual Needs

■ large-print Christmas prayer service

Auditory Needs

■ headphones and recordings of carols

Tactile–Motor Needs

■ peer helper for *Las Posadas*

Supplemental Resources

Christmas: the Complete Gospel of Luke (video)
William H. Sadlier, Inc.
9 Pine Street
New York, NY 10005
(1-800-221-5175)

"*Vamos Todos a Belén,*" words and music from *Misal Del Día* for Advent

93A

14

Lesson Plan: Beginning

OBJECTIVES

To help the young people

- understand the meaning of Christmas and its customs and symbols;
- share in a Christmas prayer.

Focusing Prayer

Play the carol "O Come, All Ye Faithful" as the young people arrive. Gather them for prayer and sing "O come let us adore Him" from the carol.

Our Life

Celebrating *Las Posadas*

Tell the young people about the beautiful custom of *Las Posadas*. Remind them that when Mary and Joseph reached Bethlehem before Jesus was born, there was no room for them anywhere. They finally found shelter in a stable that was probably a cave in the hillside.

Encourage the group members to talk about their own family customs and to tell what Christmas means to them.

Sharing Life

Customs Around the World

If possible, show pictures of Christmas customs in other parts of the world. Then invite responses to the two questions.

Materials needed: pictures of Christmas customs

---

14 Celebrating Christmas

O come let us adore him, Christ the Lord!

OUR LIFE

In some Latin American countries the people celebrate a lovely Christmas custom called *Las Posadas* ("the dwellings"). Two children take the parts of Mary and Joseph as they look for a place to stay in Bethlehem. All the other children escort them as they go from house to house in the neighborhood. At each door all sing a carol. Then Mary and Joseph ask for a room. They are turned away until they come to the last house. Here they are welcomed in, and all join in singing a joyful carol. A party usually follows! Does your family have any special Christmas customs? Tell about them. Encourage specific examples. Share yours with the group!
Share what Christmas means to you. Answers will vary.

SHARING LIFE

Share what you know about Christmas customs in other countries. Why do you think people celebrate Christmas in different ways? Because they came from different backgrounds
Discuss: what is the most important thing to remember in our Christmas celebrations? The birth of Jesus—God became human like us.

ENRICHMENT

A World of Song

Some fifth graders might enjoy learning Christmas carols from other countries—for example, "Stille Nacht" in German, "Il Est Né" in French, and "Vamos Todos a Belén" in Spanish. Let them present the carols to another group.

Materials needed: foreign language versions of Christmas carols

14

Lesson Plan: Middle

Our Catholic Faith

Jesus, the Savior

Invite the group to look at the illustration on these pages before a volunteer reads aloud the first two paragraphs.

Then ask, "How do you think Joseph knew about the child Mary was to have?" Read the story of the angel's message to Joseph in a dream and how Joseph and Mary named the new baby, Jesus. Ask, "Why do you think Jesus was just the right name for Him?" Read the meaning of the name Jesus.

Tell the young people about the Jewish custom of bringing a new baby to the temple to give thanks. Then have them read to find out what happened when Jesus was brought to the Temple. Ask, "How do you think Simeon knew that Jesus was the Savior?" Elicit from the young people that the Holy Spirit led Simeon to recognize Jesus as the Savior.

◆ ENRICHMENT ◆

Spreading Christmas Joy!

Encourage your fifth graders to share the gift of song at this glorious time of year by caroling in the neighborhood or at a nearby nursing home. Remind the fifth graders that sharing song with those who are alone or away from their families at holiday time is a thoughtful act that follows the Law of Love. Invite the young people's families or other religious groups to join the caroling. As always, the proper permissions should be sought beforehand.

Materials needed: song lyrics; permission of parents or guardians

---

Our Catholic Faith

Stress the underlined text.

Newborn Savior of All People

On Christmas Day, we celebrate the birth of Jesus. We remember that the Son of God, the second Person of the Blessed Trinity, became one of us and was named Jesus, because he is our Savior. Jesus brings God's life and love to all people.

Here is what we read in the gospel about Jesus receiving his name.

Before Jesus was born, an angel appeared to Joseph in a dream to tell him that Mary would have a Son. The angel told Joseph, "You are to name him Jesus, because he will save his people from their sins."

Based on Matthew 1:18–22

The name Jesus means "God saves."

A week after Jesus' birth, Joseph, his foster father, followed the Jewish custom and named the newborn Savior Jesus.

Later the Holy Family went to the Temple in Jerusalem to present Jesus to God. A man named Simeon, who had been praying for the Promised Savior, took Jesus in his arms. Praising God, Simeon said, "Now, Master, . . . my eyes have seen your salvation, . . . a light for revelation to the Gentiles. . . ."

Based on Luke 2:21–32

People of many different languages, customs, and races celebrate the birth of Jesus because he is the Savior of all people. When we celebrate Christmas, we remember that Jesus Christ has united us to God and to people all over the world.

Lesson Plan: Middle

The Savior of All People

Now have the group read the section "Celebrating the Birth of Jesus" to discover the meaning of the different Christmas customs. Ask:

- Why do we have lights?
- What does the tree remind us of?
- Why do we send cards and give gifts?

Emphasize that the best way to celebrate the meaning of Christmas is by sharing God's love with others.

You may wish to use pages 31–32 in the activity book for *Coming to God's Life*.

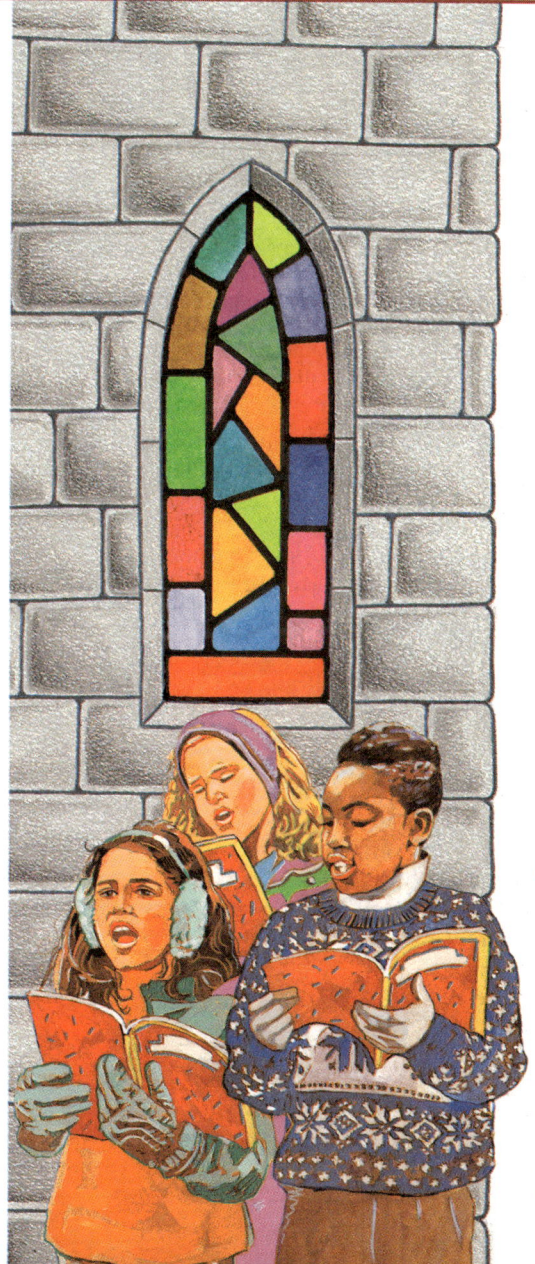

Celebrating the Birth of Jesus

During the first years of Christianity, pagans in Rome celebrated a feast of the sun on December 25. Our Church may have chosen that same day on which to celebrate Jesus' birth because we believe that Jesus is the true Light of the World.

Today Christians around the world celebrate Christmas in many different ways. All our Christmas preparations, customs, and decorations should help us to remember the meaning of Christmas.

The lights on our Christmas trees and in our windows remind us of Christ, the Light of the World. The Christmas tree, which is usually an evergreen tree, reminds us that Jesus brought us life that lasts forever. The Christmas cards and gifts that we give remind us that God shared his own life and love with us.

During the Christmas season, we celebrate that God loved us so much that his only Son became one of us. We celebrate Christmas best by sharing God's love with others.

Coming to Faith

Tell the story of Jesus' name.

Then have a *Las Posadas* procession. Choose someone to be Mary and someone to be Joseph. Go from group to group in your parish center asking for a room and singing carols like "O Come All Ye Faithful" and "Away in a Manger." Let the last "house" be the place where your group meets. Some of you can be the "hosts" who welcome Mary and Joseph. When all are gathered, share the prayer service.

ENRICHMENT

Coming to Christmas

The young people might enjoy creating a Christmas mural with the nativity scene in the center of a piece of shelving paper and people from around the world coming towards it. Everyone's Christmas customs could make up the background. Call the mural "O come let us adore Him" and display it in your parish church, if possible.

Materials needed: shelving paper; crayons and markers

14

Lesson Plan: End

Coming to Faith

Las Posadas

Invite volunteers to tell the story of Jesus' name.

Have a *Las Posadas* procession through the building or neighborhood, or possibly at a parish Mass. Go over the carols in advance and try to have one of them in Spanish in honor of the people whose custom this is.

NOTE: It would be wise to have *Las Posadas* and the Christmas prayer service from the *Practicing Faith* section at two separate sessions.

Materials needed: costumes for Mary and Joseph; lyrics for carols

Faith Summary

Use the annotations to review the *Faith Summary* on page 97. See if the young people can express, in their own words, what they have learned.

Practicing Faith

A Christmas Prayer

Go over the carols so that the group will be comfortable with them. Select readers and young people for the other roles and have them go over their readings in advance. Choose Mary and Joseph and have them at the center of the group. Then gather the young people for Christmas prayer.

Materials needed: costumes for Mary, Joseph; doll wrapped in cloths

EVALUATING YOUR LESSON

■ Do the young people understand the meaning of Christmas?

■ Have they participated in the prayer experiences?

Practicing Faith

Mary and Joseph kneel beside an empty crib. All the rest gather around them and sing:

> O little town of Bethlehem
> How still we see thee lie.
> Above thy deep and dreamless sleep
> The silent stars go by.
> Yet in thy dark streets shineth
> The everlasting light—
> The hopes and fears of all the years
> Are met in thee tonight!

Reader 1: While Mary and Joseph were in Bethlehem, the time came for Mary to have her baby. She gave birth to a son, wrapped him in cloths and laid him in a manger because there was no room for them in the inn.

(Someone places a wrapped doll or an image of the baby in the manger.)

Reader 2: There were shepherds in the area, living in the fields and keeping watch over their flock. An angel of the Lord appeared to them and the glory of the Lord shone around them, and they were very much afraid. The angel said to them:

Angel: You have nothing to fear. I come to proclaim good news to you to be shared by all the people. This day a Savior has been born to you. Let this be a sign to you: in a manger you will find an infant wrapped in swaddling clothes.

Angels: Glory to God in high heaven, peace on earth to those on whom God's favor rests!

Shepherds: Let us go over to Bethlehem and see this event that has come to pass, which the Lord has made known to us!

Reader 3: The shepherds went with haste and found Mary and Joseph—and the baby lying in the manger.

All sing "Silent Night"
(in Spanish, if possible):

> Noche de paz, noche de amor.
> Todo duerme en derredor.
> Entre los astros que esparcen su luz,
> Bella anunciando al niñito Jesús
> brilla la estrella de paz,
> brilla la estrella de paz.

Talk with your catechist about ways you and your family might use the "Faith Alive" pages. Ask family members to help create prayers for the tree, the lights, the star.

Optional Activities

Christmas Customs (for use with page 93)

Some fifth graders might enjoy researching different Christmas customs. To excite their interest, share the following information with them:

- The word *Noel* or *Nowell* is a contraction of the phrase "All is well." First it was shortened to "Now's well" and eventually to "Noel" in French and "Nowell" in English.

- *Carol* originally meant a round or ring dance, not a song. Many European countries had ring dances with accompanying songs that were joyful. Christmas songs were called "carols" because they are joyful.

- The first *Christmas crib*, or *manger scene*, was created by Saint Francis of Assisi in the thirteenth century. He wanted the townspeople to enter more fully into the Christmas story so he set up a manger scene with real people portraying Mary, Joseph, shepherds, and kings. All the people came in procession singing songs.

- *Las Posadas* is typically a celebration of nine days in which the people march through the town with "Mary" and "Joseph" looking for a room. On the last night, they find a place and all share refreshments.

Light of the World (for use with page 94)

Remind the young people that Jesus came to bring light to the world in the darkness of sin. The light of a wondrous star led the shepherds and wise men to Him. Simeon said He was a "light to all the nations."

Have the young people draw and cut out a Christmas star. On it they could write a brief description of someone who is a star for them, that is, someone who leads them to Jesus. Hang the stars from string or yarn in the room.

Materials needed: gold or silver paper; yarn or string; markers; scissors

Our Own Nativity Scene (for use with page 95)

Have the fifth graders make their own nativity scene using clay or papier-mâché, and pipe cleaners. Scraps of fabric can be used for clothes. Set up the scene in the room and surround it with greenery and candles.

Materials needed: clay or papier-mâché; pipe cleaners; fabric scraps; glue; greenery; candles

Faith Alive

AT HOME AND IN THE PARISH

In this lesson your son or daughter was reminded that the name Jesus means "God saves." Jesus came to be our Savior and his saving grace is for all people. All Christians celebrate Christmas and, though customs differ in different parts of the world, we all rejoice in the truth that God loved us so much that his Son came to dwell among us and to be like us in all things, except sin.

Talk together as a family about your Christmas customs that recall the true meaning of Christmas—the lights that remind us that Christ is the light of the world; the Christmas tree, an evergreen, that reminds us of life that lasts forever; the Christmas crib that reminds us that Christ came to us in poverty and peace. If you have special Christmas customs from your own childhood, be sure to share them with your children. Explore parish customs as well, and how you plan to be a part of parish events on a continuing basis.

✝ Family Prayer

Jesus, help us to follow the star
And find the place where now you are—
No longer lying in manger bed,
But in our human hearts instead.

Learn by heart — Faith Summary

What does the name Jesus mean?
- The name Jesus means "God saves."

Why do we decorate with lights at Christmas?
- Jesus is the Light of the World.

Of what does the Christmas tree remind us?
- Jesus came to bring us everlasting life.

Make up a short prayer to say with your family as you:

- put up your Christmas tree (everlasting life).
- put lights in your window (Light of the World).
- put the star on your tree (finding Christ).

___

___

___

___

___

Review

Go over the *Faith Summary* together and encourage your fifth grader to learn it by heart, especially the first statement. Then complete the *Review*. The answers to numbers 1–4 appear on page 216. The response to number 5 will show how well your child understands the deeper meaning of Christmas.

Circle **T** (True) or **F** (False).

1. The name *Jesus* means "Immanuel."   T   **(F)**

2. Simeon had been praying for the promised Savior.   **(T)**   F

3. All Christians celebrate Christmas the same way.   T   **(F)**

4. Jesus Christ came to unite all people to God.   **(T)**   F

5. How do you think Jesus wants us to celebrate Christmas?

_____

_____

_____

_____

_____

FAMILY SCRIPTURE MOMENT

Gather and if possible, light a large candle. Then **Listen** to the true meaning of Christmas.

In the beginning was the Word,
  and the Word was with God,
  and the Word was God.
He was in the beginning with God.
All things came to be through him,
  and without him nothing came to be.
What came to be through him was life,
  and this life was the light of the human race;
  the light shines in the darkness,
  and the darkness has not overcome it.
And the Word became flesh
  and made his dwelling among us, . . .

John 1:1–5, 14

Share Ask: What images of Jesus do we hear in this passage? What do people think "the Word became flesh" means for us?

Consider for family enrichment:

■ In these opening words of John's Gospel, Jesus is proclaimed as the eternal living Word, who reveals God to us.

■ At Christmas we welcome Jesus as the Word made flesh, who makes his home in us.

Reflect As disciples of Jesus Christ, how might we reveal the glory of God's only Son in our daily lives?

Decide How will our family welcome the Word among us this Christmas?

SUMMARY 1 • REVIEW

Ask: How does Jesus Christ reveal God?

Lesson 1—Jesus Christ Reveals God

- Jesus Christ is both human and divine.
- Jesus showed us that "God is love" by the things he said and did.
- God works through us and others to show his love in the world.

Ask: What is the good news? How does Jesus bring about the kingdom of God?

Lesson 2—Jesus Christ and the Kingdom of God

- Jesus announced the good news of the kingdom, or reign, of God. The good news is that God loves us and will always love us.
- The reign of God is the power of his life and love in the world.
- Jesus lived his whole life for the reign of God and calls us to do the same.

Ask: How does Jesus Christ bless our lives?

Lesson 3—Jesus Christ Blesses Our Lives

- Jesus invited everyone to live for the reign of God.
- Forgiveness heals the separation from God and from others that sin causes.
- Like Jesus, we try to forgive those who hurt us, no matter how great the hurt.

Ask: How does the Church carry on Jesus' mission? Who helps the Church?

Lesson 4—The Church Carries on Jesus' Mission

- The Holy Spirit helps the Church carry on the mission of Jesus to all people.
- Jesus is the head of the Church, his body, and we are its members.
- Like Jesus, the Church serves people and brings them Jesus' healing and forgiveness.

Ask: What are the seven sacraments?

Lesson 5—The Sacraments and the Church

- A sacrament is an effective sign through which Jesus Christ shares God's life and love with us.
- There are seven sacraments: Baptism, Confirmation, Eucharist, Reconciliation, Anointing of the Sick, Matrimony, and Holy Orders.
- We receive God's grace in the sacraments.

SUMMARY 1 • REVIEW

Ask: What do we receive at Baptism? What does Baptism call us to do?

Lesson 8—Jesus Christ Brings Us Life (Baptism)

- We receive new life at Baptism when we are reborn of water and the Holy Spirit.
- At Baptism we are initiated into, or begin to become members of, the Church, the body of Christ.
- Our Baptism calls us to live for the reign of God.

Ask: What is Confirmation?

Lesson 9—Jesus Christ Strengthens Us (Confirmation)

- Confirmation is the sacrament in which we are sealed with the Gift of the Holy Spirit and strengthened to give witness to the good news of Jesus Christ.
- In Confirmation the Holy Spirit fills us with the gifts that we need to live our Christian faith.
- We live our Confirmation when we become witnesses to the reign of God in the world.

Ask: What is the Eucharist? How do we respond to this gift?

Lesson 10—Jesus Christ Feeds Us (Eucharist)

- The Eucharist is the sacrament of the Body and Blood of Christ.
- Jesus is the Bread of Life. The food that Jesus gives us is his own Body and Blood.
- We respond to the gift of the Eucharist by living for the reign of God.

Ask: What happens during the Liturgy of the Word? During the Liturgy of the Eucharist?

Lesson 11—Our Church Celebrates the Eucharist (The Mass)

- The two major parts of the Mass are the Liturgy of the Word and the Liturgy of the Eucharist.
- During the Liturgy of the Word, we listen to God's word from the Bible.
- During the Liturgy of the Eucharist, the priest offers gifts of bread and wine to God. They will become the Body and Blood of Christ.

Ask: What are the Church's liturgical seasons? What does the liturgical year remind us of?

Lesson 12—The Church Remembers (The Liturgical Year)

- The liturgical seasons of the Church year are Advent, Christmas, Lent, the Easter Triduum, Easter, and Ordinary Time.
- During the liturgical year we also honor and pray to Mary and the other saints.
- The liturgical year reminds us that we always live in the presence of God.

SUMMARY 1 • TEST

Circle the correct answers.

1. Jesus is like us in every way except
   a. that he never laughed.
   b. that he never got angry.
   c. that he never sinned.
   d. that he never died.

2. We say that Jesus is divine because
   a. he is the Son of God.
   b. he is loving.
   c. he is kind and merciful.
   d. he is Mary's son.

3. Jesus showed us how to live for the reign of God by
   a. building church buildings.
   b. becoming Catholic.
   c. living the Law of Love.
   d. writing the Gospels.

4. The sacraments of initiation are
   a. Matrimony and Holy Orders.
   b. Baptism, Confirmation, and Eucharist.
   c. Reconciliation and Anointing of the Sick.
   d. Eucharist and Holy Orders.

5. Sacraments are
   a. powerful signs of Jesus' presence with us.
   b. celebrations of our Church.
   c. sources of God's grace.
   d. all of these

Complete the following sentences.

service initiation Holy Spirit
healing Body and Blood

6. Baptism, Confirmation, and the Eucharist are called sacraments of _initiation_.

7. Reconciliation and the Anointing of the Sick are called sacraments of _healing_.

8. Matrimony and Holy Orders are called sacraments of _service_.

9. In Baptism we are reborn of water and the _Holy Spirit_.

10. In the Eucharist ordinary bread and wine become the _Body and Blood_ of Jesus.

Think and decide:

Choose one of the sacraments. Write one way you will live that sacrament.

Accept individual responses.

SUMMARY 1 • TEST

Read the following sentences. Cross out the terms that are incorrect.

11. In Baptism we receive the help of (the Holy Spirit/~~holy water~~) to live our new life of grace.

12. In Confirmation the Holy Spirit gives us gifts that help us live and witness (our faith/~~our citizenship~~).

13. The (Blessed Sacrament/~~holy oil~~) is kept in the tabernacle.

14. The Fruits of the Holy Spirit are signs that we (are living/~~need help to live~~) as witnesses to our faith.

15. The food that Jesus gives us as our Bread of Life is (~~ordinary bread and wine~~/Jesus' own Body and Blood).

16. We honor Mary on December 8, the feast of (the Immaculate Conception/~~the Ascension~~).

17. Jesus first gave us the gift of his Body and Blood at (~~his ascension into heaven~~/the Last Supper).

18. During the liturgical season of (~~Christmas~~/Lent) we prepare for Easter.

19. The Easter Triduum begins on (~~Ash Wednesday~~/Holy Thursday).

20. The Church remembers and celebrates the resurrection of Jesus on (~~Good Friday~~/Easter Sunday).

Think and decide:

We have learned about many feasts of the Church's liturgical year. Choose one feast. Tell how you will celebrate it and how it helps you to live your Baptism.

Feast <u>Accept individual responses.</u>

_____

_____

_____

Possible responses:

I will celebrate the feast by

<u>going to Mass on that day.</u>

_____

_____

_____

I will live my Baptism by

<u>trying to be fair and just to</u>

<u>everyone I meet; being a friend</u>

<u>to someone who is lonely; trying</u>

<u>to be helpful at home, etc.</u>

Name _____

Your son or daughter has just completed Unit 2. Have him or her bring this paper to the catechist. It will help you and the catechist know better how to help your fifth grader grow in faith.

_____ He or she needs help with the part of the Summary/Review I have underlined.

_____ He or she understands what has been taught in this unit.

_____ I would like to speak with you. My phone number is _____ .

Signature: _____

15 Jesus Christ Forgives Us

For the Catechist: Spiritual and Catechetical Development

ADULT BACKGROUND

Our Life

Over coffee in the teachers' room, Ellen recounted a tragic story that she had heard on the news. "They bombed an elementary school," she said. "Twenty-two children were killed. It makes me sick to think of it." Martha replied in a noncommittal tone, "That's exactly why I don't watch the news. So much of it is bad, and there's nothing I can do about it. Why make yourself suffer?"

Ask yourself:

■ How might I have responded to Ellen?

Sharing Life

What evidence have you seen that grace is stronger than evil in the world?

Why are forgiveness and reconciliation so crucial to all of us?

Our Catholic Faith

Our need for the sacrament of Reconciliation grows as we come to recognize our need for forgiveness. Some contemporary Catholics seem to have lost their sense of sin, either as personal wrongdoing or as participation in social injustices. However, we cannot make sin disappear by denying its reality:

> If we say, "We are without sin," we deceive ourselves, and the truth is not in us. If we acknowledge our sins, he…will forgive our sins and cleanse us from every wrongdoing (1 John 1:8-9).

Throughout His public ministry, Jesus challenged people to recognize their sinfulness, to seek forgiveness, and to turn back to God. He warned His disciples about judging and condemning, about holding grudges and seeking revenge, about hypocrisy and power seeking. He insisted that they set no limits on the liberality of their forgiveness—"not seven times but seventy-seven times" (Matthew 18:22).

The Church reminds us of the reality of sin, both mortal and venial, and of our need for sacramental forgiveness—whether we are seriously alienated from God or simply need to confront sinful attitudes and habits (see John 5:16–17).

We also need to recognize the existence of social sin in our world, and to accept our share of responsibility for it. Examples of social sin include denial of human rights, racism, religious persecution, sexism, institutional violence, and inequitable distribution of resources.

Reconciliation can be a channel of grace, growth, and healing for believers as well as for the communities to which they belong.

Coming to Faith

How are Christians called to respond to social sin?

How does the Church's teaching on forgiveness and reconciliation challenge you to change?

Practicing Faith

In what way(s) will you be reconciled this week?

How will you try to help your fifth graders appreciate Reconciliation?

CATECHISM OF THE CATHOLIC CHURCH

The Theme of This Chapter Corresponds with Paragraph 1443

LITURGICAL RESOURCES

Since the early centuries of the Church, the beautiful prayer of praise to the risen Christ, "Kyrie Eleison," has been sung or recited during the Mass. In the penitential rite, we express our need for forgiveness before we join together in praising God's glory.

The Kyrie, or "Lord, have mercy," may be used as the guiding prayer of a reflection on forgiveness to be shared by the fifth graders. If possible, begin by teaching a simple musical setting for the prayer from your parish missalette or hymnal.

Ask the group members to write what they think boys and girls their age might need to be forgiven for. Have them read these thoughts aloud. After each, respond, "Lord, have mercy."

Now sing "Lord, have mercy," and pause for volunteers to name signs of sin or evil in the world. Repeat "Lord, have mercy" after each sign. End with the Our Father or a sign of peace.

JUSTICE AND PEACE RESOURCES

Describing the ministry of reconciliation shared by all Christians, Saint Paul says that we are "ambassadors for Christ." We are to speak for Christ as though He were appealing through us.

"We implore you on behalf of Christ, be reconciled to God" (2 Corinthians 5:20).

Write "ambassador" on the chalkboard or newsprint. Ask the fifth graders what they think it means. Focus on an ambassador as an "authorized negotiator" sent on a mission. Discuss how ambassadors are often sent by our government to help make peace between enemies. Challenge small groups to role-play ways they could serve as ambassadors of reconciliation between family members who are not speaking to each other; two teen gangs that are threatening each other; community leaders who are "at war" because of racial or religious insults.

103B

15

Teaching Resources

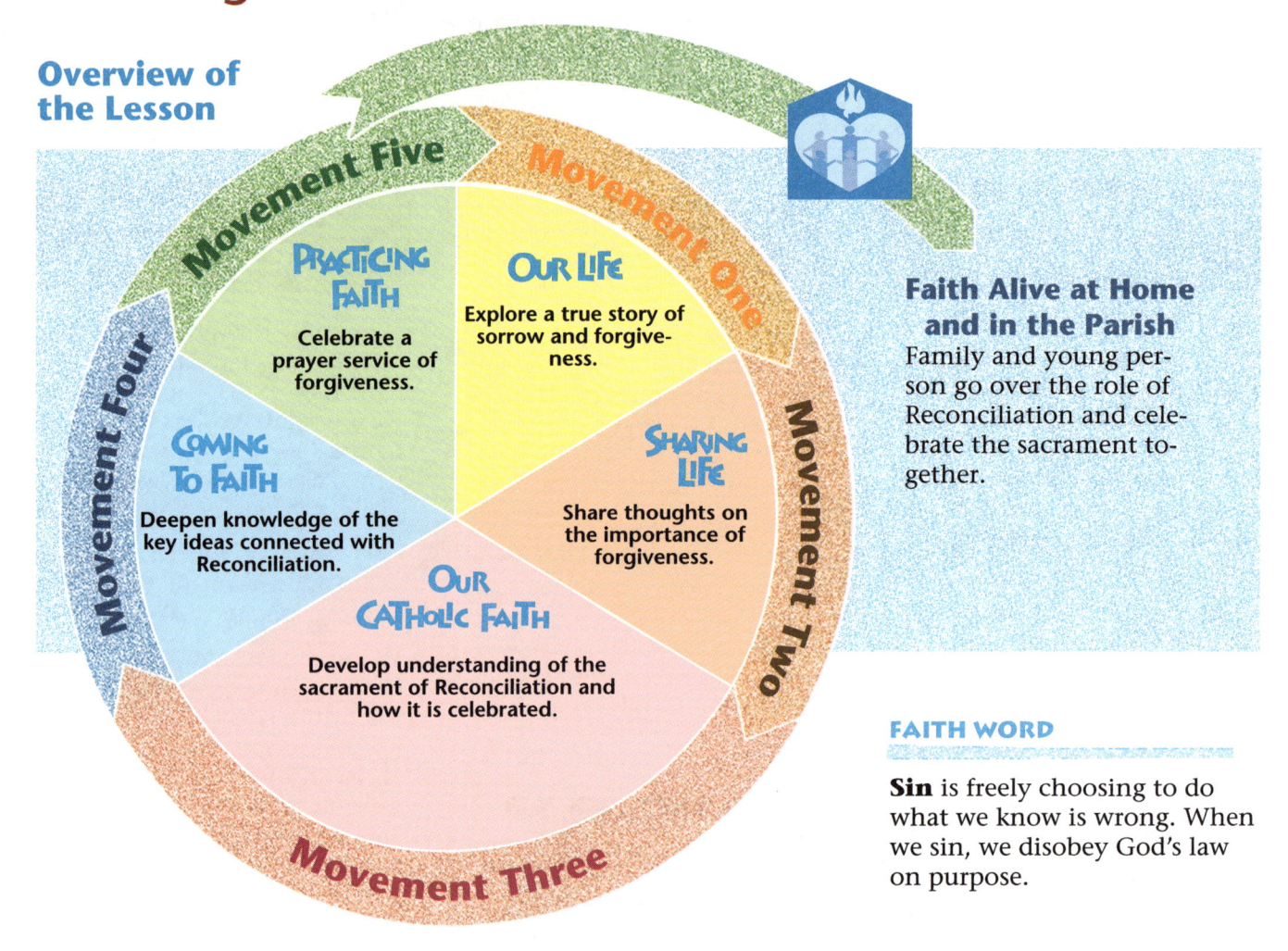

Overview of the Lesson

Movement One — Our Life: Explore a true story of sorrow and forgiveness.

Movement Two — Sharing Life: Share thoughts on the importance of forgiveness.

Movement Three — Our Catholic Faith: Develop understanding of the sacrament of Reconciliation and how it is celebrated.

Movement Four — Coming To Faith: Deepen knowledge of the key ideas connected with Reconciliation.

Movement Five — Practicing Faith: Celebrate a prayer service of forgiveness.

Faith Alive at Home and in the Parish
Family and young person go over the role of Reconciliation and celebrate the sacrament together.

FAITH WORD

Sin is freely choosing to do what we know is wrong. When we sin, we disobey God's law on purpose.

Teaching Hints

To make the concepts presented in this lesson on Reconciliation more relevant, have the group experience Reconciliation themselves. This can be done individually, communally, or in a paraliturgy of reconciliation. Along with the prayer or sacramental experience, plan some sort of social celebration to follow the forgiveness action. This will enhance the young people's awareness that we are grateful for and celebrate God's forgiveness in our lives.

Special-Needs Child

When teaching visually impaired young people, encourage oral interaction and response.

Visual Needs
- recording of *Our Catholic Faith* section, *Faith Summary* and *Faith Word*

Auditory Needs
- use of gestures
- role-play opportunities

Tactile–Motor Needs
- large, thick markers

Supplemental Resources

Signs and Sacraments (videostrip)

Lord of Mercy: Reconciliation (video)
Brown-ROA
2460 Kerper Blvd.
P.O. Box 539
Dubuque, Iowa 52004–0539
(1-800-922-7696)

Lesson Plan: Beginning

Objectives

To help the young people

- understand how to celebrate Reconciliation;
- know that God always forgives us when we are sorry;
- recognize Reconciliation as a healing sacrament.

Focusing Prayer

Gather the young people quietly for prayer. Tell them that today you will be exploring together how God wants us to forgive and to be forgiven. Slowly pray the words of the Our Father at the top of page 103.

Our Life

Receiving Forgiveness

Introduce the *Our Life* section by telling the young people that they are about to hear a true story. Invite volunteers to read aloud the story of John Newton. Read slowly the verse of "Amazing Grace." Ask, "Why did Newton say he once was lost and that he once was blind?" Use the questions following the story to lead the young people in a discussion of the healing power of God's forgiveness.

Sharing Life

Describing Forgiveness

Read aloud the first direction in this section. See the annotation. Have the young people share their responses. Then read and discuss the remaining forgiveness questions.

Enrichment

Words of Grace

Make copies of the second verse of "Amazing Grace," which follows. Discuss it with the young people. Elicit from them what the words say about sorrow and God's forgiveness.

> Through many dangers,
>   toils and snares
> I have already come.
> T'was grace that brought
>   me safe thus far,
> And grace will lead me
>   home!

Materials needed: copies of song verse

---

15 Jesus Christ Forgives Us
(Reconciliation)

Jesus, forgive us our trespasses as we forgive those who trespass against us.

Our Life

John Newton was a Scottish sea captain in the middle of the 19th century. He became very prosperous because of the cargo he carried—human cargo. Newton was a slave trader. He took people from Africa and sold them to slave traders in the new world. He did this for some years.
Then something happened to change him. Later he called it "grace."

Newton took a close look at his life and saw clearly the evil he was doing. He left the sea and the slave trade and spent his days in prayer asking God's mercy. As time went by he experienced great peace; he knew that he was forgiven. Newton tried to express in words the amazing grace of God's forgiving love. What he wrote has become one of the most loved Christian hymns in the world.

> Amazing grace, how sweet the sound
> That saved a wretch like me.
> I once was lost, but now am found;
> Was blind, but now I see.

He changed and had peace.
What two "amazing" things did God's grace do for Newton?
Tell how you feel when you are forgiven.
happy, relieved, peaceful, joyful

Sharing Life

Discuss with one another what it means to be truly forgiven. Begin by saying, "True forgiveness means . . . ."
Encourage specific responses.
What part do you think forgiveness should play in the life of a Christian? in a family? in a parish? **Accept reasonable responses.**

103

15

Lesson Plan: Middle

Our Catholic Faith

Faith Word

Write the word *sin* on the chalkboard or show it on a flash card. Tell the young people to watch for the word and its meaning as they read.

Our Need for Healing

Read aloud the first paragraph under "Reconciliation, A Sacrament of Healing" on page 104.

Have the young people locate the word *sin* at the top of page 105, and read the definition together. Then ask a volunteer to read aloud the second paragraph on page 104 to emphasize the importance of the word and its meaning.

Have the young people silently read the next three paragraphs. Help them to understand the difference between mortal and venial sin. Explain that mortal sin deprives us of God's life because we freely and knowingly choose to reject God's life. Venial sin is less serious, but should also be avoided because it causes damage to ourselves and to others, and weakens our relationship with God.

Social Sin

Ask how social sin happens, and have the young people silently read the next paragraph. Encourage volunteers to discuss their responses.

Help your fifth graders to better understand the difference between a sin of commission—a wrong caused by doing something—and a sin of omission—a wrong caused by not doing something that we should do and could do. For example:

Commission:
Spreading dangerous rumors

Omission:
Not defending someone who is hurt by rumors

Invite the young people to discuss what they would do in such situations. Help them to see that by not doing anything to stop an injustice, one shares in the injustice.

Hurting the Community

Read aloud the next paragraph. Emphasize that our sins hurt the whole community. Discuss how we can heal the hurts caused by our sins.

Healing the Hurt

Invite volunteers to read aloud the next two paragraphs. Remind the young people that the two sacraments of healing are Reconciliation and the Anointing of the Sick. Have the group think about and discuss how forgiveness is a healing action. Help the young people begin to see our need for spiritual healing. Emphasize that

---

OUR CATHOLIC FAITH

Stress the underlined text.

Reconciliation, A Sacrament of Healing
Jesus announced the good news that God always forgives our sins when we are sorry for them.

We sin when we freely choose to do what we know is wrong. We disobey God's law on purpose. When we sin, we fail to live as we should as members of the Church and disciples of Jesus.

The Catholic Church teaches us that we can sin in thought, in word, or in action. Some sins are so serious that by doing them we turn completely away from God's love. We call them mortal sins. We must confess all mortal sins in order to recover our friendship with God.

A sin is mortal when:

- what we do is very seriously wrong;
- we know that it is wrong and that God forbids it;
- we freely choose to do it.

Other sins are less serious. These are called venial sins. By them we do not turn away completely from God's love. But they still weaken our relationship with God and they can cause hurt to others and to the Church.

All sins are personal sins. But whole groups of people can sin, too. We call this social sin. Social sin happens when groups of people choose not to do God's loving will. For example, members of a group commit social sin when they treat unfairly people who are poor or different from them.

Sin is never just between God and one person. Our sins always hurt someone else. We must try to heal the hurt we cause by our sin. We must do and say things that show we

104

---

are truly sorry. We must try not to sin again.

Reconciliation, or Penance, is one of the two sacraments of healing. This sacrament is a powerful and effective sign through which Jesus shares with us God's mercy and forgiveness of our sins. We know we are united again, or reconciled, to God and to our Church community.

When we celebrate Reconciliation, we praise and worship God. In this sacrament we receive God's help to do his loving will, to avoid all forms of sin, and to live as God's people. For this reason, we celebrate Reconciliation even when we are not guilty of serious sin.

We can celebrate Reconciliation individually or communally. These ways, or rites, of celebrating Reconciliation are given in the chart on page 107. In both rites, we meet with a priest privately. By the power of the

104

Lesson Plan: Middle

the sacrament is an act of prayer and worship, and an opportunity to grow in holiness.

Celebrating Reconciliation

Read aloud the next three paragraphs. Ask how we can be reconcilers. Invite volunteers to share their responses.

Call attention to the chart on page 105. Have the young people silently read each of the points listed. Print each of the chart elements on large paper pennants and display them in sequential order. Call on several young people to explain the main parts of the sacrament of Reconciliation. Have two volunteers act out the giving of absolution. Then have the young people look at the picture. Ask what part of the sacrament is shown.

Materials needed: paper pennants; pencils or pens

Call attention to the chart on page 107 that clarifies the similarities and differences between the two rites of Reconciliation. Have several young people read each step aloud. Explain that an act of contrition may be made in one's own words as long as it expresses sorrow for sin and the sincere intention to avoid sin in the future. Allow time for discussion of these two rites.

Our Catholic Identity

Use page 9 from the *Our Catholic Identity* section in the back of the book. Ask the students whether they appreciate people who can keep secrets. Point out that one of the wonderful things about the sacrament of Reconciliation is the "seal of Confession." Go on to the story of Saint John Nepomucene. Answer any questions the youngsters might have.

You may wish to use pages 35–36 in the activity book for *Coming to God's Life.*

Holy Spirit, the priest acts in the name of Christ and the Church to forgive sins in God's name.

We thank God for Reconciliation in our everyday lives. We try to bring God's peace to our families, our school, and our parish community.

FAITH WORD

Sin is freely choosing to do what we know is wrong. When we sin, we disobey God's law on purpose.

Sacrament of Reconciliation

Examination of Conscience: We ask the Holy Spirit to help us think about how well we are doing God's loving will.

Contrition: We say an Act of Contrition to tell God that we are sorry for our sins. We promise to try harder to avoid sin and to love others as God loves us.

Confession: We confess our sins to God by telling them to the priest in private. We make sure that we confess all mortal sins to the priest. He advises us how to live each day for the reign of God as Jesus wants. The priest will never tell anyone what he heard in confession.

Penance: Our penance can be a prayer or a good deed that helps make up for the hurt caused by our sins. We do the penance the priest gives us to show God that we are sorry and want to change. Doing our penance helps us to avoid sin and grow closer to God.

Absolution: By the power of the Holy Spirit, the priest gives us God's forgiveness, or absolution. He makes the sign of the cross over us and says in part, "Through the ministry of the Church may God give you pardon and peace, and I absolve you from your sins in the name of the Father, and of the Son, ✝ and of the Holy Spirit." We respond, "Amen."

ENRICHMENT

A Scripture Search

Invite the young people to work in three groups to search the Gospels for signs of Jesus forgiving others. To get them started, suggest that they look at Luke 15:1–7 and 8–10, and John 8:3–11.

Let them present their gospel stories as plays or dramatic readings.

Materials needed: Bible

15

Lesson Plan: End

Coming to Faith

Remembering Reconciliation

Prepare several sets of flash cards. Each set should include the words *conscience, contrition, Reconciliation, absolution, penance,* and *confession,* with the definitions on the backs of the cards. Form several groups and have the group members quiz each other with the flash cards.

Materials needed: **sets of flash cards**

Faith Summary

Use the annotations to review the *Faith Summary* on page 107. See if the young people can express, in their own words, what they have learned.

Practicing Faith

Praying for Forgiveness

Choose a reader and a leader for the prayer service, and have them practice their lines. You may want to read the "reflection" part yourself. Gather the young people for prayer. Begin and end the service by singing "Amazing Grace."

EVALUATING YOUR LESSON

■ Do the young people know how to celebrate Reconciliation?

■ Do they appreciate the value of forgiveness?

■ Have they decided how to seek and offer forgiveness?

ENRICHMENT

A Pastoral Visit

Invite your pastor or one of the priests in the parish to talk to the group about celebrating the sacrament of Reconciliation individually and communally. Hearing about the options of confession face-to-face or behind a screen would help the young people. If possible, have the pastor meet with the young people in church so they can visit the Reconciliation room.

Coming To Faith

Challenge one another's knowledge of the key ideas of Reconciliation. Choose a card. Ask a group member to explain the term on the card. Check the answer by reading the definition on the back of the card. Key words are: conscience, contrition, Reconciliation, absolution, penance, confession.

Practicing Faith

Gather in a circle. Sing "Amazing Grace."

Reader: God calls us to come back to him. He loves us and blesses us always.

Reflection: Be very still. Talk to Jesus about forgiveness you need to receive, or forgiveness you need to give. Ask Jesus to help you do what you need to do.

Leader: To show our thanks for the amazing grace of God's mercy and forgiveness, let us offer one another a sign of God's peace. (Turn to those on your right and left and give a handshake of peace.)

Closing: All sing (or say) another verse of "Amazing Grace."
Through many dangers, toils, and snares
We have already come;
'Tis grace has brought us here thus far
And grace will lead us home.

Talk with your catechist about ways you and your family might use the "Faith Alive" pages. Invite a family member to celebrate Reconciliation with you.

106

106

Optional Activities

An Essay about Forgiveness (for use with page 103)

Invite the young people to write one-page personal essays about a time when someone refused to forgive them and how that experience affected them.

Materials needed: writing paper; pens or pencils

A Musical Meditation (for use with page 104)

As a musical meditation on forgiveness, play a song such as "Believe and Repent," by Ken Meltz (from the album *Until He Comes,* World Library Publications) or "Hosea," by Gregory Norbet (from the album *Listen, Weston Priory*).

Materials needed: music source

Overcoming Social Sins (for use with page 104)

Form small groups. Have them cut out pictures, headlines, and stories from newspapers and magazines to make collages illustrating such social sins as prejudice, greed, or failure to help the poor and homeless. Display the collages, and discuss how people are trying to overcome these social sins.

Materials needed: magazines; newspapers; newsprint; scissors; markers; glue

Celebration Booklets (for use with page 105)

Have the young people create "Celebrating Reconciliation" booklets illustrating the importance of both the individual and communal rites of Reconciliation. The elements should be described briefly, and may be illustrated with stick figures or simple sketches.

Materials needed: construction paper; pencils; crayons and/or markers

A Forgiveness Prayer Service (for use with page 106)

Gather at the prayer table. As you pray the litany that follows, ask the group to respond "Forgive us, Lord Jesus" to each petition.

- For the times we have hurt others. . . .
- For the times we have held a grudge. . . .
- For the ways we have refused to be reconciled. . . .

Allow the young people to add other petitions if they wish, then pray the Our Father together.

106A

Faith Alive AT HOME AND IN THE PARISH

This chart will help your fifth grader celebrate the sacrament of Reconciliation either individually or communally. Go over both ways to make sure he or she understands each rite.

Individual Rite of Reconciliation

- Before entering the Reconciliation room, we examine our conscience.
- The priest welcomes us in the name of Jesus Christ and the Church. We make the sign of the cross together.
- We listen to a reading from the Bible.
- We confess our sins to the priest individually. We receive our penance from the priest and he gives us absolution from our sins in the name of Jesus.
- We pray an Act of Contrition like the one on page 205.
- In the name of God and the Church, the priest says the words of absolution and makes the sign of the cross. We know that God has forgiven us. We answer, "Amen."
- The priest then tells us to go in peace.
- We make sure to do the penance the priest gave us.

Communal Rite of Reconciliation

- We gather as a community and sing a song. The priest greets us and we pray together for God's mercy.
- We listen to readings from the Bible. The priest or deacon gives a homily, reminding us of God's mercy and our need for forgiveness.
- We examine our conscience by thinking about our sins. We pray an Act of Contrition together. We may pray a litany or sing a song. We tell God that we are sorry and ask for forgiveness.
- We pray the Our Father
- We confess our sins to the priest individually. We receive our penance from the priest and he gives us absolution from our sins in the name of Jesus.
- We gather together after our individual confessions. We show our thanks to God by singing or praying.
- The priest blesses us and we leave in God's peace to do our penance and try to sin no more.

Learn by heart — Faith Summary

What is the sacrament of Reconciliation?
- Reconciliation is the sacrament in which we are forgiven by God and the Church for our sins.

What are important steps in the celebration of Reconciliation?
- Examination of conscience, contrition, confession, penance, and absolution are important steps in the celebration of Reconciliation.

What do we receive in Reconciliation?
- In Reconciliation we receive God's help to do God's loving will, to avoid sin, and to live as God's people.

Review

Go over the *Faith Summary* together and encourage your fifth grader to learn it by heart, especially the first statement. Then have him or her do the *Review*. The answers to numbers 1–4 appear on page 216. The response to number 5 will show how well your son or daughter understands that being sorry also means making up with those we may have hurt by our sins. When the *Review* is completed, go over it together.

1. Order from 1–5 the steps in the individual rite of sacrament of Reconciliation.

    _2_ We confess our sins to the priest.

    _5_ The priest gives us absolution, in the name of Jesus.

    _1_ We are welcomed in Jesus' name.

    _4_ We pray an Act of Contrition.

    _3_ The priest gives us a penance.

2. All sins are
    a. venial.
    (b.) personal.
    c. mortal.
    d. social.

3. Reconciliation is a sacrament of
    a. initiation.
    (b.) healing.
    c. service.
    d. witness.

4. If we totally reject God we commit
    a. venial sins.
    b. personal sins.
    (c.) mortal sins.
    d. social sins.

5. How can you try to heal the hurt caused by sin?

    _____

    _____

FAMILY SCRIPTURE MOMENT

Gather and ask each family member to recall an experience of being forgiven. How does receiving forgiveness change us? Then **Listen** closely to the first words that the risen Lord says to the disciples.

On the evening of that first day of the week, . . . Jesus came and stood in their midst and said to them, "Peace be with you." When he had said this, he showed them his hands and his side. The disciples rejoiced when they saw the Lord. [Jesus] said to them again, "Peace be with you. As the Father has sent me, so I send you." And when he had said this, he breathed on them and said to them, "Receive the holy Spirit. Whose sins you forgive are forgiven them, and whose sins you retain are retained."
John 20:19–23

Share how each person feels about these words from the risen Christ.

Consider for family enrichment:

■ The risen Christ gives his frightened disciples the gift of his peace and sends them forth as reconcilers of others.

■ Our Church celebrates this ministry of forgiveness in the sacrament of Reconciliation, a sacrament of healing.

Reflect and **Decide** How might the Holy Spirit be calling us to "breathe" peace and forgiveness into other people's lives? What will be our response?

16 Jesus Christ Helps Us in Sickness and Death

For the Catechist: Spiritual and Catechetical Development

Adult Background

Our Life

Lorraine had called the pastor to the bedside of her dying husband, Louis. "He has been waiting for you," she quietly said to the priest. Louis's breathing was shallow.

Father Berube immediately anointed and absolved his old friend. He proclaimed from John 10:9 (Jesus the Good Shepherd): "Whoever enters through me will be saved, and will come in and go out and find pasture" (John 10:9).

A minute later, Louis stopped breathing. Lorraine and her family prayed over him as he journeyed toward new life.

When Father Berube offered the night prayer of the Church, the words spoke to him of his friend. "Lord, now you let your servant go in peace; your Word has been fulfilled. . . ."

Ask yourself:

■ Who or what has helped me in times of sickness or of a loved one's death?

Sharing Life

What effects do you believe sacramental anointing has?

Our Catholic Faith

At a parish celebration of the sacrament of Anointing of the Sick, the pastor offered this opening prayer:

Father, your Son accepted our suffering to teach us the virtue of patience in human illness. Hear the prayer we offer for our sick brothers and sisters. May all who suffer pain, illness, or disease realize that they are joined to Christ in His suffering for the salvation of the world. . . .

The prayer summarizes for us the purpose and value of the sacrament. Since Vatican II, the sacrament of the Anointing of the Sick has been celebrated both individually and communally for the sick and dying. These sacramental celebrations assure the sick of the compassionate concern of their faith community.

In its faithfulness to the healing mission of Jesus, the Church invites the sick and dying to come to Him, seeking physical and spiritual health. The anointing of heads and hands with holy oil is a powerful sign of the Lord's loving presence to the one who suffers.

Catechesis for this sacrament encourages us to visit the sick and those who are confined by illness, praying for them and with them. It challenges us to do more than sit passively by the bedside of one who is facing death. By compassionate listening, we can encourage the dying person to express fears, doubts, hopes, and cherished memories. By keeping an active vigil with the dying, we are faithful to Jesus, who invited His disciples to "Remain here and keep watch with me" (Matthew 26:38).

Coming to Faith

What insights on Anointing would you share with the sick or dying?

How might parishes celebrate this sacrament more effectively?

Practicing Faith

How will you serve the sick, aged, or dying this week?

What will you do to help your group understand this sacrament?

CATECHISM OF THE CATHOLIC CHURCH

The Theme of This Chapter Corresponds with Paragraph 1514

LITURGICAL RESOURCES

You may choose to involve the fifth graders in an enactment of a parish celebration of the Anointing of the Sick. Form three groups to portray the sick and dying, their companions on this faith journey, and the celebrants.

Have each group make and wear large tags identifying its role. If possible, supply the "sick" with canes, crutches, or other symbols of infirmity.

Provide the celebrants with any oil or lotion.

As each member of the first group comes forward with a companion, the celebrant makes the sign of the cross in oil on the forehead and hands of the sick while saying the following Anointing Prayer:

(name)_____, through this holy anointing may the Lord in his love and mercy help you with the grace of the Holy Spirit.

May the Lord who frees you from sin save you and raise you up. (Amen)

JUSTICE AND PEACE RESOURCES

Involve the fifth graders in an ongoing commitment to visiting the sick of the parish. With the help of the pastor or parish council, make a list of those who are in hospitals and nursing homes, or who are housebound and would welcome young visitors.

Form the class into small groups or sets of partners who, with an adult, will visit assigned patients. Invite the young people to participate in creating simple prayer services to share with the sick. These might include the telling of gospel stories of healing; singing or sharing poetry; a blessing for the patient; and praying the Our Father together while holding hands.

16

Teaching Resources

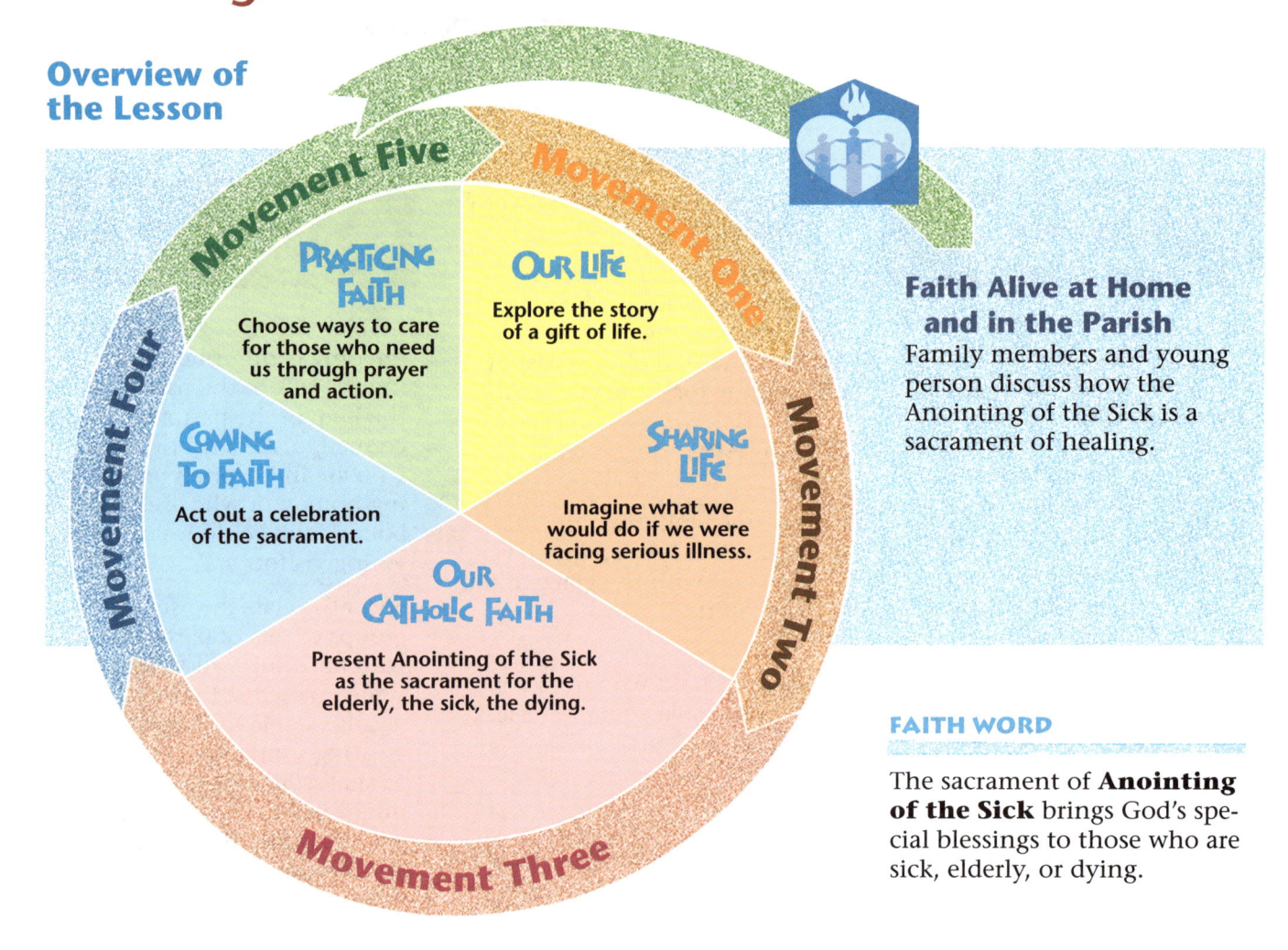

Overview of the Lesson

Movement One — Our Life: Explore the story of a gift of life.

Movement Two — Sharing Life: Imagine what we would do if we were facing serious illness.

Movement Three — Our Catholic Faith: Present Anointing of the Sick as the sacrament for the elderly, the sick, the dying.

Movement Four — Coming to Faith: Act out a celebration of the sacrament.

Movement Five — Practicing Faith: Choose ways to care for those who need us through prayer and action.

Faith Alive at Home and in the Parish
Family members and young person discuss how the Anointing of the Sick is a sacrament of healing.

FAITH WORD
The sacrament of **Anointing of the Sick** brings God's special blessings to those who are sick, elderly, or dying.

Teaching Hints

If the parish is planning a communal celebration of the Anointing of the Sick, try to involve your group in this sacramental experience. They can publicize, invite, and even accompany the sick and elderly.

Another way to make the sacrament of the Anointing of the Sick more relevant to the young people is to plan a visit to a home for the aged and prepare the group in advance for this visit. Point out the importance of just listening to the elderly and praying with them.

Special-Needs Child

Provide felt-tipped pens or thick-lead pencils for visually impaired young people.

Visual Needs
- preferential seating
- large-print flash card

Auditory Needs
- headphones for music recording

Tactile–Motor Needs
- nonslip-fabric desk covering
- peer assistants

Supplemental Resources

The Book of Luke: Early Ministry (video)
(from *The New Media Bible* series)
Mass Media Ministries
2116 North Charles St.
Baltimore, MD 21218
(1-800-828-8825)

109C

16

Lesson Plan: Beginning

OBJECTIVES

To help the young people

■ know what Anointing of the Sick means;

■ appreciate that this sacrament carries on Jesus' mission of healing;

■ choose to help the sick and respect their own bodies.

Focusing Prayer

Explain that God blesses us with His strength and hope when we are ill. Gather the young people and pray together the prayer at the top of page 109.

Our Life

God's Healing Power

Have the young people look at the illustrations. Explain that the young boy in the hospital bed is Danny Cardo, who was about the same age as the fifth graders when the events recounted in the *Our Life* story took place. Then read the story aloud. Use the follow-up questions to discuss the story. Point out how the prayers of so many people contributed to Danny's healing.

Sharing Life

Reflecting on Dying

Read aloud the questions under *Sharing Life*. Have the young people think about and share their responses. Use the annotated material as a guide.

---

16 Jesus Christ Helps Us in Sickness and Death
(Anointing of the Sick)

You, O God, are our strength and our hope.

OUR LIFE

Ten-year-old Danny Cardo was dying. Leukemia was destroying his blood cells and without a bone marrow transplant his life would end in a matter of weeks. No one in his family was a close enough match to his bone marrow for a transplant—not even his twin sister. His family turned to God in prayer. His school friends and his whole parish joined in.

In California, far away from Danny's home in Vermont, a young woman named Clare had recently become a bone marrow donor. The computer linked her blood type with Danny's as a real match. The surgery was done "just in time," the doctor said.

Today Danny is a healthy, active eleven-year-old. He would like to meet Clare someday. "I thank God for my life," Danny says. "I would like to thank her, too."

Possible responses:
Why do you think Danny's family and parish turned to God in prayer? *They believed God could help Danny and his family.*
How do you think Danny felt to know so many people were praying for him? *Very grateful and happy.*
What or who helps you when you are sick? *My parents, friends, the parish etc.*

SHARING LIFE
Possible response:
Imagine you were Danny. How would it make you feel to be facing death? *Sad, frightened etc.*
What would you want your family and friends to do? *Whatever they could do to help me get well.*
Discuss together the best way to handle serious illness.

The subject of serious illness is often difficult for young people to deal with. Be sensitive to their feelings, and try to be conscious of those who may have a loved one who has a serious illness.

ENRICHMENT

Stories of Healing

Invite the young people to do a gospel search for stories of people whom Jesus helped or healed. Some suggestions to get them started are:
Luke 7:1–10; Matthew 8:14–15; Mark 7:31–37; John 5:1–9.

Have them share their findings through dramatic readings, plays, or drawings.

Materials needed:
Bibles; drawing paper; crayons and/or markers

16

Lesson Plan: Middle

Our Catholic Faith

Faith Word

Write *Anointing of the Sick* on the chalkboard or newsprint. Pronounce the term, and have the young people listen for it in today's lesson.

Healing Work

Read aloud the first two paragraphs under "Anointing of the Sick, a Sacrament of Healing" on page 110. Ask why our Church celebrates the sacrament of Anointing of the Sick. Call on volunteers to answer.

Have the group locate the term *Anointing of the Sick* at the top of page 111. Read the definition together.

Ask how this sacrament helps the sick, and invite volunteers to read aloud the next three paragraphs on page 110. Discuss responses while emphasizing that the effects of the sacrament may be felt physically or spiritually, and at times in both ways.

Celebrating Anointing of the Sick

Have the young people silently read the next two paragraphs on page 110. Discuss where the sacrament can be celebrated.

Then call attention to the illustration on page 113. Explain that the items pictured are used by the priest when celebrating the sacrament of Anointing. The candles, crucifix, white cloth, and cotton should be placed on a table near the sick person before the priest comes

◆ Enrichment ◆

Counter AD-tack

Remind the fifth graders how important it is to take care of our bodies by following rules of good health. Discuss the differences between good drugs—chemicals prescribed by a doctor when we are sick–and bad drugs—nonprescription chemicals that can change the way we act and think.

Then challenge the young people to make posters that advertise alternatives to alcohol and other drug use. For example: An illustration of a fifth grader bicycling and the words "Use your skills, not drugs!"

Display the posters where others can see them.

Materials needed: paper; pencils; crayons or markers

110

Our Catholic Faith

Stress the underlined text.

Anointing of the Sick, A Sacrament of Healing

In his public ministry, Jesus showed great care and compassion for people who were sick. His most frequent miracles were those of healing. Jesus told his disciples to carry on this ministry of healing.

Jesus gave his Church the work of bringing God's healing power to the sick, the elderly, and the dying. By the power of the Holy Spirit, the Church carries on this mission of healing in the sacrament of the Anointing of the Sick.

Anointing of the Sick is one of the two sacraments of healing. This sacrament is a powerful and effective sign of Jesus' presence that brings strength and healing to the elderly, the sick, and the dying.

The celebration of this sacrament sometimes helps sick people to get well again. When that does not happen, the sacrament helps the sick face their illness with faith and trust. It also helps dying people to continue their journey to God in heaven.

Saint James writes in his New Testament letter that in this sacrament our sick bodies can be healed and our sins forgiven. He wrote that if anyone was sick the Church elders would come and pray for and rub oil on the sick person in the name of the Lord. James said: "The prayer of faith will save the sick person, and the Lord will raise him up. If he has committed any sins, he will be forgiven."
James 5:15

The sacrament of Anointing of the Sick often takes place during a Mass after the Liturgy of the Word. Family, friends, and other members of the parish come together with the sick and elderly to pray for and support them.

Anointing of the Sick is also given at home and in the hospital to those who are very ill or dying. The picture on page 113 shows how to prepare for this sacrament.

The two most important signs of the sacrament are the laying on of hands

110

16

Lesson Plan: Middle

to a home. The priest will bring the "Rites of Anointing" book, Viaticum, and the holy oil.

Ask volunteers to read aloud the remaining paragraphs on page 110 and the first column on page 111. Discuss how the sacrament is celebrated and the significance of the laying on of hands and the anointing with oil.

Call attention to the picture on page 110, and ask volunteers to explain what is happening in it.

Continuing Jesus' Healing Mission

Have the group silently read the first three paragraphs under "Living the Sacrament" on page 111. To guide the reading and the discussion of the key concepts, ask how we can take care of our bodies. Call on several young people to share their responses. You may want to discuss why alcohol and drugs are so appealing to many young people. Ask what it takes to say "No" to drinking and taking drugs.

Read aloud the remaining paragraph in this section, emphasizing how we can continue Jesus' mission of healing. Then call attention to the pictures. Ask the young people what they have to do with Jesus' mission of healing.

Our Catholic Identity

Use page 11 from the *Our Catholic Identity* section in the back of the book. Ask the students whether a priest has ever visited their home to anoint someone who was very sick. Let volunteers share their stories. Talk about the way the early Christians visited the sick and how it continues today in the sick calls that our priests make so often. Suggest to the youngsters that they offer to help prepare the table for a sick call if a priest ever visits their home to anoint someone.

You may wish to use pages 37–38 in the activity book for *Coming to God's Life*.

---

and anointing with oil. The priest first lays his hands on the head of the sick or elderly person. This is a sign of God's blessing.

He then anoints the person's forehead with oil, saying,
"Through this holy anointing
may the Lord in his love
and mercy help you
with the grace of the Holy Spirit."

He then anoints the person's hands, saying, "May the Lord who frees you from sin save you and raise you up."

Every Catholic should understand how this sacrament is celebrated. When a Catholic is seriously ill, a priest should be notified. In this way we help our friends and relatives who are sick.

FAITH WORD

The sacrament of **Anointing of the Sick** brings God's special blessings to those who are sick, elderly, or dying.

Living the Sacrament

God wants us to respect our bodies by taking care of them. Some sickness or disease cannot be avoided. Other illnesses can be avoided if we eat healthful foods, get enough sleep, and exercise properly.

Most importantly, we must not abuse or harm our bodies. Drinking alcohol to excess and using tobacco are dangerous and bad for our health.

No matter what our friends do or ask us to do, God will give us the courage to say no to illegal drugs. God will also help us to try again if we fail.

We can continue Jesus' mission of bringing God's healing power to all the world. We can respect our bodies. We can support our Church's efforts to eliminate disease, suffering, hunger, homelessness, and war in our world.

111

ENRICHMENT

Experiencing the Sacrament

Invite someone who has experienced the sacrament of the Anointing of the Sick to tell the class about his or her experience. Beforehand, have the group prepare interview questions. After the visit, have the young people write to thank the visitor for sharing her or his experience. Tell the young people to mention in their notes what they found to be most instructional.

111

16

Lesson Plan: End

Coming to Faith

Recalling Our Mission of Healing

Read aloud the first direction under *Coming to Faith* on page 112. Allow time for the young people to prepare.

Then read the second direction and invite them to think about and discuss responses.

Faith Summary

Use the annotations to review the *Faith Summary* on page 113. See if the young people can express, in their own words, what they have learned.

Practicing Faith

Caring For Others

Help the young people to brainstorm and list on the chalkboard or newsprint those who need help and how to help them.

◆ ENRICHMENT ◆

Visiting the Sick

As a way to express care for sick children, have your group take games and toys to hospitalized youngsters. You will need to get permission both from the hospital and the parents of your fifth graders.

Invite the young people to share their reactions after the visit.

Materials needed: games and toys

112

Praying for the Sick

Distribute slips of paper and ask each young person to write the name of someone who is sick. As the young people gather for prayer, have them place the slips in a bowl on the prayer table. Play appropriate music such as "Lay Your Hands" by Carey Landry. Select a leader and pray together the blessing from the text.

Materials needed: slips of paper; bowl

⌐ EVALUATING YOUR LESSON ¬

■ Do the young people know what Anointing of the Sick means?

■ Do they recognize how it carries on Jesus' healing?

■ Have they chosen to respect their bodies and help the sick?

COMING TO FAITH

Act out a celebration of the sacrament of Anointing of the Sick.

(1) Tell how we can live this sacrament in our daily lives.

PRACTICING FAITH

Ask your catechist about some people in your parish who are in need of your loving care. People in hospitals, nursing homes, "shut-ins", etc.
Decide together some things that you, your friends, or your family will do to help these people.

† Praying for the Sick

Place in a bowl on a prayer table the names of people who are sick. Pray this blessing from the Bible for all these people.

Leader: In the name of the Father, and of the Son, and of the Holy Spirit. Amen.

All: The LORD bless you and keep you!
The LORD let his face shine upon you
 and be gracious to you!
The LORD look upon you kindly
 and give you peace!

Numbers 6:24–26

Take turns praying for your special person by name.
(1) Possible responses:

Respect our bodies by taking care of them; support our Church's efforts to eliminate disease, suffering, and war, etc.

Talk with your catechist about ways you and your family might use the "Faith Alive" pages. Ask your family to pray the prayer with you.

Optional Activities

A Meditation Song (for use with page 109)

Invite the young people to close their eyes and listen to the words of a meditation song such as "I Believe in the Sun," by Carey Landry (NALR) or "Lay Your Hands: A Song of Anointing and Forgiveness," also by Carey Landry. After a brief silence, pray the Our Father for all sick and suffering young people.

Materials needed: music source

A Caring Church (for use with page 110)

Invite the young people to write, tell, or illustrate why they think the Church, the people of God, should always be deeply involved in caring for the sick, elderly, and dying.

Materials needed: paper; pens; pencils; crayons and/or markers

Identifying Unhealthy Products (for use with page 111)

Challenge the young people to make collages illustrating products and practices that are not healthy for our bodies. Display these and discuss them briefly.

Materials needed: magazines; scissors; glue; markers; construction paper

Caring for Our Bodies (for use with page 112)

Show a video or filmstrip on the consequences of smoking, using drugs, or abusing alcohol.

Invite a guest who works with young people in any of these problem areas to respond to the fifth graders' questions.

Materials needed: video or filmstrip

Helping Others (for use with page 112)

Have the young people complete the following statements in their faith journals. Allow time for thoughtful response.

■ I can help an elderly neighbor by _____.

■ I can help a handicapped young person by _____.

■ I can help a sick person by _____.

Invite volunteers to share their completed statements.

112A

FAITH ALIVE AT HOME AND IN THE PARISH

In this chapter your fifth grader has learned more about the sacrament of Anointing of the Sick. Many Catholics will recognize this sacrament by its former name, Extreme Unction. The change of name came from the renewal of the sacraments called for by the Second Vatican Council. Now the Church has returned to the early Christian understanding of this sacrament as one of healing, and not simply a sacrament limited to the dying. This is why the sacrament is called Anointing of the Sick.

In its faithfulness to the healing mission of Jesus, the Church invites the sick and dying to come to him, seeking physical and spiritual health. The anointing of heads and hands with holy oil is a powerful sign of Jesus' loving presence to the one who is suffering.

When Holy Communion is given to a dying person, it is called Viaticum. Viaticum means "food for the journey."

Ask your fifth grader to tell your family about the Anointing of the Sick. Then let him or her use this drawing to show how your family should prepare for and celebrate this sacrament when it is needed by someone in your home.

† Family Prayer

God of compassion,
you take every family under your care
and know our physical and spiritual needs.
Transform our weakness by the strength
  of your grace
and confirm us in your covenant
so that we may grow in faith and love.
(From *Pastoral Care of the Sick*)

Learn by heart Faith Summary

What is the sacrament of Anointing of the Sick?

● The sacrament of Anointing of the Sick brings God's special blessings to those who are sick, elderly, or dying.

What type of sacrament is the Anointing of the Sick?

● Anointing of the Sick is one of the two sacraments of healing.

How can we carry on Jesus' healing mission?

● We must respect our bodies by caring for them. We must work to eliminate sickness and evil from the world.

Candle — Crucifix — Candle

Holy Water — White Cloth — Water — Cotton — Lemon

(Both are used to clean the oil from the priest's hands.)

Review

Go over the *Faith Summary* together and encourage your fifth grader to learn it by heart, especially the first statement. Then have him or her do the *Review*. The answers to numbers 1–4 appear on page 216. The response to number 5 will help you to see how well your fifth grader understands that one way we live this sacrament is by caring for our bodies. When the *Review* is completed, go over it together.

Circle the letter beside the correct answer.

1. Our Church cares for the sick, especially in the sacrament of
   a. Reconciliation.
   b. Anointing of the Sick.
   c. Baptism.
   d. Confirmation.

2. Anointing of the Sick can be celebrated
   a. during Mass.
   b. at home.
   c. in a hospital.
   d. all of the above

3. The two most important signs in Anointing of the Sick are
   a. laying on of hands and anointing.
   b. water and oil.
   c. the words and actions of absolution.
   d. bread and wine.

4. We live the sacrament of Anointing of the Sick when we
   a. ignore the homeless.
   b. take illegal drugs.
   c. respect our bodies.
   d. eat only "junk" foods.

5. Tell how you will respect your body.

_____
_____
_____
_____

FAMILY SCRIPTURE MOMENT

Gather and ask: How does our faith affect our hopes for someone who has died? Then **Listen** as Jesus visits a friend whose brother has just died.

When Martha heard that Jesus was coming, she went to meet him; but Mary sat at home. Martha said to Jesus, "Lord, if you had been here, my brother would not have died. [But] even now I know that whatever you ask of God, God will give you." Jesus said to her, "Your brother will rise." Martha said to him, "I know he will rise, in the resurrection on the last day." Jesus told her, "I am the resurrection and the life; whoever believes in me, even if he dies, will live, and everyone who lives and believes in me will never die."
John 11:20–26

Share what you heard in this reading for your life.

Consider for family enrichment:

■ Jesus invites Martha to express her faith in him as "the resurrection and the life."

■ In the sacrament of Anointing of the Sick, the Catholic Church extends Jesus' healing love to the sick and dying.

Reflect How might we better minister to the sick and dying in our parish?

Decide How will we reach out to any who are sick or elderly in our family?

114

17 Jesus Christ Helps Us to Love

For the Catechist: Spiritual and Catechetical Development

Adult Background

Our Life

At a seminar on Christian marriage, all were invited to complete the following statement in three different ways:

"A good marriage is like _____."

Participants could respond with images ("A good marriage is like a good wine that improves as it matures") or with comparisons to marriages they admired.

Ask yourself:

■ What three responses would I give?

Sharing Life

What obstacles to marriage do you see in today's world?

How do you want the Church to guide and support married persons?

Our Catholic Faith

In a profound and visible way, the sacrament of Matrimony is a sign of Christ's love present among us. Because of its very ordinariness, we often take it for granted. However, the making of a good marriage—the authentic day-by-day living of the sacrament—is an extraordinary accomplishment.

The United States Bishops, in their 1993 pastoral letter *Follow the Way of Love,* recognized the great difficulties facing married couples today. They invited families to share with the Church their ways of working to "stay married" and their suggestions about how the Church can support lasting marriages.

Follow the Way of Love discusses four basic challenges in family life:

■ *Living faithfully*
This section urges married couples to repeatedly renew their commitment to love; to seek pastoral help as needed; to develop virtues like humility and trust that bind them together.

■ *Giving life*
Here the bishops explore the responsibilities of parenting and nurturing. They describe ways of giving life in a society that "devalues life."

■ *Growing in mutuality*
This section emphasizes that husband and wife are "equal in dignity and value." It encourages the sharing of household duties and of decision making.

■ *Taking time*
The bishops challenge married persons to be present to one another, to build intimacy, and to create family memories.

By taking the bishops' message to heart, Catholic families will strengthen their binding covenant of married love.

Coming to Faith

What insights from the above message will you share?

Practicing Faith

How will you choose to affirm the values of Christian marriage?

What will you do to communicate to your group the value of friendship as a long-range preparation for marriage?

115A

CATECHISM OF THE CATHOLIC CHURCH

The Theme of This Chapter Corresponds with Paragraph 1603

LITURGICAL RESOURCES

Share with your group the bishops' challenge to families to strengthen marriages by "taking time." (See *Our Catholic Faith* on the preceding page.) Display on the board Psalm 143:5.

I remember the days of old;
I ponder all your deeds;
the works of your hands
I recall.
(Psalm 143:5)

Seek suggestions on how the fifth graders can help their families create memories by planning a "We Remember" meal at which each person shares one memory of how God has been present to the family.

JUSTICE AND PEACE RESOURCES

Challenge your fifth graders to consider how they can "give life" to their parents or guardians. Elicit from them ways in which parents can be drained of life or energy (overwork, worry, squabbles with spouses or children, too much routine, too little appreciation).

Have each person make a written commitment to surprise parents and "give life" by learning a helpful skill, doing extra chores around the house, keeping peace with siblings, writing and decorating a Prayer for My Parents, or offering some other handmade gift.

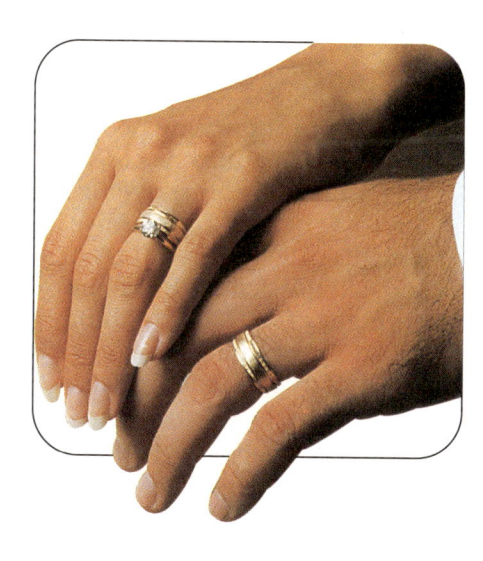

115B

Teaching Resources

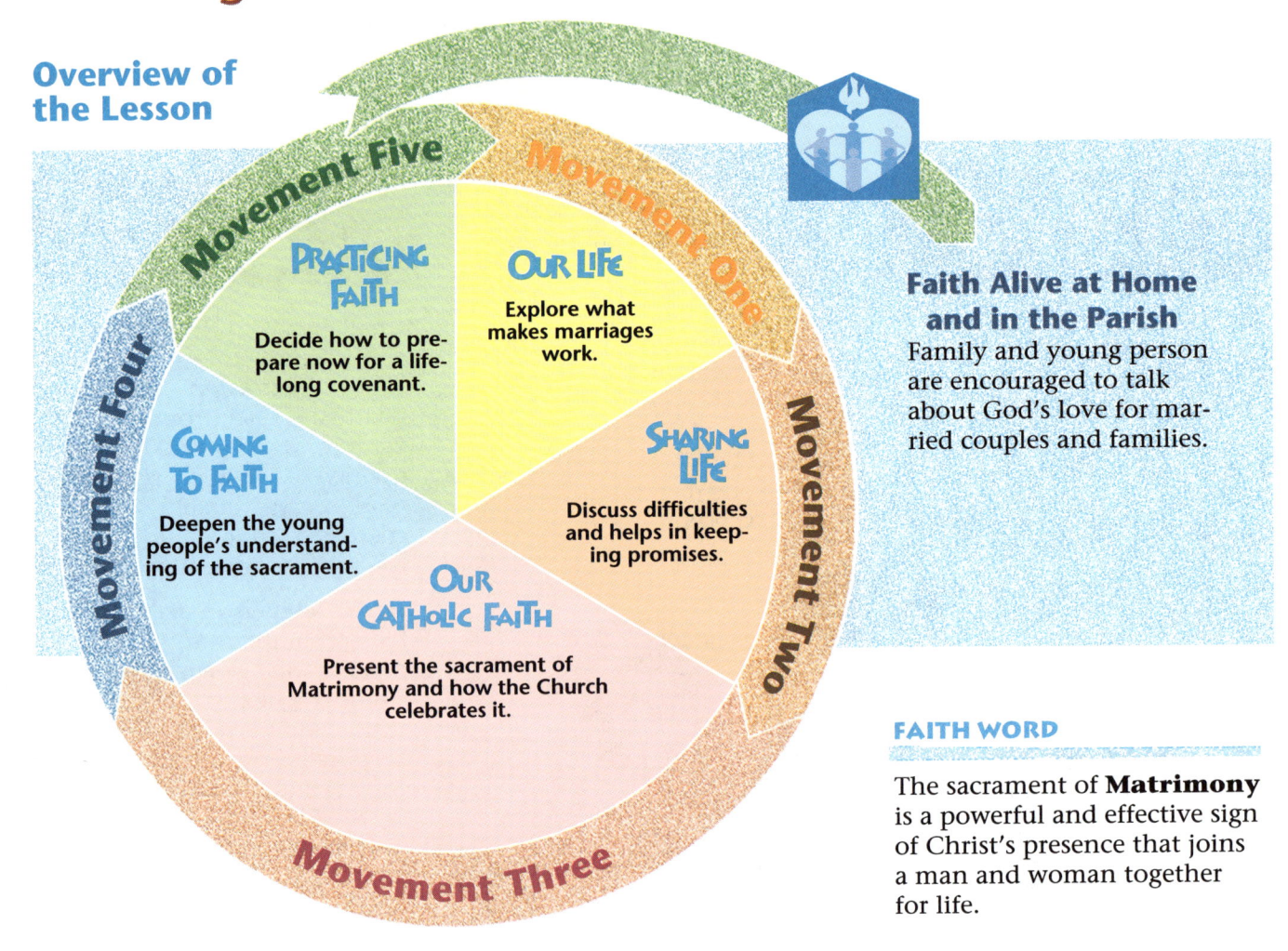

Overview of the Lesson

Movement One — **Our Life**: Explore what makes marriages work.

Movement Two — **Sharing Life**: Discuss difficulties and helps in keeping promises.

Movement Three — **Our Catholic Faith**: Present the sacrament of Matrimony and how the Church celebrates it.

Movement Four — **Coming to Faith**: Deepen the young people's understanding of the sacrament.

Movement Five — **Practicing Faith**: Decide how to prepare now for a life-long covenant.

Faith Alive at Home and in the Parish

Family and young person are encouraged to talk about God's love for married couples and families.

FAITH WORD

The sacrament of **Matrimony** is a powerful and effective sign of Christ's presence that joins a man and woman together for life.

Teaching Hints

Recall with the young people that by our Baptism we are each called to holiness. Point out that married couples live out this call in a special way. Married life demands a commitment of love and faithfulness. Explain that the young people can prepare for such a commitment by growing in their ability and willingness to be faithful in their relationships now.

Special-Needs Child

If a socially maladjusted young person is mainstreamed with your group, be sure to provide opportunities for success and positive feedback from the group.

Visual Needs
- magnifying glass

Auditory Needs
- headphones for recorded music

Tactile–Motor Needs
- large, thick crayons or markers

Supplemental Resources

The Changing Sacraments: Marrying Melvin, Marriage
St. Anthony Messenger/
Franciscan Communications
1615 Republic Street
Cincinnati, OH 45210
(1-800-488-0488)
(1-800-989-3600)

115C

Lesson Plan: Beginning

OBJECTIVES

To help the young people

- know the meaning of the sacrament of Matrimony;
- understand that it involves a lifelong covenant;
- recognize that they can prepare for Matrimony by practicing unselfish love.

Focusing Prayer

After gathering the young people, ask why it is important to keep promises. Then pray together the prayer at the top of page 115.

Our Life

Marriage Is Work

Read aloud the first paragraph. Emphasize that although it may be difficult, it is important for people to be true to their word and to keep their promises. Have volunteers read the four responses. Ask the first follow-up question and invite the group to respond. Read the last question and have the young people write their responses in their faith journals. See the annotations.

Sharing Life

Keeping Promises

Have the young people work in two groups. Assign one of the discussion topics from this section to each group. See the annotations. Allow time for discussion, then have the groups share their responses.

---

17 Jesus Christ Helps Us to Love
(Matrimony)

Loving God, help us to grow as people who understand and keep our promises.

OUR LIFE

Most fairy tales end with the prince and princess "living happily ever after." It is an ending we expect. Real life, however, can be very different. People who get married plan to live happily ever after, too. The couples promise to stay together "until death us do part." But real life is full of good times and bad times, joys and sorrows, sickness and health.

How do couples make marriage work? Here are some responses from real people.

- "We try to love each other. That's what is most important."
(Jennifer and Steven, newlyweds)
- "We keep trying to grow and change together—we're partners in everything."
(Gilberto and Maria, married 10 years)
- "When we have problems, we work them out. Marriage takes *work*!"
(Roy and Linda, married 21 years)
- "We are best friends. We always will be."
(Jim and Tiana, married 46 years)

What do you think about what these couples are saying about marriage? **Marriage takes love, work, and friendship.**

Then ask yourself: How well do I keep promises? **Ask for a range of examples of promises from small to greater. Introduce the group to the saying, "Say what you mean and mean what you say."**

SHARING LIFE

Discuss together: **Encourage the group to use made-up names for couples they use as examples.**

- things that make it difficult for couples to keep their promises **Economic hardship, long hours, illness, addictions, etc.**
- things couples might do to help them keep their promises **Prayer, spending more time together, solving problems by listening to each other, etc.**

ENRICHMENT

A Christian Perspective

Saint Paul spoke about the Christian way of life, often in specific terms. In Ephesians 5:21–33, he urged married Christians to live a strong, mutual love. Paul himself recalled for his readers the words of Genesis 2:24: "That is why a man leaves his father and mother and clings to his wife, and the two of them become one body." Paul saw marriage as divinely instituted. He regarded Christian marriage as symbolizing the intimate relationship of love between Christ and the Church. Christian marriage is to reflect this intimate love between Christ and His Church.

17

Lesson Plan: Middle

Our Catholic Faith

Faith Word

Sketch two intertwined rings on the chalkboard or newsprint. Inside, write *Matrimony*. Ask the group to watch for the word in today's lesson.

Loving in a Special Way

Have the young people silently read the first paragraph under "Matrimony, a Sacrament of Service" on page 116. Review the Law of Love with the group.

Call attention to the *Faith Word* section at the top of page 117. Read the definition of *Matrimony* and have the group repeat it together.

Invite volunteers to read aloud the next two paragraphs on page 116. Ask how Matrimony is a sacrament of service, and how married couples can serve the Church. Discuss the group's responses.

Ask what happens in the sacrament of Matrimony, and then read aloud the next two paragraphs. Invite volunteers to tell, in their own words, what happens in Matrimony. Explain that a covenant is a special agreement that joins two people together forever. Emphasize that married love becomes a great sign of God's love in the world.

Celebrating the Sacrament

Have the young people silently read the next three paragraphs on this page. Discuss with the group the special roles of the bride and groom as ministers of this sacrament. Point out that holding hands and saying the marriage vows are signs that the two people have made a lifelong covenant with each other.

Signs of Union

Ask the group to silently read the next four paragraphs on page 117. Discuss how the bride and groom become united in love. Invite the young people to name the signs used in the sacrament of Matrimony (holding hands, saying the vows, exchanging rings). Explain how they symbolize the union of the couple.

Be sensitive to those in the group who may come from homes where parents are divorced or separated. Stress that God's covenant with us never fails. God always loves us.

OUR CATHOLIC FAITH

Matrimony, A Sacrament of Service

God who created us out of love calls us to love. Love is the vocation of every human being. The Church celebrates the call to love in a special way in the sacrament of Matrimony, or marriage.

Matrimony is one of the two sacraments of service. Married couples promise to serve each other with love and to serve the whole Church. They enter into a lifelong covenant of love. This is their vocation.

Stress the underlined text.

They serve the Church by their love and share in God's creation in a very special way when they give birth to children. Every married couple must be ready to welcome and raise lovingly the children God wishes them to have. In Matrimony God gives a man and woman the special grace and blessings to build a truly Christian family together.

In the sacrament of marriage, the Church brings God's love and blessing to the newly married couple. Their love is a sign of God's absolute and unfailing love for us. Jesus himself becomes a special partner in their relationship. Jesus wants to help every couple live out their marriage covenant.

The Holy Spirit gives the couple the grace to live this sacrament faithfully and well.

Catholics celebrate marriage as a sacrament. It is usually celebrated in the parish of the bride or groom. In the Catholic celebration of marriage, the couple themselves are the ministers of the sacrament. After the Liturgy of the Word, the bride and groom stand before the priest or deacon, who witnesses the couple's promises for Christ's community, the Church.

Individually they vow to each other, "I, (Name), take you, (Name), to be my wife [or husband]. I promise to be true to you in good times and in bad, in sickness and in health. I will love you and honor you all the days of my life." These are called the marriage vows, or promises.

Jesus comes to the couple and unites them in love as Christ loves his Church. The Holy Spirit strengthens and blesses their love.

Lesson Plan: Middle

Preparing for Marriage

Ask, "How can friendship help us to prepare for marriage?" Invite several volunteers to read aloud the two paragraphs under "Learning to Love," then encourage the young people to share their responses to your previous question. Point out that being faithful to our friends and working together as equal partners prepare us for marriage.

To prompt discussion, ask questions such as: "In what ways can young people your age work together as equal partners?" and "How can you promote greater equality at home?"

Our Catholic Identity

Use page 12 from the *Our Catholic Identity* section in the back of the book. After going through the page, stress the importance of the priest's presence. He represents the whole faith community and receives the consent of the couple in its name.

If you wish, let each youngster cut a large "wedding ring" from yellow construction paper or from poster board colored with a gold or yellow marker. Have them write an inscription and their name on each ring.

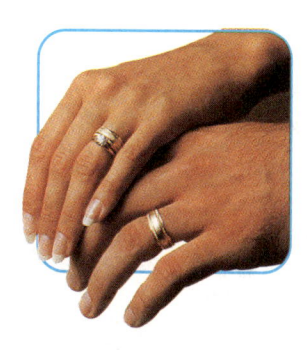

FAITH WORD

The sacrament of **Matrimony** is a powerful and effective sign of Christ's presence that joins a man and woman together for life.

Their married love becomes a sign of God's love for the world.

After they exchange their vows, the bride and groom usually give each other wedding rings as signs of their new union.

After the Our Father of the Mass, the priest or deacon gives the nuptial blessing. In this prayer, the Church asks God to help the couple love each other as Jesus loves us, share their love with their children, and raise them to be Jesus' disciples.

As another sign of their union, the bride and groom, if both are Catholics, may receive Holy Communion together. They ask Jesus to help them live their marriage promises with love all their lives.

Sometimes husbands and wives struggle in their marriages. But children are not to blame when their parents separate or divorce. Separation or divorce does not mean people are bad. This is a very difficult time for the whole family.

No matter what happens, God continues to love each person and always offers the help that is needed.

Learning to Love

Marriage is a long way off for us. We can prepare now for this sacrament by learning to love, respect and care for our family and friends in the same way that God always loves us.

We should learn to practice unselfish love. Parents often place their children's needs before their own. We can practice this kind of unselfish love now by doing things generously for our parents, for our brothers and sisters, and for our friends.

ENRICHMENT

The Marriage Rite

If possible, use slides and background music to enhance the presentation of the marriage rite. Have the young people read aloud and comment on the promises of the bride and groom and the prayers of the celebrant. Ask those who have taken part in a wedding ceremony:

■ What was the best part of the ceremony?

■ Did you wish that anything had been done or said differently? Why?

Call on volunteers to explain how the promises of the bride and groom tell us something about God's love for us. Incorporate their responses in a summary statement on how a Christian husband and wife can reflect God's loyalty, patience, compassion, mercy, and love.

Lesson Plan: End

Coming to Faith

Promising and Preparing

Read aloud the first paragraph under *Coming to Faith* on page 118. Have the young people silently reread the marriage vows and then share their descriptions with the group. Read the question that follows, and have the young people write their responses in their faith journals. Ask volunteers to share what they have written.

Faith Summary

Use the annotations to review the *Faith Summary* on page 119. See if the young people can express, in their own words, what they have learned.

Practicing Faith

Praying for Married Couples

Select four leaders for the prayer service. Begin with a song such as "That's What Friends Are For," by Bacharach-Bayer Sager, or "You've Got a Friend," by Carole King. Invite the young people to name couples for whom they will pray, then conduct the prayer service.

EVALUATING YOUR LESSON

- Do the young people know what married couples promise to do?
- Do they appreciate that married love is a sign of God's love in the world?
- Have they chosen to prepare for Matrimony?

ENRICHMENT

What Is Love?

Ask the young people to read the following lines from 1 Corinthians 13:4–5, then have them tell what each line means:

> Love is patient.
> Love is kind.
> Love is not jealous.
> Love is not selfish.
> Love forgives.

Finally, have the young people write in their faith journals about circumstances that might make it difficult to live these words. Elicit from them that God's love enables us to accomplish these goals.

Materials needed: faith journals

Coming To Faith

Reread the marriage vows on page 116. These are the promises the man and woman make to each other on their wedding day and forever. Describe in your own words what they are promising. **Accept individual answers.**
Why do you think the Church considers Matrimony a sacrament of service? **Because it strengthens people to help each other and all they meet.**

Practicing Faith

† Praying for Married Couples

Praying for married couples is one of the most important ministries, or services, young people can offer.

Offer the following prayer together.

Leader 1: Jesus, you shared the joy and laughter of wedding celebrations.

All: Share your joy with all married couples—especially those who are closest to us.

Leader 2: Jesus, you treated women and men equally.

All: Help wives and husbands to live together as equal partners and loving friends.

Leader 3: Jesus, you want marriage to last forever, like God's love for us.

All: Guide those whose marriages are in trouble. Help divorced or separated couples.

Leader 4: Jesus, help all your disciples to follow your command to love and to be faithful friends.

All: Amen.

Talk with your catechist about ways you and your family might share the "Faith Alive" pages together. Before doing the activity you might ask family members for their ideas.

Optional Activities

Book Reviews (for use with page 115)

Invite the young people to prepare oral or written book reviews on the theme of marriage (both happy and unhappy). You might suggest the following titles: *Sarah, Plain and Tall*, by Patricia MacLachlan (Harper & Row); *What I Heard*, by Mark Geller (Harper & Row).

Talk Show Host (for use with page 116)

Select a young person to play the part of a talk show host. He or she may use a real or imaginary microphone to interview members of the studio audience (the other group members). Have the host ask questions such as:

■ Why do you think a man and woman decide to marry?

■ What do you think is the most important thing about getting married?

Involve as many young people as possible in this activity.

Materials needed: microphone

A Marriage Booklet (for use with pages 116–117)

Challenge the young people to write an ending that will complete any of the following statements in a meaningful way. (The statements may be serious or humorous.)

■ A good marriage is like _____.

■ The best wife or husband is one who _____.

■ True married love requires _____.

Collect the completed statements in a Marriage Booklet that might be reproduced for parents.

Materials needed: writing paper; pens or markers

Serving Friends (for use with page 117)

Distribute index cards and have the young people write ways in which they will serve a friend during the next three days. Play a friendship song as they place these cards on the prayer table.

Materials needed: index cards; pens or pencils; music source

Remembering Married People (for use with page 118)

On a large sheet of newsprint, have the young people write the names of married people they care about, are concerned about, or admire. Invite them to draw marriage symbols to accompany the names. Then gather at the prayer table, and sing together "They'll Know We Are Christians." Have the group think about how these words apply to the people named.

Materials needed: newsprint; pens or pencils; markers; song lyrics

118A

FAITH ALIVE AT HOME AND IN THE PARISH

Your fifth grader has learned more about the sacrament of Matrimony. Invite her or him to tell you what the sacrament means, and what young people can do now to learn to prepare for marriage if that is their vocation. The Second Vatican Council described marriage as a covenant of life and love.

Read the Bible story of the marriage feast at Cana from John 2:1–11. Talk about God's love for married couples and families. Also talk about the fact that God does not abandon families separated by death or divorce.

Decide and share what each of you will do this week to grow in unselfish love for and service to one another in your parish.

Do the activity below together to help your fifth grader grow in understanding what marriage really means.

✝ Family Prayer

May the Lord Jesus, who was a guest at the wedding in Cana,
bless my family and friends.

Learn by heart Faith Summary

What is the sacrament of Matrimony?
- The sacrament of Matrimony is a powerful and effective sign of Christ's presence that joins a man and woman together for life.

What do married couples promise?
- Married couples promise to serve each other and the whole Church. Matrimony is a sacrament of service.

How can we prepare now for Matrimony?
- We can prepare now for Matrimony by trying to love others as God loves us.

Designing a Wedding Ring

Write what you would like printed inside a family member's wedding ring to remind him or her of the marriage covenant of love and service.

_____
_____
_____
_____

Review

Go over the *Faith Summary* together and encourage your fifth grader to learn it by heart, especially the first statement. Then have him or her do the *Review*. The answers to numbers 1–4 appear on page 216. The response to number 5 will show how well your fifth grader understands that one must prepare now for the marriage promise of unconditional love and service. When the *Review* is completed, go over it together.

Complete the following statements.

1. Matrimony is a sacrament of service. The best service Christians can give the world is *love.*

2. In the marriage vows a man and a woman promise to *be true at all times and love one another forever.*

3. Jesus Christ unites a husband and wife in love as Christ loves *His Church.*

4. Married love is a sign of *God's love for the world.*

5. How will you prepare now to be a good marriage partner someday?

   _____
   _____
   _____
   _____

FAMILY SCRIPTURE MOMENT

Gather and recall memories of a family wedding. Ask: For Catholic couples, what difference should their faith make to their marriage? Then **Listen** to a wedding story from John's Gospel.

There was a wedding in Cana in Galilee, and the mother of Jesus was there. Jesus and his disciples were also invited. . . . When the wine ran short, the mother of Jesus said to him, "They have no wine." His mother said to the servers, "Do whatever he tells you." Jesus told them, "Fill the jars with water." So they filled them to the brim. Then he told them, "Draw some out now and take it to the headwaiter." . . . The headwaiter called the bridegroom and said to him, ". . . you have kept the good wine until now." Jesus did this as the beginning of his signs . . . and so revealed his glory.
John 2:1–3, 5, 7–11

Share Imagine being at the wedding feast at Cana. Describe what you learn from the experience.

Consider for family enrichment:

■ In the Bible, a wedding feast often symbolizes the kingdom of God, in which love, peace and joy flow freely.

■ Catholics believe marriage is a sacrament and a sign of God's reign of love.

Reflect and **Decide** How might we turn the "water" of poverty or sorrow into the "wine" of gratitude or gladness for a married couple? For whom will we do this? When?

120

18 Jesus Christ Calls Us to Serve

For the Catechist: Spiritual and Catechetical Development

ADULT BACKGROUND

Our Life

When their auxiliary bishop died of cancer, the people of the diocese flocked to his funeral Mass. They wanted to show their gratitude for his unselfish service. He was remembered as a shepherd who fought for justice at great expense to himself, as a reconciler of opposing groups, and as a wise mentor to priests.

A year before his death, Bishop Amedee Proulx observed, "All I ask is that God grant me the grace to follow where he leads."

Ask yourself:

■ How have priests or bishops enabled me to follow where God leads?

Sharing Life

What hopes do you have for priests and deacons? Why?

Our Catholic Faith

Jesus Christ is the source of ministry in the Church. He has given His own mission and authority to the Church so that the word of God and the message of salvation may reach to the ends of the earth.

No one can take on a ministry in the Church by personal authority but only through Christ's authority.

In the sacrament of Holy Orders, a man is called to share in a unique way Jesus' mission of "sanctifying, teaching, and building the Christian community." Although all the faithful are members of the royal priesthood of Christ through Baptism, the ordained priest "becomes—in the Church and for the Church—a real, living, and faithful image of Christ, the priest" (*Directory on the Ministry and Life of Priests*, Vatican Congregation for the Clergy, 1994).

The Catholic Church ordains bishops, priests, and deacons to serve the people of God. Bishops are the successors of the apostles. They are ordained to teach, sanctify, and govern as chief pastors of their dioceses. But the bishop does not act alone in this ministry. For all the bishops together throughout the world make up what is called the episcopal college, or body, which acts in union with the pope, the bishop of Rome and successor of Saint Peter. Together and in agreement with the pope, the college of bishops has been given by Christ full authority over the universal Church.

Gathered around the bishops are the priests, co-workers with the bishops in their dioceses. Like the bishops, the priests exercise their ministry in the person of Christ. When baptizing, for example, they say, "I baptize you. . ." When forgiving sins in the sacrament of Reconciliation, they say, "I absolve you. . ." Priests act under the direction of a bishop, and it is in the Eucharist that priests exercise to the greatest degree their sacred ministry.

Deacons, too, are part of the hierarchy of the ordained ministry and also receive the sacrament of Holy Orders. They are ordained to serve and assist the bishops and priests in their ministry.

Coming to Faith

What does it mean to say that the priest acts in the person of Christ?

Practicing Faith

How will you encourage your group to appreciate the ordained?

CATECHISM OF THE CATHOLIC CHURCH

The Theme of This Chapter Corresponds with Paragraph 1572

LITURGICAL RESOURCES

Display on a large poster or banner these words of Jesus: "The harvest is abundant but the laborers are few; so ask the master of the harvest to send out laborers for his harvest" (Luke 10:2).

Distribute drawing materials. Have the group create symbols of the harvest or the harvester. On each symbol have the young people write a prayer for vocations to the ordained ministry. Display these on the banner or poster.

JUSTICE AND PEACE RESOURCES

Jesus fulfilled Isaiah's description of God's chosen servant as one who would persist "until he brings justice to victory." In him all people will hope, Isaiah says. (Matthew 12:20-21)

Consider the ways in which your parish or diocesan priests have given people hope by furthering the cause of justice. Share the witness of these priests with your group. Have the fifth graders write letters of appreciation to them, with promises of prayer support.

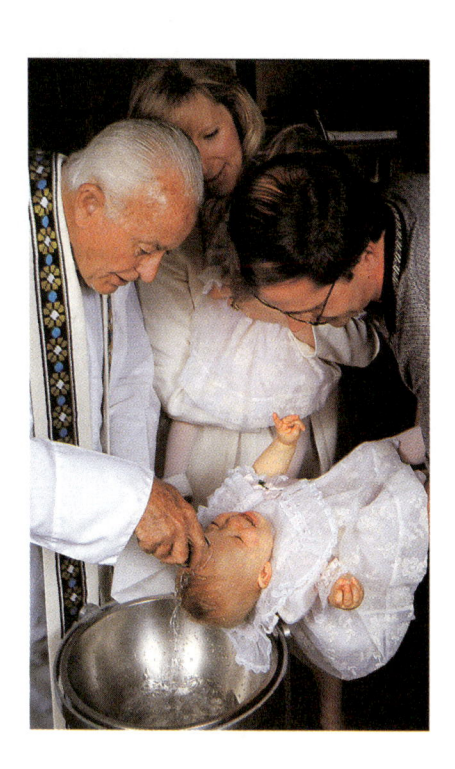

Teaching Resources

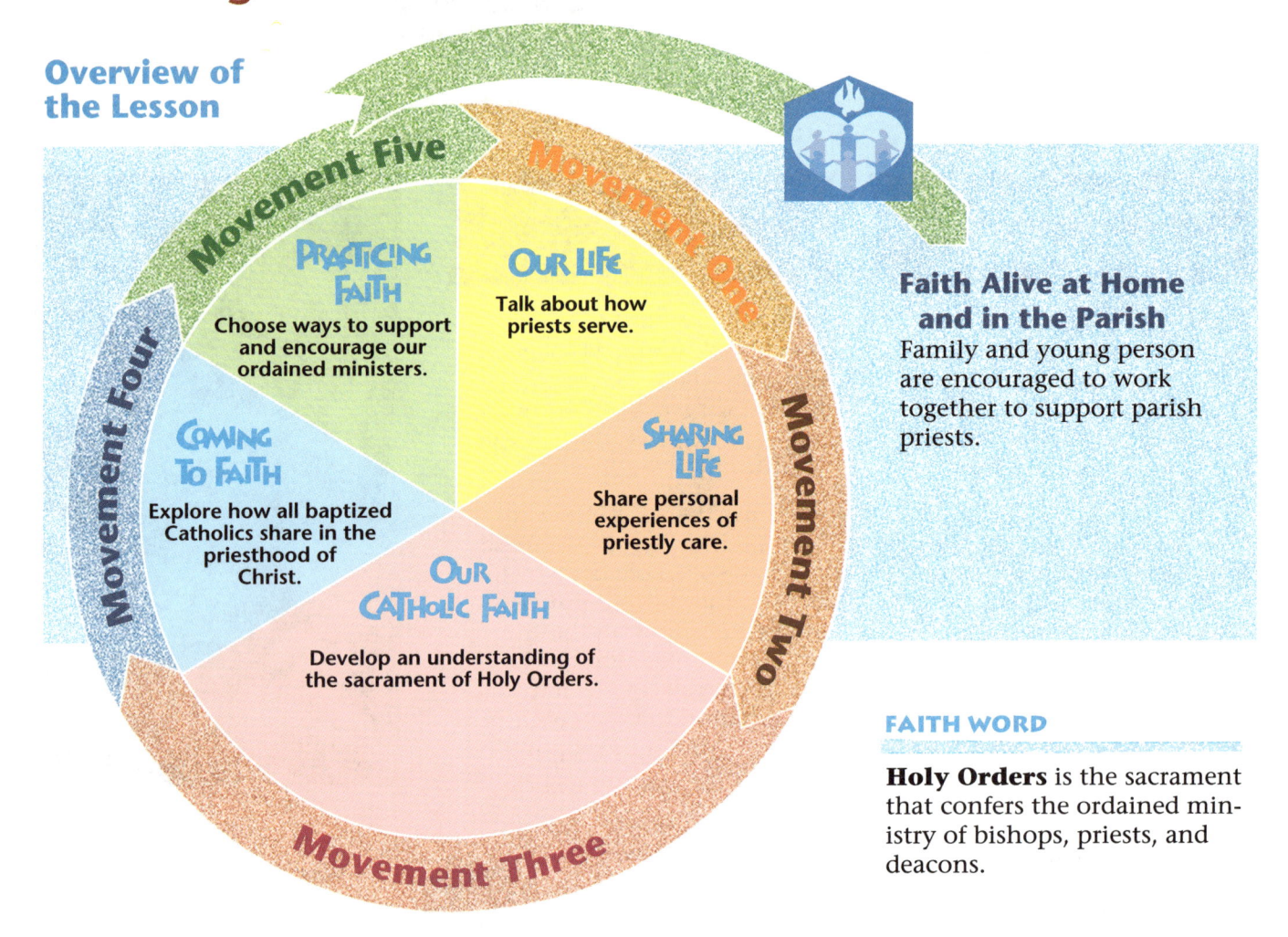

Overview of the Lesson

Movement One — Our Life: Talk about how priests serve.

Movement Two — Sharing Life: Share personal experiences of priestly care.

Movement Three — Our Catholic Faith: Develop an understanding of the sacrament of Holy Orders.

Movement Four — Coming to Faith: Explore how all baptized Catholics share in the priesthood of Christ.

Movement Five — Practicing Faith: Choose ways to support and encourage our ordained ministers.

Faith Alive at Home and in the Parish
Family and young person are encouraged to work together to support parish priests.

FAITH WORD
Holy Orders is the sacrament that confers the ordained ministry of bishops, priests, and deacons.

Teaching Hints

The lesson on Holy Orders will be more meaningful if a priest or deacon visits the young people to tell them about his vocation and to describe for them the work he is called to do in the Church. The priest or deacon may wish to share with the group a video, home movie, or photos of his ordination.

If such a visit cannot be arranged, choose some young people to interview an ordained person and report to the group on what they have learned.

Special-Needs Child

Visually impaired young people may not see you looking at or pointing to them. Call each one by name to gain her or his attention.

Visual Needs
- large-print *Faith Word*

Auditory Needs
- preferential seating

Tactile–Motor Needs
- role-playing opportunities

Supplemental Resources

Sacraments of Vocation (video)
Brown-ROA
2460 Kerper Blvd.
P.O. Box 539
Dubuque, IA 52004
(1-800-922-7696)

Lesson Plan: Beginning

OBJECTIVES

To help the young people

- know that Holy Orders is a sign of the special priesthood of Jesus;
- appreciate that we all share in Jesus' priesthood;
- choose ways to support our ordained ministers.

Focusing Prayer

Explain that today the young people will learn about the leaders Jesus gives us to help His Church. Then pray together the prayer at the top of page 121.

Our Life

Ministering Service

Read aloud the first paragraph and call attention to the pictures. Invite the young people to share their responses. Then read the final direction and allow time for the group to respond.

Sharing Life

Deciding How to Serve

Have the young people read the first question under *Sharing Life*. Have them circle a ministry in which they might want to serve. Read aloud the next paragraph. Allow time for the young people to respond. Then read aloud the closing paragraph, and encourage the young people to share their responses. See the annotations.

ENRICHMENT

Outstanding Servant

Read a story or tell an anecdote about a priest or bishop who is outstanding for his service to others. One example is Archbishop Romero, who was murdered because of his advocacy of the poor. Another is Father John Drumgoole, who spent his life providing care for homeless and abandoned children in New York. A third example is Father Flanagan, the founder of Boys Town.

Materials needed: story about a priest or bishop

---

18 Jesus Christ Calls Us to Serve
(Holy Orders)

Loving God, fill your Church with the spirit of courage, love, and service.

OUR LIFE

In each of these pictures a priest is ministering, or offering some service, to his parish. Tell:
- how each priest is serving.
- what difference the priest may be making in the lives of the people served.

Possible responses:
Name other ways by which priests minister to, or serve, their people. Helping the poor, explaining God's word; praying with people

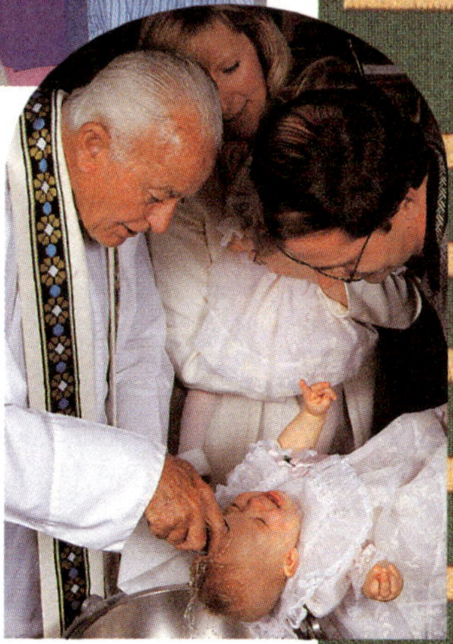

SHARING LIFE

If you were a priest, what would you want to do for those you serve? Circle one of the priestly ministries listed below.

baptizer   confessor   teacher
preacher   leader   friend
Mass Celebrant and presider   spiritual guide

Think of a priest who has served you or your family in this ministry. How did he help? Accept individual answers.

Discuss as a group what qualities are needed to be a good priest. Why? Have the young people freely express their views and give reasons for them.

18

Lesson Plan: Middle

Our Catholic Faith

Faith Word

Write on the chalkboard or newsprint *Holy Orders*. Pronounce the term, and ask the group to listen for it in today's lesson.

Leading the Church

Ask, "Who did Jesus choose to lead His Church?" Then read aloud the first two paragraphs under "Jesus Christ Gives Us Leaders" on page 122. Now invite volunteers to respond to your previous question. Call attention to the word *apostle*, and discuss its meaning. Emphasize that, by His words and actions, Jesus showed His apostles that they were not to seek power and glory over others, but were to serve others.

Ask who continued the work of the apostles, and have the young people silently read the next two paragraphs to find the answer. Discuss responses. Note that the apostles led the Church in teaching and in worship. Have the young people recognize that the successors to the apostles are called bishops, and that the first bishop of Rome, Saint Peter, was our first pope. Have the group silently read the remainder of the section, and then discuss how priests help our parishes.

Encourage the young people to imagine what is happening in the picture.

Defining a Sacrament of Service

Ask, "What is the sacrament of Holy Orders?" Invite a volunteer to read aloud the first paragraph under "Holy Orders, a Sacrament of Service" on page 122. Then have the group reread the paragraph together. Call on several volunteers to read aloud the second paragraph. To focus the reading and to guide a discussion of responses, ask how priests serve the community.

Celebrating Holy Orders

Have the group silently read the next five paragraphs. Encourage the young people to explain, in their own words, what happens during the sacrament of Holy Orders. Invite volunteers to list on the chalkboard or newsprint the key actions in the ordination of a priest.

Have the young people look at the photograph. Lead them in a discussion about the celebration of this sacrament. You may wish to point out that the candidates promise to respect and obey their bishop, to celebrate the sacraments faithfully, to preach and explain the Catholic faith, and to give their lives in service to God.

OUR CATHOLIC FAITH

Stress the underlined text.

Jesus Christ Gives us Leaders

From among the disciples, Jesus chose twelve special helpers, called apostles, to be the first leaders of his Church. He showed them that being a leader means being a servant, not one who is served.

Jesus told them, "Whoever wishes to be great among you will be your servant. . . . For the Son of Man did not come to be served but to serve and to give his life as a ransom for many."
Mark 10:43–45

The Church grew so rapidly that soon more helpers were needed. The apostles, with the help of the Christian community, chose others to continue their work of teaching and leading the Church in worship and service. The apostles laid their hands on them and prayed that they would be strengthened by the Holy Spirit.

In time these successors of the apostles were called bishops. The bishops ordained still others as priests to help them. Deacons also were chosen to make sure that the needs of the poor, the lonely, the widowed, and the orphaned were met. The leader of the apostles was Saint Peter. As bishop of Rome, the pope carries on the ministry of Saint Peter. He is the Vicar, or representative, of Christ on earth.

Today our bishops, priests, and deacons continue the mission of the apostles. Our pope, together with the bishops, leads the whole Catholic Church. Bishops lead and serve our dioceses.

In our parish, priests help us to be a Christian community caring for one another. They lead us in celebrating the sacraments and teach us how to live Jesus' good news. They serve the whole community and encourage us to use our gifts in service, too. Deacons have a special concern and ministry for the poor and those in need.

Holy Orders, A Sacrament of Service

Holy Orders is the sacrament through which the ordained ministry of bishops, priests, and deacons is conferred by the laying on of hands followed by the prayer of consecration.

Our ordained ministers serve the Catholic community in four ways:

• They preach and teach the good news of Jesus Christ.

• They lead us in celebrating the sacraments.

• They lead us in working together to build up the Christian community.

• They help us to serve the poor and all those in need.

Lesson Plan: Middle

To reinforce the meaning of this sacrament of service, have the group read together the definition of *Holy Orders* at the top of page 123.

Sharing in the Priesthood

Ask the young people what our Baptism calls us to do, and invite volunteers to read aloud the last paragraph. Emphasize that by Baptism we share in the priesthood of Jesus Christ and are called to preach and teach the good news.

Multicultural Awareness

Remind the group that Jesus calls each of us—He calls us to be holy and to minister to one another. Tell the fifth graders that if we put on Christ, then we will minister to *all* those in need. Elicit from the group that it is easy to minister to those we like or those with whom we feel comfortable. Explain that only because of Christ can we minister to *all*.

Our Catholic Identity

Use page 13 from the *Our Catholic Identity* section in the back of the book. Explain that the Church still has specially ordained men who serve as deacons. If your parish has a deacon, show the youngsters a parish bulletin that contains the deacon's name. See if anyone is familiar with the deacon's work. Perhaps you can arrange for a deacon to visit your group – especially if there is no deacon serving in your parish right now.

ENRICHMENT

A Call to Orders!

Explain to the young people that in America, only a few young men are entering seminaries to study for the priesthood. Ask what the fifth graders think are some of the joys of being a priest, such as the ability to follow Jesus' disciples in doing His work, the privilege of leading the celebration of the Eucharist, or the knowledge that one works to help others. Then challenge the young people to write want ads inviting young men to consider the priesthood. Share the following example, then let the fifth graders proceed on their own:

Wanted—Young men who wish to dedicate their lives to Christ's mission, to be co-workers with the bishops, and to celebrate the sacraments in a spirit of love and service. Must be prayerful, willing, strong, creative, and able to deal with different situations. Rewards are greater than you can imagine.

Bishops, priests, and deacons are ordained in the sacrament of Holy Orders. The sacrament of Holy Orders is celebrated during Mass. Only a bishop can ordain another bishop, priest, or deacon.

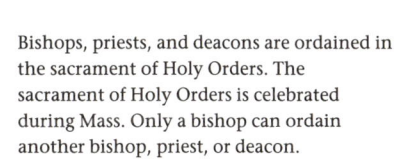

In ordaining priests, the bishop lays his hands on the head of each candidate and prays silently. This is the most important sign of the sacrament of Holy Orders. Then the bishop prays a prayer of consecration, or the prayer that "makes holy."

Each candidate for the priesthood is also anointed with holy oil. This is a sign of his special sharing in Christ's own priesthood through the ordained ministry.

Each receives a paten and chalice. With these the priest leads the community in celebrating the Eucharist.

Through the sacrament of Holy Orders, priests receive the grace to share, in the fullest way, in Christ's work of salvation. They are Christ's representatives on earth.

FAITH WORD

Holy Orders is the sacrament that confers the ordained ministry of bishops, priests, and deacons.

Like Baptism and Confirmation, Holy Orders confers an indelible character and cannot be repeated. We need to ask the Holy Spirit to give those called to the ordained priesthood the strength to accept and live this vocation.

By Baptism each of us is given a share in the priesthood of Jesus Christ. We are not ordained ministers. But we, too, are called to share the good news of Jesus Christ and carry on his mission.

18

Lesson Plan: End

Coming to Faith

Serving the Church

Form groups and then read aloud the directions under *Coming to Faith*. Allow the groups time to discuss and write their ideas. Have each group share its responses with the others. See the annotation.

Faith Summary

Use the annotations to review the *Faith Summary* on page 125. See if the young people can express, in their own words, what they have learned.

Practicing Faith

Helping Our Priests

Explain the *Practicing Faith* activities. Allow time for the young people to think about and discuss their responses. Invite them to share how they have decided to help their parish priests. Encourage the young people to be realistic and specific in their responses.

Gather the young people for prayer. Ask them to close their eyes and listen as you read John 10:11–16, "Jesus the Good Shepherd." After a brief silence, pray together the prayer for vocations on page 125.

Materials needed: Good News Bible

◆ ENRICHMENT ◆

Saying "Thank You"

Encourage the young people to write individual notes of thanks to the pope, to their bishop, and to their pastor. They should be specific in naming what they are especially grateful for. Make sure the notes get mailed.

Materials needed: writing paper; pens or pencils; envelopes; addresses; stamps

124

EVALUATING YOUR LESSON

■ Do the young people know that Holy Orders celebrates Christ's priesthood?

■ Do they appreciate how ordained ministers serve the Church?

■ Have they decided how to support their priests?

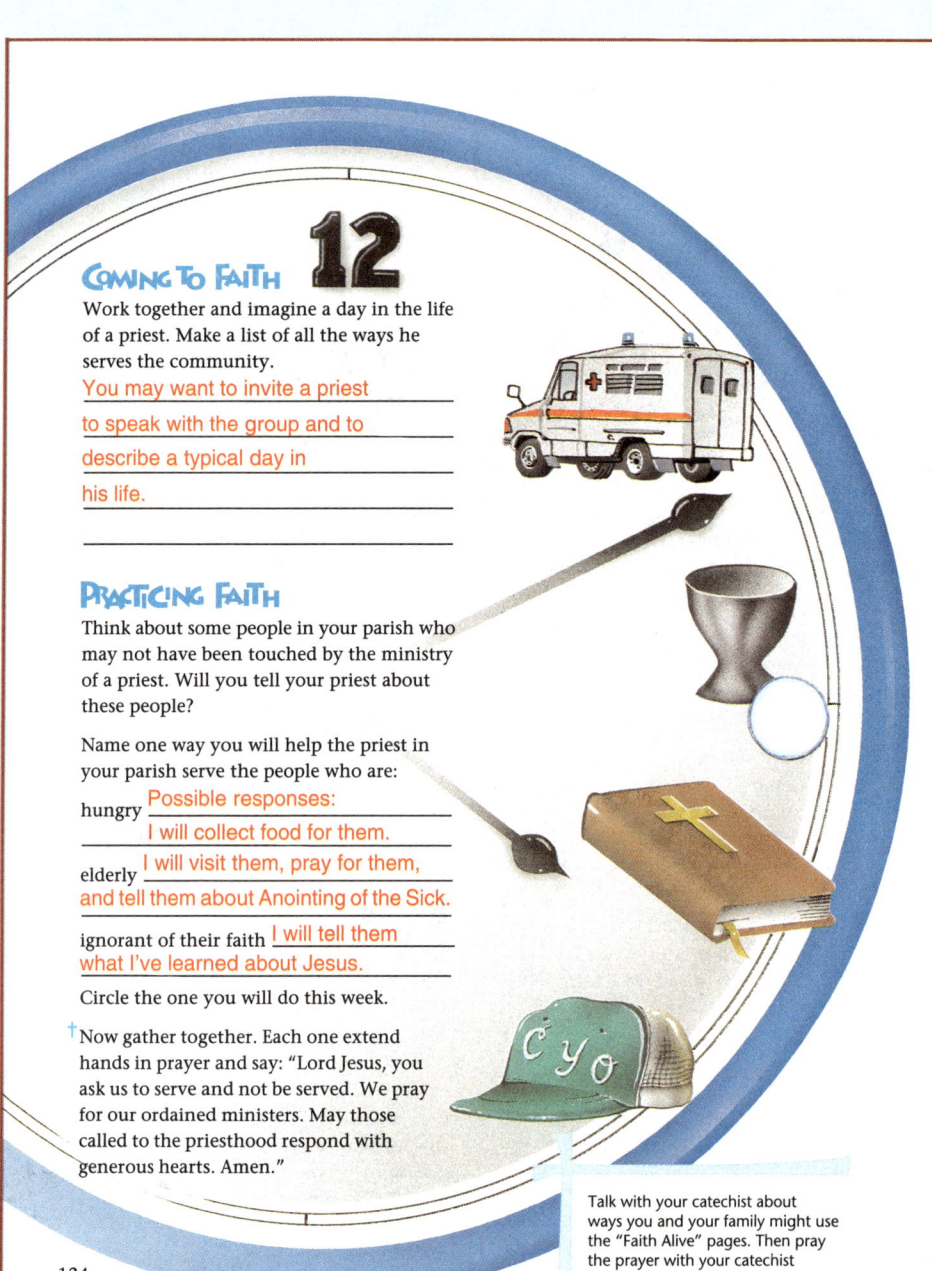

COMING TO FAITH 12

Work together and imagine a day in the life of a priest. Make a list of all the ways he serves the community.

You may want to invite a priest to speak with the group and to describe a typical day in his life.

PRACTICING FAITH

Think about some people in your parish who may not have been touched by the ministry of a priest. Will you tell your priest about these people?

Name one way you will help the priest in your parish serve the people who are:

hungry *Possible responses: I will collect food for them.*

elderly *I will visit them, pray for them, and tell them about Anointing of the Sick.*

ignorant of their faith *I will tell them what I've learned about Jesus.*

Circle the one you will do this week.

† Now gather together. Each one extend hands in prayer and say: "Lord Jesus, you ask us to serve and not be served. We pray for our ordained ministers. May those called to the priesthood respond with generous hearts. Amen."

Talk with your catechist about ways you and your family might use the "Faith Alive" pages. Then pray the prayer with your catechist and friends.

124

Optional Activities

An Ordained Visitor (for use with page 122)

Invite a priest or deacon to visit with the fifth graders. Begin informally, allowing young people to get to know the guest and question him about his duties in the parish. Then invite the priest or deacon to relate anecdotes from his experience of parish ministry.

A Prayer for Priests (for use with page 123)

Play quiet background music related to service or priesthood such as "Peace Prayer," by John Foley, S.J., (NALR) or "Like a Shepherd," by Bob Dufford, S.J. (NALR).

Help the young people to understand that a priest's life can be a lonely one. Explain that loneliness takes many forms—it does not necessarily mean solitude. People can experience loneliness if they are not appreciated by those around them, or if they are taken for granted, or if they begin to feel invisible.

Invite the group to pray silently for ordained men who are suffering from loneliness or lack of appreciation.

Materials needed: music source

Prayer Support (for use with page 124)

Write the names of area priests, deacons, and the bishop of your diocese on strips of paper. Place the names in a bowl and have each fifth grader draw one. Invite the young people to pray for their chosen ordained person, asking God to strengthen and support him.

Materials needed: name strips; bowl

Expressing Our Thoughts (for use with page 124)

Have the young people think about and respond to the following questions in their faith journals:

- How will I live my Baptism?
- How will I help my parish priest?
- What do I most want a priest to do for me? Why?

Invite volunteers to share their responses.

Materials needed: faith journals; pens or pencils

FAITH ALIVE AT HOME AND IN THE PARISH

Talk to your fifth grader about ways each one of us experiences the sacrament of Holy Orders through the ministry of the priests and deacons in our parish.

Discuss ways your family can support the ordained ministers in your parish. For example:

- pray for them, especially at Mass.
- help them in one of your parish programs.
- show appreciation for their service.
- contribute your own talents to the ministry of the parish.

Now ask each member of the family to write down what she or he will do this week to support your parish priest.

Then do these activities together:

- Create a poster showing how a priest you know serves.
- As a family, write a thank-you note to the priest illustrated on your poster.

✝ Family Prayer

Father,

in your plan for our salvation you provide shepherds for your people.

Fill your Church with the spirit of courage and love.

Raise up worthy ministers for your altars and ardent but gentle servants of the gospel.

(From the Mass for Priestly Vocations)

Learn by heart — Faith Summary

Whom did Jesus choose to lead our Church?

- Jesus chose the twelve apostles to lead our Church in service and worship.

Who are ordained in Holy Orders?

- Bishops, priests, and deacons are ordained in the sacrament of Holy Orders.

How do our ordained ministers lead us?

- Our ordained ministers lead us in building up the Christian community.

How Father _____ Serves

Review

Go over the *Faith Summary* together and encourage your fifth grader to learn it by heart. Then have him or her do the *Review*. The answers to numbers 1–4 appear on page 216. The response to number 5 will show how well your fifth grader understands our responsibility to help our priests. When the *Review* is completed, go over it together.

Complete the following sentences.

1. Jesus chose the twelve ____apostles____ to be the first leaders of our Church.

2. ____Bishops____ are the successors of the apostles.

3. Those ordained ministers who have a special concern and ministry for the poor are called ____deacons____.

4. The sacrament of Holy Orders is conferred through the ____laying on of hands____ and the prayer of consecration.

5. Tell some ways you will support a priest who serves the people in your parish.

_____
_____
_____
_____

FAMILY SCRIPTURE MOMENT

Gather and ask: How do we know for sure that someone loves us? Then **Listen** as Jesus questions Peter.

. . . Jesus said to Simon Peter, "Simon, son of John, do you love me more than these?" He said to him, "Yes, Lord, you know that I love you." He said to him, "Feed my lambs." He then said to him a second time, "Simon, son of John, do you love me?" He said to him, "Yes, Lord, you know that I love you." He said to him, "Tend my sheep." He said to him the third time, "Simon, son of John, do you love me?" . . . he said to him, "Lord, you know everything; you know that I love you."
John 21:15–17

Share how you would respond to Jesus asking you this same question.

Consider for family enrichment:
■ Because Peter had denied knowing Jesus three times before the crucifixion, Jesus gave his chosen "Rock" three opportunities to express faithful love.
■ We honor and respect our pope as he carries on the ministry of Saint Peter today.

Reflect and **Decide** How might Jesus expect us to show support for our ordained ministers? How will we respond as a family in our parish?

19 WE SHARE JESUS CHRIST'S PRIESTHOOD

For the Catechist: Spiritual and Catechetical Development

ADULT BACKGROUND

Our Life

When Thomas Merton entered the strict monastic order popularly known as the Trappists, he was prepared to give up his original vocation as a writer. Instead he became one of the most influential spiritual writers of the twentieth century. Merton believed that every human being has a vocation to transform the world and draw out the spiritual glory which has been hidden in it by our Creator.

Ask yourself:

- What is my primary vocation?
- How do I live it?

Sharing Life

In what ways does the Church enable you to "transform the world" as Merton says?

Our Catholic Faith

While the Church clearly distinguishes between the ordained priesthood and the priesthood of the faithful, the Church stresses that both share in the common priesthood of Christ through Baptism.

There are myriad ways in which contemporary Christians can serve God and others as members of the priesthood of the faithful. Some serve as professional lay ministers. They may be hired by a diocese or a parish to administer a parish or such programs as religious education, social services, youth ministry, or family counseling. They are generally involved full time in a service for which they have particular skills and training.

Many single men and women live as religious brothers and sisters. They give their lives to God and serve as members of religious communities. They work tirelessly to advance the message of Christ in many settings—hospitals, parishes, missions, schools, and justice and peace organizations.

Many people serve the parish as volunteers in lay ministries. They serve as lectors, visit the sick, work on the parish council, become eucharistic ministers, or serve as catechists. Others who cannot commit themselves to a continuing ministry may volunteer for occasional community-building efforts (for example: special liturgies, fundraising events for social justice causes, parish socials).

All Christians can participate in lay ministry by living out their baptismal vows, giving witness to their faith, and serving others in Jesus' name. Their conviction is nourished by a strong prayer and sacramental life.

Pope John Paul II has emphasized the need for all the faithful to participate in the re-evangelization of developed countries where there is a "constant spreading of an indifference to religion, of secularism and atheism." He also calls on the laity to participate in the mission "of bringing the gospel to the multitudes—the millions and millions of men and women—who as yet do not know Christ the Redeemer of humanity" (*Christifideles Laici*, III, December 30, 1988).

We are members of the priesthood of the faithful who embody the word of God as married or single persons, religious sisters or brothers, or members of secular institutes (living a vowed life in society). Together we build up the reign of God on earth.

Coming to Faith

How might your parish participate in the re-evangelization of our country?

Practicing Faith

How will you encourage others to participate in Christ's priesthood?

In what ways will you lead your fifth graders to value their ministries and vocations?

CATECHISM OF THE CATHOLIC CHURCH

The Theme of This Chapter Corresponds with Paragraph 871

LITURGICAL RESOURCES

The primary place in which we share the priesthood of Jesus Christ is the "domestic church." It is in our homes that we learn to love God in one another and to practice the gospel values Jesus embodied.

Invite your fifth graders to reflect on and respond in writing to the following:

- What do I love, admire, or appreciate about each member of my family?
- How have I experienced the love of God in my family?
- What have I learned about love in my family that I want to share with others?

Pray together: "Jesus, help us to see You in our loved ones and share You with those who do not know You."

JUSTICE AND PEACE RESOURCES

With the help of a few parents, the fifth graders can organize an evening or Sunday-after-Mass program called "We Are Witnesses." Invite several persons involved in the ministry of justice and peace (professionals, volunteer lay ministers, religious) to participate in a panel discussion.

Ask participants to inspire, encourage, or challenge parishioners to work for justice and peace. They might also enlist volunteers for particular programs, projects, or other forms of witness.

19

Teaching Resources

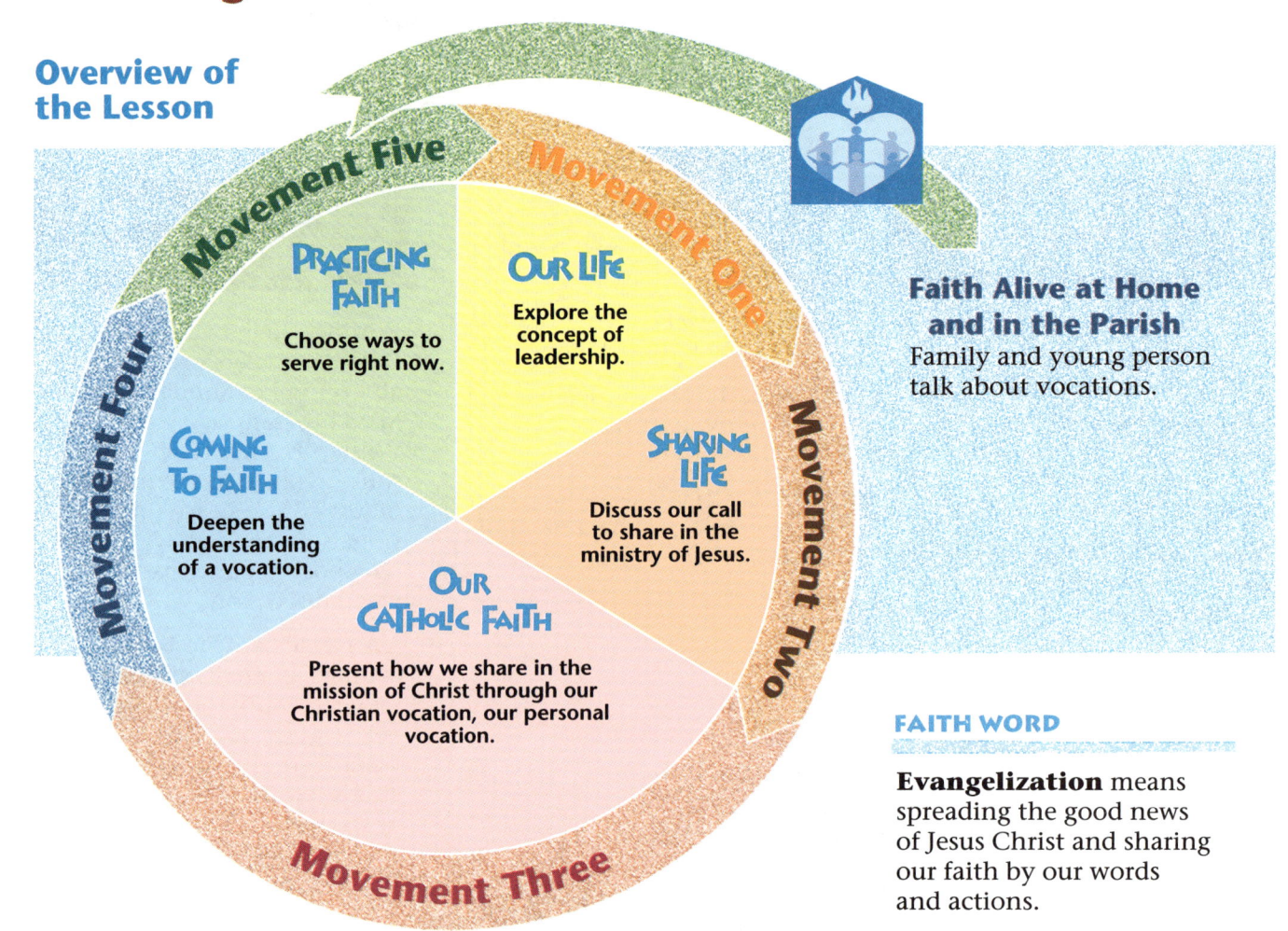

Overview of the Lesson

Movement Five — **Practicing Faith**: Choose ways to serve right now.

Movement One — **Our Life**: Explore the concept of leadership.

Movement Two — **Sharing Life**: Discuss our call to share in the ministry of Jesus.

Movement Three — **Our Catholic Faith**: Present how we share in the mission of Christ through our Christian vocation, our personal vocation.

Movement Four — **Coming To Faith**: Deepen the understanding of a vocation.

Faith Alive at Home and in the Parish
Family and young person talk about vocations.

FAITH WORD

Evangelization means spreading the good news of Jesus Christ and sharing our faith by our words and actions.

Teaching Hints

This lesson on ministry provides an excellent opportunity to develop awareness of the various lifestyles within the Church.

Encourage the young people to pray each day that they may know God's call in their lives, and to pray, too, for the grace needed to respond to this call.

Special-Needs Child

For those young people with auditory needs, make a special effort to face the group and make full use of facial expressions and gestures.

Visual Needs
- sandpaper letters of *Faith Word*

Auditory Needs
- preferential seating

Tactile–Motor Needs
- peers to assist in writing responses

Supplemental Resources

The Church as Sacrament (videostrip)
(from *Signs and Sacraments*)
Brown-ROA
2460 Kerper Blvd.
P.O. Box 539
Dubuque, IA 52004–0539
(1-800-922-7696)

Lesson Plan: Beginning

Objectives

To help the young people

■ know that we all are called to continue Jesus' mission;

■ appreciate that each has a specific Christian vocation;

■ recognize the many ways by which we can serve.

Focusing Prayer

Gather the group quietly, then pray together the prayer at the top of page 127.

Our Life

Reaching Out as a Parish

Introduce the *Our Life* story by writing the term *parish council* on the board. Discuss what it means and ask what the council does. Read the first paragraph to the group. Call on volunteers to share why they think so many young people and adults are inactive in the Church. Then have volunteers read aloud the next three paragraphs. Give the group time to think about the final question before calling for responses. Emphasize the mutual responsibility of all parish members to reach out to those who are no longer active in the Church. See the annotation.

Sharing Life

Determining Needs

Read aloud the questions under *Sharing Life*. Allow time for thoughtful response. You may wish to have the young people answer the last question in their faith journals. Invite volunteers to share responses. See the annotations.

19 We Share Jesus Christ's Priesthood
(Ministry)

Holy Spirit, help us to carry on the mission and ministry of Jesus.

Our Life

The parish council of St. Rose's Parish was upset to learn that so many young people between the ages of 18 and 30 and adults aged 30 to 45 seemed not to be active in the Church.

The council decided to invite these people back to the Church with a very special "Come Home for Easter!" celebration. Then they began to talk about who had the responsibility to organize the drive. This is what different members of the parish council said:

1. "Father Thomas is the priest and pastor. So he's the only one who can bring Catholics back to the Church. Of course, Sister Teresa and Mrs. Brown, the pastoral ministers, could help him."
2. "We're the people of the parish. Let's all work together with our ministers to build up our parish."

What answers do you think each of the following would give and why?

    Your parish council   You
    Your parents   Jesus

Help the young people realize that everyone in the parish has responsibility.

Sharing Life

Why do you think the Church needs priests, religious brothers and sisters, and lay pastoral ministers? Encourage the young people to see everyone is called to help serve.

Discuss how Baptism calls all Christians to share in the ministry of Jesus. In Baptism, we are all given the love and life of Jesus to share with all people.

What are some of the gifts that you can share with your parish community? Help the group name at least one gift for each member of the group.

Enrichment

Quick Response

Play an association game. Have the fifth graders complete the following service statements with the first thing that comes to mind.

I can serve:

■ an unpopular fifth grader by . . . .

■ a handicapped person by . . . .

■ my grandparents by . . . .

■ the people of my parish by . . . .

■ my family by . . . .

127

19

Lesson Plan: Middle

Our Catholic Faith

Faith Word

Write *evangelization* on the chalkboard or newsprint. Pronounce the word and have the group repeat it. Alert the young people to look for the word as they read.

Sharing in Jesus' Ministry

Ask what Jesus wanted his followers to do, and read aloud the opening paragraph under "Sharing Christ's Priestly Mission" on page 128. Call on volunteers to respond to your question.

Choose volunteers to read aloud the next four paragraphs. Have another volunteer write the meaning of vocation on the chalkboard or newsprint. Discuss how Confirmation and the Eucharist help us to live our vocations.

Ask what the priesthood of the faithful is, and read aloud the next two paragraphs. Discuss responses to the question. Emphasize that each one of us has a vocation to help carry on Jesus' mission.

Have the young people silently read the last paragraph on page 128. Then call attention to the *Faith Word* section at the top of page 129; have the group read the definition together. If possible, show some articles from the diocesan newspaper or parish bulletin that illustrate evangelization.

Materials needed: diocesan newspaper or parish bulletin

ENRICHMENT

Christians At Work

Have the young people work in pairs, using want-ad sections from your local newspaper. Ask each pair to read through the ads and mark those listing any special requirements for a position, such as "computer literacy a must," "data processing," "college degree," "teaching license required," "at least three years experience," or "must type 50+ words per minute." Have the pair cut out such ads, tape them to newsprint, then write beside each one how someone in that vocation might do God's work. Allow time for all the pairs to share ads and information.

Materials needed: newspaper want ads; scissors; tape; newsprint; pencils

128

OUR CATHOLIC FAITH

Sharing Christ's Priestly Mission

Before Jesus ascended into heaven, he said to his disciples, "Go, therefore, and make disciples of all nations, baptizing them in the name of the Father, and of the Son, and of the holy Spirit, teaching them to observe all that I have commanded you. And behold, I am with you always, until the end of the age."

Matthew 28:19–20

Stress the underlined text.

Jesus wants his work to be carried on by all who are baptized. By Baptism all of us share in the great mission of Jesus to bring about the reign of God. This means that each of us has been called to live a holy life of service in our Church and our world.

This call is named our *Christian vocation*. Our Christian vocation begins at Baptism, the first sacrament of initiation. At Baptism we receive God's life of grace and are called to bring this life to others.

In Confirmation we are sealed with the Gift of the Holy Spirit and strengthened to live our Christian faith with courage.

In the Eucharist we are given the daily help we need to carry out our vocation as Christians.

Through Baptism every Christian shares in Jesus' priestly mission. We call this the *priesthood of the faithful*. This means that every baptized person has a vocation to live as Jesus lived. As disciples, we share in the priesthood of Jesus Christ.

The priesthood of the faithful is not the same as the ordained priesthood. Through the priesthood of the faithful, each one of us helps to carry on Jesus' mission in the world. Our pope and bishops have written special letters to all Catholics, reminding us of our responsibility to share the good news of Jesus. This responsibility is called evangelization. Every Christian has many opportunities to share his or her faith with others.

128

Lesson Plan: Middle

Carrying on Jesus' Mission

Invite the young people to share what they would like to be when they grow up. Read aloud the first sentence under "Carrying on Jesus' Mission" on page 129. (You may wish to have representatives of the various vocations speak to the group about the ways they serve the Church and follow Jesus.) Point out that as baptized Catholics Jesus calls us to work for the reign of God in whatever vocation we follow. Then invite several young people to read aloud the descriptions of each of the vocations.

You might wish to tell your group about the three vows that members of religious communities publicly make to God. Religious men and women—religious priests, brothers, and sisters—make these perpetual vows of poverty, chastity, and obedience after long years of preparation and study. They do this not alone, but always in the context of their community.

Read aloud the last paragraph, and emphasize the key message about individual vocations. Share something important about your own vocation.

Carrying on Jesus' Mission

These are some of the vocations to which Jesus calls his people.

Married People: Jesus calls many women and men to the vocation of marriage and being parents.

Single People: Some people have a vocation to serve the Church as single, or non-married, men and women. By their daily words and actions, single people can show the world what it means to follow Jesus.

Ordained Ministers: Those who receive the sacrament of Holy Orders are called by Jesus to serve His Church as bishops, priests, and deacons. They share in Christ's priesthood in a special way.

FAITH WORD

Evangelization means spreading the good news of Jesus Christ and sharing our faith by our words and actions.

Religious: For many hundreds of years, men and women have joined religious communities as religious sisters, brothers, or priests. Religious serve our Church in parishes, hospitals, schools, and anywhere the good news needs to be preached. They make promises, or vows, of poverty, chastity, and obedience.

Laity: These are the single or married people in our Church. They serve our Church in many ways. Some dedicate years in serving as lay missionaries or as volunteers with religious communities in our country and around the world.

Pastoral Ministers: Pastoral ministers are religious brothers or sisters and lay people who have received special training to serve the needs of our Church. Some dedicate their entire lives to the tasks of parish leadership and education. Others serve by working with the poor and the homeless and for justice and peace.

Each of us has been called by Jesus to continue his mission of building up the reign of God on earth. All of us have a vocation to do something that only we can do.

129

ENRICHMENT

The Vowed Life

For many centuries religious men and women have professed what we have come to know as the *evangelical counsels*: poverty, chastity, and obedience. In Catholic tradition, they are called "evangelical" because they conform to the gospel call to "perfection" in following Jesus. All Christians are called to live the evangelical counsels. But some are called to witness in a more visible and prophetic way to these counsels. Poverty does not deny the good things of creation but challenges an over-possessiveness of natural goods. The virtue of chastity helps all Christians to live unselfishly and responsibly. For religious, chastity also means renouncing marriage as a personal option. Obedience emphasizes the Lord's call to serve others and to listen to true authority and not just ourselves.

129

19

Lesson Plan: End

Coming to Faith

Using Our Talents for Others

Read the first paragraph on page 130. Call on volunteers to respond. Read the rest of this section and allow time for the young people to reflect and respond. Discuss their responses. See the annotation.

Faith Summary

Use the annotations to review the *Faith Summary* on page 131. See if the young people can express, in their own words, what they have learned.

Practicing Faith

Choosing to Serve

Read aloud the first paragraph under *Practicing Faith*. Have the young people silently read the choices listed and reflect on their choice of service. Be prepared to offer suggestions if needed. Then read aloud the questions to help plan the group project.

Gather the group for prayer. Play and sing aloud "Reach Out," by Carey Landry (from the album *Hi God,* NALR). Have the group silently pray for God's help in carrying out its project. Then read together the prayer on page 130.

◆ Enrichment ◆

Preparing for Vocations

Remind the young people that they can start preparing right now for a future decision about their vocations. They can pray each day for direction; talk to adults in different walks of life; and develop their personal gifts.

Have each person make a "vocation cross" on which to write what his or her vocation might be and a prayer asking for God's help.

Materials needed: construction paper; markers; scissors

Evaluating Your Lesson

■ Do the young people know that we are called to continue Jesus' mission?

■ Do they realize that each has a special vocation?

■ Have they chosen to prepare for their vocations?

Coming to Faith

Tell what a vocation is.
What is the Christian vocation of a baptized person? *to live as Jesus lived.*

List the talents and abilities God has given you. How can you use them to help others? *Encourage awareness of talents and abilities, such as: getting along with others; listening well; making others happy; being sympathetic; etc.*

Practicing Faith

Work together in your group to choose one of the following ways you will serve others this week.

- Offer to visit the sick with a eucharistic minister.
- Offer to help your catechist.
- Volunteer to work in a community project for the poor or the homeless.
- Volunteer as a tutor for younger or handicapped children.
- Other: _____

Write the plan for your project.
What will you do?
How and when will your group do it?
Who will lead the project?

† Loving God, help us to live our Christian vocation in following Jesus.

Talk with your catechist about ways you and your family might use the "Faith Alive" pages. Encourage family members to support you in what you and your group plan to do. Then pray the prayer for vocations with your catechist and friends.

Optional Activities

Listening to Jesus (for use with page 127)

Invite the group to listen while you read the story of Martha and Mary from Luke 10:38–42.

After the reading ask, "What do you think Jesus is saying is most important for us to do—whether we are married or single, young or old?"

Emphasize that we need to spend time listening to Jesus (in prayer, in the Liturgy of the Word, in reading the Gospels). Explain that if we listen, our service to others will be more meaningful.

Materials needed: Bible

Spreading the Good News (for use with page 128)

Share with the group this story about Saint René Goupil:

René Goupil was a young Frenchman who had studied medicine. He wanted to help in the work of evangelization among the Native Americans in the New World.

In 1638 he went to Quebec, where he worked for four years. During this time, Goupil became a Jesuit brother. Then, while on a journey with a Jesuit priest, Father Isaac Jogues, he was captured by the Iroquois and killed near Albany, New York. René Goupil was the first of the North American martyrs.

After the story, discuss with the young people why they think people like René Goupil are willing to risk their lives to serve others.

You may wish to follow up this story by recalling the life or showing a video about someone who has admirably carried out Jesus' priestly mission—for example Mother Teresa, Jean Donovan, Archbishop Oscar Romero, or Dorothy Day.

Materials needed: appropriate book or video

Vocation Posters (for use with page 129)

Have the young people make posters illustrating the vocations their parents are pursuing. Help them to understand that mothers and fathers who remain at home to care for young children have chosen to do so as their vocation. Display the posters around the room.

Materials needed: posterboard; crayons and/or markers

A Vocation Illustration (for use with page 129)

Have the young people make drawings, paintings, or collages that illustrate the vocations they think Jesus might be calling them to live.

Materials needed: construction paper; newsprint; magazines; scissors; glue; paints; markers

FAITH ALIVE AT HOME AND IN THE PARISH

In this lesson your fifth grader has deepened his or her understanding that each of us has a particular vocation to build up the reign of God on earth. Ask your fifth grader to describe the different vocations presented in the lesson. It is not too early for fifth graders to consider what their special vocation might be. Encourage your fifth grader to pray and read about this vocation and to talk to those who follow it. Then discuss how she or he can prepare now for a life of service to others. Use this list to help you.

- Celebrate the sacraments often so as to live each day better as a disciple of Jesus.
- Pray each day that the Holy Spirit will guide you and give you courage to accept the vocation God has for you.
- Read the Bible frequently.
- Spend time trying to understand what is in this religion book so that you can explain it to others.
- Listen carefully to the homilies at Mass and the faith stories told by your family.
- Read the lives of your favorite saints.

✝ Family Prayer

Pray about a vocation you admire. Talk to those who follow this vocation. Say this prayer to help you know and follow your own vocation.

Holy Spirit, help me to know my special vocation in carrying on the mission of Jesus.

Learn by heart Faith Summary

To what does Jesus call each of us?
- Jesus calls each of us to a specific vocation to carry on his priestly mission.

What is the meaning of evangelization?
- Evangelization means spreading the good news of Jesus Christ and sharing our faith by our words and deeds.

What kinds of vocations are there?
- There are many vocations—married, ordained, religious, and single life. We are all called to carry on Jesus' mission.

Working for Justice and Peace

Select and write one way you will serve others by working for justice and peace.

_____
_____
_____
_____

Peace in the world starts with me.

Play by the rules.

Give of your time. Help the homeless.

Review

Go over the *Faith Summary* together and encourage your fifth grader to learn it by heart, especially the first two statements. Then have him or her go over the *Review*. The answers to numbers 1–4 appear on page 216. The response to number 5 will show how well your fifth grader understands the vocation we have right now through our Baptism to work for God's reign. When the *Review* is completed, go over it together.

1. Circle true (**T**) or false (**F**).

   We must be ordained in order to carry on Jesus' mission.   T   **(F)**

   The laity includes men and women who are single and married.   **(T)**   F

   All baptized Catholics are called to work for God's reign.   **(T)**   F

2. Our call to live a holy life of service is called our _vocation_.

3. Our share in Jesus Christ's priestly mission is called _the priesthood of the faithful_.

4. Spreading the good news of Jesus by our words and deeds is called _evangelization_.

5. How will you work for God's reign right now?

   _____
   _____
   _____

FAMILY SCRIPTURE MOMENT

Gather and share what acts of service we do for one another in our family. **Listen** to a Last Supper story.

So when he had washed their feet [and] put his garments back on and reclined at table again, he said to them, "Do you realize what I have done for you? If I, therefore, the master and teacher, have washed your feet, you ought to wash one another's feet. I have given you a model to follow, so that as I have done for you, you should also do. Amen, amen, I say to you, no slave is greater than his master nor any messenger greater than the one who sent him. If you understand this, blessed are you if you do it."

John 13:12, 14–17

Share Imagine you are in this gospel scene. What would you learn from Jesus' washing of your feet?

Consider for family enrichment:

■ Jesus teaches his disciples the joy of service in ministry. The story of Jesus washing the feet of his disciples has become a treasured ritual during Holy Week.

■ We are called to be "foot washers" who are willing to serve others even in simple ways.

Reflect and **Decide** What feelings does this gospel passage arouse in us? How will we help one another to put Jesus' example into practice in our family? in our parish?

132

20 CELEBRATING LENT

CATECHISM OF THE CATHOLIC CHURCH

The Theme of This Chapter Corresponds with Paragraph 1164

For the Catechist: Spiritual and Catechetical Development

Our Life

Saint Vincent's soup kitchen ran an ad proclaiming a "Special Lenten Offer to Christians." It said: "Make a worthwhile investment with no earthly returns. You will not receive a tax deduction. Your name will not appear in the newspaper. You may not be thanked by our clients. But your investment of time and care will be rewarded."

Ask yourself:

■ How might I respond to this ad?

Sharing Life

What Lenten "investments" will help you to prepare for Easter?

Our Catholic Faith

Prayer, fasting, and almsgiving are the traditional Lenten practices by which the Church has prepared itself to commemorate the passion, death, and the resurrection of Jesus. Almsgiving not only opens our hearts to those not as well off as we are, but also effectively unites us with the poverty of Christ, who advised the rich young man, "Sell all that you have and distribute it to the poor, and you will have a treasure in heaven" (Luke 18:22).

Lent is also a time to arm ourselves against temptation as Jesus did when He prayed and fasted in the desert. It is a time to seek forgiveness and be reconciled with our God.

Lent is a time for us to pray with and for those persons preparing for Baptism. It is a retreat time for us to use wisely so that we may come to a deeper sense of who we are, what we believe, and why we support others who are preparing to join us as members of the Church in our parish.

Coming to Faith

What is Lent a time for in your life?

Practicing Faith

How will you encourage your fifth graders to observe Lent?

Teaching Resources

Teaching Hints

This lesson aims to help the young people realize that they are called by Baptism to share their food and possessions with those in need. Encourage them to be generous during this season of Lent. Besides giving material donations, urge the young people to think of other ways they can reach out and help others.

Special-Needs Child

Find out if any of your fifth graders are required to take medication. Be informed of possible side effects.

Visual Needs

■ large-print copy of prayer service readings

Auditory Needs

■ headphones and recorded Scripture story

Tactile–Motor Needs

■ nonslip-fabric desk covering

Supplemental Resources

"The Road to Jerusalem" (video) (from *Following Jesus Through the Church Year*)
Twenty-Third Publications
P.O. Box 180
Mystic, CT 06355
(1-800-321-0411)

133A

Lesson Plan: Beginning

OBJECTIVES

To help the young people

- know that Lent is a time to prepare for Easter;
- appreciate more deeply the new life they received at Baptism;
- participate in a Lenten prayer service.

Focusing Prayer

Greet the young people and tell them that today we will learn how we can follow Jesus more closely during Lent. Gather together and pray the prayer of petition at the top of page 133.

Our Life

Looking at Reports

Read aloud slowly and with emphasis the first paragraph under *Our Life*. Have a volunteer read the second paragraph aloud. Invite several young people to respond to the questions that follow. You might like to start the discussion of the second question by responding to it yourself.

Sharing Life

Sharing with Others

Conduct a quick opinion survey of the group using the first set of questions under *Sharing Life*. Have several individuals explain their responses.

Read aloud each set of remaining questions. Allow time for the young people to respond thoughtfully. Encourage volunteers to share their ideas with the group.

Call attention to the pictures. Ask the young people what they think is happening in each picture.

ENRICHMENT

A Lenten Collage

Have the group find magazine and newspaper pictures of people who are without food, health care, homes, or peace. Make a Lenten collage of these pictures to remind the young people of where they will find Jesus in today's world.

Materials needed: magazines; newspapers; construction paper; scissors; glue or paste

---

20 Celebrating Lent

Jesus, help us to follow you this Lent so that we may live in Easter joy.

Our Life

A report tells us that during one year the average person in the United States eats about:

- 144 pounds of meat
- 81 pounds of vegetables
- 63 pounds of sugar
- 22 pounds of cheese
- 18 pounds of ice cream

It is also reported that during an average year people spend about:

- 26 billion dollars on television products
- 8.6 trillion dollars on clothes
- 20 billion quarters on video games

Accept individual responses.
What do you think about this report?
Note: You might like to begin discussion by responding yourself.
Which of your possessions is the last you would give away? Why?

Sharing Life

Discuss with your group whether there are people who have:

- not enough food and things?
- just enough food and things?
- more than enough food and things?

Why are things the way they are, and what can be done about them? Encourage individual responses.
Do you believe that Jesus wants us to share with others, especially the poor? Why or why not? Yes; because Jesus shared with others

133

Lesson Plan: Middle

Our Catholic Faith

Jesus' Temptation

Have volunteers read aloud the Scripture story under "Jesus In the Desert" on page 134.

Afterwards engage the young people in a discussion of the event. Invite several volunteers to tell how Jesus was tempted not to do God's will. Challenge the young people to tell why they think Jesus was tempted in this way. Have them discuss how they think Jesus' temptation prepared Him for preaching the good news.

This would be an opportune time to point out that temptation itself is never sinful. Explain that we must freely choose to give in to the temptation for it to become sinful. Also help the young people to see that temptation is often "masked" as something good. Encourage them to pray to the Holy Spirit for guidance in times of temptation.

Lead the young people in a discussion of how they might be tempted to show off their talents instead of using them to help others; endanger their lives and those of others by taking unnecessary risks to impress people; consider things other than God to be more important to their happiness.

ENRICHMENT

Temptation Tips

Ask the fifth graders to think of ways people can fight off temptation rather than giving in to it. For example, one person might suggest counting from one to twenty-five; another might suggest reciting a favorite prayer; a third might say to focus on a field of flowers or a beach; and a fourth might suggest reciting the alphabet backward! Each suggestion would indeed take one's mind off the temptation for the moment, and would be a better choice than just giving in easily. Invite the fifth graders to illustrate their thoughts with poetry, music, or art.

Materials needed: paper; pencils; crayons and markers

134

OUR CATHOLIC FAITH

Jesus in the Desert

Before Jesus began to preach the good news of God's love to the people, he went into the desert to prepare himself. After many days Jesus was very hungry, and the devil tempted him by saying that if he was God's Son, he should turn the stones into bread.

Jesus must have looked at the rocks around him. Some of them may even have been shaped like loaves of bread. How easy it would have been to hold a rock in his hands and turn it into a hot, good-smelling loaf of bread.

But Jesus told the devil that a person does not live only on bread, but needs every word that God speaks.

The devil next took Jesus to Jerusalem. Setting him on the highest point of the Temple, the devil told Jesus to throw himself down, and if he was God's Son, God would send angels to hold him up so that even his feet would not be hurt.

Jesus told the devil that the Scripture says, "You shall not put the Lord, your God, to the test."

The devil finally took Jesus to a very high mountain, and showing him all the kingdoms of the world, said he would give Jesus all this if Jesus would kneel down and worship him.

Jesus told Satan to go away! The Scripture says that no one but God should be worshiped.

Then the devil left Jesus.
Based on Matthew 4:1–11

After this, Jesus went out and began to preach the good news to all the people.

What do you learn from this story of Jesus being tempted?

Stress the underlined text.

A Time for Preparing

During the season of Lent we prepare for Easter. Lent helps us to understand the meaning of the death and resurrection of Jesus. We remember that in our Baptism we die to sin and rise to new life in Jesus. During Lent we try to prepare ourselves to live better the new life we received in Baptism. We also pray for those who are about to be baptized.

Sometimes we spend too much time eating, shopping, and playing games. We become so busy with our possessions that we can forget about God and others.

134

Lesson Plan: Middle

Preparing for Easter

Ask, "For what does Lent prepare us?" Then read aloud the first paragraph under "A Time for Preparing" on page 134. Seek and discuss responses to your previous question. Have the young people silently read the remaining four paragraphs. Stress that Lent is a time when we try to grow in unselfish love by doing things for others without expecting something in return. Initiate a discussion by having the group tell how our Lent is like Jesus' time in the desert.

Give a simple introduction to the RCIA (Rite of Christian Initiation of Adults). Explain that, during Lent, the parish community continues the preparation of those who are getting ready to enter fully into the life of Jesus' community, the Church. After a long period of prayer and instruction, the catechumens (those preparing for the sacraments of initiation) receive the sacraments of initiation during the Easter Vigil. You may wish to invite some parish sponsors of catechumens to speak to the group.

You may wish to use pages 45–46 in the activity books for *Coming to God's Life*.

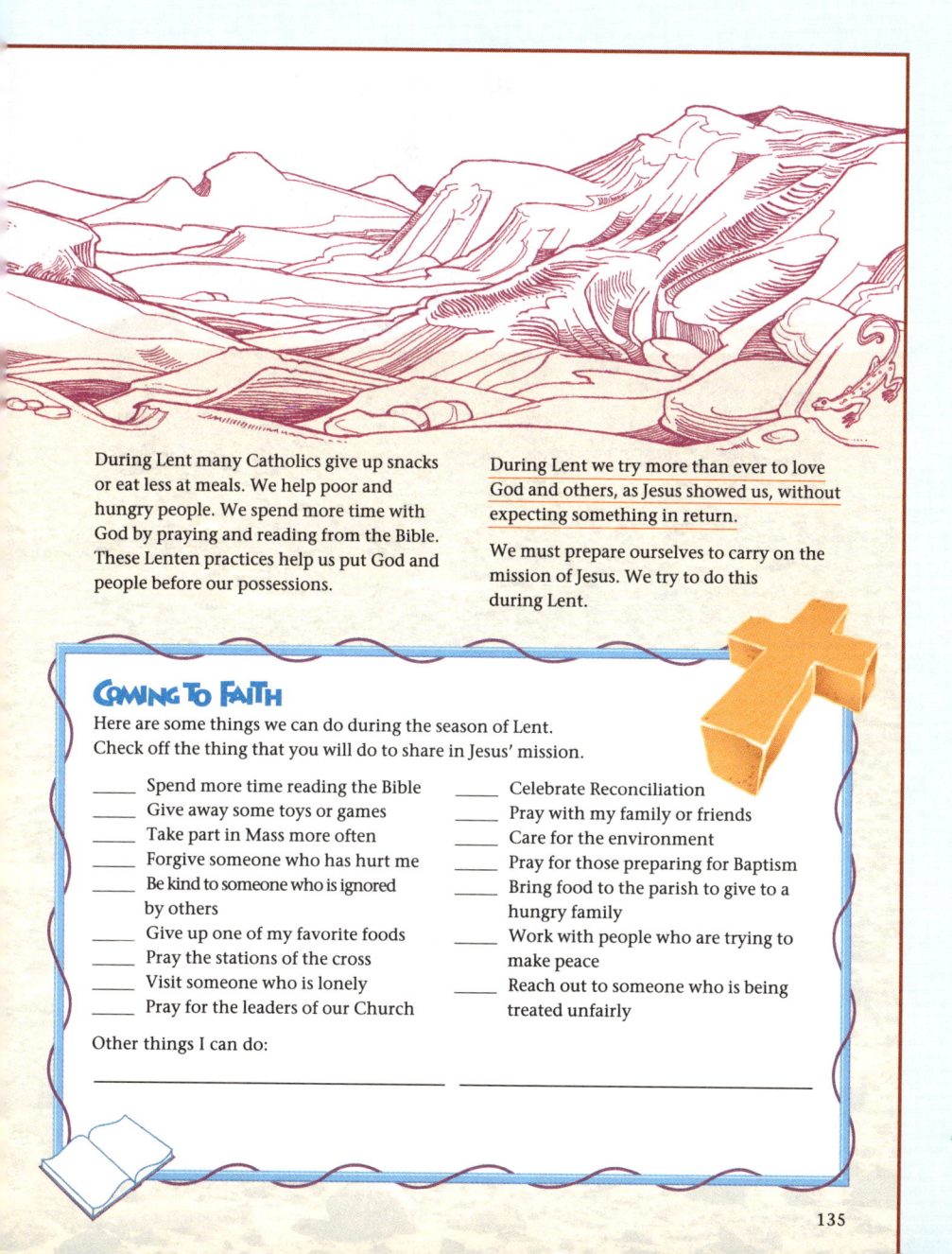

During Lent many Catholics give up snacks or eat less at meals. We help poor and hungry people. We spend more time with God by praying and reading from the Bible. These Lenten practices help us put God and people before our possessions.

During Lent we try more than ever to love God and others, as Jesus showed us, without expecting something in return.

We must prepare ourselves to carry on the mission of Jesus. We try to do this during Lent.

Coming To Faith

Here are some things we can do during the season of Lent. Check off the thing that you will do to share in Jesus' mission.

____ Spend more time reading the Bible
____ Give away some toys or games
____ Take part in Mass more often
____ Forgive someone who has hurt me
____ Be kind to someone who is ignored by others
____ Give up one of my favorite foods
____ Pray the stations of the cross
____ Visit someone who is lonely
____ Pray for the leaders of our Church
____ Celebrate Reconciliation
____ Pray with my family or friends
____ Care for the environment
____ Pray for those preparing for Baptism
____ Bring food to the parish to give to a hungry family
____ Work with people who are trying to make peace
____ Reach out to someone who is being treated unfairly

Other things I can do:
_____   _____

135

ENRICHMENT

Sharing the Mission

Have the fifth graders work together to make a large cardboard cross and cover it with wood-grain adhesive paper. Have each person write on a small piece of paper one thing he or she will do during Lent to share in Jesus' mission. Tape the pieces of paper to the cross, then make it the centerpiece of the prayer service.

Materials needed: cardboard; wood-grain adhesive paper; scissors; paper; tape

135

Lesson Plan: End

Coming to Faith

Living Our Baptism

Have the young people read the activity on page 135 to explore particular ways they can prepare during Lent to better live their Baptisms. Explain the checklist and allow ample time for completing the activity.

Practicing Faith

Celebrating a Prayer Service

Take a few moments to go over "A Prayer Service for Lent." Choose a prayer leader and a Scripture reader, and give them time to prepare. While they are preparing, practice the opening and closing hymns with the rest of the group.

When all are ready, celebrate the prayer service. Observe a short time of silence after the gospel reading. Decide together what your Lenten acts will be and have the young people write them in their textbooks. Have everyone read together the final prayer and then what they have written.

EVALUATING YOUR LESSON

- Do the young people know how Catholics prepare for Easter?
- Do they appreciate that Lenten practices help us to better live our Baptisms?
- Have they decided how to carry on Jesus' mission?

PRACTICING FAITH
A Prayer Service for Lent
† Gather in a circle.

Opening Hymn
"Come Back to Me" (Hosea) or "Earthen Vessels"

Prayer
Leader: Jesus, we come together to begin our preparation for Easter. During the season of Lent, we want to renew our desire to live the way you taught us.

Gospel
Leader: A reading from the holy gospel according to Mark.
(Read Mark 1:12–15)

Time for Reflection
Think about the Gospel reading. Read over the list of Lenten practices you checked on page 135. Now discuss together quietly what your group might do together to join in Jesus' mission this Lent.

Then pray the following prayer together.

Jesus, during these forty days of Lent, help us to follow you. Help us to live more fully the new life we received in Baptism. As your disciples, we have decided to do the following acts:

We will pray more by _____

We will act as peacemakers by _____

We will serve the poor and hungry by _____

Closing Hymn
"Let There Be Peace on Earth" or "Prayer of Saint Francis"

Talk with your catechist about ways you and your family might use the "Faith Alive" pages together. Share with family members ways your family can pray, fast, and give to the poor.

Optional Activities

Role-Playing (for use with page 134)

Invite the young people to role-play what they would do in the following circumstance:

You have not had anything to eat all day. Someone offers you a candy bar if you will tell the principal a "little white lie" to keep him or her out of trouble.

Have the young people discuss why an offer like this is called a temptation.

Sharing Views (for use with page 134)

Have the young people write one paragraph telling why Jesus might have been tempted as part of His preparation to go out to preach the good news.

Play any Lenten recording quietly in the background as the group works.

Materials needed: paper; pens or pencils; music source

A Prayer for Help (for use with page 135)

Gather the young people at the prayer table and pray together:

Leader: You know what it is to be tempted. Help us to turn away from the false gods of greed, envy, and selfishness. For this we pray.

All: Lord, hear our prayer.

End with the Sign of the Cross.

Lenten Cartoons (for use with page 135)

Challenge the young people to draw three- or four-panel comic strips illustrating how they might resist a particular temptation during Lent. Have the cartoonists display and explain their work.

Materials needed: drawing paper; crayons or markers

FAITH ALIVE
AT HOME AND IN THE PARISH

This lesson has explored more deeply the significance of the Lenten season in the life of a Christian. Your fifth grader has learned that Lent is a time to strengthen our hearts and wills against temptation as Jesus did when He prayed and fasted in the desert. Prayer, fasting, and almsgiving are traditional Lenten practices to help us renew the gift of faith that we first received in Baptism. Besides fasting on Ash Wednesday and Good Friday, Catholics also abstain from meat on these days and the other Fridays of Lent.

Your child has also learned that during Lent we join in prayer with those preparing for Baptism. We share our beliefs and give our support to people preparing for membership in our Church.

You might want to discuss with your family how you will deepen your own practice of prayer, fasting, and almsgiving this Lent.

Praying with the Bible

Prayers do not have to be long and wordy. The Bible often gives us short prayers that are very powerful. For example: "Lord, you know everything; you know that I love you." (John 21:17)

Find other short prayers in your Bible, such as John 20:28, Luke 22:42, Psalm 23:1, Psalm 34:1, Isaiah 6:3.

Write your favorite short prayer here.

Learn by heart Faith Summary

What does Lent prepare us to do?
- Lent prepares us to enter more fully into the passion, death, and resurrection of Jesus.

What do we do during Lent?
- During Lent we try to love God and others without expecting something in return.

Review

Go over the *Faith Summary* together and encourage your fifth grader to learn it by heart, especially the first statement. Then have him or her do the *Review*. The answers to numbers 1–4 appear on page 216. The response to number 5 will indicate your child's growing understanding of the Lenten challenge. When the *Review* is completed, go over it together.

Circle the letter beside the correct response.

1. Before Jesus began preaching he
   a. went into the desert.
   b. was tempted by Satan.
   c. fasted from food.
   d. all of the above

2. Satan tempted Jesus to
   a. eat stones.
   b. turn stones into bread.
   c. turn bread into stones.
   d. turn Satan into stone.

3. Satan tempted Jesus to
   a. worship him instead of God.
   b. leave him.
   c. fight with the angels.
   d. none of the above

4. We rise to new life in Jesus
   a. during Lent.
   b. in Baptism.
   c. in the desert.
   d. when we pray.

5. Tell one way you can put God and others before possessions.

   _____
   _____
   _____

FAMILY SCRIPTURE MOMENT

Gather and discuss what you think it means to live the truth. Then **Listen** to a Lenten story.

So Pilate . . . summoned Jesus and said to him, "Are you the King of the Jews?" Jesus answered, "My kingdom does not belong to this world. If my kingdom belonged to this world, my attendants [would] be fighting to keep me from being handed over to the Jews. . . ." So Pilate said to him, "Then you are a king?" Jesus answered, "You say I am a king. For this I was born and for this I came into the world, to testify to the truth. Everyone who belongs to the truth listens to my voice."
John 18:33, 36–37

Share why you associate Jesus with the truth and what it means to belong to the truth of Jesus.

Consider for family enrichment:
■ Although Pilate's question is intended as an insult, Jesus responds by telling the truth about his kingdom and identity.
■ By his example, Jesus teaches us to be truthful, courageous, and nonviolent in confronting sin or evil.

Reflect How can we show during Lent that we are people who "belong to the truth"?

Decide Pray together: Jesus, may we use each day of Lent as an opportunity to become more truthful, courageous, and nonviolent in opposing evil.

21 Celebrating Easter

CATECHISM OF THE CATHOLIC CHURCH

The Theme of This Chapter Corresponds with Paragraph 1165

For the Catechist: Spiritual and Catechetical Development

Our Life

Have you ever placed your hopes in a leader or mentor and been disappointed? When? Who was it?

Have you ever placed your hopes in a leader or mentor and been rewarded? When? Who was it?

Ask yourself:

- Who among these leaders or mentors has seemed to fail but later triumphed?

Sharing Life

Which of these experiences was most rewarding?

Which came closest to the experience that the friends of Jesus had in His leadership?

Our Catholic Faith

When Jesus entered Jerusalem on the first Palm Sunday, He was triumphantly hailed as king. Six days later, as He hung on the cross, the words "Jesus of Nazareth, King of the Jews" were displayed above His head.

Especially during the Easter Triduum, we too hail Jesus as the King of Kings and Lord of Lords. We honor Him as the eternal embodiment of the kingdom of God. In His life, death, and glorious resurrection, Jesus depicts for us the meaning of the reign of God in our lives.

We celebrate Easter, the greatest feast of the Church year, with songs and bells, lilies and alleluias. We extend our liturgical celebration by rededicating ourselves to the cause of God's kingdom come and the salvation of all humanity.

Coming to Faith

What Easter hopes will you pray for and act on this year?

Practicing Faith

How will you encourage your group to celebrate Easter?

Teaching Resources

Teaching Hints

This lesson centers around the rich liturgical experiences of Holy Week. Encourage the young people to participate in the celebrations of the liturgy during the Easter Triduum. Review your parish Holy Week schedule with the group.

Special-Needs Child

The process of shared Christian praxis encourages maximum interaction and dialogue. Mainstreamed young people can find success in such an environment of openness and dialogue.

Visual Needs

- large-print prayer readings

Auditory Needs

- preferential seating for role-playing

Tactile–Motor Needs

- helper for movement in prayer services

Supplemental Resources

The Risen Lord (video)
(from *Jesus of Nazareth*)
Vision Video
2030 Wentz Church Road
PO Box 540
Worcester, PA 19490
(1-800-523-0226)

The Book of Luke: Easter (video)
(from *The New Media Bible* series)
Mass Media Ministries
2116 North Charles St.
Baltimore, MD 21218
(1-800-523-0226)

Lesson Plan: Beginning

OBJECTIVES

To help the young people

- know the celebrations of Holy Week;
- understand more deeply the paschal mystery;
- celebrate an Easter prayer service.

Focusing Prayer

Create an environment of Easter joy. If possible, display flowers and play happy music as the young people gather. When all are settled, pray together the prayer at the top of page 139.

Our Life

Giving New Life

Read aloud the story under *Our Life* on page 139. Then ask the follow-up question and discuss the story. Read the direction after the question and have volunteers share their responses.

Sharing Life

The Joy of New Life

Ask the first *Sharing Life* question and elicit from the group their experiences of new life. After all volunteers have shared their stories, ask the second question and discuss responses.

---

21 Celebrating Easter

Alleluia! Jesus is risen and is still with us. Alleluia, alleluia!

Our Life

It was a forgotten patch of earth almost lost among the dingy apartments. Full of weeds, garbage, and abandoned junk, it was just another piece of ugliness in this very tough part of the city. But not to Mr. Catelli. He had a dream. This plot of earth could live again. So one day Mr. Catelli went out and began to work.

Some neighbors saw what he was doing and offered to help. Soon the garbage was packed into bags and left for the sanitation trucks. Young people in the neighborhood started to drop by to help with the weeding. Soon Mr. Catelli was laboriously turning the soil and adding loam. By now the whole neighborhood was involved, and Mr. Catelli had gifts of seeds, plants, and even trees. The planting began. "Now what?" the children asked. "Now we wait and water and let God work," Mr. Catelli answered.

Spring came and the lot was now a park full of flowers and grass and young trees. "Our park is beautiful!" everyone said. Mr. Catelli smiled. What was dead had come back to life.

What do you learn from this story of Mr. Catelli? *What seemed dead can come back to life, and can give joy and hope.*

Name some things that give you new life. *Encourage specific responses.*

Sharing Life

Have you ever helped something that seemed dead have new life? Tell about it. *Accept individual responses.*

Why are these experiences so full of surprise and joy? *Because they bring hope where there seemed to be none.*

ENRICHMENT

A New Life Challenge

Talk to the group about becoming involved in an environmental project this spring. Explain that our belief in Christ's resurrection challenges us to try to bring new life into every situation in our lives. Working to protect and nurture our planet is truly a new life challenge.

Have the group choose a project. Then help them to devise a plan and carry it out over the remainder of the school year.

139

Lesson Plan: Middle

Our Catholic Faith

A Parade for Jesus

Ask, "What is Passion, or Palm, Sunday?" Then read aloud the first two paragraphs under "Honoring Christ, Our Savior" on page 140. Call on volunteers to respond to your previous question.

Invite a volunteer to read aloud the gospel story of Jesus' triumphant entry into Jerusalem. Ask another volunteer to read aloud the paragraph after the story. Ask what happened to Jesus on the first Passion Sunday, and discuss responses. Invite the young people to speculate about how they might have felt and what they might have done had they been in the crowd that day in Jerusalem. Have the group silently read the last paragraph in this section, then ask the group members how we celebrate Passion Sunday.

Our Catholic Faith

Honoring Christ, Our Savior

The Sunday before Easter Sunday is called Passion, or Palm, Sunday. Passion Sunday is the first day of Holy Week. It prepares us for the Easter Triduum, the three days that begin on Holy Thursday evening and end with Evening Prayer on Easter Sunday.

On Passion Sunday we remember that Jesus and his friends went to the city of Jerusalem shortly before his arrest and crucifixion. The Gospel of Mark tells us the story as follows:

Jesus, riding on a donkey, came into the city of Jerusalem. As Jesus rode by, people spread their cloaks before him on the road. Others cut branches off the trees and laid these on the road in front of Jesus. Others followed Jesus, shouting,

"Blessed is he who comes in the name of the Lord! . . .
Hosanna in the highest!"
Based on Mark 11:1–11

Jesus came into the city of Jerusalem in triumph. He was honored and welcomed by the crowds. But within a few days, he would suffer, be crucified, and die.

On Passion Sunday, palm branches are blessed and given to us. We walk in procession into the church, singing and waving palm branches to honor Jesus.

The Easter Triduum

During the Easter Triduum we celebrate the paschal mystery. The word *paschal* means "passing over" or "passover." The paschal mystery is a remembering and celebrating of the events of Jesus' "passing" through suffering and death to new life in his resurrection.

On Holy Thursday evening we celebrate the Mass of the Lord's Supper. We remember that Jesus gave us the gift of himself in the Eucharist.

On Good Friday in the Celebration of the Lord's Passion, we remember that Jesus was crowned with thorns, suffered, and died on the cross for our sins.

On Holy Saturday night we celebrate the Easter Vigil. We await the resurrection of Jesus and remember that we are baptized into his death and resurrection. On this night we welcome new members into the Church through the sacraments of initiation.

On Easter Sunday we celebrate the resurrection of Jesus and our new life in Christ. The Easter Triduum concludes with Evening Prayer on this day. Then all during the Easter season, we remember how Jesus Christ brought us the fullness of God's life and love.

Lesson Plan: Middle

The Easter Triduum

Read aloud the first paragraph under "The Easter Triduum." Call on several young people to explain what is meant by the paschal mystery. Then have volunteers read the next four paragraphs on page 140 that describe the Easter Triduum. Have everyone underline in the text what we remember and celebrate during this most important time of the Church year. Then recall that the word *triduum* means "three days." The three days begin with the Evening Mass of the Lord's Supper on Holy Thursday and concludes with Evening Prayer on Easter Sunday evening.

Emphasize that the Easter season does not last just one day. It starts on Easter Sunday and ends on Pentecost Sunday. It is a season of fifty days. In fact, *Pentecost* means "fiftieth."

Recall with the group that the catechumens in the RCIA program celebrate the sacraments of initiation during the Easter Vigil and so are fully initiated into the life of the risen Christ and the Church community.

Coming to Faith

Below is a list of some important celebrations of the Easter Triduum. Tell what we remember and celebrate during each. Write how you can take part in each celebration.

Evening Mass of the Lord's Supper
We celebrate *the Mass of the Lord's Supper. We remember that Jesus gave us the gift of himslf in the Eucharist.*
I can _____

Celebration of the Lord's Passion
We celebrate *and remember that Jesus was crowned with thorns, suffered, and died on the cross for our sins.*
I can _____

Easter Vigil
We celebrate *as we await the resurrection of Jesus, and we remember that we are baptized into His death and resurrection.*
I can _____

ENRICHMENT

Easter Dramatizations

Invite volunteers to do dramatic readings of the Easter accounts in Matthew 28:1–10 and John 20:1–18.

Explain that a dramatic reading usually involves a narrator and different readers for each voice part. Tell readers that they do not act the scene out physically, but try to convey the actions and feelings with their voices only. Compare this to the difference between radio and television dramas.

Lesson Plan: End

Coming to Faith

Celebrating the Easter Triduum

Explain the *Coming to Faith* chart. Let the young people know that thoughtful and specific responses are called for. Play quiet background music while they work.

Involve the entire group in a sharing of the "We celebrate" and "I can" statements. Tell the group how you will celebrate one of the holy days.

Practicing Faith

Participating in an Easter Celebration

Take a few moments to go over "An Easter Celebration" on page 142. Select the reader and the narrator, and have the rest of the young people form two groups. Have the young people silently familiarize themselves with the material before the celebration is actually conducted. Gather around the prayer table and have the young people silently reflect on what they are about to celebrate. Then have the leader stand before the prayer table and begin the service. Take time for quiet reflection after the presentation of the Easter story and after the renewal of the baptismal promises. End the celebration by having the group sing an appropriate Easter hymn.

Materials needed: bowl; holy water

Evaluating Your Lesson

- Do the young people know what we recall in Holy Week?
- Do they appreciate Jesus' sacrifice of Himself to bring us new life?
- Have they decided how they will celebrate Easter?

Practicing Faith
An Easter Celebration

Opening Prayer
Leader: Jesus, we have prepared ourselves to share in the joy of your resurrection. Open our hearts to receive your new life.

An Easter Story
Group 1: Are you the only visitor in Jerusalem who does not know what things happened there to Jesus of Nazareth?

Group 2: What things?

Group 1: We had hoped that Jesus was the one who would set Israel free. But he was crucified. After his death, some women in our group went to the tomb and told us, "He is alive!"

Group 2: How slow to believe you are! Wasn't it necessary for the Messiah to suffer these things?

Narrator: Jesus explained many other things to them. As they came near the village toward which they were going, Jesus acted as if he were going on.

Group 1: Stay with us. It is getting dark.

Narrator: Jesus sat down to eat with them, took the bread, and said the blessing; then he broke the bread and gave it to them. Their eyes were opened and they recognized Jesus. Jesus then disappeared from their sight.

Based on Luke 24:13–32

Renewal of Baptismal Promises
Leader: Do you reject Satan?
All: I do.

Leader: And all his works?
All: I do.

Leader: And all his empty promises?
All: I do.

Leader: Do you believe in God, the Father Almighty, creator of heaven and earth?
All: I do.

Leader: Do you believe in Jesus Christ, God's only Son, our Lord, who was born of the Virgin Mary, was crucified, died and was buried, rose from the dead, and is now seated at the right hand of the Father?
All: I do.

Leader: Do you believe in the Holy Spirit, the holy Catholic Church, the communion of saints, the forgiveness of sins, the resurrection of the body, and life everlasting?
All: I do.

Blessing with Holy Water
All come to a prayer table on which a small bowl containing holy water has been placed. All bless themselves with the holy water by making the sign of the cross to remember the gift of new life given in Baptism.

Optional Activities

A Bible Story (for use with page 139)

Have three volunteers prepare to role-play Mark 14:3–9, "Jesus Is Anointed at Bethany," for the group:

> When he was in Bethany reclining at table in the house of Simon the leper, a woman came with an alabaster jar of perfumed oil, costly genuine spikenard. She broke the alabaster jar and poured it on his head. There were some who were indignant. "Why has there been this waste of perfumed oil? It could have been sold for more than three hundred days' wages and the money given to the poor." They were infuriated with her.
>
> Jesus said, "Let her alone. Why do you make trouble for her? She has done a good thing for me. The poor you will always have with you, and whenever you wish you can do good to them, but you will not always have me. She has done what she could. She has anticipated anointing my body for burial. Amen, I say to you, whenever the gospel is proclaimed to the whole world, what she has done will be told in memory of her."

A Parade for Jesus (for use with page 140)

Form an impromptu parade behind two leaders carrying aloft a large picture or statue of Jesus, or a cross, or a Bible. Sing "Are Not Our Hearts," by Carey Landry (NALR) or any other spirited Jesus song. Accompany the song with any available instruments (piano, tambourine, or drums). Place the Jesus symbol on the prayer table. Then in Jesus' honor, pray the Our Father.

Materials needed: picture or statue of Jesus, cross, or Bible; music source; instruments

Honoring Jesus (for use with page 140)

Invite the young people to imagine themselves with Jesus at one of the events in the Easter Triduum. Have them place themselves in the scene. What do they see? hear? What do they do? What do they say to Jesus? Ask them to write their thoughts in their faith journals.

Materials needed: faith journals; pens or pencils

The Paschal Mystery (for use with page 141)

Invite the young people to illustrate one of the events of the paschal mystery. Discuss and display the completed works.

Materials needed: drawing paper; pencils; crayons and/or markers

FAITH ALIVE AT HOME AND IN THE PARISH

This lesson is an immediate preparation for the Easter experience of moving with Jesus through death to new life. Your child was given a deeper understanding of the events of Palm Sunday and the Triduum—which begins with the Evening Mass of the Lord's Supper on Holy Thursday and ends Easter Sunday with Evening Prayer.

Easter is the greatest celebration of the Church year. It is a feast full of joy and triumph—the triumph in Jesus Christ of life over death. The resurrection of Jesus is the ultimate foundation of Christian faith.

If possible, have your family join with the parish in celebrating the Easter Triduum.

✝ Family Prayer

Lord of all hopefulness, Lord of all joy,
Whose trust ever childlike no cares can destroy,
Be there at our waking and give us, we pray,
Your Easter joy that forever will stay.

Learn by heart Faith Summary

What does the paschal mystery celebrate?
- The paschal mystery celebrates the events of Jesus' "passing" through suffering and death to new life.

What do we celebrate on Holy Thursday, Good Friday and Easter?
- On Holy Thursday we celebrate the gift of the Eucharist. On Good Friday we remember Jesus' suffering and death. On Easter we celebrate Jesus' resurrection.

We Are Easter People

Talk with your family about what it means when we say that Christians are "Easter" people. List all the ideas that are mentioned. Some might be: hope, joy, life, love. Perhaps you might make an Easter flag for your home using these ideas.

Review

Go over the *Faith Summary* together and encourage your fifth grader to learn it by heart. Then have him or her do the *Review*. The answers to numbers 1–4 appear on page 216. The response to number 5 will help you see how well your child understands the paschal mystery. When the *Review* is completed, go over it together.

Complete the sentences.

1. On Holy Thursday we celebrate __the Mass of the Lord's Supper__.

2. On Good Friday we celebrate __and remember the Lord's Passion.__

3. At the Easter Vigil and on Easter Sunday we celebrate __the resurrection of Jesus and our new life in Christ__.

4. The above celebrations make up what is called the __Easter Triduum__.

5. What do you think it means to be "baptized into Christ's death and resurrection"?

FAMILY SCRIPTURE MOMENT

Gather and recall the joy when loved ones have paid surprise visits. Then **Listen** to an Easter story.

Mary stayed outside the tomb weeping. And as she wept, she bent over into the tomb and saw two angels in white.... And they said to her, "Woman, why are you weeping?" She said to them, "They have taken my Lord, and I don't know where they laid him." ... She turned around and saw Jesus there, but did not know it was Jesus. Jesus said to her, "Woman, why are you weeping? Whom are you looking for?" ... Jesus said to her, "Mary!" She turned and said to him in Hebrew, "Rabbouni," which means Teacher. Mary of Magdala went and announced to the disciples, "I have seen the Lord."
John 20:11–16, 18

Share Imagine you are at the tomb with Mary Magdalene. What are your feelings?

Consider for family enrichment:

■ In John's Gospel, Mary Magdalene is the first disciple to see and proclaim the risen Lord. Christ has a glorified body, which she, in her sorrow, does not recognize.

■ We rejoice with Mary in the risen Christ and go to share our faith with others.

Reflect and **Decide** How are we like Mary Magdalene? What will we do to proclaim the Easter message with others in our parish?

144

UNIT 3 · REVIEW

Ask: What is the sacrament of Reconciliation? How is it celebrated?

Jesus Christ Forgives Us (Reconciliation)

The Church celebrates all the sacraments by the power of the Holy Spirit. In the sacrament of Reconciliation, Jesus Christ shares God's forgiveness of our sins. Reconciliation is one of the sacraments of healing.

Reconciliation, or Penance, may be celebrated individually or communally. In both rites, or forms of celebration, we confess our sins to a priest in private.

Examination of conscience, confession, contrition, penance, and absolution are important parts of Reconciliation.

Ask: How does the church carry on Jesus' healing mission?

Jesus Christ Helps Us in Sickness and Death (Anointing of the Sick)

In the sacrament of Anointing of the Sick, the Church carries on Jesus' mission of bringing God's healing power to the sick and dying. Anointing is one of the sacraments of healing. The two most important signs of this sacrament are the laying on of hands and anointing with oil.

We also carry on Jesus' mission of healing when we take care of and respect our bodies, and when we support our Church's efforts to eliminate disease and suffering in our world.

Ask: What is the sacrament of Matrimony? What do the bride and groom promise?

Jesus Christ Helps Us to Love (Matrimony)

Matrimony is a sacrament of service. It is a powerful sign of God's love and faithfulness. In Matrimony a bride and groom enter into a lifelong marriage covenant. They promise to love each other and serve the Church. We can prepare for Matrimony by being faithful in our friendships and practicing unselfish love.

Ask: Who is ordained? How can we help them?

Jesus Christ Calls Us to Serve (Holy Orders)

Jesus Christ chose twelve apostles to lead his Church. In time, the Church chose other leaders called bishops, priests, and deacons.

Holy Orders is a sacrament of service. Our bishops, priests, and deacons are ordained in the sacrament of Holy Orders to lead our Church in service and worship. The Pope, together with the bishops, leads the whole Church. We support our ordained leaders by praying for them and helping them.

Ask: How does each baptized person share in Jesus' priestly mission?

We Share Jesus Christ's Priesthood (Ministry)

Through Baptism every Christian shares in Jesus' priestly mission and ministry and is called to serve the Church. Each person has a vocation, or call, to serve others. There are many vocations: married, ordained, religious, and single persons. Our preparation for a life of service begins now.

UNIT 3 • TEST

Circle the correct answers.

1. The sign of receiving God's forgiveness in Reconciliation is the
    a. Act of Contrition.
    (b.) absolution.
    c. penance.
    d. examination of conscience.

2. The sacraments of healing are
    a. initiation and service.
    b. Anointing of the Sick, Baptism.
    (c.) Reconciliation, Anointing of the Sick.
    d. Confirmation, Eucharist.

3. The sacrament that brings God's healing to the sick, and dying is
    a. Holy Orders.
    b. Confirmation.
    c. Eucharist.
    (d.) Anointing of the Sick.

4. Through Baptism all Christians share in
    a. marriage.
    b. ordination.
    (c.) the priesthood of the faithful.
    d. confession.

5. Every baptized person has
    a. ordination.
    (b.) a vocation.
    c. vows.
    d. anointing.

6. The ministers of the sacrament of Matrimony are
    a. bishops.
    (b.) the bride and groom.
    c. deacons.
    d. priests.

7. The sacraments of service are
    (a.) Holy Orders and Matrimony.
    b. Baptism and Matrimony.
    c. Holy Orders and Confirmation.
    d. Eucharist and Reconciliation.

Answer the following questions.

8. Two ways to celebrate Reconciliation are
   the Individual Rite and the Communal Rite.

9. How does the Church continue Jesus' ministry of healing?
   through the sacraments of Reconciliation and Anointing of the sick.

Think and decide:

What vocation do you think you will follow? Tell how you will prepare for it.
   Accept individual responses.

Name _____

Your son or daughter has just completed Unit 3. Have him or her bring this paper to the catechist. It will help you and the catechist know better how to help your fifth grader grow in faith.

_____ He or she needs help with the part of the Review I have underlined.

_____ He or she understands what has been taught in this unit.

_____ I would like to speak with you. My phone number is _____.

Signature: _____

22 BECOMING A CATHOLIC
(The Marks of the Church)

For the Catechist: Spiritual and Catechetical Development

ADULT BACKGROUND

Our Life

The assignment seemed simple enough. "Write a one-page essay on 'What I Love About the Catholic Church.'"

Sister Joan wondered how several members of her small Christian community would respond and what they might discover in the process.

Ask yourself:

■ What points would I make in such an essay?

Sharing Life

What one quality of the Catholic Church makes you especially glad to be a member?

What one quality would you most like to see grow?

Our Catholic Faith

Whenever we pray the Nicene Creed, we call to mind the four marks that traditionally have characterized the Church. We remind ourselves that the Church is one, holy, catholic, and apostolic. These marks, which are not merely abstract words but also dynamic realities, tell us who we are as Catholics and what our mission is. They speak of what we are and of what we should strive to be.

To be Catholic is to respond to the prayer of Jesus at the Last Supper:

"I pray...that they may all be one, as you, Father, are in me and I in you, that they also may be in us, that the world may believe that you sent me" (John 17:20-21).

By this oneness, achieved through mutual love and a common faith, we testify to the Son's identity. Our primary experience of unity is in celebrating the Eucharist, which is a sign and a cause of our oneness.

Though God alone is holy, the Holy Spirit calls all of us to share in that holiness. Our communal life of prayer, sacraments, and ministry enables us to conform our lives more closely to Christ's life and to reflect His holiness.

The catholicity of our Church is a response to Christ's universal call to salvation. The Gospels are to be preached to all people in every time and culture. Thus, despite a diversity of time and place, the same Catholic faith is shared by all.

The Church is apostolic in that it traces its origins to Christ and the twelve apostles. It has preserved a continuing fidelity to the vision of God's kingdom, to Christ's saving message, and to the ministry and teaching of the apostles. Through the succession of bishops, priests, and deacons, this fidelity has been maintained.

Coming to Faith

How might the Church communicate these marks more effectively to the world?

How do you hope your ministry as a catechist has helped you to grow in holiness?

Practicing Faith

How will you choose to communicate the oneness of the Church?

In what ways will you make holiness appealing to your group?

CATECHISM OF THE CATHOLIC CHURCH

The Theme of This Chapter Corresponds with Paragraph 811

LITURGICAL RESOURCES

The author Donald Nicholl emphasizes how much more important the influence of a genuinely holy person is than countless books about holiness. The seeds of holiness are watered by daily prayer.

If possible, invite each fifth grader to plant several seeds in a paper cup. Each young person is responsible for watering his or her seeds while praying for personal growth in holiness.

JUSTICE AND PEACE RESOURCES

One of the marks of holiness is a willingness to share in the menial tasks of family or community life. (Picture Jesus on His knees, washing the disciples' well-traveled feet.)

Prompt your group members to ask themselves: "Do I always try to avoid doing certain jobs at home that I don't like? Is it fair or just of me not to do my share of the unappealing chores? Would I be a holier (better) person if I sometimes did these jobs so that others would not have to?"

Teaching Resources

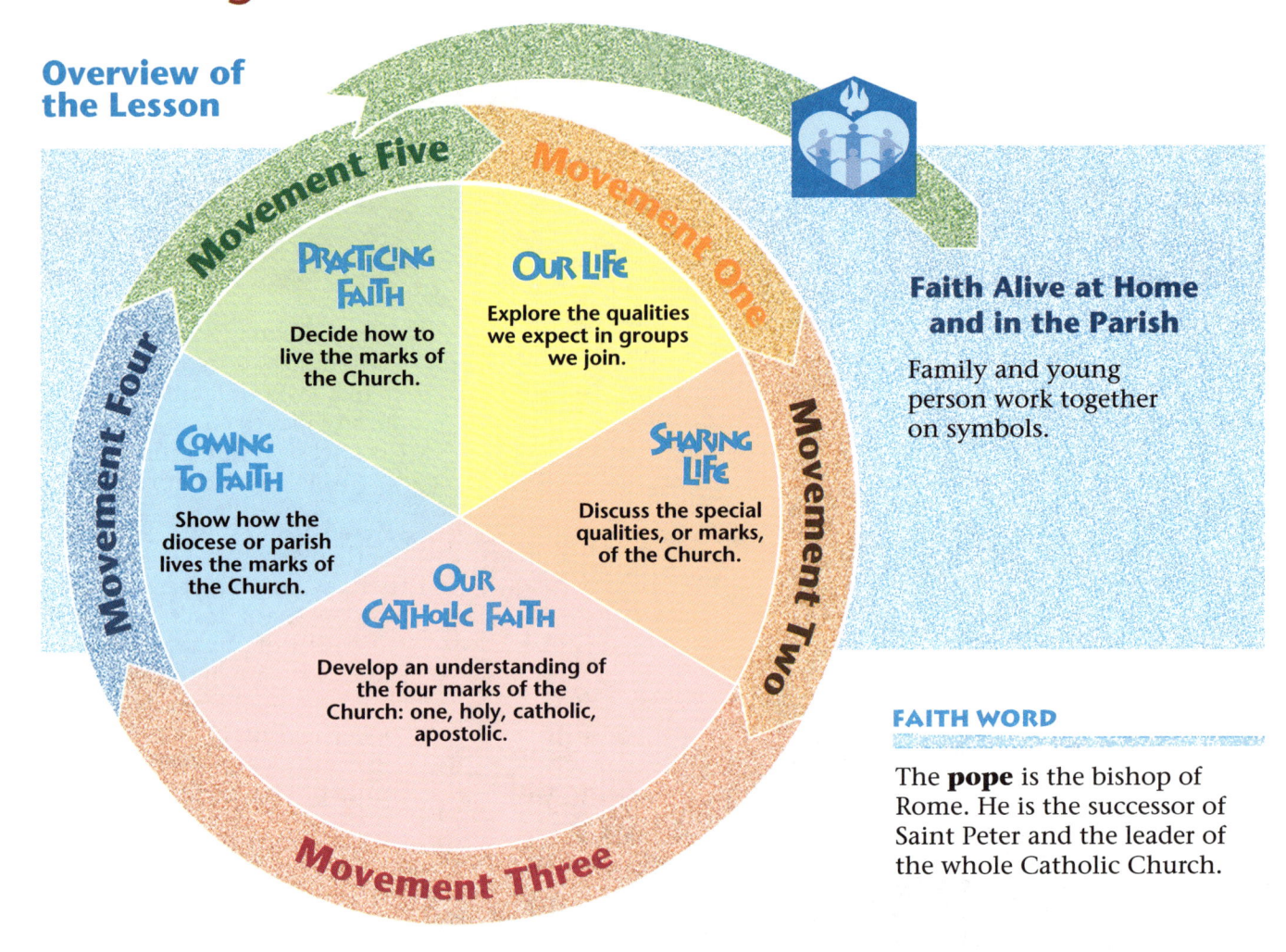

Overview of the Lesson

Movement One — Our Life: Explore the qualities we expect in groups we join.

Movement Two — Sharing Life: Discuss the special qualities, or marks, of the Church.

Movement Three — Our Catholic Faith: Develop an understanding of the four marks of the Church: one, holy, catholic, apostolic.

Movement Four — Coming To Faith: Show how the diocese or parish lives the marks of the Church.

Movement Five — Practicing Faith: Decide how to live the marks of the Church.

Faith Alive at Home and in the Parish

Family and young person work together on symbols.

FAITH WORD

The **pope** is the bishop of Rome. He is the successor of Saint Peter and the leader of the whole Catholic Church.

Teaching Hints

It is important that the young people understand that the marks of the Church are meant to be lived by each Catholic in his or her daily life. In this lesson, stress the truth that the Church is the people of God.

When we say that the Church is one, holy, catholic, and apostolic, we are actually saying that each member of the Church is trying to be one in faith and love; to be holy as Jesus was holy; to welcome everyone into the Church; and to live the faith given to us by the apostles.

Special-Needs Child

The mainstreamed young person will flourish in an environment that is supportive and loving but firm and orderly.

Visual Needs
■ large-print copy of "A Prayer to the Holy Spirit"

Auditory Needs
■ peer helper for brainstorming activity
■ tape recording of the Nicene Creed

Tactile–Motor Needs
■ peer helper for writing activities

Supplemental Resources

Peter and Paul (video)
Vision Video
2030 Wentz Church Road
PO Box 540
Worcester, PA 19490
(1-800-523-0226)

147C

Lesson Plan: Beginning

OBJECTIVES

To help the young people

■ know the marks of the Church;

■ appreciate that they, the people of God, are the Church;

■ choose ways to live the marks every day.

Focusing Prayer
Recall with the young people that Jesus invites each of us to share in His priestly ministry. Pray together the prayer at the top of page 147.

Our Life

Choosing Descriptive Marks
Read aloud the first paragraph under *Our Life* on page 147.

Have the young people choose partners, then ask them to read silently the rest of the section. Allow time for partners to discuss and write down their ideas. Afterwards, have them discuss their ideas with the entire group.

Sharing Life

Describing Our Church
Read the opening statement under *Sharing Life*. Have the young people silently read the three following questions and think about their answers. Then call on several volunteers to share their responses with the group.

ENRICHMENT

Who Are You?
Tell the young people that they have two minutes to jot down five important things that identify who they are. Tell them that their names should not be counted, but do not define the instructions further. Let them decide what the important identifiers are.

Share responses, keeping track of how many times "Catholic" is listed. Then ask:

■ What does belonging to the Catholic Church mean in your life?

■ How do you feel about being Catholic?

Materials needed: paper; pencils

---

22 Becoming a Catholic
(The Marks of the Church)

Loving God, bless the Church. Help us to live as your people.

OUR LIFE
Groups such as youth organizations and sports teams have marks, or qualities, that clearly show what kind of a group each one is or would like to be. Choose one of the following situations and work with a partner to draw up your expectations, qualities, or "marks" for each one.

• You are putting together a "dream team" in any sport you wish.

• You are a musician and are assembling a band or an orchestra.

• You are organizing a youth service group.

What qualifications would you expect from individual members? from the group as a whole? **Encourage specific responses.**

SHARING LIFE
We are members of the Church. Discuss together: What marks, or qualities, do you think the Church should have? Make a list. **Accept reasonable responses.**
Do you show that our Church has these qualities? How?

Lesson Plan: Middle

Our Catholic Faith

Faith Word

Display a picture of the pope, and under it write the word *pope*. Find out how many young people can name the pope. Alert the group to listen for this word in today's lesson.

Materials needed: picture of the pope

The Marks of the Church

Ask what the marks of the Church are, then read aloud the opening paragraph on page 148. Repeat your question and call on volunteers to respond. Then display the four marks of the Church on flash cards, and have the group say each one.

The Church Is One

Read the heading "The Church Shows It Is One" to the group, and call on a volunteer to read the first paragraph under it. Then ask what we mean when we say the Church is one, and have the group silently read the next two paragraphs before discussing responses.

Have a volunteer read aloud the last two paragraphs under this heading. Stress that although all Catholics are Christians, not all Christians are Catholics.

The Church Is Holy

Ask, "How is the Church holy?" Have the young people silently read the first three paragraphs under "The Church Shows It Is Holy," then repeat your question and let a volunteer respond. Emphasize that, although only God is perfectly holy, we all share in God's holiness through Jesus.

Ask, "How can we grow in holiness?" Invite a volunteer to read aloud the final two paragraphs of this section, then discuss responses to your question. You may wish to conclude this section by having the young people give specific examples of how we can show that the Church is holy. Ask a volunteer to list them on the chalkboard or newsprint.

Our Catholic Faith

Stress the underlined text.

The Marks of the Church

The Church has four great identifying "marks," or qualities, that let people know the kind of community Jesus began. We say that the Church is one, holy, catholic, and apostolic. We must always keep trying to live these marks.

The Church Is One

Jesus wants all his disciples everywhere to be one with him and with one another in the Holy Spirit.

When we say that the Church is one, we mean that all baptized persons are united in the body of Christ. We, though many, are made part of the one body of Jesus Christ through Baptism.

As Catholics we are united by the leadership of the pope and bishops. We celebrate our unity with Jesus and with one another in the Eucharist. We are united in faith and in love with Jesus Christ and one another.

But not all Christians share the same beliefs and practices. Over the centuries, some Christians became separated from the Catholic Church.

Today all Christians are called to pray and work for the full unity of the Church. Saint Paul once described the unity we should have: "One Lord, one faith, one baptism; one God and Father of all, who is over all and through all and in all."

Ephesians 4:5–6

The Church Is Holy

God alone is perfectly holy. The Church is holy because it is the body of Christ and because the Holy Spirit is present in the Church.

Jesus called his disciples to live holy lives, as he did. The holy lives of the apostles, the saints, and of all disciples of Jesus show the holiness of the Church.

God says to us, "Be holy, for I, the Lord, your God, am holy" (Leviticus 19:2).

We begin to share in God's holy life when we are baptized. The Church helps us to grow in holiness, especially through the sacraments.

We can show that the Church is holy by leading holy lives and by working for the reign of God in the world. We try to put God first in all we say and do. We try to live the Law of Love and work for justice and peace.

Lesson Plan: Middle

The Church Is Catholic

Invite several volunteers to read the four paragraphs under "The Church Shows It Is Catholic" on page 149. Ask how the Church is catholic and how it shows this. Conclude by having a volunteer write the definition of the word *catholic* on the chalkboard or newsprint.

The Church Is Apostolic

Read aloud the first paragraph under "The Church Shows It Is Apostolic." Call attention to the *faith word* at the top of the page. Display the Holy Father's picture again, and have the group read the definition together.

Have volunteers read the final three paragraphs on this page. Pause to let volunteers respond to these questions: "How does the Church show it is apostolic?" and "What can we do to show that the Church is apostolic?" Conclude by having the young people thoughtfully pray the Nicene creed together. You may wish to pass out missalettes or write the creed on the chalkboard or newsprint.

FAITH WORD

The **pope** is the bishop of Rome. He is the successor of Saint Peter and the leader of the whole Catholic Church.

Today the Church continues to show it is catholic. Missionaries carry the good news to every country on earth. The Church works for the salvation of all people everywhere. We try to share our faith and welcome everyone to Jesus' community of disciples.

The Church Is Apostolic

When Saint Paul wrote to the early Christians, he reminded them that they were "built upon the foundation of the apostles and prophets," with "Christ Jesus himself as the capstone" (Ephesians 2:20). The Church is apostolic, because it was founded on the apostles and tries to be faithful to the mission and beliefs Jesus gave them. The Church can trace itself back to the apostles.

Saint Peter led the first apostles as they carried on Jesus' mission. In the Catholic Church, Peter's successors are the popes. Today our Holy Father, the pope, carries on the work of Saint Peter. The other bishops carry on the work of the first apostles.

We can show that our Church is apostolic by learning all we can about our Catholic faith. We can pray for and help our missionaries. We can do our part in carrying out the mission Jesus gave to the first apostles.

Each time we pray the Nicene Creed at Mass, we say that we believe in the one, holy, catholic, and apostolic Church. Jesus asks each one of us to develop these marks, or qualities, in our own lives. In this way we show others that we are true disciples of Jesus Christ.

The Church Is Catholic

The word *catholic* means "universal" or "worldwide." The Church is to be a community in which all people of every race, color, nationality, and background are welcome. All are to hear the good news of Jesus Christ.

Jesus invited everyone to belong to his community and to follow him. He commanded his disciples to be just as welcoming and to include everyone in carrying on his mission.

Before his ascension into heaven, Jesus told his disciples, "Go into the whole world and proclaim the gospel to every creature" (Mark 16:15). The disciples carried out Jesus' command.

ENRICHMENT

The Catholic Church

What is the relationship between the Catholic Church and the Church founded by Christ? The Second Vatican Council tells us that the Church Jesus founded is found in its fullness in the Catholic Church. The Council's Document on the Church says in part: "This is the unique Church of Christ which in the Creed we avow as one, holy, catholic, and apostolic. After His Resurrection our Savior handed her [the Church] over to Peter to be shepherded (John 21:17), commissioning him and the other apostles to propagate and govern her (cf. Mt. 28:18 ff.). He erected Her for all ages as 'the pillar and mainstay of the truth' (1 Tim. 3:15). This Church, constituted and organized in the world as a society, subsists in the Catholic Church, which is governed by the successor of Peter and by the bishops in union with that successor." *The Church,* #8

Lesson Plan: End

Coming to Faith

Writing a TV Commercial

Read the first direction under *Coming to Faith* on page 150. Invite four volunteers to each write one of the names on the chalkboard or newsprint.

Read the next paragraph explaining the activity. Distribute the necessary art materials, and have the young people work in small groups to complete their TV commercials.

Faith Summary

Use the annotations to review the *Faith Summary* on page 151. See if the young people can express, in their own words, what they have learned.

Practicing Faith

Living the Marks

Form two groups and have them face each other. Read the first paragraph and explain that after each side reads its part aloud, there will be a moment of silence as everyone reads and thoughtfully considers each action idea. Then invite the young people to pray the prayer and sing an "Amen" or an "Alleluia" at the end.

EVALUATING YOUR LESSON

- Do the young people know the marks of the Church?
- Do they appreciate that, as God's people, they must try to live the marks?
- Have they decided how they will try to be one, holy, catholic, and apostolic?

ENRICHMENT

Singing the Marks

To the tune of "He's Got the Whole World," sing the following:

We are the catholic Church, yes we are. (Repeat three times.)
We are one and holy.

We are the apostolic Church, yes we are. (Repeat three times.)
We are one and holy.

Form concentric circles, that will move in opposite directions during the singing.

Coming To Faith

Tell the name of:
your diocese, bishop, parish, pastor.

Now imagine that your bishop has asked your group to make a short TV spot showing how your diocese or parish tries to live the marks of the Church today. Plan your ideas together. Use the marks of the Church as an outline. You may draw sketches, write a script, or act it out. *Encourage originality and creativity.*

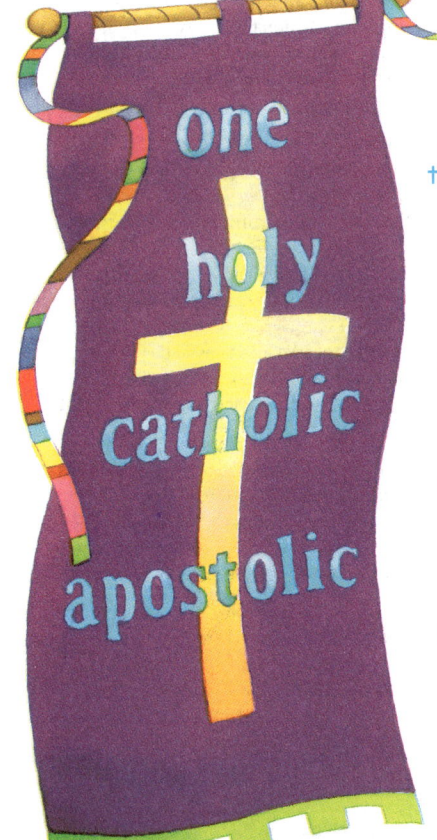

Practicing Faith

† Gather in a prayer circle. Be very still and let the Holy Spirit guide us.

Side 1: May the Holy Spirit help us to live in unity with Jesus and one another.
(*Action idea*: Decide to help someone who is sick or lonely or poor this week.)

Side 2: May the Holy Spirit guide us to be like Jesus in all things.
(*Action idea*: Decide to set aside time for prayer this week.)

Side 1: May the Holy Spirit help us to be open and welcoming to all people.
(*Action idea*: Invite a friend, who does not usually go to Mass, to come with you this week.)

Side 2: May the Holy Spirit give us courage to proclaim the good news of Jesus.
(*Action idea*: Read a gospel story with a friend or family member. Talk about what it means.)

All: We believe in the one, holy, catholic, and apostolic Church. Amen.

Talk with your catechist about ways you and your family can use the "Faith Alive" pages. Ask a family member to do the activity with you.

Optional Activities

A Campaign Button (for use with page 147)

Invite each young person to make a campaign button illustrating his or her favorite quality of the Church. Have them cut out the buttons and wear them.

Materials: construction paper; markers; scissors; straight pins

A Report on Holiness (for use with page 148)

Have the young people work in pairs or small groups to prepare brief reports or descriptions of individuals or groups who they believe live the mark of holiness.

The Church Is Catholic (for use with page 148)

You might want to provide your group with a more complete explanation of what it means when we say the Church is catholic. Explain it to them as follows:

If we want to know why the Church must be catholic, we can find our answer in the Gospels and in the other New Testament writings describing the life of the early Christians. From the beginning, Jesus made it clear that He had not come for some small exclusive group but for all people. His words and His actions reached out to include everyone who would listen to Him and believe the good news of God's kingdom. When He chose the twelve apostles, He included Matthew, a tax collector, a member of a profession that most people looked down on or despised. One of His close friends was a woman who had been a public sinner, and another was a wealthy religious leader. When He wanted to reveal He was the Messiah, did He tell a fellow Jew? No, He revealed that good news to a foreigner—a Samaritan woman. When He wanted to teach what it meant to be a real neighbor, did He use a fellow Jew as an example? No, He used a kind Samaritan. Jesus wanted to welcome all people—Greeks and Romans, Mexicans and Japanese, Ugandans and Americans, poor and rich, black and white, female and male—into God's kingdom.

All of these people, whether they were born in the first century or the twentieth, would share one Baptism and one faith. That's why the Church also has to be apostolic. It has to be true to the message of Jesus as it was handed down by the apostles and their successors. By its faithfulness to the teachings of the apostles, the Church keeps the good news alive and well in the Christian community.

A Flash-Card Quiz (for use with page 149)

Distribute four index cards on which partners will write one question for each of the four marks of the Church. These questions should reflect the material in the text and go beyond the mere definition of the marks. Then have one pair quiz another using the cards.

Materials needed: index cards

Faith Alive AT HOME AND IN THE PARISH

In this lesson your fifth grader has learned more about the four marks of the Church. The Church is one, holy, catholic, and apostolic. Beyond a confession of faith, these four marks are challenges that the whole Church and every member is called to live faithfully. Ask your son or daughter to name and describe each mark. Discuss with the family how each of you as a member of the Church can live these marks today. Use this list to help you.

■ We can show that we are *one* with others in our parish by celebrating the Eucharist each week with them. We can pray for the unity of all Christians. We can forgive others.

■ We can show that we are *holy* by loving God, praying frequently, and celebrating the sacraments. We can grow in holiness by treating all people justly and by living in peace with them.

■ We can show that we are *catholic* by welcoming everyone and treating them as important because they, too, are loved by God.

■ We can show that we are *apostolic* by learning how to live our Catholic faith and working for the reign of God. We can pray that the Holy Spirit will guide our pope and bishops. We can ask the Holy Spirit to help us and our parish to carry out the mission of Jesus Christ.

Then do the activity together.

✝ Family Prayer

May the Holy Spirit help us to show we are holy by loving the people in our family, our parish, and our neighborhood.

Living Symbol

Choose one of the four marks. Create a symbol that expresses what that sign means to you.

Learn by heart Faith Summary

What are the marks of the Church?
● The marks of the Church are one, holy, catholic, and apostolic.

How does the Church show it is one and holy?
● The Church of Jesus Christ shows it is one and holy when we are united in faith and live holy lives.

How does the Church show it is Catholic and apostolic?
● The Church of Jesus Christ shows it is catholic and apostolic by welcoming all and being faithful to the mission and beliefs Jesus gave to the apostles.

Review

Go over the *Faith Summary* together and encourage your fifth grader to learn it by heart, especially the first statement. Then have him or her do the *Review*. The answers to numbers 1–4 appear on page 216. The response to number 5 will help you see how well your fifth grader is trying to grow in holiness. When the *Review* is completed, go over it together.

Complete the following sentences with the words below.

catholic   one   holy   apostolic

1. We, though many, are made part of the _____ one _____ body of Jesus Christ through Baptism.

2. The second mark of the Church reminds us that we are called to be _____ holy _____.

3. The third mark of the Church reminds us that we are a universal, or _____ Catholic _____, Church.

4. The fourth mark of the Church, _____ apostolic _____, reminds us that we are a community founded on the apostles.

5. This week I will help to show that our Church is holy by
_____
_____
_____

FAMILY SCRIPTURE MOMENT

Gather and ask: What beliefs do we share with Christians who are not Catholic? Then **Listen** as Jesus speaks to us of his hope for unity.

A thief comes only to steal and slaughter and destroy; I came so that they might have life and have it more abundantly. I am the good shepherd, and I know mine and mine know me, just as the Father knows me and I know the Father; and I will lay down my life for the sheep. I have other sheep who do not belong to this fold. These also I must lead, and they will hear my voice, and there will be one flock, one shepherd.
John 10:10, 14–16

Share what each one heard Jesus saying.

Consider for family enrichment:

■ Shepherds often had to save their flock from predators. Jesus, our Good Shepherd, protects us and wants all to belong to his one flock.

■ As members of the one, holy, catholic, and apostolic Church, we welcome all people into our faith community.

Reflect and **Decide** How might we help others outside Jesus' flock to hear his voice? Will we join with people in our parish to reach out to them?

23 ALL PEOPLE ARE GOD'S PEOPLE

For the Catechist: Spiritual and Catechetical Development

ADULT BACKGROUND

Our Life

Rebecca and Kevin grew up as good neighbors. They shared the same friends and interests. When they were in the fifth grade, a new student from a distant city moved into the neighborhood. He began making fun of Rebecca for reasons Kevin did not understand. After school, the newcomer asked Kevin, "Why do you hang around with Rebecca? You're not a Jew, are you?"

Ask yourself:

- If I were Kevin, how would I respond?

Sharing Life

In what ways have you experienced or observed religious or racial prejudice?

What do you think causes these kinds of prejudice?

Our Catholic Faith

At the heart of the Church's social doctrine is the concept of our human dignity. The sacredness of each person is affirmed by the biblical authors:

Then God said: "Let us make man in our image, after our likeness"
(Genesis 1:26).

You formed my inmost being;
you knit me in my
mother's womb
(Psalm 139:13).

Human beings are the pinnacle of God's visible creation, and their spiritual, psychological, emotional, and bodily integrity must be respected.

Intolerance and prejudice of any kind—whether sexual, racial, economic, cultural, or religious—denies the human dignity of another. When practiced knowingly and purposely, prejudice is a sin. It is a direct denial of the example of Jesus, who welcomed women, Gentiles, tax collectors, and social outcasts of every kind into His friendship. Religious intolerance is especially harmful to the body of Christ. While recognizing the uniqueness of the Catholic Church, we should initiate dialogues with Jews and members of other Christian churches in our communities. Jesus expects no less of us.

Coming to Faith

What does the Church's teaching on the dignity of persons challenge you to do?

Practicing Faith

How will you help your group to recognize the sinfulness of prejudice?

CATECHISM OF THE CATHOLIC CHURCH

The Theme of This Chapter Corresponds with Paragraph 839

LITURGICAL RESOURCES

Meditation on selected Scripture passages can be an effective antidote to attitudes of intolerance that may arise without our recognizing them. A prayerful reading of 1 John 4:7–21, for example, might be followed by a period of silence in which you ask the Spirit to uncover hidden prejudices in your mind or heart.

You might choose to share with the group a few lines from your reading, such as:

- "There is no fear in love, but perfect love drives out fear."
- "If anyone says, 'I love God,' but hates his brother, he is a liar."

Invite the young people to interpret these lines in light of their own experiences.

JUSTICE AND PEACE RESOURCES

From a directory of local churches and synagogues, have the fifth graders select several that they would like to know more about. With the permission of your pastor, have the fifth graders write letters of invitation in which they explain that they are studying about respect for other religions and would like to have a church or synagogue member come to visit the group. (If the representatives are well-informed young people, the fifth graders will profit by the example of peer faith-sharing.)

After welcoming the visitors, your group might break the ice by singing a simple interfaith song like "Halle, Halle, Halle" (from *Many and Great*, Iona Community album, GIA) or an alleluia. The guests could then give brief talks or simply answer prepared questions. Close by sharing refreshments.

Encourage your group and the visitors to stay in touch with one another.

153B

Teaching Resources

Overview of the Lesson

Movement One — Our Life
Talk about experiences of acceptance or prejudice.

Movement Two — Sharing Life
Discuss how God wants us to treat one another.

Movement Three — Our Catholic Faith
Develop an understanding of why and how we are to show respect for all people.

Movement Four — Coming to Faith
Consider why prejudice is sinful and how we can avoid it.

Movement Five — Practicing Faith
Do an activity that helps us choose how to deal with prejudice.

Faith Alive at Home and in the Parish
Young person and family discuss ways to be more tolerant of others.

FAITH WORD
Racism is a sin of prejudice.

Teaching Hints

In a spirit of ecumenism, the Catholic Church fosters a deep respect and affection for our brothers and sisters in other Christian Churches and communities. Through our common Baptism, we are members of the one body of Christ. At the same time, however, we must make it clear that the Catholic Church is unique and that our Catholic faith is a gift from God to be treasured. Help the young people never to be indifferent to their faith—to learn it and live it well.

Special-Needs Child

If a mainstreamed child has difficulty in maintaining concentration, help him or her focus on the main theme of the lesson.

Visual Needs
- preferential seating

Auditory Needs
- clear and precise directions
- peer helper for activities

Tactile–Motor Needs
- tape to hold materials in place

Supplemental Resources

Saint Martin de Porres (video)
W. H. Sadlier, Inc.
9 Pine Street
New York, NY 10005-1002
(1-800-221-5175)

Prejudice (filmstrip)
Warren Schloat Productions
151 White Plains Road
Tarrytown, NY 10591

Lesson Plan: Beginning

OBJECTIVES

To help the young people

- know that all people are made in God's image;
- appreciate the ways in which people of other religions worship God;
- recognize why prejudice is sinful.

Focusing Prayer

Remind the young people that Jesus said to the first Christians, "As I have loved you, so you also should love one another" (John 13:34). Then pray together the prayer at the top of page 153.

Our Life

Demonstrating Prejudice

To help your group understand prejudice, announce that: everyone with blue eyes will have a written assignment. Ask those singled-out how they feel. Guide the discussion to elicit the word *prejudice*.

Then read aloud the *Our Life* story and discuss responses to the questions.

Sharing Life

Overcoming Prejudice

Read aloud the first set of *Sharing Life* questions, and have the young people respond in their faith journals. Discuss the last question with the group.

---

23 All People Are God's People

Dear Jesus, help us to love one another as you love us.

Our Life

It was almost the last day of the summer Olympics. Some athletes who had just completed the track and field competition were being interviewed for TV.

"Let me ask you," the interviewer said looking at the group that included young people from many different countries. "What is the highlight of this experience for you?"

What do you think was the answer?

The athletes did not talk about competition, or gold medals, or national honor. To a person they said their deepest memory would be of meeting people from different cultures, different backgrounds, different races, different languages, and discovering how very much they all shared in common.

"The Olympic circles are the color of the races of the world," one athlete remarked, "but they are all linked together as one."

What do you think this story says about prejudice? **Prejudice (ignorance and fear) can be overcome by getting to know others.** How do you try to live this "Olympic" dream? **By getting to know others and learning what we have in common**

Sharing Life

Is there any person or group of people that you find hard to treat as equals? Why is this so? Who can help you?

Discuss together: How does God want you to treat people who are different from you? Explain. **Ask the group to recall the Law of Love.**

ENRICHMENT

Recording Our Uniqueness

If possible take instant pictures of the young people. Using a stamp pad, have them put their fingerprints on index cards and then write their names on the cards. Help the young people to see how unique each picture and set of fingerprints is. Ask them to write thumbnail sketches of their unique attributes. Display the sketches, the photos, and the fingerprints, and ask the group to title the display.

Materials needed: instant camera; stamp pad; index cards; paper; pencils

Lesson Plan: Middle

Our Catholic Faith

Faith Word

Write the word *racism* on the chalkboard or newsprint. Explain that the young people will learn the meaning of this word in today's lesson.

The Meaning of Prejudice

Read aloud the first paragraph under "Respecting Other Religions" on page 154. Ask the young people what prejudice is, then invite a volunteer to read aloud the answer in the next paragraph. Have the entire group repeat the definition in unison. Emphasize that prejudice is a dislike or hatred of people because they differ from us.

Have the young people locate the *faith word* at the top of page 155. Read the definition, and discuss the sin of racism with them. Point out examples of racism that may be in the news.

Read the next paragraph on page 154. Give the young people the opportunity to discuss prejudice and to ask questions about it.

Our Relationship with Jewish People

Ask the young people what beliefs Christians and Jews share, and have them listen for the answer as you read the next two paragraphs.

Call on volunteers to list on the chalkboard or newsprint the three beliefs we share with the Jewish people. Then ask what is happening in the picture on page 154.

Multicultural Awareness

Read the following to your group:

The LORD. . . executes justice for the orphan and the widow, and befriends the alien, feeding and clothing him. So you too must befriend the alien, for you were once aliens yourselves in the land of Egypt (Deuteronomy 10:17-19).

Discuss with the fifth graders different intolerances that people have had throughout history and still have today. Have the fifth graders use their Bibles to find other references that show that God loves all people. Remind them that any prejudice denies the human dignity of a person.

OUR CATHOLIC FAITH

Stress the underlined text.

Respecting Other Religions

We meet many people who differ from us in color, religion, age, language, or wealth. Although people are different, all are created in God's image and likeness. We must treat everyone with respect.

Prejudice is a dislike for or hatred of people because they are different from us in race, sex, religion, age, or any other way. The Catholic Church condemns all prejudice as a sin.

God calls us to reject prejudice of any kind. This also includes religious prejudice. This is a dislike for people who worship God differently from the way we do, or who do not worship God at all. There are many religions in the world other than Christianity. Jesus wants us to respect all people, even those who do not believe in him.

We have a special relationship with the Jewish people. Jesus himself was a Jew and grew up practicing the Jewish religion. Mary his mother, Saint Joseph, and the apostles were all devoted Jews. Christians must have a great respect for the Jewish people, who are still God's chosen people.

Christians and Jews share these beliefs:

- Both religions believe in the one true God, who is our creator.
- Both religions read, study, and believe the Jewish Scriptures, which Christians call the Old Testament.
- Both religions follow the Ten Commandments.

Christianity itself is made up of all the baptized disciples of Jesus. Originally, there was only one Church. However, over the centuries, divisions took place among Christians.

Among the Christian Churches that became separated from the Catholic Church are the Eastern Orthodox Churches and the Protestant Churches (for example, the Lutheran and Episcopal). Some other Protestant Churches found in America today include the Baptist, Congregationalist, Methodist, and Presbyterian.

By Baptism all Christians are united as brothers and sisters in Christ. We share many important beliefs:

- We believe in and worship the one true God: Father, Son, and Holy Spirit.

Lesson Plan: Middle

The Unity of Christians

Ask, "What is Christianity?" and have the group silently read the next two paragraphs on page 154. Invite the young people to share any knowledge they have of other Christian churches.

Ask a volunteer to read aloud the last paragraph on page 154. Then, have six young people each read one of the beliefs Christians share. Write these beliefs on the chalkboard or newsprint.

Have another volunteer read the paragraph on ecumenism. Write the word *ecumenism* on the chalkboard or newsprint. Discuss the pictures on this page.

Working Against Prejudice

Ask how we can work against prejudice before having one of the young people read the last three paragraphs on the page.

Then have the young people underline in their texts the things they can do to work against prejudice and discuss these things. Encourage the young people to be open to all people, both young and old, in their neighborhood, their parish, or their school.

You may wish to use pages 51–52 in the activity book for *Coming to God's Life*.

FAITH WORD

Racism is a sin of prejudice.

- We believe in Jesus Christ, who is both divine and human. Jesus died out of love for us and to save us from our sins. He rose from the dead to bring us new life.
- We believe that the Bible is the inspired word of God.
- We believe in one Baptism for the forgiveness of sins.
- We believe that we are to live the Ten Commandments and the Law of Love, and to carry on Jesus' mission in the world.
- We believe in the resurrection of the dead on the last day and in everlasting life.

Ecumenism is the search for the reunion of the Christian Churches. The Catholic Church is very involved in this work. All of us must work and pray for Christian unity.

Working Against Prejudice

Prejudice is an offense against God. Prejudice of any kind prevents us from living the way Jesus taught. To avoid being guilty of prejudice, we can learn about people whom we consider "different." We can be friendly with the children in our neighborhood or parish or school who are of another color or religion.

As we get older, we can study more about other Christian traditions and about other religions. Learning what they believe and how they worship God can enrich our own faith.

We can talk about our faith to our friends who are not Catholic. We can pray each day that some day all Christians will be united in one Church.

155

ENRICHMENT

Praying a Psalm

If photos or fingerprints have been taken during this session, display them on the prayer table with a large candle in the middle. Gather around the table to pray Psalm 139:1–5:

LORD, you have probed me,
   you know me:
   you know when I sit and
      stand;
   you understand my
      thoughts from afar.
My travels and my rest you
      mark;
   with all my ways you are
      familiar.
Even before a word is on my
      tongue,
   LORD, you know it all.
Behind and before you encircle
      me
   and rest your hand upon
      me.

Materials needed: candle

155

23

Lesson Plan: End

Coming to Faith

Avoiding Prejudice

Ask the first two questions under *Coming to Faith* on page 156. Invite volunteers to share and discuss their responses. Then form small groups and have them do the final activity in this section.

Faith Summary

Use the annotations to review the *Faith Summary* on page 157. See if the young people can express, in their own words, what they have learned.

Practicing Faith

United in God's Love

Read the first paragraph under *Practicing Faith*. Give each group a paper circle and explain that all the circles will be joined together into one. Have each group read its part and join its circle to the others.

◆ Enrichment ◆

A Banner for Justice

Have the young people work in groups to cut out the previously stenciled letters of a quote from Pope Paul VI: "If you want peace, work for justice." Have the young people glue the letters to fabric to make a banner that can be used in the closing prayer. It might also be hung in the church later on.

Materials needed: letter stencils; scissors; fabric; glue

After the final paragraph has been read, you may wish to distribute copies of the following prayer or write it on the chalkboard or newsprint.

> Lord, we know that prejudice is like quicksand. Once we get stuck in it, it takes a real effort to get out. Help us to see our own prejudices. Help us to root them out. We pray in Jesus' name. Amen.

Gather the group around the prayer table and pray together the above prayer.

EVALUATING YOUR LESSON

■ Do the young people know what prejudice is?

■ Do they appreciate our special bond with Jewish people and our hope of unity with all Christians?

■ Have they decided to work against prejudice?

Coming To Faith Possible responses:

Discuss: Why does our Catholic faith teach that all prejudice is a sin? **Because prejudice is a sin against the Law of Love**
What can we do to avoid prejudice? **Get to know others**

Challenge one another to name the beliefs all Christians have in common.

Practicing Faith

Form five groups, each representing a group that faces prejudice. Cut five large circles out of different-colored paper.

Group 1: Our circle stands for the physically and mentally challenged. Things are sometimes harder for us. But we are just like everyone else.

Group 2: Our circle stands for those who face prejudice because of their skin color. Jesus' followers must be "color blind." (Group 2 makes a slit in its circle and joins it with Group 1's.)

Group 3: Our circle stands for those who face prejudice because of their religious beliefs. We know that God loves all people. (Group 3 joins circles with Group 2.)

Group 4: Our circle stands for those who meet prejudice because of gender. Men and women, girls and boys are equal in God's eyes. (Group 4 joins circles with Group 3.)

Group 5: Our circle stands for poor and homeless people. We have very few material things, but Jesus calls us his very own people. (Group 5 joins with Group 4 and Group 1, linking all circles together.)

All: In Christ, there is no east or west,
In him no north or south,
One great family bound by love
Throughout the whole wide earth!

Talk with your catechist about ways you and your family might use the "Faith Alive" pages. Talk with family members about ways to fight prejudice.

Optional Activities

An Illustration of Our Unity (for use with page 153)

Invite the young people to illustrate the good news that all people are made in God's image. Play an appropriate recording such as "We Are the World," while the group is working. Display the completed drawings.

Materials needed: paper; markers; music source

Recognizing Prejudice (for use with page 153)

Have the young people look through newspapers or magazines for stories of people who are being subjected to prejudice. Encourage them to cut out the stories and glue them on a long piece of shelf paper. Have the young people write a caption across the top of the display.

Materials needed: magazines or newspapers; shelf paper; glue; markers

Getting the Message Across (for use with page 154)

Challenge the young people to use humor in fighting prejudice. Have them make up comic strips, cartoons, puppet skits, jokes, or bumper stickers to get the message across. Help them to understand how laughter (both directed at ourselves and at others) can enable people to change bad habits or negative views.

Materials needed: arts and crafts supplies

Fighting Prejudice (for use with page 155)

Have the young people prepare oral book reports on the lives of famous people who fought to overcome prejudice (for example: Mahatma Gandhi, Martin Luther King, Jr., Elizabeth Cady Stanton).

A Community Mural (for use with page 155)

On a large sheet of newsprint or shelf paper, have the group create a mural illustrating the various churches and faiths represented in the local community. They might use signs or symbols to indicate which churches have basic beliefs in common.

Materials needed: newsprint or shelf paper; markers

An Essay on Prejudice (for use with page 156)

Challenge the young people to write one-page essays on the theme of prejudice. Encourage them to share their essays with the group.

Materials needed: paper; pencils or pens

FAITH ALIVE AT HOME AND IN THE PARISH

Children are not born prejudiced or bigoted. Others teach them this sin. In this lesson your fifth grader has learned that any kind of prejudice is evil. It is an offense against God's love. Our world and our society constantly face the sin of prejudice—racial, religious, gender prejudice, and prejudice against those who are physically or mentally challenged, against the elderly, against the ill, or against the poor. Prejudice is usually the result of ignorance and fear, both of which can be overcome by God's grace and our good will. We must work to ensure that our own lives and our parish are free of all prejudice.

To deepen your fifth grader's respect for and understanding of other religions, invite to your home neighbors who practice other religions. Ask them to talk about and show pictures illustrating what they believe and how they worship God.

† Family Prayer

Talk together about the fact that our natural differences as family members are a blessing for our family. Pray together:

O God, thank you for all the people in my family, for all the gifts that make us different, and for your grace that makes us one.

Learn by heart Faith Summary

What must we do about prejudice?
- As Catholics we must fight against prejudice in our lives.

How do we act toward people of other religions?
- We respect those who worship God in other religions.

How do we relate to those who do not share our Catholic faith?
- We have a special bond with the Jewish people. We seek unity with all Christians.

Make a list of friends who worship differently from you. Put a check when you have told a friend why you are proud to be a Catholic, and your friends have told you about their religion.

FRIEND	RELIGION	TALKED ( )

Review

Go over the *Faith Summary* together and encourage your fifth grader to learn it by heart, especially the first statement. Then have him or her do the *Review*. The answers to numbers 1–4 appear on page 216. The response to number 5 will show how well your fifth grader understands the evil of prejudice, and what he or she can do today to help end it. When the *Review* is completed, go over it together.

Circle whether each is True or False. Then make a false statement true.

1. Prejudice is acceptable in some circumstances.   T   **(F)**
2. Not all Christians believe in Jesus.   T   **(F)**
3. Christians and Jewish people both follow the Ten Commandments.   **(T)**   F
4. Ecumenism is the search for unity among all Christians.   **(T)**   F
5. Name a group that suffers from prejudice in our society. Tell some ways you will help to end this prejudice.

_____
_____
_____
_____
_____
_____

FAMILY SCRIPTURE MOMENT

Gather and have family members list ways they have "been blind" about other people. Then **Listen** to a gospel story about blindness.

As he passed by he saw a man blind from birth. His disciples asked him, "Rabbi, who sinned, this man or his parents, that he was born blind?" Jesus answered, "Neither he nor his parents sinned; it is so that the works of God might be made visible through him. We have to do the works of the one who sent me while it is day. Night is coming when no one can work. While I am in the world, I am the light of the world."
John 9:1–5

Share how Jesus is the Light of the World for each person.

Consider for family enrichment:
■ By assuming that the blind man was disabled through his own or his parents' fault, the disciples showed their own "blindness."
■ Since all people are made in God's image, prejudice toward anyone for any reason is sinful.

Reflect and **Decide** What is our vision of a world without prejudice of any kind? How will we help to make that vision a reality in our parish, our Church, and our nation?

24 THE GIFT OF FAITH

For the Catechist: Spiritual and Catechetical Development

ADULT BACKGROUND

Our Life

Have you ever walked on water? Peter managed it admirably—until he took his eyes off Jesus and tried to go it alone. "O you of little faith," Jesus complained, "why did you doubt?" (Matthew 14:31).

Have you ever achieved the impossible in other ways?

Maybe you overcame a handicap of some kind or helped a dying person to gain peace of mind or learned a skill that others claimed was "beyond you."

Ask yourself:

■ In what ways have I "walked on water"?

Sharing Life

Why is faith (in God, in self, in others) an indispensable virtue?

What sometimes prevents you from living as a person of faith?

Our Catholic Faith

Faith implies a relationship of trust. Peter was able to walk on water because he trusted Jesus, who had said to him, "Come." When Peter's trust wavered, his relationship with the Lord lost its newfound intensity, and he started to sink.

The theological virtue of faith enables us to trust and believe in God, to accept God's revelation, and to live according to God's will. As the theologian Paul Tillich has pointed out, faith involves our will, knowledge, and emotions. It is a gift from God that must be practiced if it is to grow and remain strong.

Dominican preacher Meister Eckhart once observed, "You can never trust God too much." The more we practice the virtue of faith, the more fruit it will bear. Faith requires a deep personal commitment that survives despite doubts and difficulties. It is an assent to Jesus' request: "You have faith in God; have faith also in me" (John 14:1).

The Catholic Church as a community voices the truths of its faith in various creeds. In the Apostles' Creed, for example, we reiterate what we believe about each of the three Persons of the Blessed Trinity. We also reaffirm our belief in the Church itself, in the communion of saints, and in the final resurrection of the dead.

Coming to Faith

In what ways do you need to practice the virtue of faith?

Why is it important for us to recognize, express, and seek guidance on any doubts we may have about the truths of our faith?

Practicing Faith

How will you trust God in a new or deeper way this week?

How will you communicate the value of faith to your fifth graders?

159A

CATECHISM OF THE CATHOLIC CHURCH

The Theme of This Chapter Corresponds with Paragraph 198

LITURGICAL RESOURCES

Invite the fifth graders to prayerfully consider the question: "What one impossible thing do I wish I could do for God (or God's people)?" Remind them that Jesus says in Matthew 17:20 that true faith can move a mountain! Distribute drawing materials and have the young people illustrate their impossible wishes in any way they choose. Then have them turn their wishes into a "Prayer for Faith That Can Move Mountains."

JUSTICE AND PEACE RESOURCES

Saint James's letter to the early Christians contains a timeless message for us. Observing that faith without actions is dead, he wrote:

> If a brother or sister has nothing to wear and has no food for the day, and one of you says to them, "Go in peace, keep warm, and eat well," but you do not give them the necessities of the body, what good is it?
> (James 2:15-16)

The fifth graders might invite another group to join them in conducting a neighborhood clothing drive for the needy. They can make up a slogan, draw posters, and come up with an identifying armband to wear during the drive. They can also sort and pack the clothing for the Saint Vincent de Paul Society or a local thrift shop.

Teaching Resources

Overview of the Lesson

Movement One — Our Life
Read a Scripture story about faith.

Movement Two — Sharing Life
Share thoughts about faith and reasons why we believe.

Movement Three — Our Catholic Faith
Present the virtue of faith and the Apostles' Creed.

Movement Four — Coming to Faith
Deepen the understanding of faith and the Apostles' Creed.

Movement Five — Practicing Faith
Fashion symbolic expressions of faith.

Faith Alive at Home and in the Parish

Family and young person are encouraged to practice the virtue of faith.

FAITH WORD

Faith is a virtue that enables us to trust and believe in God, to accept what God has revealed, and to live according to God's loving will.

Teaching Hints

This lesson provides an opportunity to strengthen the young people's understanding of the virtue of faith. Present it so that the group understands these three basic truths: The virtue of faith begins as a gift from God; it must be practiced if it is to grow and remain strong; and if we really have faith in God, we will believe even when we find it hard to do so.

Special-Needs Child

Try to involve mainstreamed children in every activity. Collaboration with others is very helpful to such children.

Visual Needs
- large-print Apostles' Creed chart

Auditory Needs
- headphones for musical selections

Tactile–Motor Needs
- peer helper to assist with activities

Supplemental Resources

Peter (God's Story series)(video)
Mass Media Ministries
2116 North Charles Street
Baltimore, MD 21218
(1-800-288-8825)

Lourdes: Pilgrimage and Healing
(video)
Palisades Home Video
P.O. Box 2794
Virginia Beach, VA 23450-2794
(1-800-989-8576)

24

Lesson Plan: Beginning

Objectives

To help the young people

- know the Apostles' Creed;
- understand that faith is a virtue that enables us to believe in God;
- decide how to put faith into action.

Focusing Prayer

Gather the young people quietly. Remind them that our faith in Jesus Christ is the greatest gift we have. Pray together the prayer at the top of page 159.

Our Life

To Whom Would We Go?

Today's lesson begins with this beautiful Scripture story from John's Gospel. Read it to the group. Ask, "Why do you think the people found it so hard to understand what Jesus was saying?" and "What was so wonderful about Peter's answer?" Then ask the closing question. Help the young people to see that faith means believing even when we do not completely understand.

Sharing Life

I Believe

Use these questions to initiate a discussion about the nature of belief. Help the young people to put into words the reasons for their belief in God. They might first write their reasons in their faith journals and then share them with the group.

Enrichment

Read All About It!

Tell the young people to read the newspapers for one week. Then tell them that they will make up their own newspaper. Explain that their newspaper will be a Newspaper of Faith, that is, all the articles will center around faith.

Bring in an appropriate newspaper and review the different sections. Have the young people work in groups to write and edit articles about faith. If possible, you might have them input their articles on a computer and "publish" their newspaper.

Materials needed: sample newspaper; writing paper; pens or pencils

---

24 The Gift of Faith

Lord Jesus, we believe that you have the words of eternal life.

Our Life

Jesus said to the people, "I am the living bread that came down from heaven; whoever eats this bread will live forever." Many of his followers could not understand this teaching. They turned away from him. So Jesus asked the twelve disciples, "Do you also want to leave?"

Simon Peter answered for all of them. "Master," he said, "to whom shall we go? You have the words of eternal life. We have come to believe and are convinced that you are the Holy One of God."

Based on John 6:51–69

What do you learn from this Scripture story?

Suppose Jesus asked you, "Do you also want to leave?" What would be your answer?

Sharing Life

Talk together about these ideas.
Possible responses:
- What is it about a person that makes us believe in him or her? Honesty, trustworthiness, kindness, keeping his or her word, etc.
- What is the hardest thing about believing in someone? People may disappoint us.
- Share the reasons why you believe in God.
Ask: When do you know that God is with you? How does God help you?

159

24

Lesson Plan: Middle

Our Catholic Faith

Faith Word

Write the word *faith* on the chalkboard or newsprint. Explain that this word is used in a special way in this lesson. Invite the group to listen for it and to consider how it is used.

Gifts from God

Read aloud the first two paragraphs on page 160. Emphasize the definition of virtue given in the first paragraph and have the group underline it. Then have a volunteer write on newsprint or the chalkboard the names of the three virtues—faith, hope, and love—that we practice each day. Circle the word *faith,* and explain that we will learn what a special gift from God this virtue is and how necessary and important it is in our lives.

Have the young people locate the *faith word* on page 161 and learn the definition by heart.

The Gift of Faith

Have volunteers read the next three paragraphs. Emphasize God's great goodness in giving us the gift of faith. Ask, "What do we mean by the mysteries of faith?" Encourage the young people to share any mysteries of faith that they find difficult to believe. Encourage them to pray for help in believing them.

◆ Enrichment ◆

Believing Without Seeing

As you discuss the virtue of faith with the fifth graders, paraphrase the story of doubting Thomas (from John 20:24–29).

Ask the young people why they think Thomas could not believe that Jesus had risen from the dead. (It seemed impossible; no dead person had come back before.) Help them to understand that sometimes we must have faith and believe, despite what others say or do.

Materials needed: Good News Bible

Our Catholic Faith

Stress the underlined text

The Virtue of Faith

A *virtue* is the habit of doing something good. We find virtues such as courage, honesty, and justice in many people.

In our relationship with God we are asked to practice the special virtues of faith, hope, and love every day. Each of these virtues is a gift from God.

Our Catholic faith is a gift from God. Jesus taught us that faith is necessary for us to gain eternal life. Faith comes to us only because God gives us this gift. We do not earn the gift of faith.

In response to God's love, we live our faith as disciples of Jesus Christ and as God's own people. Jesus is the greatest teacher of our faith. Jesus also gave us the Church to help us learn about and live our faith together.

Sometimes it is difficult to understand everything about God and our faith. Many things about God are called mysteries of faith, such as the Blessed Trinity. No one can fully understand these mysteries. We believe them because God has revealed, or made them known, to us. The Church teaches them to us, and they are part of our faith.

Our Church has several prayers called creeds that summarize what we believe. We pray the Nicene Creed at Mass.

On the next page is another creed. It is called the Apostles' Creed because it developed from the very early teachings of the Church. The Apostles' Creed describes the most important truth of our Catholic faith: There is one God but three divine Persons in the one God. We call this truth the mystery of the Blessed Trinity.

Our faith requires that we practice what we believe and put our faith into action. Here are some ways we can do this:

- We should learn as much as we can about our faith.
- We should celebrate the sacraments often, especially Eucharist and Reconciliation.
- We should make decisions each day that show we are living the Law of Love and building up the reign of God.
- We should avoid all forms of prejudice.
- We should try to be peacemakers in our lives and pray for peace in the world.

Perugino, *Consegna delle Chiavi*, Sistine Chapel, Vatican

160

Lesson Plan: Middle

What We Believe

Read aloud the next paragraph. Then ask if anyone remembers the part of the Mass during which we pray the Nicene Creed.

Before continuing the reading, emphasize that the mystery of the Blessed Trinity is the most important truth of our faith. As you read the next paragraph, have the young people underline the sentence that describes the mystery of the Blessed Trinity.

Finish up the reading on page 160. Have five volunteers each read one of the ways we can practice what we believe.

The Apostles' Creed

Read aloud the Apostles' Creed on page 161. Then have three pairs of young people present the parts of the creed by having one partner read the prayer and the other partner read the corresponding explanation.

Encourage the young people to learn the Apostles' Creed by heart a section at a time. By the end of the year, they should know the whole creed. Profess it together now aloud.

Our Catholic Identity

Use page 14 from the *Our Catholic Identity* section in the back of the book. Point out that saints were persons who understood perfectly that faith is something to be lived. Comment on the actions of the saints you have read about on the page. Answer any questions the group might have.

You may wish to use pages 53–54 in the activity book for *Coming to God's Life*.

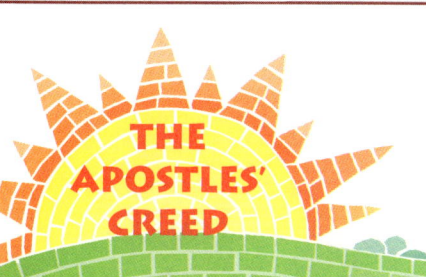

THE APOSTLES' CREED

FAITH WORD

Faith is a virtue that enables us to trust and believe in God, to accept what God has revealed, and to live according to God's loving will.

I believe in God, the Father almighty, creator of heaven and earth.

The Apostles' Creed tells the story of God's love for us. It is divided into three parts. The first part of the Apostles' Creed tells us about God the Father, who gives us life.

I believe in Jesus Christ,
his only Son, our Lord.
He was conceived by the power
of the Holy Spirit
and born of the Virgin Mary.
He suffered under Pontius Pilate,
was crucified, died, and was buried.
He descended to the dead.
On the third day he rose again.
He ascended into heaven,
and is seated at the right hand of the Father.
He will come again to judge
the living and the dead.

The second part speaks of God the Son, who became our Savior and the Savior of all people. God the Son became one of us to save us from sin. Jesus died on the cross and rose from the dead to bring us new life. He redeemed us and freed us from the power of sin. He is the perfect sign of God's love for us.

The third part of the Apostles' Creed talks first of God the Holy Spirit, who is our sanctifier, the one who makes us holy.

I believe in the Holy Spirit,
the holy, catholic Church,
the communion of saints,
the forgiveness of sins,
the resurrection of the body,
and the life everlasting.
Amen.

Then the Creed reminds us that we are to believe that the Church was founded by Jesus. We are in union with all baptized persons, living and dead.

We believe that our sins will be forgiven if we are truly sorry for them, and that we will rise again to live with God forever in heaven.

ENRICHMENT

Stating Our Beliefs

Challenge the young people to compose "I Believe" statements about their Catholic faith to share with their friends and families. Remind them that these beliefs require actions in their daily lives.

Have the young people print their statements on large sheets of posterboard or strips of shelving paper. Display them in the room or, if appropriate, in the vestibule of your parish church.

Materials needed: posterboard or shelving paper; markers

24

Lesson Plan: End

Coming to Faith

Learning the Creed

Have the young people share their beliefs about the Father, Son, and Holy Spirit. Then have them work in pairs to help each other start learning the Apostles' Creed by heart.

Practicing Faith

Symbols of Faith

Allow time for the young people to work on their symbolic expressions of faith and to share them with one another. Find space to display these in the room under the title "We Believe."

Direct the group to page 199, the section in the back of the book called *Sharing the Faith* where the truths of the faith are incorporated. Explain that these truths are here to help the young people remember what they have learned about their Catholic faith by the time they have completed fifth grade.

Evaluating Your Lesson

- Do the young people know the Apostles' Creed?
- Do they understand what faith enables us to do?
- Have they decided how they will live their faith?

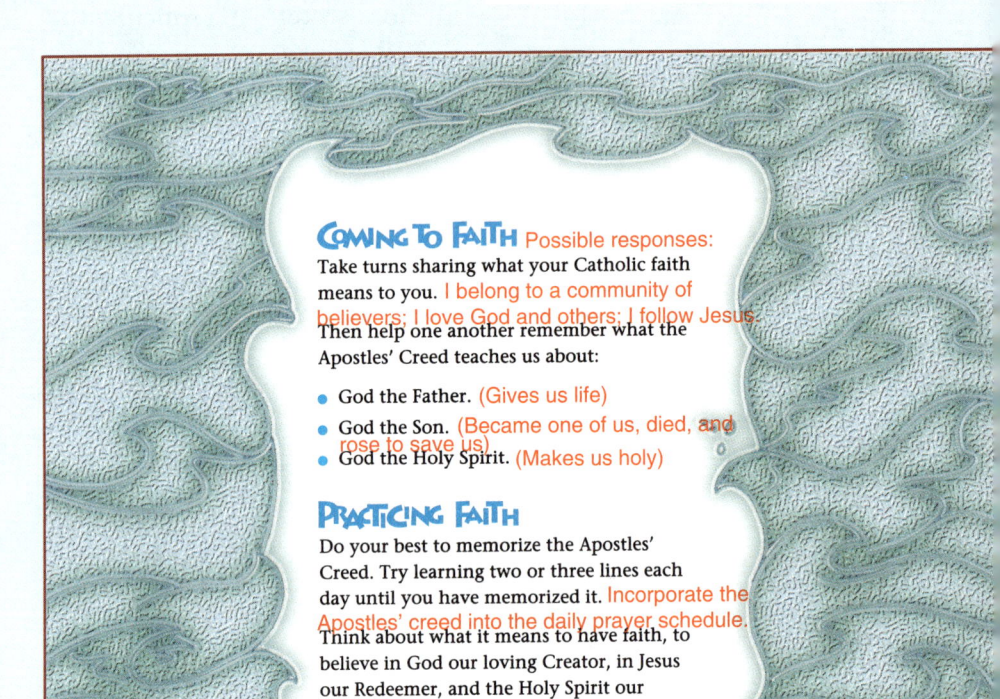

Enrichment

The Rewards of Faith

Form groups and have the young people do a Scripture search to find how Jesus rewarded faith. For example, have them read Luke 7:1–10; 8:40–48; 8:49–56.

They can present their findings to the whole group as dramatic readings or role-plays.

Materials needed: Good News Bibles

Coming to Faith
Possible responses:
Take turns sharing what your Catholic faith means to you. *I belong to a community of believers; I love God and others; I follow Jesus.* Then help one another remember what the Apostles' Creed teaches us about:

- God the Father. *(Gives us life)*
- God the Son. *(Became one of us, died, and rose to save us)*
- God the Holy Spirit. *(Makes us holy)*

Practicing Faith

Do your best to memorize the Apostles' Creed. Try learning two or three lines each day until you have memorized it. *Incorporate the Apostles' creed into the daily prayer schedule.* Think about what it means to have faith, to believe in God our loving Creator, in Jesus our Redeemer, and the Holy Spirit our Sanctifier. Then express your faith by drawing a symbol or by writing a poem, or by just writing key words that say what your faith means to you.

Take turns sharing what you have made. Listen carefully as your friends speak. We can help one another strengthen our faith.

✝ Close by praying together the words of the Apostles' Creed.

Talk with your catechist about ways you and your family might use the "Faith Alive" pages. Pray the prayer together.

Optional Activities

A Modern-Day Parable (for use with page 160)

Read Matthew 14:22–33 to the group. Ask the young people to write similar, modern-day stories. Explain that their characters should trust in God up to a certain point and then begin to doubt. Have them finish their stories by stating how the doubting person comes to believe once again.

Materials needed: paper; pens or pencils

Faith in Action (for use with page 161)

Invite your group to think about how the following people might respond to the question, "How do we put faith into action in our lives?"

- an elderly person
- a second grader
- a priest or missionary
- a parent

Have them role-play their responses.

A Mural of the Creed (for use with page 161)

Your group might enjoy drawing or painting on newsprint or shelf paper a large, three-panel mural presenting the major divisions of the Apostles' Creed. The first panel could illustrate God the Father as Creator and Giver of life. The second could depict the life, death, and rising of Jesus our Savior. The third panel could focus on the Holy Spirit and the Church (holy, united with the saints, and forgiving). Display the completed mural.

Materials needed: art supplies

A Group Project (for use with page 162)

Have the young people choose one of the following group projects:

- Improvise a skit based on the story of Jesus walking on the water (Matthew 14:22–33) or any other gospel story illustrating faith.
- Make a booklet that could be used to teach the main ideas of the Apostles' Creed to young children.
- Make flash cards to define the terms *faith*, *virtue*, *creed*, *Blessed Trinity*, and *mysteries of our faith*.

Materials needed: drawing paper; markers; cardboard for flash cards

Living Faith (for use with page 162)

Challenge the young people to write short stories or to draw comic strips or posters illustrating Saint James's statement, "If faith includes no good actions, then it is dead." Have them share their work with the group.

Materials needed: paper; pens; pencils; posterboard; markers

162A

FAITH ALIVE AT HOME AND IN THE PARISH

In this lesson your fifth grader has learned more about the virtue of faith and its necessity for our salvation. This is the first of the three great virtues that are at the core of our Catholic identity. They are sometimes called the theological virtues because they pertain to our relationship with God.

Read together the Bible story of Jesus walking on the water (Matthew 14:22–33). In this story Jesus asks Peter to have faith and trust in him and to walk on the water, too. But Peter doubted Jesus, lost faith, and began to sink. So Jesus said to him, "O you of little faith, why did you doubt?" (Matthew 14:31).

As a family, think about the hard times that each family member has faced in trying to practice her or his Christian faith. Then talk about the times that family members, like Peter, relied only on themselves instead of trusting in Jesus' love and care.

Discuss the fact that once we have done the best we can, we have to place ourselves in God's hands, trusting in God's promise of loving care. This is how we and our whole parish practice the virtue of faith.

✝ Family Prayer

Jesus, we believe in you because you are the way, the truth, and the life. Amen.

Learn by heart Faith Summary

What virtues are gifts from God?
- The virtues of faith, hope, and love are gifts from God.

What is faith?
- Faith is a virtue that enables us to trust and believe in God, to accept what God has revealed, and to live according to God's will.

What do the creeds of the Church do?
- The creeds of the Church summarize what we believe.

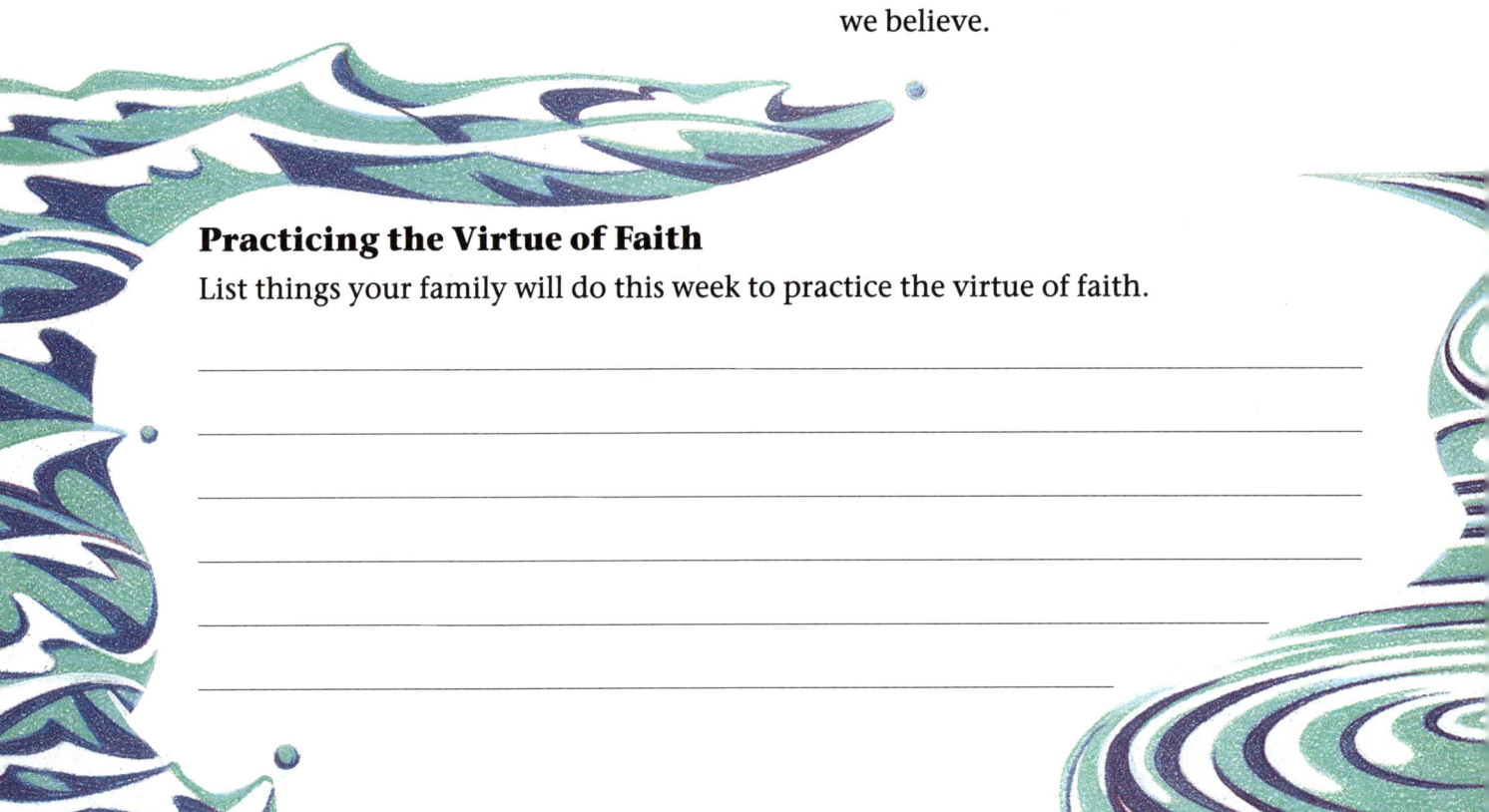

Practicing the Virtue of Faith

List things your family will do this week to practice the virtue of faith.

_____
_____
_____
_____
_____

Review

Go over the *Faith Summary* together and encourage your fifth grader to learn it by heart, especially the first two statements. Then have him or her do the *Review*. The answers to numbers 1–4 appear on page 216. The response to number 5 will show how well your fifth grader accepts responsibility for living the faith. When the *Review* is completed, go over it together.

Circle the letter beside the correct answer.

1. The habit of doing good is called
   a. a sacrament.
   b. a virtue.
   c. the Apostles' Creed.
   d. a mystery.

2. A mystery is something we do not fully
   a. pray about.
   b. learn about.
   c. understand.
   d. care about.

3. Faith enables us to
   a. trust and believe in God.
   b. accept what God has revealed.
   c. live according to God's loving will.
   d. all of the above

4. The Apostles' Creed includes
   a. Jesus walking on water.
   b. the virtue of love.
   c. the mystery of the Blessed Trinity.
   d. the virtue of hope.

5. How will you show this week that you accept the responsibility to live your Christian faith?

_____
_____
_____

FAMILY SCRIPTURE MOMENT

Gather and have family members name persons and things in which they have faith and tell why. Then **Listen** to the story of doubting Thomas.

The other disciples said to him [Thomas], "We have seen the Lord." But he said to them, "Unless I . . . put my finger into the nailmarks and put my hand into his side, I will not believe." Now a week later. . . . Jesus came . . . and said, "Peace be with you." Then he said to Thomas, "Put your finger here and see my hands, and bring your hand and put it into my side, and do not be unbelieving, but believe." Thomas answered . . . "My Lord and my God!" Jesus said to him, "Have you come to believe because you have seen me? Blessed are those who have not seen and have believed."

John 20:25–29

Share what family members heard in this reading for their own lives.

Consider for family enrichment:
■ Thomas is afraid to believe in the good news of Jesus' resurrection.
■ Jesus praises all who, like us, believe in him without demanding that we first see his glorified body.

Reflect and **Decide** What can we as a family do to deepen our faith in Jesus? Pray together: "My Lord and my God!"

25 GOD FILLS US WITH HOPE

For the Catechist: Spiritual and Catechetical Development

ADULT BACKGROUND

Our Life

Like many other inner-city Catholic schools, St. Francis de Sales Academy survives on hope. The budget is always on the edge of disaster. Neighborhood crack addicts vandalize the building regularly. Teachers sometimes "burn out" and leave. Despite the obstacles, students have high aspirations. Their shared beliefs and values enable them to believe that "there's a new day coming."

The principal, Brother Mark, says, "The kids share our hope that they will reshape their own world."

Ask yourself:

■ What enables me to keep hope alive?

Sharing Life

What obstacles to hope do you think young people encounter today?

What differences do beacons of hope like St. Francis de Sales Academy make?

Our Catholic Faith

Although we offer our hopes in our daily conversations, when we speak of the virtue of hope we are going beyond our wishes, dreams, and expectations. Hope is the virtue that enables us to trust in all God's promises. Paul's letter to the Romans, describing the surety of future glory that can make our present suffering seem insignificant, puts it this way:

> For in hope we were saved. Now hope that sees for itself is not hope.... But if we hope for what we do not see, we wait with endurance (Romans 8:24-25).

The Second Vatican Council reaffirmed the need of all Christians to exercise continually the theological virtues of faith, hope, and love. (We call them theological virtues because they are gifts of God and help to direct our lives toward Him.) As we participate in the building of God's kingdom, our aspirations for lasting riches, rather than for the wealth of the passing world, are strengthened. Naturally, along the way we will encounter setbacks and failures, obstacles and difficulties.

> Among the struggles of this life, they find strength in hope, convinced that "the sufferings of the present time are not worthy to be compared with the glory to come that will be revealed in us" (Romans 8:18).
> (*Decree on the Apostolate of the Laity*, 4)

The Blessed Virgin Mary, as the first and greatest disciple, is a sign and model of hope for us. She believed in God's promises, followed her Son to the cross, and rejoiced in His resurrection. Her Magnificat is a song of hope for the reversal of worldly values and the reign of God in our lives.

Coming to Faith

Why do you think hope is crucial to a follower of Jesus?

How do you think the Church can be a more effective sign of hope for the world?

Practicing Faith

What will you do for someone or some group that is suffering from a lack of hope?

How will you help your most disinterested fifth graders to experience hope?

CATECHISM OF THE CATHOLIC CHURCH

The Theme of This Chapter Corresponds with Paragraph 1817

LITURGICAL RESOURCES

As a simple meditation on the virtue of hope, distribute art materials and invite the group to consider these words:

> You are my hope, Lord;
>   my trust, GOD, from my
>   youth
> (Psalm 71:5).

Have the fifth graders fashion symbols of persons, places, or things that have helped them to put their hope in Jesus. Display these and offer the prayer together. Urge the young people to learn it by heart.

JUSTICE AND PEACE RESOURCES

In the Magnificat, Mary sings of how God has had mercy on those who hope in God. The mighty have been dethroned; the proud have been scattered. The hungry have been fed, all their needs provided for. God has "lifted up the lowly" (Based on Luke 1:52).

Engage the fifth graders in a dialogue on how they can "lift up the lowly." Help them to identify the lowly (the poor, those who have no influence, those who are dependent on others for everything, those who have no hope).

Have each person decide on a gift of hope to be given to one of the "lowly" this week.

25

Teaching Resources

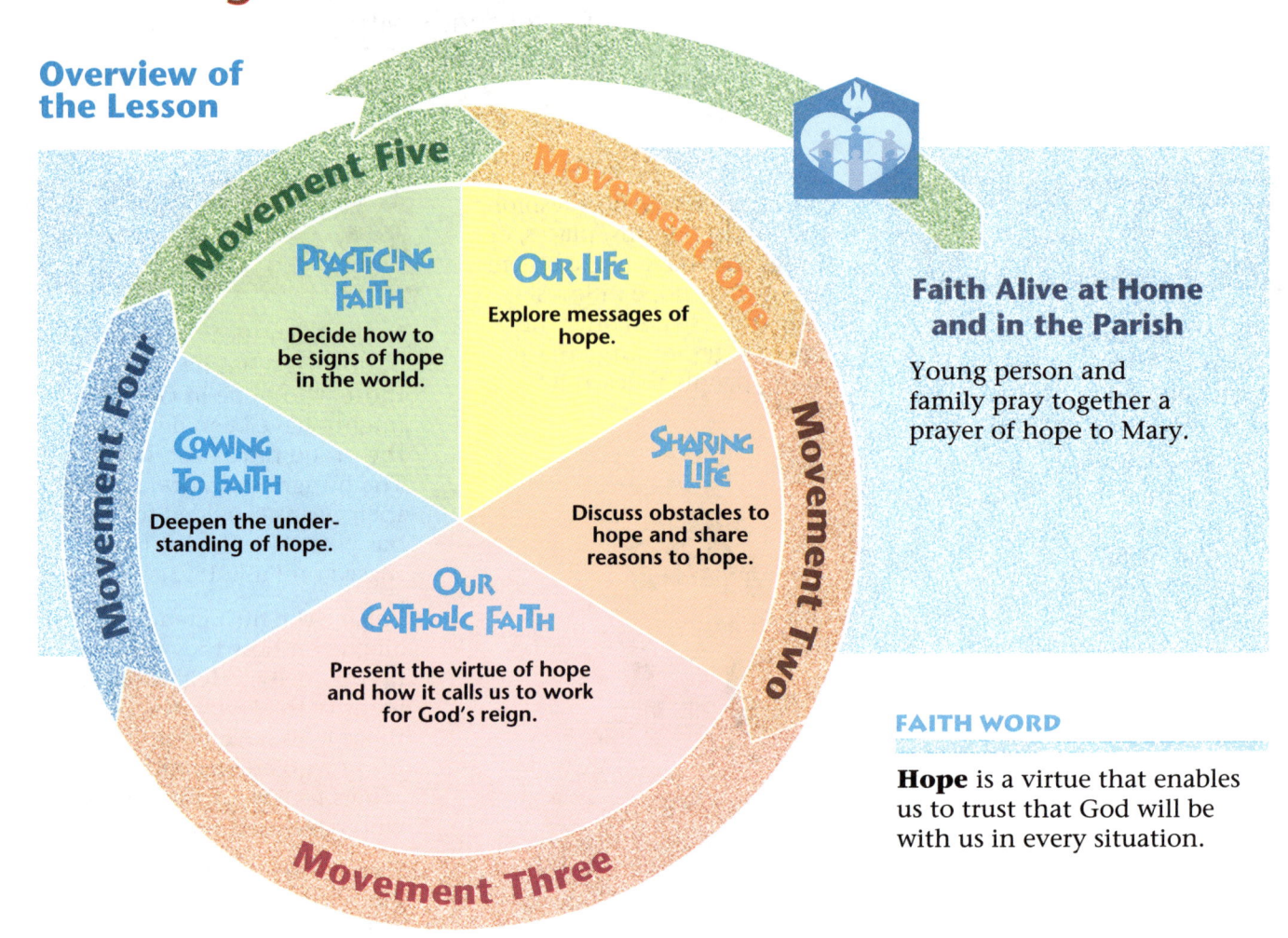

Overview of the Lesson

Movement One — Our Life: Explore messages of hope.

Movement Two — Sharing Life: Discuss obstacles to hope and share reasons to hope.

Movement Three — Our Catholic Faith: Present the virtue of hope and how it calls us to work for God's reign.

Movement Four — Coming To Faith: Deepen the understanding of hope.

Movement Five — Practicing Faith: Decide how to be signs of hope in the world.

Faith Alive at Home and in the Parish

Young person and family pray together a prayer of hope to Mary.

FAITH WORD

Hope is a virtue that enables us to trust that God will be with us in every situation.

Teaching Hints

This lesson provides an opportunity to strengthen the young people's awareness that they can grow in the virtue of hope through prayer, receiving Holy Communion, and practicing a hopeful attitude toward our life today. The virtue of hope should be presented in such a way as to encourage them to feel free to express their fears. Once they have expressed their fears, help them to decide what they can do to alleviate them.

Special-Needs Child

Hope may be a difficult virtue for the special-needs young person. Create an environment of support and encouragement.

Visual Needs
- blind person to speak to the group on hope

Auditory Needs
- hearing-impaired person to speak to the group on hope

Tactile–Motor Needs
- peer helper to assist with activities

Supplemental Resources

God So Loved the World (video)
(from the *Gospel* series)
Brown-ROA
2460 Kerper Blvd.
P.O. Box 539
Dubuque, IA 52004–0539
(1-800-922-7696)

The Cloak of Juan Diego (video)
Vision Video
2030 Wentz Church Road
PO Box 540
Worcester, PA 19490
(1-800-523-0226)

165C

Lesson Plan: Beginning

OBJECTIVES

To help the young people

- know the meaning of hope;
- understand that hope is a virtue that enables us to trust God;
- choose ways to be signs of hope.

Focusing Prayer

Gather the young people quietly, then pray together the prayer at the top of page 165.

Our Life

Messages of Hope

Play a recorded song (suggestions: "Wind Beneath My Wings" or "You Will Know") and ask the young people to tell what the song says about hope. Now have the young people look at the picture on page 165. Explain that they are going to hear about how young people respond to Pope John Paul II's message of hope. Then call on volunteers to read aloud the first five paragraphs of *Our Life*. Use the follow-up questions to guide a group discussion on the subject of hope.

Materials needed: music source

Sharing Life

Reflecting on Hope

Have the young people share and discuss their responses to the *Sharing Life* questions and ideas. Conclude by asking how they think people their age can grow in hope in God. Invite several volunteers to respond.

---

25 God Fills Us with Hope

Jesus, we place all our hope in you.

Our Life

Pope John Paul II loves young people. He enjoys being with them and hearing what they have to say about their lives and about their faith. He always brings them a message of hope.

After meeting with the Holy Father, here is what a group of young people had to say:

"I think the pope is great! He makes me feel that things are better than I thought."

"Wow! He told us how much the Church needs us and how important we are. That's cool!"

"He told us that we are the future of the Church. He made me feel that young people like us can make a difference."

Do you know anyone who is filled with hope? Tell about him or her. **Accept individual responses. Include your own.** What do you think it means to be a person of hope? **To keep going when discouraged, to trust that God will help** What does hope mean in your life now? **Accept reasonable responses.**

Sharing Life

Have you ever been in a situation in which you felt hopeless? Tell about it. Explain what you did and why. **Include your own example.**

Talk together and share reasons why Christians should always have hope. **Because we follow Jesus from death to life**

ENRICHMENT

Symbols of Hope

Encourage the young people to use drawings, prose, or poetry to illustrate symbols of hope. Set a ten-minute limit for this activity. Tell the group to focus on ideas that suggest how they can be signs of hope to the world. Share the results and display the symbols under the heading of "Hope."

Materials needed: art supplies; paper; pens or pencils

Lesson Plan: Middle

Our Catholic Faith

Faith Word

Write the word *hope* on the chalkboard or newsprint. Alert the group to listen for this word in today's lesson.

The Virtue of Hope

Have a volunteer read the first paragraph under "The Virtue of Hope" on page 166. Invite the young people to respond to the question, "What is the virtue of hope?" Observe that when we "wish" for something, we are not sure it will happen.

Explain that in this lesson we are not talking about hope as wishing—the virtue of hope means we trust that what we hope for *will* happen.

Have the young people locate the *faith word* at the top of page 167. Invite a volunteer to read the definition of *hope* to the group. Then return to page 166, and read aloud the second and third paragraphs.

Before continuing, ask the young people to name some of the things God has promised us. For example:

■ If we live a good life, we will live forever with God in heaven.

■ If we do our part, God will help us to avoid sin.

Explain that when we trust that God will fulfill these promises, we are practicing the virtue of hope.

◆ ENRICHMENT ◆

Filled With Hope

Have your fifth graders conduct a survey about people's hopes. Ask each young person to fold a piece of paper in half lengthwise, then in half widthwise. Explain that fifth graders will write in seven of the eight sections—four on each side of the paper—a person's answers to the following questions: "What is your greatest hope for yourself? for your family? for America? for the world? What do you hope the world will be like in 50 years? Do you think it's important to always have hope for the future? Why or why not?" Have the young people bring their survey results back to share with the group. Find out if most people surveyed hope for a better life in the future.

Materials needed: paper; pencils

Our Catholic Faith

Stress the underlined text.

The Virtue of Hope

Often we use the word hope to mean "wish and expect." When we say, "I hope it will be nice this weekend," we are wishing for good weather. The virtue of hope means much more than this kind of wishing or expecting.

<u>We practice the virtue of hope when we trust that God will help us in every situation, no matter what our problem is.</u>

Hope, like faith, is a gift from God. We are able to have hope because <u>God promises to love us always.</u> Our confidence in God helps us to live as people with hope.

Michelangelo, *Pietá*, (15th century)

<u>Jesus is our greatest source of hope.</u> We trust in Jesus' promise that our actions will make a difference. When Christians hope that God's reign will really come, we are not just wishing. We do all that we can each day to make it happen. With the help of the Holy Spirit, we do our best to do God's loving will, knowing that our lives can make a difference.

Everyday we read about sadness and suffering. We are tempted to wonder whether God has forgotten us. To hope does not mean to wait for God to solve all our problems. <u>With the help of God's grace, we must work together for the reign of God.</u>

Two thousand years ago, Saint Paul also lived in a world filled with problems. Christians were being persecuted and killed for their faith in Jesus Christ. It looked as if the Church, which had just begun, would not last. *Stress that hope enables us to act and to solve problems.* In Romans 8:39, Saint Paul wrote to the Christians in Rome to encourage them to have hope, telling them that there was nothing in all creation that would ever be able to separate them from the love of God which was theirs—and is ours—through Christ Jesus our Lord.

<u>As Christians we have the hope of eternal life as well. This hope encourages us to pray for the souls in purgatory. At Mass we pray for those who have died in the hope of rising again.</u> We also hope to enjoy forever the vision of God's glory in heaven.

166

Lesson Plan: Middle

Living in Hope

Read carefully the remaining paragraphs of this section. Ask, "When is it most difficult to hope?" and "How do we live in a world filled with problems?"

Read aloud again the words of Saint Paul.

A Special Sign of Hope

Discuss with the young people why they think Mary is often called "Our Lady of Hope." Then read aloud the first three paragraphs under "Mary, a Sign of Hope." Stress the connection between Mary's assumption and our own hope that we will live forever with God. Try to instill in the young people a sense of gratitude for the gift God has given us in Mary.

Showing Hope Today

Read aloud the last paragraph on page 167. Encourage volunteers to share and discuss their responses. Emphasize that hope is a virtue that should motivate us to action. Each of us is called to do his or her part to bring about God's reign.

Call attention to the picture on this page. Ask, "How do we show we have hope?" Engage the group in a discussion of the joy that this virtue can bring to our lives.

Our Catholic Identity

Use page 15 from the *Our Catholic Identity* section in the back of the book. Ask the youngsters to identify the candle in the illustration. If possible, show them a real paschal candle. Recall that the candle is a symbol of Jesus, the Light of the World. Ask if any students have attended the Easter Vigil. Have them share what they remember of the blessing of the new fire and the procession and lighting of candles. Talk about the Service of Light as a wonderful sign of the good we can do as Christians.

ENRICHMENT

A Woman of Hope

Invite the young people to discover in the Gospels how Mary was a woman of hope. Have them work in four groups, each with one of these gospel stories: Luke 1:26–38, and 1:39–56; John 2:1–11, and 19:25–27.

Each group should present, in its own words, its story to the whole group. Have the young people select a key phrase or sentence from the Gospel account for all to remember Mary as a woman of hope.

Materials needed: Bible

Mary, A Sign of Hope

Mary is a special sign of hope for us. The Blessed Virgin Mary was Jesus' first and greatest disciple. Mary is the Mother of the Church.

The Church teaches that at the end of her life, Jesus brought Mary, body and soul, to be with Him forever in heaven. We call this Mary's assumption. We celebrate this event on August 15. Mary's assumption strengthens our hope that we, too, will live forever in heaven.

We can ask Mary to help us hope that we can make things better in the world. Then one day our hope will be fulfilled. We, too, like Mary, will enjoy life with God forever in heaven.

The Church today continues to bring a message of hope to the whole world. Each time we pray and celebrate the sacraments with our parish community, we show that we have hope that God's reign will come.

FAITH WORD

Hope is a virtue that enables us to trust that God will be with us in every situation.

167

Lesson Plan: End

Coming to Faith

Living Hope

Explain the *Coming to Faith* activity on page 168. Allow time for the young people to write their responses. Then invite volunteers to read aloud what they would do in each of the situations outlined.

Affirm their responses, and encourage them to be signs of hope for their families and other people.

Practicing Faith

Living as Signs of Hope

Explain the *Practicing Faith* activity on page 168. Encourage generous but realistic decisions about how to be signs of hope. Have the young people share what they have decided to do. You may also wish to share with the young people how they have been signs of hope for you.

A Prayer of Hope

Select five leaders for the prayer service. Gather the young people at the prayer table and invite them to take a moment to think about God, to whom they are about to pray. Then celebrate the prayer service.

Enrichment

Letters of Hope

Have the young people work in four groups. Give each group one letter of the word *hope*. Each group should take its assigned letter and use it as the opening letter of a statement about hope. Have the young people share their work, then write the statements on a poster for the parish church.

Some ideas:
*H*ave trust in God.
*O*pen your hearts to trust.
*P*ersevere in confidence.
*E*ternal joy will be ours.

Materials needed: posterboard; markers

Evaluating Your Lesson

■ Do the young people know what hope is?

■ Do they understand that hope enables us to trust in God?

■ Have they decided ways to be signs of hope?

Talk with your catechist about ways you and your family might use the "Faith Alive" pages.

Coming to Faith

As Christians we can show hope in God in many ways. Discuss what you would do to live the virtue of hope in each of these situations. Why?
  Possible responses:
• Everything at home seems hopeless. No one seems to understand you. You feel like running away. Talk with someone you trust.
• People are being treated unfairly and with prejudice because of their race or religion. Refuse to join in, try to help.
• Violence seems to be a way of life; young people are losing their lives on our streets. Pray for peace, work out conflicts peacefully.

Practicing Faith

Share with one another ways you can be signs of hope in your homes and neighborhood. Write on the candle one way you will do this. Then gather in a circle with your friends. Take turns holding up your candle and reading aloud your decision of hope. Pray together:

†**Leader:** Let us pray for hope for others and for ourselves.

All: We are people of hope.

Leader: God, our Creator, help those who have given up hope.

All: We are people of hope.

Leader: Jesus Christ, our Redeemer, help those who suffer from addiction. Free them from their hopeless actions.

All: We are people of hope.

Leader: Holy Spirit, our Sanctifier, help all people, especially those our age, who want to hurt themselves or even end their lives. Take away their hopelessness.

All: We are people of hope.

Leader: Loving God, help each one of us to be a person of hope.

All: Amen.

Optional Activities

A Hope Slogan (for use with page 165)

Invite the young people to design posters bearing slogans about the need for hope in today's world. Have volunteers share their posters with the group.

Materials needed: posterboard; rulers; markers

A Poem/Song of Hope (for use with page 166)

Challenge the fifth graders to write poems or songs on the theme of hope. Then have the poets and lyricists present their work to the entire group.

An Essay on Hope (for use with pages 166–167)

Have the young people write one-page essays on "How (or Why) Jesus Gives Me Hope." Select several essays to be read to the group and/or duplicated to share with others. (The local or diocesan newspaper might be interested in publishing the best ones.)

Role-Playing Hope (for use with page 168)

Invite the young people to role-play how they would try to encourage and give hope to:

- a parent or neighbor who has lost his or her job;
- a friend who keeps failing at something;
- a priest or teacher who is overworked and seems depressed.

Praying for Hope (for use with page 168)

Invite three volunteers to each read one of the following verses from the Book of Psalms:

Those who fear the LORD
    trust in the LORD,
  who is their help and shield.
(Psalm 115:11)

I will walk freely in an open space
    because I cherish your precepts.
I will speak openly of your decrees
    without fear even before kings.
I delight in your commands,
    which I dearly love.
I lift up my hands to your commands;
    I study your laws, which I love.

Remember your word to your servant
    by which you give me hope.
This is my comfort in affliction,
    your promise that gives me life.
(Psalm 119:45-50)

My soul, be at rest in God alone,
    from whom comes my hope.
(Psalm 62:6)

Gather at the prayer table. Have the young people proclaim their verses. Between each proclamation, have the group respond with a sung "Amen."

FAITH ALIVE AT HOME AND IN THE PARISH

In this lesson your fifth grader has learned more about the virtue of hope. Ask him or her to tell you what hope means and how to live it each day at home and in the parish.

As Christians, we usually know when we sin against faith or love, but we are not nearly as conscious of sins against hope. Yet hope, too, is one of the great and central virtues of our faith.

Help your family to understand that in Christian faith, the life, death, and resurrection of Jesus are our greatest source of hope. Because of Easter, we know that Jesus will help us to avoid sin and do God's loving will. We can live in hope because we know that we can always rely on God.

Discuss as a family how you feel about news items you see, hear, or read that report situations which appear to be hopeless.

Share how your family feels about the life, death, and resurrection of Jesus as the greatest source of hope for our world. To help your fifth grader see this, read or tell the Bible story of when Jesus appeared to Mary Magdalene and told her to tell everyone he had been raised from the dead (John 20:1–18).

Then talk about things your family can say and do to be a sign of hope. Help your family look to Mary as a sign of hope by doing the activity below together.

✝ Family Prayer

O Mary, help us never to give up on your Son's love. We have hope that his kingdom will come, and that we will live forever with him in heaven.

Honoring Mary

Design a banner honoring Our Lady, an example of hope for all Christians.

Learn by heart Faith Summary

What is hope?
- Hope is the virtue that enables us to trust that God will be with us in every situation.

Who is our greatest source of hope?
- Jesus is our greatest source of hope.

What is Mary a sign of?
- Mary, the Mother of the Church, is a sign of hope for us.

169

Review

Go over the *Faith Summary* together and encourage your fifth grader to learn it by heart, especially the first two statements. Then have him or her do the *Review*. The answers to numbers 1–4 appear on page 216. The response to number 5 will help you see how well your fifth grader is growing as a person of hope. When the *Review* is completed, go over it together.

Circle the letter beside the correct answer.

1. Hope enables us to
   - **a.** trust in God's promises.
   - b. doubt God's promises.
   - c. worry about God's promises.
   - d. deny God's promises.

2. On August 15, Catholics celebrate
   - a. Pentecost.
   - b. Christmas.
   - c. the birth of Mary.
   - **d.** the Assumption.

3. Jesus' first and greatest disciple is
   - a. Saint Peter.
   - **b.** Mary.
   - c. Saint Paul.
   - d. Saint John the Baptist.

4. We can be signs of hope by
   - a. praying.
   - b. celebrating the sacraments.
   - c. trying our best to do God's loving will.
   - **d.** all of the above

5. What will you do to show you are a person of hope?

   _____
   _____
   _____
   _____
   _____

FAMILY SCRIPTURE MOMENT

Gather and ask: What part do we want Mary to play in our lives? Then **Listen** as a family to one of the very last things Jesus did before he died on the cross.

Standing by the cross of Jesus were his mother and his mother's sister, Mary the wife of Clopas, and Mary of Magdala. When Jesus saw his mother and the disciple there whom he loved, he said to his mother, "Woman, behold, your son." Then he said to the disciple, "Behold, your mother." And from that hour the disciple took her into his home.
John 19:25–27

Share what you learned from the words of Jesus on the cross.

Consider for family enrichment:

■ John is the beloved disciple to whom Jesus entrusts his mother. John is the symbol of the entire Church; Mary is to be the mother of us all.

■ Mary is a sign of hope to us that we, too, will conquer death and live forever with the risen Lord.

Reflect and **Decide** What might we do to make Mary an ever-present member of our family? Pray together: Thank you, Lord, for sharing your mother with us.

26 The Gift of God's Love

For the Catechist: Spiritual and Catechetical Development

Adult Background

Our Life

A fifth grader in Oceanside, California, decided to have his head shaved while he was undergoing chemotherapy. When his classmates heard about it, thirteen boys had their heads shaved, too. They did not want their friend to feel like "he didn't fit in." Inspired by his students' example, the teacher followed suit.

Ask yourself:

■ What is my response to this story?

■ How have I shown (or been shown) unselfish love?

Sharing Life

Why do we sometimes fail to love others as generously as we love God?

How do you hope your life gives witness to the virtue of love?

Our Catholic Faith

Love is the third theological virtue, and the most significant of the three. In one of Saint Paul's best-known passages ("Love is patient, love is kind…"), we are reminded that while we are awaiting the day when we shall see God face-to-face, we can "know God" through the practice of faith, hope, and love "but the greatest of these is love" (1 Corinthians 13:13).

Whatever other gifts we may have—skill at teaching or preaching, great knowledge, or physical abilities—they mean little if we have not love. Saint Paul insists that even if we were to give away all of our possessions to the poor and seek martyrdom itself, our acts would have no value in God's eyes unless they were motivated by love. Love is the outstanding virtue of a mature Christian who has outgrown "childish ways."

Our Catholic tradition provides us with specific ways to embody God's love for others. The Corporal Works of Mercy challenge us to provide for the physical needs of our sisters and brothers in the human family. The Spiritual Works of Mercy call us to prayer, patience, forgiveness, and other acts of sharing that draw people to God.

Guided by the example of Jesus Christ, the Church has always emphasized our need to commit ourselves to works of mercy and charity. These works are evident in the lives of the saints, the histories of religious orders, the services of charitable organizations, and the ministry of all Christians who are guided by God's Law of Love.

Coming to Faith

Why is love the greatest of the theological virtues?

How will you encourage and practice the works of mercy in your parish?

Practicing Faith

What will you do to communicate to your group the value of selfless love for others?

CATECHISM OF THE CATHOLIC CHURCH

The Theme of This Chapter Corresponds with Paragraph 1823

LITURGICAL RESOURCES

Among the saints few surpass Francis of Assisi as an exemplar of Christlike love. Francis stands as an excellent model for people of all ages because he combined his great love for God with an equally great love for other human beings.

Ask volunteers (or those who have prepared in advance) to share any stories they know about how Saint Francis showed his love for Jesus, the poor, the lepers, nature, and all creatures.

Provide materials for the group to make Franciscan greeting cards illustrating his prayer: "Grant that I may not so much seek to be loved as to love."

JUSTICE AND PEACE RESOURCES

When the young Joan of Arc had to confront the French dauphin in his illustrious court, the voices of her companion saints advised her, "Go boldly." Out of love for God and country, Joan did just that.

Tell or read a story of Saint Joan of Arc to your group. Then brainstorm how the young people might "go boldly" to work for the cause of justice, peace, or freedom. (For instance, they might speak up to public officials on behalf of the homeless; write letters for Amnesty International; design a poster or radio campaign for life issues, and so on.)

Teaching Resources

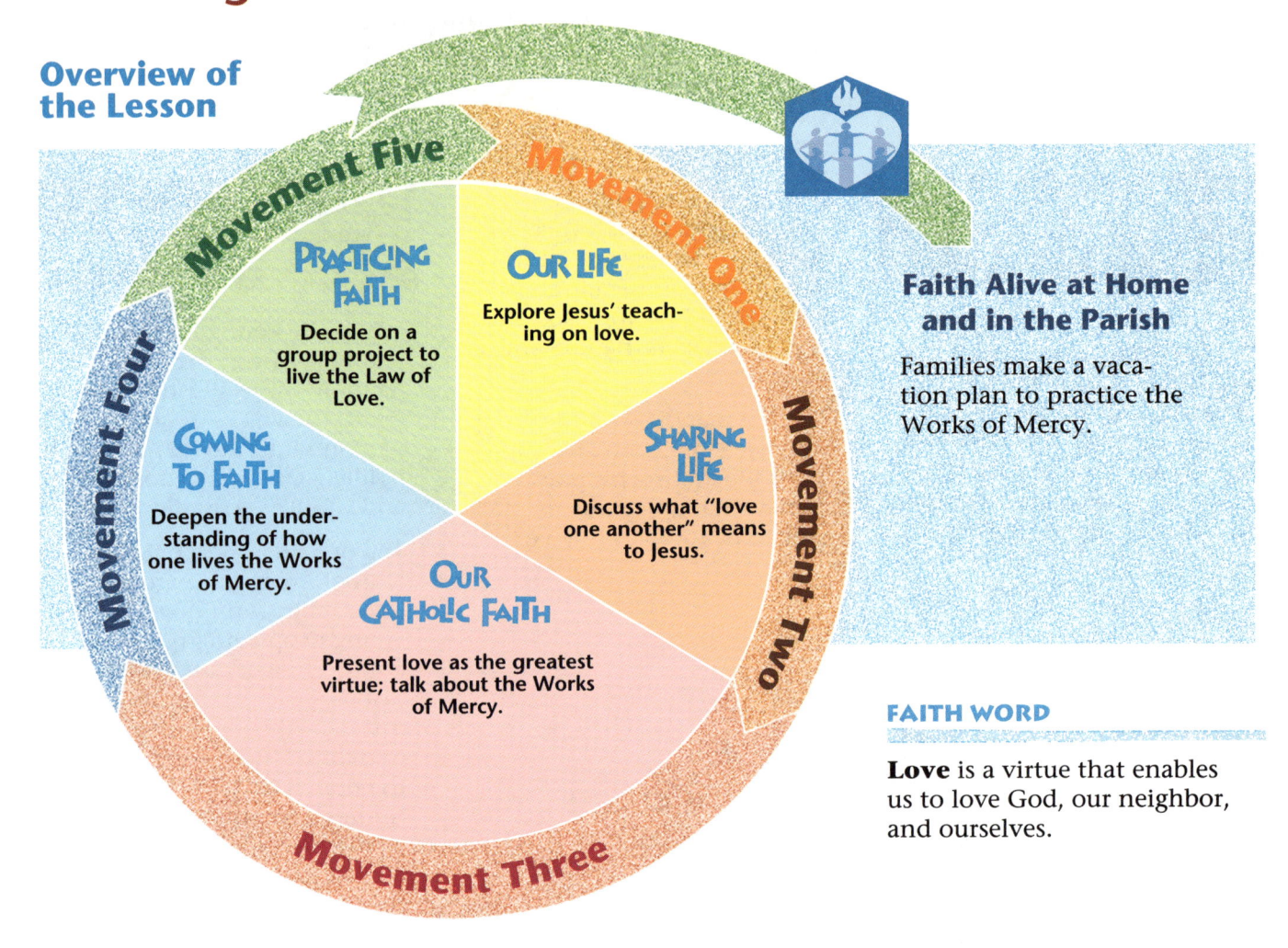

Overview of the Lesson

Movement One — Our Life: Explore Jesus' teaching on love.

Movement Two — Sharing Life: Discuss what "love one another" means to Jesus.

Movement Three — Our Catholic Faith: Present love as the greatest virtue; talk about the Works of Mercy.

Movement Four — Coming To Faith: Deepen the understanding of how one lives the Works of Mercy.

Movement Five — Practicing Faith: Decide on a group project to live the Law of Love.

Faith Alive at Home and in the Parish

Families make a vacation plan to practice the Works of Mercy.

FAITH WORD

Love is a virtue that enables us to love God, our neighbor, and ourselves.

Teaching Hints

This lesson provides an excellent opportunity to help the group understand that one person can make a difference in the world. Encourage the young people to begin to make a difference in little ways by doing "random acts of kindness."

Be sure to emphasize the practical ways that young people can live the Spiritual and Corporal Works of Mercy in their daily lives.

Special-Needs Child

If you have a mainstreamed young person with motor-control disabilities, think of ways to include this person in the group's projects.

Visual Needs

■ recorded story about a blind person (for example, Helen Keller) who made a difference

Auditory Needs

■ book about Beethoven, a deaf composer

Tactile–Motor Needs

■ large crayons or markers for activities

Supplemental Resources

The Selfish Giant (video)
Mass Media Ministries
2116 North Charles St.
Baltimore, MD 21218
(1-800-828-8825)

Skate Expectations
(from *The McGee and Me* series)
(video)
Vision Video
2030 Wentz Church Road
PO Box 540
Worcester, PA 19490
(1-800-523-0226)

171C

Lesson Plan: Beginning

OBJECTIVES

To help the young people

- know the meaning of Jesus' teaching on love;
- understand that the virtue enables us to love God, neighbor, and self;
- choose ways to live this virtue through Works of Mercy.

Focusing Prayer

Gather the young people in quiet. Tell them that today you will be talking together about the simplest, yet most difficult of Jesus' teachings. Then pray together the prayer at the top of page 171.

Our Life

A Letter from Saint John

Read aloud the first paragraph on page 171, then ask for responses to the question. Ask the young people to listen to John's letter as if he were writing directly to each of them. Then read John's letter slowly and reverently. Have the group respond to the two final questions.

Sharing Life

Love One Another

Have the young people work in two groups to discuss the ideas presented here. Then have them share their collective thoughts with the whole group.

---

26 The Gift of God's Love

Jesus, help us to love others as you love us.

OUR LIFE

The apostle John once wrote a long letter to the Christians of the early Church. He was concerned that some might be overcome by the pressures of the world and forget the most important teaching of Jesus' way of life.

What do you think is the most important teaching of Jesus about the way we should live?

Here is a part of John's letter. Listen to it as if he is writing it directly to you.

> Beloved, let us love one another, because love is of God; everyone who loves is begotten by God and knows God. Whoever is without love does not know God, for God is love. In this way the love of God was revealed to us: God sent his only Son into the world so that we might have life through him. In this is love: not that we have loved God, but that he loved us and sent us his Son as expiation for our sins. Beloved, if God so loved us, we also must love one another.
>
> 1 John 4:7–11

What did you hear from John's letter for your life? *God loves us, God is love, we are children of God, God sent the Son to us.*
John uses the word *love* ten times! What do you think John means by *love*? *God's love for us in sending the Son, forgiveness*

SHARING LIFE

Discuss: how can we love those who are
- strangers to us?
- different from us?

Treat others fairly, with kindness, understanding, etc.

What does Jesus, and John, expect of us when they say "love one another"? *We should live the Law of Love.*

ENRICHMENT

Campaign for Kindness

A university professor in California was so dismayed by the hate he read about in the newspaper that he decided to start a campaign to encourage people to do acts of kindness for others, even strangers, every day. Many have joined him. Encourage your young people to join, too. All they have to do is perform "random acts of kindness and senseless acts of beauty" for other people, without expecting anything in return. Challenge your group to come up with ideas about what fifth graders might do. Have the group make a chart on posterboard or newsprint listing the different ideas. Display the chart in the room.

Materials needed: posterboard or newsprint; markers

171

Lesson Plan: Middle

Our Catholic Faith

Faith Word

Write the word *love* on the chalkboard or newsprint. Ask the group what symbol you should use to represent this word. Have the young people decide whether or not a cross is a better symbol than a heart. Tell them to listen for the word in today's lesson and to remember its meaning.

The Virtue of Love

Read aloud the first two paragraphs under "The Virtue of Love" on page 172. Discuss with the young people examples of sacrifices that they might be called upon to make to show their love for God and others. Have the young people locate the *Faith Word* at the top of page 173. Invite the group to read together the definition of *love* and to learn it by heart.

A Bible Story About Love

Have volunteers read aloud the next five paragraphs. Have the young people underline Jesus' response to the question. Stress that Jesus means that whatever we do for others, we do for Him.

◆ ENRICHMENT ◆

Love Is . . .

Remind the young people that through the ages humans have tried to describe what love is in words and music. Explain that people also have defined the word *love* by actions of affection and mercy, such as those performed by the yearly winners of the Andrew Carnegie Hero Award. These heroes receive a medal inscribed "Greater love hath no man than to lay down his life for a stranger." Then challenge the fifth graders to compose songs, poems, or sayings that describe love and/or loving actions.

Materials needed: paper, pencils

172

OUR CATHOLIC FAITH

Stess the underlined text.

The Virtue of Love

<u>The virtue of love is one of God's greatest gifts to us.</u> Because we are created in God's image and likeness, we are made to love and be loved. Living the virtue of love is what makes us most like God.

We practice the virtue of love not just with words and feelings, but especially by what we do for others. We should not give to others or do for others only when it is convenient for us. To live the virtue of love we must often sacrifice, or give up something, to show our love for God and others.

Jesus' whole life was an act of love. He once told his followers this powerful story to help them better understand how important the virtue of love is in living for God's reign.

Jesus said that at the end of time he will say, "Come, you who are blessed by my Father. Inherit the kingdom prepared for you from the foundation of the world. For I was hungry and you gave me food, I was thirsty and you gave me drink, a stranger and you welcomed me, naked and you clothed me, ill and you cared for me, in prison and you visited me."

172

Lesson Plan: Middle

Read the final paragraph. Invite responses to the question, "What does love require of us?" Then ask the young people to discuss how the woman in the illustration is showing love.

Works of Mercy

Read aloud the first three paragraphs under "The Greatest Virtue." Invite several young people to read aloud the Corporal and Spiritual Works of Mercy. After each has been read, ask, "Can a fifth grader live this work today? If so, how can you do it?"

Interpreting Pictures

Direct the young people's attention to the illustration on pages 172. Ask what they think Jesus is telling the crowd of people. Then ask the young people what they think Jesus meant by "the least important. . . ." since all people are equally important to Him.

You may wish to use pages 57–58 in the activity book for *Coming to God's Life*.

The followers will ask, "Lord, when did we do all these things for you?"

Jesus will reply, "Whatever you did for one of these least brothers of mine, you did for me."
Based on Matthew 25:31–40

Jesus was teaching his disciples that love demands action. The virtue of love demands that we reach out to others, especially to people in need. The true love that Jesus taught us demands that we treat others fairly and with justice.

FAITH WORD

Love is a virtue that enables us to love God, our neighbor, and ourselves.

The Greatest Virtue

In our Catholic tradition, we know some very specific ways to practice the virtue of love. These are called the Corporal and Spiritual Works of Mercy.

The Corporal Works of Mercy show us how to care for the physical well-being of our neighbors. The Spiritual Works of Mercy show us how to care for their spiritual well-being.

When we practice the virtue of love, we come to know why Saint Paul ends his description of love by saying that of the three virtues of faith, hope, and love, "the greatest of these is love" (1 Corinthians 13:13).

Corporal Works of Mercy
- Feed the hungry.
- Give drink to the thirsty.
- Shelter the homeless.
- Clothe the naked.
- Care for the sick.
- Help the imprisoned.
- Bury the dead.

Spiritual Works of Mercy
- Share knowledge.
- Give advice to those who need it.
- Comfort those who suffer.
- Be patient with others.
- Forgive those who hurt you.
- Give correction to those who need it.
- Pray for others.

173

◆ ENRICHMENT ◆

Pennants of Mercy

Have the young people create fourteen paper pennants, one for each work of mercy. Each pennant should carry an action-word heading that suggests the activity (for example: *Feed, Help, Comfort, Forgive, Counsel*). Under the heading have the young people write the specific Work of Mercy. Display the pennants in the room.

Materials needed: construction paper; scissors; markers

Lesson Plan: End

Coming to Faith

An Individual Plan of Action

Explain the activity on page 174 and give the group time to complete it. Provide appropriate background music while the young people work.

Invite them to share their Action Plans.

Materials needed: music source

Practicing Faith

A Group Plan of Action

Now invite the young people to work together to plan a project the group could do collaboratively as "workers of mercy" in the weeks ahead.

◆ **ENRICHMENT** ◆

Living the Virtue

Reinforce the *Practicing Faith* activity by organizing the young people into a planning committee. Have them choose one of the following acts of love, and then plan how to carry it out:

■ Help younger children to learn a skill.

■ Teach a gospel story to children in primary grades.

■ Collect canned goods or clothing for the poor.

■ Visit someone at a nursing home.

■ Make cards for those in mourning.

174

Close by rereading together the words of Saint John on page 171. Then have the group listen to a recording such as "The Cry of the Poor," from the *Wood Hath Hope* album, North American Liturgy Resources.

Materials needed: music source

EVALUATING YOUR LESSON

■ Do the young people understand the virtue of love?

■ Do they know the Works of Mercy?

■ Have they decided how they will practice the virtue of love?

Coming To Faith

Rewrite these Corporal and Spiritual Works of Mercy as action statements so that it is easier for you to practice them. For example, you could rewrite "Comfort those who suffer" as "I can invite someone who is suffering from prejudice to spend time with my group of friends."

MY ACTION PLAN

■ Share knowledge.
I can help someone with schoolwork or read to younger children.

■ Be patient with others.
I can try to understand people who are younger or older than I.

■ Feed the hungry.
I can share my lunch with a classmate or help in a food drive.

■ Shelter the homeless.
I am willing to play or work with everyone—not just my best friends.

■ Pray for others.
I can pray for my family, my friends, and others who may need prayers.

Practicing Faith

Talk together about a work of mercy that you might take on as a group project this coming week. For example:

• Does your parish work for the poor and homeless? How can you help?

• Could a catechist use some help with younger children?

Plan what you can do. Then do it! End by listening again to the words from Saint John's letter on page 171.

174

Talk with your catechist about ways you and your family might use the "Faith Alive" pages. Pray the family prayer with your catechist and friends.

Optional Activities

The Light of Love (for use with page 171)

Gather at the prayer table. Pray together the Christophers' motto ("It is better to light one candle than to curse the darkness"), and follow up with a Scripture reading. An appropriate selection would be John 8:12:

Jesus spoke to them [the Pharisees] again, saying, "I am the light of the world. Whoever follows me will not walk in darkness, but will have the light of life."

Materials needed: Bible; song lyrics

A Plan to Change the World (for use with page 171)

Invite the young people to imagine themselves as young adults who have been provided with an opportunity to do something to change the world. Have each write a short paragraph telling what she or he would change and how.

A Reading About Love (for use with page 172)

Point out to the group that Saint Paul wrote one of the most beautiful definitions of love that the world has ever known. Have a volunteer read aloud the passage from 1 Corinthians 13:4–7, and invite the young people's comments.

Materials needed: copies of Scripture selection

A Works of Mercy Search (for use with page 173)

Have the young people search newspapers and magazines for stories in which a person or a group is doing one of the Corporal or Spiritual Works of Mercy. Have the young people cut out the stories, mount them on construction paper, and staple them together to make a Works of Mercy booklet.

Materials needed: newspapers and magazines; scissors; glue; construction paper; stapler

Works of Mercy Drawings (for use with page 174)

Have the group members draw a series of illustrations depicting the Corporal or Spiritual Works of Mercy as they can be carried out by young people. Display these as an aid to memory and an incentive to action.

Materials needed: drawing paper, markers

FAITH ALIVE AT HOME AND IN THE PARISH

In this lesson your fifth grader has learned more about the greatest virtue of all, love. Ask her or him to tell you what Jesus and John mean by love. Know that in our Catholic tradition love always demands justice; true love means much more than a sentimental feeling.

As a family read and talk about this description of real love written by Saint Paul:

Love is patient, love is kind. It is not jealous, [love] is not pompous, it is not inflated, it is not rude, it does not seek its own interests, it is not quick-tempered, it does not brood over injury, it does not rejoice over wrongdoing but rejoices with the truth. Love never fails.

1 Corinthians 13:4–6,8

Discuss with your fifth grader ways you and your parish can live the virtue of love. Conclude by helping to complete this activity.

† Family Prayer

O God, we love you above all things. Help us to love one another and ourselves as Jesus taught us to do.

Growing in Love

During vacation keep a weekly calendar. Write one way you will try to practice the virtue of love each day. Use the Spiritual and Corporal Works of Mercy for suggestions.

Learn by heart — Faith Summary

What is love?
- Love is a virtue that enables us to love God, our neighbor, and ourselves.

What are the Corporal and Spiritual Works of Mercy?
- The Corporal and Spiritual Works of Mercy are some very specific ways to practice the virtue of love.

What does Saint Paul tell us about love?
- Saint Paul tells us that love is the greatest Christian virtue.

Monday
_____
_____

Sunday
_____
_____

Tuesday
_____
_____

Wednesday
_____
_____

Thursday
_____
_____

Friday
_____
_____

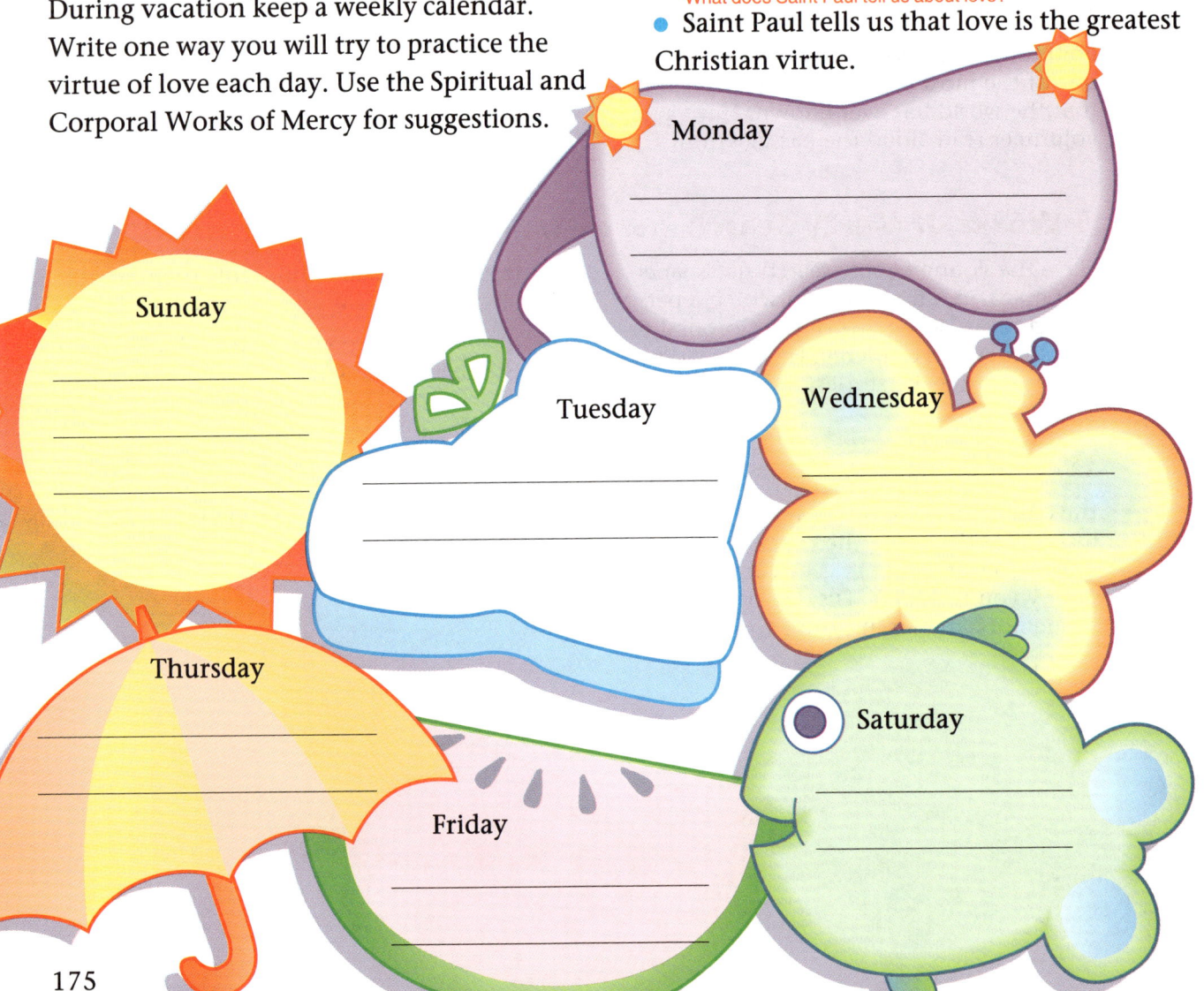

Saturday
_____
_____

Review

Go over the *Faith Summary* together and encourage your fifth grader to learn it by heart, especially the first statement. Then have him or her complete the *Review*. The answers to numbers 1–4 appear on page 216. The response to number 5 will help you to see how well your fifth grader is trying to practice the virtue of love. When the *Review* is completed, go over it together.

Circle the letter beside the correct answer.

1. Saint Paul said the greatest virtue is
   a. hope.
   b. love. *(circled)*
   c. faith.
   d. truth.

2. By his example, Jesus revealed that we practice love in our
   a. words.
   b. feelings.
   c. actions.
   d. all of the above *(circled)*

3. The Corporal Works of Mercy include
   a. praying for others.
   b. comforting those who suffer.
   c. caring for the sick. *(circled)*
   d. sharing knowledge.

4. The Spiritual Works of Mercy include
   a. forgiving those who hurt you. *(circled)*
   b. feeding the hungry.
   c. caring for the sick.
   d. sheltering the homeless.

5. How will you practice the virtue of love this week?

_____
_____
_____
_____

FAMILY SCRIPTURE MOMENT

Gather and have each person tell a story about a time someone showed him or her genuine love. Ask: How do people who truly love us affect who we are? Then **Listen** as Jesus gives us a new commandment.

"My children, I will be with you only a little while longer. You will look for me, and as I told the Jews, 'Where I go you cannot come,' so now I say it to you. I give you a new commandment: love one another. As I have loved you, so you also should love one another. This is how all will know that you are my disciples, if you have love for one another."

John 13:33–35

Share the signs by which people know that you are Jesus' disciples.

Consider for family enrichment:

■ In the Old Testament, God had commanded, "You shall love your neighbor as yourself" (Leviticus 19:18). At the Last Supper Jesus adds that his disciples must love as he has loved them.

■ We show that we are Christians by our love.

Reflect and **Decide** As a family, what attitudes or habits prevent us from loving as Jesus loved? What first step will we take in overcoming these obstacles?

27 SACRAMENTALS

CATECHISM OF THE CATHOLIC CHURCH

The Theme of This Chapter Corresponds with Paragraph 1668

For the Catechist: Spiritual and Catechetical Development

Our Life

For as long as she could remember, Rosaria had seen the faded foot-tall statue of Our Lady of Guadalupe standing by Grandmother Luisa's bed. She knew that her grandmother spoke with the Lady every night before going to sleep. Now as Luisa lay dying, she nodded toward the statue and said to Rosaria, "I want you to have my Lady. She will bring you many blessings."

Ask yourself:

- What sacramentals do I associate with loved ones in my life?

Sharing Life

How have sacramentals enriched your faith?

Our Catholic Faith

Sacramentals are blessings, actions, or objects that help us to remember God, Jesus, Mary, and the saints. They include blessings and medals, relics and shrines, statues and rosaries. They are material, visible realities that help us to become aware of the invisible presence of God, and of our relationship to Mary and the saints.

We never worship sacramentals. We look instead to the reality for which they stand. They help us to recognize that all of life can be holy. As was pointed out at Vatican II, "There is hardly any proper use of material things which cannot thus be directed toward the sanctification of all and the praise of God."

Coming to Faith

How would you explain sacramentals to someone who was not a Catholic?

Practicing Faith

How will you encourage your group to use sacramentals?

Teaching Resources

Teaching Hints

The Church specifically calls some things sacramentals. Other things can be sacramental by their very nature.

If you feel your group is ready for the concept, you can explore with the young people the possibility that all of creation can be sacramental. A sunrise or sunset can remind us of the beauty of the God who created us.

Special-Needs Child

Encourage the mainstreamed young person to participate as fully as possible in all group activities.

Visual Needs
- preferential seating

Auditory Needs
- recorded lesson; headphones

Tactile–Motor Needs
- large markers

Supplemental Resources

Mary and *The Rosary for Young Catholics* (filmstrips)
Twenty-Third Publications
P.O. Box 180
Mystic, CT 06355

The Holy Rosary with the Pope (video)
Vision Video
2030 Wentz Church Road
PO Box 540
Worcester, PA 19490
(1-800-523-0226)

Lesson Plan: Beginning

OBJECTIVES

To help the young people

- know what sacramentals are and how they help us;
- understand the value of the rosary in our lives;
- choose qualities of the saints to emulate.

Focusing Prayer

Gather the young people. When all are quiet, pray together the prayer at the top of page 177.

Our Life

Remembering Famous Catholics

Read aloud the opening paragraph under *Our Life* on page 177. Have volunteers each read one of the names of famous Catholics. Ask the follow-up questions, and list the young people's responses to the last question on the chalkboard or newsprint.

Sharing Life

Special Reminders

Ask the *Sharing Life* questions. Invite volunteers to tell how some of the things in the parish church help them to remember Jesus, Mary, and the saints.

Call attention to the picture on this page. Encourage several young people to tell what the stained-glass window reminds them of and how it makes them feel.

ENRICHMENT
A Blessing to Remember

Have the young people look up and learn by heart one of the following blessings from the Bible. Invite them to share the blessings with their families.

> The LORD bless you and keep you!
> The LORD let his face shine upon you, and be gracious to you!
> The LORD look upon you kindly and give you peace!
> Numbers 6: 24-26

Grace, mercy, and peace from God the Father and Christ Jesus our Lord.
2 Timothy 1:2

Materials needed: Bible

---

27 Sacramentals

Jesus, help us to see signs of your love in our daily lives.

OUR LIFE

Our country honors people in many ways. One special way is by placing statues of two people from each state in the National Statuary Hall located in the Capitol building in Washington, D.C. Among those selected for this honor are thirteen Catholics—so far.

Arizona: Father Eusebio Kino, Jesuit
California: Father Junipero Serra, Franciscan
Hawaii: Father Damian of Molokai, Sacred Heart Fathers
Illinois: General James Shields
Louisiana: Justice Edward D. White
Maryland: Charles Carroll
Nevada: Patrick A. McCarren
New Mexico: Dennis Chavez
North Dakota: John Burke
Oregon: Dr. John McLoughlin
Washington: Mother Mary Joseph Pariseau, Sister of Charity of Providence
West Virginia: John E. Kenna
Wisconsin: Father Jacques Marquette, Jesuit

Father Damian of Molokai

Do you know why any one of these Catholics is honored this way?

What things do you or your family have that remind you of someone? *Answers will vary. Some may have articles of clothing, jewelry, pictures or even furniture.*

SHARING LIFE

What things in your parish church help you to remember Jesus, or Mary, and the saints? *Statues, windows, crucifix, etc.*
Why are these things a help? *Remind the class of the saying, "A picture is worth a thousand words." What does it mean?*

177

27

Lesson Plan: Middle

Our Catholic Faith

Using Sacramentals

Ask: "What things in our daily lives remind us of God?" Then have the young people silently read the first paragraph under "Sacramentals" on page 178. Call on volunteers to share responses to the question.

Invite several young people to read aloud the remaining paragraphs of this section. Pause during the reading to ask, "What does holy water remind us of?" and "What does the altar symbolize?" Allow time to discuss responses. Invite a volunteer to demonstrate how we bless ourselves with holy water. As the reading continues, ask, "What sacramentals do we use during the liturgical year?"

Praying the Rosary

Invite the young people to think about five of the most joyful events or times in their lives. Have them share these events with the group and tell what helps them to remember these happy times; for example, pictures, souvenirs, postcards.

◆ ENRICHMENT ◆

Sacra-MENTAL

Help your fifth graders to understand that sacramentals are not objects of worship but things that help us to remember God. Tell the young people that these blessings, actions, or objects jog our memories of God, Jesus, Mary and the saints. Brainstorm with your group to come up with a list of sacramentals and write the suggestions on the chalkboard or newsprint. Ask each group member to write a brief paragraph explaining why a specific object or sign could be called a sacramental.

Materials needed: paper; pencils

Our Catholic Faith

Stress the underlined text.

Sacramentals

There are many things in our daily lives that remind us of God. Our Church uses blessings, actions, and objects to help us remember God, Jesus, Mary, and the saints. We call these *sacramentals*.

We bless ourselves with *holy water* as we enter the church. Holy water is a sacramental that reminds us that we have been baptized by water and the Holy Spirit and have become God's own children.

The *altar* in our church is also a sacramental. The altar is the symbol of Jesus Christ. It is sometimes called the Lord's table because it reminds us of the Last Supper.

We may wear a *cross* to help us remember the death and resurrection of Jesus. Or we may wear a *medal* to help us remember Mary or the saints. Looking at a *statue* of Jesus, Mary, or one of the saints while we are praying helps us to remember their love and care for us.

Lesson Plan: Middle

Explain that in the next part of the lesson we will find out more about a sacramental that helps us to remember the major events in the lives of Jesus and Mary. Have the young people silently read "The Rosary," then ask volunteers to explain how we pray the rosary.

Read over the joyful, sorrowful, and glorious mysteries with your group. Help the fifth graders to see that the fifteen mysteries basically present an outline of the life of Jesus. Encourage them to try to memorize the mysteries. Explain that when we pray the rosary and reflect on these key points, it strengthens our will to follow Jesus.

You may wish to use pages 59–60 in the activity book for *Coming to God's Life*.

We also use sacramentals during the liturgical year. We light *Advent candles* to help us remember that Christ is the Light of the World. On Ash Wednesday we receive *ashes* on our foreheads. This reminds us to turn away from sin and to turn to the good news of Jesus. On Good Friday we kiss the *crucifix* as a sign of respect and love for Jesus crucified.

During the Easter season we light the *Paschal*, or *Easter Candle* to remember the resurrection of Jesus.

The Rosary

The *rosary* is also a sacramental. Praying the rosary helps us to remember the lives of Jesus and Mary.

We begin praying the rosary with the sign of the cross. The rosary has a cross on which we then pray the Apostles' Creed and remember the beliefs of our faith. The cross is followed by one large bead and three smaller beads. We pray the Our Father on the large bead and one Hail Mary on each of the small beads.

Then there is a circle of five groups of beads, or "decades." Each decade has one large bead and ten smaller ones. We pray an Our Father on each of the large beads and one Hail Mary on each of the small beads. We end each decade by praying the Glory to the Father.

As we pray the rosary, we think about the joyful, sorrowful, and glorious events in the lives of Jesus and Mary. We call these the mysteries of the rosary. There are fifteen mysteries of the rosary. They are:

The Five Joyful Mysteries
1. The annunciation
2. The visitation
3. The birth of Jesus
4. The presentation of Jesus in the Temple
5. The finding of Jesus in the Temple

The Five Sorrowful Mysteries
1. The agony in the garden
2. The scourging at the pillar
3. The crowning with thorns
4. The carrying of the cross
5. The crucifixion and death

The Five Glorious Mysteries
1. The resurrection
2. The ascension
3. The descent of the Holy Spirit upon the apostles
4. The assumption of Mary into heaven
5. The coronation of Mary as Queen of heaven

179

◆ Enrichment ◆

Searching for Sacramentals

Plan a visit to your parish church. Encourage the young people to walk around very quietly and to list all the sacramentals they find. Then have them share their lists.

Point out sacramentals they might have missed, such as stained glass windows and the church bells. Explain that when a church is consecrated, these things are blessed as sacramentals.

27

Lesson Plan: End

Coming to Faith

Remembering God's Presence

Ask the first question under *Coming to Faith* and invite the young people to share their responses.

Then explain the next two activities. Encourage specific personal responses. Invite the young people to share their responses and pictures. Elicit from them how sacramentals can help them to grow in holiness.

Materials needed: paper; markers

Practicing Faith

Living Like the Saints

Read the first two paragraphs, and introduce the activities under *Practicing Faith*. As the young people read about Saint Thomas More and Saint Frances Cabrini, encourage them to keep in mind a particular quality they might like to develop in their own lives. Then have them write responses to the questions that follow each story. Invite volunteers to share their responses, and encourage the young people to carry out their "saintly" decisions.

A Closing Prayer

Place a candle, a crucifix, and a bowl of holy water on the prayer table. Play a recording of any familiar faith song as the young people gather at the table in pairs and silently make the sign of the cross on each other's forehead. Pray together the Hail Mary.

Materials needed: candle; crucifix; bowl of holy water; music source

EVALUATING YOUR LESSON

- Do the young people know the meaning of sacramentals?
- Do they understand how to pray the rosary?
- Have they chosen qualities of the saints to emulate?

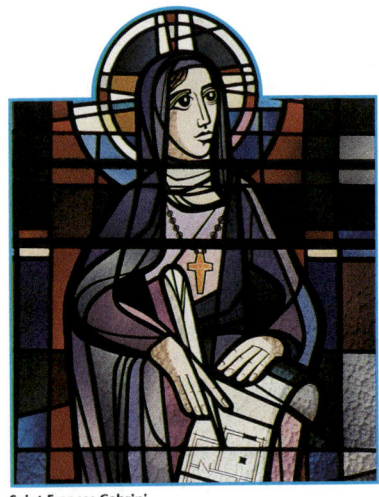

Saint Frances Cabrini

Coming to Faith

How do sacramentals help you to remember God's presence in your life?
Encourage specific responses.
Name a sacramental that you have learned about. Tell what it helps you to remember.
Possible response: A cross helps me to remember the death and resurrection of Jesus.

Draw a picture or a symbol of your favorite sacramental. Then gather together and share your ideas.

Practicing Faith

Statues and medals remind us of the saints who were faithful disciples of Jesus. Their lives can encourage us and remind us of how we can live our faith today.

Read about the saints below and then share together your ideas about ways you can be like them, faithful followers of Jesus Christ.

Saint Thomas More (1478–1535) was a devoted husband, parent, and a successful lawyer. He rose to great power in the government of England when Henry VIII was king. But Henry VIII made himself the head of the Church in England and demanded that Thomas More take an oath against the pope. Thomas refused and was sentenced to death. Thomas More remained loyal both to the Church and to England. He said, "I am the king's good servant, but God's first."

What quality in Thomas More's life will help you to live as Jesus' disciple?
Loyalty—he put God first.

Saint Frances Cabrini (1850–1917) was an orphan who became a school teacher. Frances Cabrini founded the Missionary Sisters of the Sacred Heart to teach orphaned children in Italy. She and some of her Missionary Sisters came to America in 1889. In America Frances founded many schools, orphanages, and hospitals to help the immigrants.

What quality in Frances Cabrini's life will help you to live as Jesus' disciple?
Compassion for others—she helped people in need.

Another saint I like is *Answers will vary.*

The quality I admire and will try to imitate in this saint's life is
Encourage individual responses.

Talk with your catechist about ways you and your family can use the "Faith Alive" pages together. Pray the Our Father with your catechist and friends.

Optional Activities

My Personal Reminder (for use with page 177)

Challenge the young people to draw or fashion from modeling clay their own reminders of Jesus, Mary, or the saints. Display the completed works.

Materials needed: paper; markers; clay

The Mysteries of the Rosary (for use with page 179)

Invite young people to copy in their faith journals the Joyful Mysteries as given on page 179. Have them also enter a symbol or a few key words to explain the meaning of each. "The annunciation" might be followed by symbols for Mary and the angel, or by the phrase "angel announces to Mary." Follow the same procedure for the Sorrowful and the Glorious Mysteries.

Materials needed: faith journals

A Rosary Prayer Service (for use with page 179)

Play a recording on a Marian theme as you explain the following prayer service. Appoint five leaders, and have each stand in a different part of the room as she or he announces one of the Joyful Mysteries. After each mystery, pray one Our Father, one Hail Mary, and one Glory Be. Close by singing "Immaculate Mary."

Materials needed: Marian recording; cassette or record player; words to hymn

Praising God (for use with page 180)

Form concentric circles at the prayer table. Sing together "Glory and Praise to Our God," by Dan Schutte, S.J. (North American Liturgy Resources).

180A

FAITH ALIVE AT HOME AND IN THE PARISH

In this lesson your fifth grader learned that sacramentals are blessings, actions, or objects that help us remember God, Jesus, Mary, the saints, and our call to discipleship. Sacramentals include, for example, blessings, medals, relics, shrines, blessed water, candles, palms and ashes, rosary beads and stations of the cross. They are material, visible realities that help us to be more aware of the invisible loving presence of God, Mary, and the saints in our lives.

We do not worship or pray to sacramentals. Rather, we look to the reality for which they stand. They help us see that all of life can be holy. Sacramentals enrich our Christian life by directing attention to God, who speaks to us through all the gifts of God's creation. Talk to your family about sacramentals and encourage family members to use and treat sacramentals with reverence and respect.

†Family Prayer

Thank you dear God, for filling our lives with your presence. With your grace, let all things remind us of you.

Learn by heart Faith Summary

What are sacramentals?
- Sacramentals are blessings, actions, and objects that remind us of God, Jesus, Mary, and the saints.

What is the rosary?
- The rosary is a sacramental that helps us reflect on the lives of Jesus and Mary.

Sacramentals

Do you have any sacramentals in your home? Do a search and make a list of what you find. If you have none, talk together as a family about having and using sacramentals as a part of your Christian family life.

Review

Go over the *Faith Summary* together and encourage your fifth grader to learn it by heart, especially the first statement. Then have him or her complete the *Review*. The answers to numbers 1–4 appear on page 216. The response to number 5 will indicate your child's understanding of sacramentals and how they help us live our faith. When the *Review* is completed, go over it together.

Complete these sentences about sacramentals.

1. _____Holy water_____ reminds us that we have become God's children in Baptism.

2. The _____crucifix_____ reminds us of Jesus' suffering and death on the cross.

3. We light the _____Paschal (or Easter) candle_____ to remember the resurrection of Jesus.

4. We receive _____ashes_____ on our foreheads at the beginning of Lent to remind us to turn from sin.

5. How can sacramentals help us live our faith?

_____
_____
_____
_____
_____

FAMILY SCRIPTURE MOMENT

Gather around a lighted candle and ask: How is Jesus the light of my world? Then **Listen** as a family to one of Jesus' descriptions of himself.

Jesus spoke to them again, saying, "I am the light of the world. Whoever follows me will not walk in darkness, but will have the light of life." So the Pharisees said to him, "You testify on your own behalf, so your testimony cannot be verified." Jesus answered and said to them, "Even if I do testify on my own behalf, my testimony can be verified. . . . I testify on my behalf and so does the Father who sent me."

John 8:12–14, 18

Share Have family members name things in the home, the church, or the community that remind them of Jesus.

Consider for family enrichment:
- In John's Gospel, Jesus is repeatedly identified with the image of light.
- Candles are a beautiful sacramental of Jesus' light among us.

Reflect Does our home reflect our faith by the presence of sacramentals?

Decide Light a candle and give one another a blessing: "May the light of Christ shine in your life!"

28 CELEBRATIONS FOR THE YEAR

CATECHISM OF THE CATHOLIC CHURCH

The Theme of This Chapter Corresponds with Paragraph 1674

For the Catechist: Spiritual and Catechetical Development

Our Catholic Faith

From the Book of Genesis ("God looked at everything he had made, and he found it very good") to the Book of Revelation ("Let us rejoice and be glad and give him glory,") the Bible celebrates God's gift of life. Psalms 149 and 150 in particular call to mind images of God's people dancing, singing, and making music to praise the Lord.

Our Catholic faith echoes the scriptural theme of celebration in its liturgies and rituals. With prayer, music, bells, vestments, and sacramental signs, we rejoice in God's presence among us. We rejoice, too, in our uniqueness, our gifts, our potential to become all that God sees in each of us.

Our catechesis celebrates not only who the young people are to become, but also who they are here and now. Pope John Paul II said that in the family, the school, and the Church, "special attention must be devoted to the children by developing a profound esteem for their personal dignity and great respect and generous concern for their rights" (*Familiaris Consortio*, 26, November 22, 1981).

Suggested Times for Use

Mass of the Holy Spirit
- At the opening or closing of the parish religion program
- Before or after the feast of Pentecost
- Before important decision-making times such as retreat days

A Way of the Cross
- During Lent or following Lesson 20
- Following Lesson 12, on the liturgical year

We Honor Our Immaculate Mother
- During the month of May
- On a feast day of Mary

Teaching Resources

Teaching Hints

Celebrations are an important way to involve young people in the experience of their faith. These suggested celebrations are meant to be used throughout the religion program at appropriate times. If it is not possible to reserve a whole religion period, you may wish to shorten the celebrations and incorporate them as part of a lesson. The supplemental resources may be used as a preparation for the celebrations or as a follow-up.

Special-Needs Child

Make it possible for a mainstreamed young person to take part in the preparations as well as in the celebrations.

Visual Needs
- large-print copies of readings

Auditory Needs
- recordings, headphones for hymns

Tactile–Motor Needs
- peer assistance

Supplemental Resources

Days of Mary (video)
(from *Celebrating the Church Year for Children* series)
Ikonographics
P.O. Box 600
Croton-on-Hudson, NY 10520
(1-800-944-1505)

183A

Lesson Plan: Beginning

Objectives

To help the young people

- understand different types of religious rituals and celebrations;

- plan, prepare, and participate in these celebrations.

Celebrations for the Year

This lesson is different from all the others in that it does not follow the praxis process. Lesson 28 presents three separate celebrations that can be prepared and celebrated at three different times during the year.

Mass of the Holy Spirit

This celebration would be appropriate at the beginning or end of the year, or around the feast of Pentecost.

It is important that the young people be completely involved in any liturgical celebration you plan for them. The first step is to win their enthusiasm and support for the idea. Then help them to organize and plan the details. Have the young people form groups to work on the various elements involved, such as music, readings, decorations.

Allow time for the preparations. As you plan the Mass, give brief explanations of the different facets of the celebration—for example, the theme of the Holy Spirit, the Liturgy of the Word and of the Eucharist, the gifts of the Spirit. Give the readers time to prepare.

Since this first celebration is a Mass, be in touch with the pastor about the preparations. Invite him to come and talk to the young people about the celebration and about their participation in it.

Allow time before the actual celebration for the young people to reflect quietly on the Holy Spirit's presence within them.

Encourage each one to participate as fully as possible by listening attentively, praying the responses, and singing the songs.

---

28 Celebrations for the Year

God, we remember and celebrate all the gifts of your love.

Mass of the Holy Spirit

Opening Hymn: Write title here.

_____

First Reading
The Holy Spirit comes to the disciples as Jesus promised. (Read Acts 2:1–11.)

Responsorial Psalm
Choose an appropriate psalm from the Lectionary or Bible, for example—Psalm 23 or Psalm 145. Write your selection here.

_____

Response: Lord, send out your Spirit, and renew the face of the earth.

Gospel
A reading from the holy gospel according to John. (Read John 20:19–23.)

Prayer of the Faithful
Leader: Come, Holy Spirit. Renew the face of the earth.
All: Come, Holy Spirit. Renew the face of the earth. *(This response is said after each of the following)*

Reader: Come, Holy Spirit. Give us the gift of wisdom.
All: (Response)

Reader: Come, Holy Spirit. Give us the gift of understanding.
All: (Response)

Reader: Come, Holy Spirit. Give us the gift of right judgment.
All: (Response)

Reader: Come, Holy Spirit. Give us the gift of courage.
All: (Response)

Reader: Come, Holy Spirit. Give us the gift of true knowledge.
All: (Response)

Reader: Come, Holy Spirit. Give us the gift of reverence.
All: (Response)

Reader: Come, Holy Spirit. Give us the gift of wonder and awe in your presence.
All: (Response)

Reader: Come, Holy Spirit. Fill our hearts with your gifts, and come upon us as you came upon the disciples on the first Pentecost.
All: Amen.

Presentation of the Gifts
Write the names of those who will carry the bread and wine to the altar.

Gift	Presenter
_____	_____
_____	_____
_____	_____

Communion Hymn

Closing Hymn

Lesson Plan: Middle

A Way of the Cross

Explain to the group that for many years Christians visited the Holy Land (previously known as Palestine, but now Israel) to follow prayerfully along the way Jesus walked to Calvary, the place of His crucifixion. The Church began the practice of the stations or way of the cross for those who were unable to visit the Holy Land. Pictures or symbols of the most important events in Jesus' passion were erected, and the people would follow them prayerfully.

If possible, show the group pictures of each station, dividing them into the four acts indicated in the text. Invite the young people's questions and comments.

Select an appropriate opening song for the first three acts and a closing Easter song. (You might wish to use "Draw Near, O Lord," or "Keep in Mind" for the first song. "Alleluia! Alleluia! Let the Holy Anthem

Enrichment

Where Jesus Walked

Pick up copies of guidebooks for Israel at your local library. Have the fifth graders work in small groups to read the sightseeing sections about Jerusalem, in which travelers are encouraged to follow the footsteps of Jesus along the way of the cross. Let each group illustrate one of the stations along the way as it looks today, complete with modern visitors, and label what is depicted. Tape the illustrations together side-by-side to make a mural, and label the entire display "Follow the Holy Footsteps."

Materials needed: travel guides for Israel; drawing paper; crayons or markers; tape

Our Catholic Faith

A Way of the Cross

Act One: Arrest and Sentencing
All: *Sing an appropriate song.*
Leader: A reading from the holy gospel according to Mark. (Read Mark 14:43–46.)

First Station
Reader: The next day Pontius Pilate sentenced you, Jesus, to be crucified. You always did God's will and lived to bring about the reign of God. Help us when others make fun of us and ignore us for doing God's loving will.
All: We adore you, O Christ, and we praise you, because by your holy cross you have redeemed the world.

Second Station
Reader: Jesus, the soldiers made fun of you. They placed a crown of thorns on your head and laughed at you. Help us when others make fun of us because we are living the Law of Love.
All: Repeat response "We adore you...."

Third Station
Reader: Jesus, you are the Son of God and one of us. The cross became too heavy and you fell under it. Help us when others tempt us to disobey the Ten Commandments. (Response)

Think and Decide:
What will you do to show that you are proud to be a disciple of Jesus?

Act Two: Helpers Along the Way
All: *Sing an appropriate song.*
Leader: A reading from the holy gospel according to Luke. (Read Luke 23:26–27.)

Fourth Station
Reader: Jesus, your mother, Mary, sees and shares in your pain and suffering. Help us turn to Mary, our mother, for strength to live as your disciples. (Response)

Fifth Station
Reader: Jesus, the soldiers order Simon to help you carry your cross. Help us to bring freedom to those suffering from injustice. (Response)

Sixth Station
Reader: Jesus, Veronica wipes the blood and sweat from your face. Help us to live the Works of Mercy. (Response)

Seventh Station
Reader: Jesus, the weight of the cross causes you to fall a second time. May the Holy Spirit help us to live your Law of Love. (Response)

Eighth Station
Reader: Jesus, you tell a group of women from Jerusalem to have hope in your promises. Help us to trust in all God's promises. (Response)

Think and Decide:
What will you do to show that you are proud to be a disciple of Jesus?

Lesson Plan: Middle

Arise" or "Ye Sons and Daughters" might be used for the Easter song.)

Choose volunteers to reverently enact the still scene at each station. Give them a picture of that station, but allow them to be creative with the enactment.

While the still scenes are being practiced, invite the rest of the young people to act as leaders or readers. Try to involve as many as possible.

Have the young people look at the *Think and Decide* sections on pages 184 and 185. Explain that during these quiet moments of personal reflection, they may wish to close their eyes and picture themselves in the scene with Jesus before deciding what they will do.

When all are ready, conduct the way of the cross with reverence and devotion.

Materials needed: pictures of stations; music source

Act Three: Darkness Over the Earth
All: *Sing an appropriate song.*
Leader: A reading from the holy gospel according to Luke. (Read Luke 23:32–34.)

Ninth Station
Reader: Jesus, you fall a third and final time on your way to Calvary. Give us strength in the Eucharist. (Response)

Tenth Station
Reader: Jesus, the soldiers stripped you and divided your clothes among themselves. Help us to forgive those who hurt us. (Response)

Eleventh Station
Reader: Jesus, the soldiers crucified you like a criminal. You asked the Father to forgive them. Help us to appreciate your love for us. (Response)

Twelfth Station
Leader: A reading from the holy gospel according to Luke. (Read Luke 23:44–46.)
Reader: Kneel and ask yourself: "How do I feel about Jesus dying out of love for me?"

Think and Decide:
What will you do to show that you are proud to be a disciple of Jesus?

Act Four: From Death to Life
Thirteenth Station
Reader: Jesus, your disciples must have felt their dreams were shattered when Joseph of Arimathea took your lifeless body down from the cross. Help us to see the signs of God's life around us. (Response)

Fourteenth Station
Reader: Jesus, as they buried your body, the disciples must have felt that their hopes were being buried, too. Help us to see the signs of God's love around us. (Response)
Leader: A reading from the holy gospel according to John. (Read John 20:11–18.)

Think and Decide:
What will you do to be a sign of God's life and love?
All: *Sing an appropriate Easter song.*

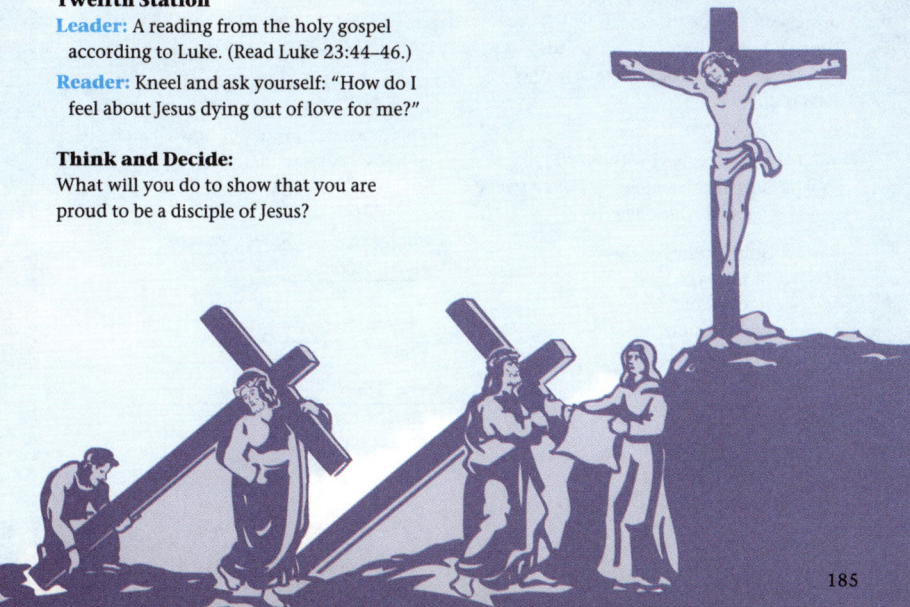

28

Lesson Plan: End

We Honor Our Immaculate Mother

Have the young people make paper flowers and a Marian banner from a strip of shelf paper to be carried in procession. They might also enjoy making a crown of stars or flowers to be placed on a statue of Mary. Flowers may be made of crepe or tissue paper, or cut from construction paper, and mounted on pipe cleaners.

Materials needed: crepe, tissue, or construction paper; scissors; pipe cleaners; shelf paper; markers; statue of Mary

Have the young people scan the sequence of the celebration in honor of Mary on page 186. Take time to explain that a litany is a prayer of petition using titles of praise and love. Some of the titles in the litany to Our Lady are very ancient expressions of devotion to Mary. Then assist the young people in making the following preparations:

- Plan the procession. (Can it be held outdoors? Who carries the banner? the flowers? the crown?)
- Invite families and other classes.
- Practice the entrance song.
- Select two leaders who will alternate in leading the prayers. Practice the response.
- Explain the "Time for Reflection" activity.
- Practice the closing hymn.

Place a large statue of Mary on the prayer table (or gather at an outdoor shrine, if possible), form the procession, and enjoy the celebration.

Evaluating Your Lesson

- Did the young people show their understanding of these religious celebrations by the way they prepared and participated?

WE HONOR OUR IMMACULATE MOTHER

Entrance Procession
You may carry flowers that you have bought, made, or grown. Put them on or next to the place that has been set up to honor Mary, our Immaculate Mother.

Opening Hymn
"Immaculate Mary"

Leader: Today, we honor the Blessed Virgin Mary as the woman God chose to be the Mother of God's own Son. We remember that the Immaculate Conception means that Mary was always sinless, even before she was born. We honor Mary as the patroness of our country on December 8, the feast of the Immaculate Conception.

In our litany prayer today, we pray to Mary, using some of the titles with which the Church honors her. These titles help us to remember Mary's role in God's plan of salvation.

Leader: Holy Mary,

All: O Mary, conceived without sin, pray for us who have recourse to you. *(This response is said after each of the following.)*

Leader: Holy Mother of God,
Mother of Christ,
Mother most pure,
Mother most lovable,
Mother of our Creator,
Mother of our Savior,
Virgin most faithful,
Cause of our joy,
Health of the sick,
Refuge of sinners,
Comfort of the afflicted,
Help of Christians,
Queen of angels,
Queen of apostles,
Queen of martyrs,
Queen of all saints,
Queen conceived without original sin,
Queen of the most holy rosary,
Queen of peace.
Pray for us, Holy Mother of God.

All: That we may be made worthy of the promises of Christ.

Time for Reflection   Possible response:
Choose one of the titles of Mary used in the litany prayer. Think about how it can help you to live as Jesus' disciple today.

Title Cause of our joy.

I will live as a disciple of Jesus by trying to make someone who seems unhappy more joyful today.

Closing Hymn
"Sing of Mary"

Optional Activities

Gifts of the Holy Spirit (for use with page 183)

Tell the young people to imagine that they have been chosen to give the homily at the Mass for the Holy Spirit. Elicit what they think are the elements necessary for a good homily. Tell them to think about the times they were at Mass and were interested in what their priest had to say. Ask them to think about why they were interested.

Then have partners work together to write a homily. Give time for each person to practice her or his homily. Remind them that the delivery has an effect on the audience. Then have them present their homilies to the rest of the group.

The Route Jesus Took (for use with page 184–185)

Have the young people work with a partner to research the area where Jesus traveled during His ministry. Tell the young people to draw a map and mark Jesus' journey. Display the maps around the room.

Materials needed: reference books; drawing paper; pencils; markers

What About Mary? (for use with page 186)

Have the young people work in small groups. Tell them to research information about devotion to Mary. Suggest that they research the different feasts of Mary, litanies, the rosary, and the scapular.

Direct each group to produce an original method of displaying the information about Mary.

Materials needed: reference books; art supplies

Picture Mary (for use with page 186)

Display pictures of Mary. Have the young people work in groups to research information about the different ways Mary has been portrayed. Have each group develop a picture of Mary as the young people see her.

Display the pictures around the room.

Materials needed: pictures of Mary; reference books; art supplies

SUMMARY 2 • REVIEW

How does the Church carry on Jesus' mission of forgiveness? What are important steps in the sacrament of Reconciliation? What do we receive in Reconciliation?

Chapter 15—Jesus Christ Forgives Us (Reconciliation)

- Reconciliation is the sacrament in which Jesus Christ shares with us God's mercy and forgiveness of our sins.
- Examination of conscience, contrition, confession, penance, and absolution are important steps in the celebration of Reconciliation.
- In Reconciliation we receive God's help to do God's loving will, to avoid sin, and to live as God's people.

How does the Church carry on Jesus' ministry of caring for the sick? How do we participate in the mission of healing?

Chapter 16—Jesus Christ Helps Us in Sickness and Death (Anointing of the Sick)

- The sacrament of Anointing of the Sick brings God's special blessings to those who are sick, elderly, or dying.
- Anointing of the Sick is one of the two sacraments of healing.
- We must respect our bodies by caring for them. We must work to eliminate sickness and evil from the world.

What is the sacrament of Matrimony? How do we prepare for Matrimony?

Chapter 17—Jesus Christ Helps Us to Love (Matrimony)

- The sacrament of Matrimony is a powerful and effective sign of Christ's presence that joins a man and woman together for life.
- Married couples promise to serve each other and the whole Church. Matrimony is a sacrament of service.
- We can prepare now for Matrimony by trying to love others as God loves us.

Whom did Jesus choose as leaders? What do our ordained ministers do?

Chapter 18—Jesus Christ Calls Us to Serve (Holy Orders)

- Jesus chose twelve apostles to lead our Church in service and worship.
- Bishops, priests, and deacons are ordained in the sacrament of Holy Orders.
- Our ordained ministers lead us in building up the Christian community.

What does Jesus call us to do? What does "evangelization" mean? What kinds of vocations are there?

Chapter 19—We Share Jesus Christ's Priesthood (Ministry)

- Jesus calls each of us to a specific vocation to carry on his priestly mission.
- Evangelization means spreading the good news of Jesus Christ and sharing our faith by our words and deeds.
- There are many vocations—married, ordained, religious, and single life. We are called to carry on Jesus' mission.

SUMMARY 2 • REVIEW

What are the marks of the Church? How is the Church one and holy? How is the Church catholic and apostolic?

Chapter 22—Becoming a Catholic (Marks of the Church)

- The marks of the Church are one, holy, catholic, and apostolic.
- The Church of Jesus Christ shows it is one and holy when we are united in faith and live holy lives.
- The Church of Jesus Christ shows it is catholic and apostolic by welcoming all and being faithful to the mission and beliefs Jesus gave to the apostles.

What can we do about prejudice? How do we treat those who worship God in other religions?

Chapter 23—All People Are God's People

- As Catholics we must fight against prejudice in our lives.
- We respect those who worship God in other religions.
- We have a special bond with the Jewish people. We seek unity with all Christians.

What virtues are gifts of God? What is faith? What do the creeds of the Church do?

Chapter 24—We Believe in God

- The virtues of faith, hope, and love are gifts from God.
- Faith is a virtue that enables us to trust and believe in God, to accept what God has revealed, and to live according to God's will.
- The creeds of our Church summarize what we believe.

What is hope? Who is our greatest source of hope? Who is a sign of hope for us?

Chapter 25—God Fills Us With Hope

- Hope is the virtue that enables us to trust that God will be with us in every situation.
- Jesus is our greatest source of hope.
- Mary, the Mother of the Church, is a sign of hope for us.

What is love? How do we practice love? what does St. Paul tell us about love?

Chapter 26—The Gift of God's Love

- Love is a virtue that enables us to love God, our neighbor, and ourselves.
- The Corporal and Spiritual Works of Mercy are some very specific ways to practice the virtue of love.
- Saint Paul tells us that love is the greatest virtue.

SUMMARY 2 • TEST

Circle the correct answer.

1. The love of married couples is
    a. not celebrated in a special sacrament.
    b. a sign of God's love in the world.
    c. not meant to last forever.
    d. meant only for them.

2. The ordained men who share in Jesus' priestly ministry are
    a. only priests.
    b. only priests and bishops.
    c. priests, bishops, and deacons.
    d. only bishops.

3. The Church is one means
    a. we receive the good news from the apostles.
    b. we welcome all people to our Church.
    c. all baptized persons are united together with Jesus Christ.
    d. we share in God's own life.

4. The virtues of faith, hope, and love are
    a. gifts from God that help us to believe, trust, and love.
    b. sacraments of the Church.
    c. parts of the Mass.
    d. prayers to say.

5. Our most important source of hope is
    a. our vocation.
    b. our bishops, priests, and deacons.
    c. our knowledge.
    d. the resurrection of Jesus Christ.

Complete the following sentences with the words below.

lifelong	Jewish	Sin
bishops	pope	Trinity
priests	contrition	hope

6. Examination of conscience, confession, __contrition__, penance, and absolution are important parts of Reconciliation.

7. __sin__ is freely choosing to do what we know is wrong. We disobey God's law on purpose.

8. A man and woman enter into a __lifelong__ covenant of love when they celebrate the sacrament of Matrimony.

9. The apostles appointed successors whom we call __bishops__.

10. Bishops ordain __priests__ to help them.

11. The __pope__ is the leader of the whole Church. He is the successor of Saint Peter and is the Bishop of Rome.

12. We have a special relationship with the __Jewish__ people and we share many beliefs with them.

13. The Apostles' Creed teaches us about the Blessed __Trinity__.

14. Mary, the Mother of our Church, is a sign of __hope__ for us.

SUMMARY 2 ▪ TEST

15. Number the following in the order in which they occur in the Individual Rite of Reconciliation.

___7___ The priest gives you absolution.

___1___ The priest welcomes you.

___6___ You pray an Act of Contrition.

___4___ You confess your sins.

___8___ The priest tells you to go in peace.

___2___ You make the sign of the cross.

___3___ You or the priest reads from the Bible.

___5___ The priest talks to you about ways to be a better Christian, and he gives you a penance.

Answer the following.

16. In what ways can you celebrate the sacrament of Reconciliation?

Two ways: Celebrating the sacrament communally; celebrating the sacrament individually

17. How can you continue Jesus' mission of healing?

By taking care of and respecting my body and by supporting the Church's efforts to eliminate disease and suffering in our world.

18. How can you prepare now for your vocation in life?

By living the Law of Love, by praying, celebrating the sacraments often, reading the Bible, reading about the lives of favorite saints, etc.

19. How do you see the sacrament of Holy Orders at work?

Our bishops, priests, and deacons continue the mission of the apostles as our ordained leaders.

20. How can you show that you share in the priesthood of Jesus?

By spreading the good news of Jesus Christ and sharing our faith by our words and deeds

Think and decide:

Tell how you will live one of the marks of the Church.
Possible responses:
Mark of the Church

The Church is holy.

I will

put God first in all I say and do; live the Law of Love, etc.

190

DAY OF RETREAT
Theme: Living the Law of Love

◀ OPENING ACTIVITY ▶

During your retreat this year, you will think about who you are and how you want to live your life as a disciple of Jesus. Imagine you could be anyone or anything for one day. For example:

- an animal
- a star athlete
- a famous entertainer
- a musical instrument
- a world leader
- a leader of our Church
- an automobile
- other _____
  _____

Who or what would you choose to be? Write it here and explain why. _____
_____
_____

On a piece of paper:

- draw or write what you would look like.
- describe what you would like to do.

After all have finished, fold your papers and place them in a container. Each member of the group takes a paper from the container, shows it to the group, and tries to guess the identity of the person described on it. Then have the person share with the group responses to the following questions:

- Why did you pick that person or thing?
- What does your choice tell others about you?

◀ JOURNAL ▶

Find a quiet place.
Think about the following questions:

- What importance or value do I see in my choice?
- What can I discover about myself from my choice?

Write your responses in the space below.

SCRIPTURE REFLECTION

Sometimes you might wonder what God really wants you to be and to do in your life. In the gospel, Jesus teaches that everything we do and say must show that we are trying to live the Law of Love. Listen carefully to what Jesus says.

Reader: A teacher of the Law tried to trap Jesus with a question. "Teacher," he asked, "which commandment in the law is the greatest?"

Jesus answered, "You shall love the Lord your God, with all your heart, with all your soul, and with all your mind. This is the greatest and the first commandment. The second is like it: You shall love your neighbor as yourself."

Based on Matthew 22:34–40

Imagine that you are one of Jesus' disciples. Later that evening you and the other disciples gather to discuss Jesus' response to the teacher of the Law. What might you say?

Take a few moments to think about the following:

- What does the Law of Love mean to me?
- What people do I know who are living the Law of Love? Tell how.
- What are the talents or the things that I do best?
- How can I use my talents to live the Law of Love?

JOURNAL

Reflect briefly on your responses in the group discussion.

Write your reflections here.

GROUP DISCUSSION

Divide into small groups and discuss your responses. Then choose a group leader to share your group's discussion with the larger group.

◀ AUDIO-VISUAL ACTIVITY ▶

On the day of your Baptism, your parents and godparents promised to help you to live the Law of Love. Now you are taking more responsibility for living that promise. After watching a videotape or filmstrip on the sacrament of Baptism, take a few minutes to reflect individually on the following:

- How does the videotape or filmstrip help me to understand my Baptism?
- How does the Law of Love guide me to live the new life I received in Baptism?
- How does the Law of Love guide me to live as a member of the body of Christ, the Church?
- Share your reflections with your group.

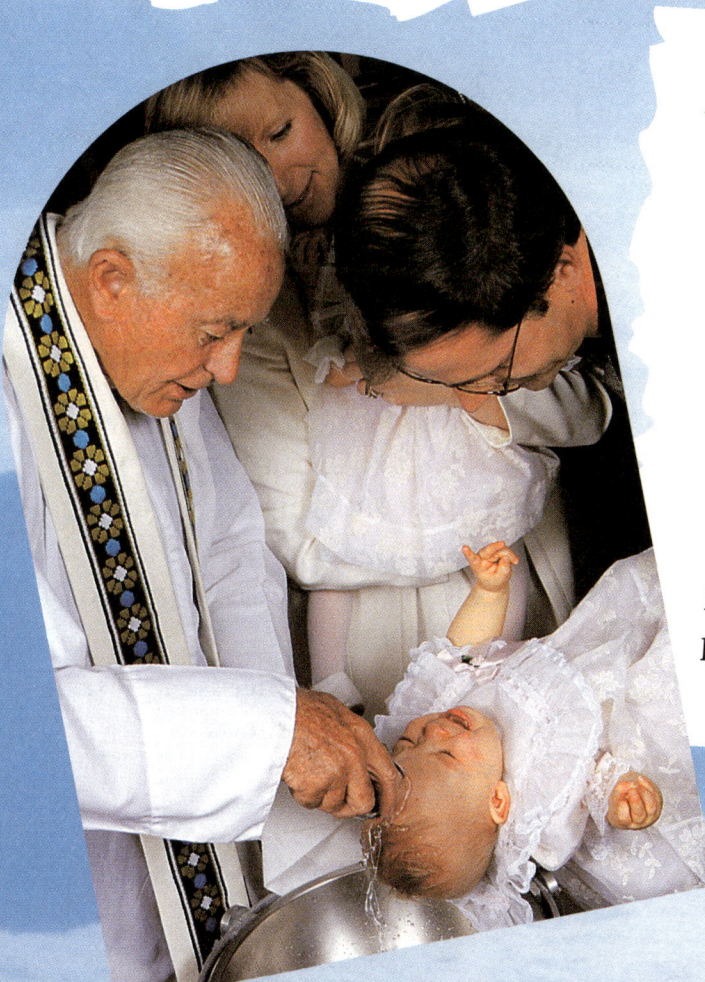

◀ LIVING THE LAW OF LOVE ▶

Divide into three groups. Each group will do one of the following projects.
- Create a word collage depicting the Law of Love.
- Illustrate a mural showing how you will live the Law of Love.
- Role-play a TV spot reporting on the Law of Love.

Each group will present its completed project during the closing prayer service.

PRAYER SERVICE

Opening Hymn

"They Will Know We Are Christians by Our Love" (or another appropriate hymn)

Scripture Reading

Reader: A reading from the holy gospel according to John.

Jesus said to his disciples, "This is my commandment: love one another as I love you. No one has greater love than this, to lay down one's life for one's friends. . . . I chose you and appointed you to go and bear fruit that will remain. . . . This I command you: love one another."

John 15:12–13, 16–17

Presentation of Projects

Each group presents and explains its project on the Law of Love.

Prayer of the Faithful

Leader: When we live our Baptism by following the Law of Love, we become signs of God's love and help bring about the reign of God. Today, we pray for the coming of the reign of God.

Prayer leader 1: For our pope, our bishop, our priests, and all who lead our Church in service and worship, we pray to the Lord.

All: Thy kingdom come; thy will be done. (Repeat this response after each petition.)

Prayer leader 2: For the leaders of our world, our nation, our state, and our communities, we pray to the Lord. (Response)

Prayer leader 3: For ourselves, that we may reach out to help the hungry, the homeless, those suffering from injustice, oppression, illness, or addiction, and for all those with special needs, we pray to the Lord. (Response)

Prayer leader 4: For the needs of those in our parish and neighborhood, especially…(Response)

Now quietly pray this prayer.

† Holy Spirit, help me to live my Baptism and follow the Law of Love by _____ _____ _____.

Amen.

◀ BLESSING ▶

Turn to a partner and trace a cross on her or his forehead, saying:

† As Christ was anointed priest, prophet, and king, so may you always live the Law of Love and bring about the reign of God.

Closing Hymn

"They Will Know We Are Christians by Our Love" (or another appropriate hymn)

Sharing our faith as Catholics

God is close to us at all times and in all places, calling us and helping us in coming to faith. When a person is baptized and welcomed into the faith community of the Church, everyone present stands with family and other members of the parish. We hear the words, "This is our faith. This is the faith of the Church. We are proud to profess it in Christ Jesus, our Lord." And we joyfully answer, "Amen"—"Yes, God, I believe."

The Catholic Church is our home in the Christian community. We are proud to be Catholics, living as disciples of Jesus Christ in our world. Each day we are called to share our faith with everyone we meet, helping to build up the reign of God.

What is the faith we want to live and to share? Where does the gift of faith come from? How do we celebrate it and worship God? How do we live it? How do we pray to God? In these pages, you will find a special faith guide written just for you. It can help you as a fifth grader to grow in your Catholic faith and to share it with your family and with others, too.

Following the Church's teachings and what God has told us in the Bible, we can outline some of our most important beliefs and practices in four ways:

WHAT WE BELIEVE — CREED

HOW WE CELEBRATE — SACRAMENTS

HOW WE LIVE — MORALITY

HOW WE PRAY — PRAYER

CATHOLICS BELIEVE...

CREED

THERE IS ONE GOD IN THREE DIVINE PERSONS: Father, Son, and Holy Spirit. One God in three divine Persons is called the Blessed Trinity; it is the central teaching of the Christian religion.

GOD THE FATHER is the creator of all things.

GOD THE SON took on human flesh and became one of us. This is called the incarnation. Our Lord Jesus Christ, who is the Son of God born of the Virgin Mary, proclaimed the reign of God by his teaching, signs, and wonders. Jesus gave us the new commandment of love and taught us the way of the Beatitudes. We believe that by his sacrifice on the cross, he died to save us from the power of sin—original sin and our personal sins. He was buried and rose from the dead on the third day. Through his resurrection we share in the divine life, which we call grace. Jesus, the Christ, is our Messiah. He ascended into heaven and will come again to judge the living and the dead.

GOD THE HOLY SPIRIT is the third Person of the Blessed Trinity, adored together with the Father and Son. The action of the Holy Spirit in our lives enables us to respond to the call of Jesus to live as faithful disciples.

We believe in **ONE, HOLY, CATHOLIC, AND APOSTOLIC CHURCH** founded by Jesus on the "rock," which is Peter, and the other apostles.

As Catholics, **WE SHARE A COMMON FAITH.** We believe and respect what the Church teaches: everything that is contained in the word of God, both written and handed down to us.

We believe in **THE COMMUNION OF SAINTS** and that we are to live forever with God.

I have also learned this year that
to believe as a Catholic means

_____
_____
_____

Catholics Celebrate...

THE CHURCH, THE BODY OF CHRIST, continues the mission of Jesus Christ throughout human history. Through the sacraments and by the power of the Holy Spirit, the Church enters into the mystery of the death and resurrection of the Savior and the life of grace.

THE SEVEN SACRAMENTS are Baptism, Confirmation, Eucharist, Holy Orders, Matrimony, Reconciliation, and Anointing of the Sick. Through the sacraments, we share in God's grace so that we may live as disciples of Jesus.

THE SACRAMENTS ARE EFFECTIVE SIGNS through which Jesus Christ shares God's life and love with us. Through the power of the Holy Spirit, they actually bring about what they promise.

The Church carries on Jesus' mission of welcoming members into the body of Christ when we celebrate Baptism, Confirmation, and Eucharist. We call these the sacraments of initiation.

The Church forgives and heals as Jesus did by celebrating Reconciliation and Anointing of the Sick. We call these the sacraments of healing.

The Church serves others and is a special sign of God's love by celebrating and living the sacraments of Matrimony and Holy Orders. We call these the sacraments of service.

IN THE SACRAMENTS, WE RECEIVE GOD'S GRACE: a sharing in the divine life, in God's very life and love. In the sacraments, Jesus shares God's life with the Church by the power of the Holy Spirit. Jesus calls us to respond by living as his disciples

By celebrating the sacraments, the Church worships and praises God In celebrating the sacraments, the Church becomes a powerful sign of Jesus' presence and God's reign in our world.

SACRAMENTS

CATHOLICS CELEBRATE...

SACRAMENTS

By participating in the celebration of the sacraments, Catholics grow in holiness and in living as disciples of Jesus. Freed from sin by Baptism and strengthened by Confirmation, we are nourished by Christ himself in the Eucharist. We also share in God's mercy and love in the sacrament of Reconciliation.

CATHOLICS CELEBRATE THE EUCHARIST AT MASS.
They do this together with a priest. The priest has received the sacrament of Holy Orders and acts in the person of Christ, our High Priest. The Mass is both a meal and a sacrifice. It is a meal because in the Mass Jesus, the Bread of Life, gives us himself to be our food. Jesus is really present in the Eucharist. The Mass is a sacrifice, too, because we remember all that Jesus did for us to save us from sin and to bring us new life. In this great sacrifice of praise, we offer ourselves with Jesus to God.

THE EUCHARIST IS THE SACRAMENT OF JESUS' BODY AND BLOOD. It is the high point of Catholic worship. It is a great privilege to take part weekly in the celebration of the Mass with our parish community.

I have also learned this year that
to celebrate as a Catholic means

_____
_____
_____
_____
_____

Catholics Live...

WE ARE MADE IN THE IMAGE AND LIKENESS OF GOD and are called to live as disciples of Jesus Christ. Jesus said to us, "Love one another as I have loved you."

When we live the way Jesus showed us and follow his teachings, we can be truly happy and live in real freedom.

To help us live as Jesus' disciples, we are guided by **THE LAW OF LOVE, THE BEATITUDES, AND THE TEN COMMANDMENTS.** The Works of Mercy and the Laws of the Church also show us how to grow in living as Jesus' disciples.

AS MEMBERS OF THE CHURCH, THE BODY OF CHRIST, we are guided by the Church's teachings that help us to form our conscience. These teachings have come down to us from the time of Jesus and the apostles and have been lived by God's people throughout history. We share them with millions of Catholics throughout the world.

THROUGH PRAYER AND THE SACRAMENTS, especially Eucharist and Reconciliation, we are strengthened to live as Jesus asked us to live. In faith, hope, and love, we as Catholic Christians are called not just to follow rules. We are called to live a whole new way of life as disciples of Jesus.

In living as Jesus' disciples, we are challenged each day to choose between right and wrong. Even when we are tempted to make wrong choices, the Holy Spirit is always present to help us make the right choices. Like Jesus, we are to live for God's reign. Doing all this means that we live a Christian moral life. As Christians we are always called to follow the way of Jesus.

I have also learned this year that
to live as a Catholic means

_____

_____

_____

MORALITY

CATHOLICS PRAY...

PRAYER

Prayer is talking and listening to God. We pray prayers of thanksgiving and sorrow; we praise God, and we ask God for what we need as well as for the needs of others.

We can pray in many ways and at any time. We can pray using our own words, words from the Bible, or just by being quiet in God's presence. We can also pray with song or dance or movement.

We also pray the prayers of our Catholic family that have come down to us over many centuries. Some of these prayers are the Our Father, the Hail Mary, the Glory to the Father, the Apostles' Creed, the Angelus, the Hail Holy Queen, and Acts of Faith, Hope, Love, and Contrition. Catholics also pray the rosary while meditating on events in the lives of Jesus and Mary.

As members of the Catholic community, we participate in the great liturgical prayer of the Church, the Mass. We also pray with the Church during the liturgical seasons of the Church year—Advent, Christmas, Lent, the Triduum, Easter, and Ordinary Time.

In prayer, we are joined with the whole communion of saints in praising and honoring God.

I have also learned this year that
to pray as a Catholic means

_____
_____
_____
_____

PRAYERS AND PRACTICES

By this time, you should know many of these prayers and practices by heart.

Sign of the Cross
In the name of the Father,
and of the Son,
and of the Holy Spirit. Amen.

Glory to the Father
Glory to the Father,
and to the Son,
and to the Holy Spirit:
as it was in the beginning,
is now, and will be for ever. Amen.

Our Father
Our Father, who art in heaven,
hallowed be thy name;
thy kingdom come;
thy will be done on earth
as it is in heaven.
Give us this day our daily bread;
and forgive us our trespasses
as we forgive those
who trespass against us;
and lead us not into temptation,
but deliver us from evil. Amen.

Hail Mary
Hail Mary, full of grace,
the Lord is with you;
blessed are you among women,
and blessed is the fruit
of your womb, Jesus.
Holy Mary, Mother of God,
pray for us sinners now
and at the hour of our death. Amen.

Morning Offering
My God, I offer you all my prayers, works, and sufferings of this day for all the intentions of your most Sacred Heart. Amen.

Evening Prayer
Dear God,
before I sleep
I want to thank you for this day,
so full of your kindness
and your joy.
I close my eyes to rest
safe in your loving care.

Grace Before Meals
Bless us, O Lord,
and these your gifts
which we are about to receive
from your bounty,
through Christ our Lord. Amen.

Grace After Meals
We give you thanks, almighty God,
for these and all your gifts
which we have received
through Christ our Lord. Amen.

Memorare
Remember, O most gracious Virgin Mary, that never was it known that anyone who fled to your protection, implored your help, or sought your intercession was left unaided. Inspired with this confidence, we fly unto you, O Virgin of virgins, our Mother. To you we come, before you we kneel, sinful and sorrowful. O Mother of the Word made flesh, do not despise our petitions, but in your mercy hear and answer them. Amen.

Apostles' Creed

I believe in God, the Father almighty,
creator of heaven and earth.

I believe in Jesus Christ,
his only Son, our Lord.
He was conceived by the power
of the Holy Spirit
and born of the Virgin Mary.
He suffered under Pontius Pilate,
was crucified, died, and was buried.
He descended to the dead.
On the third day he rose again.
He ascended into heaven,
and is seated at the right hand
of the Father.
He will come again to judge
the living and the dead.

I believe in the Holy Spirit,
the holy catholic Church,
the communion of saints,
the forgiveness of sins,
the resurrection of the body,
and the life everlasting. Amen.

Prayer to the Holy Spirit

Come, Holy Spirit,
fill the hearts of your faithful
and enkindle in them
the fire of your love.
Send forth your Spirit and
they shall be created, and
you shall renew the face of
the earth.

Nicene Creed

We believe in one God,
the Father, the Almighty,
maker of heaven and earth,
of all that is seen and unseen.

We believe in one Lord, Jesus Christ,
the only Son of God,
eternally begotten of the Father,
God from God, Light from Light,
true God from true God,
begotten, not made,
one in Being with the Father.
Through him all things were made.
For us men and for our salvation
he came down from heaven:
by the power of the Holy Spirit
he was born of the Virgin Mary,
and became man.

For our sake he was crucified
under Pontius Pilate;
he suffered, died, and was buried.
On the third day he rose again
in fulfillment of the Scriptures;
he ascended into heaven and is seated
at the right hand of the Father.
He will come again in glory
to judge the living and the dead,
and his kingdom will have no end.

We believe in the Holy Spirit,
the Lord, the giver of life,
who proceeds from the Father
and the Son.
With the Father and the Son
he is worshiped and glorified.
He has spoken through the Prophets.

We believe in one holy catholic
and apostolic Church.
We acknowledge one baptism
for the forgiveness of sins.
We look for the resurrection of the dead,
and the life of the world to come. Amen.

Act of Contrition

My God,
I am sorry for my sins with all my heart.
In choosing to do wrong
and failing to do good,
I have sinned against you
whom I should love above all things.
I firmly intend, with your help,
to do penance,
to sin no more,
and to avoid whatever leads me to sin.
Our Savior Jesus Christ
suffered and died for us.
In his name, my God, have mercy.

Prayer for My Vocation

Dear God,
You have a great and loving plan
for our world and for me.
I wish to share in that plan fully,
faithfully, and joyfully.

Help me to understand what it is
you wish me to do with my life.
Help me to be attentive to the signs
that you give me about preparing for the future.

Help me to learn to be a sign
of the kingdom, or reign, of
God whether I'm called to the
priesthood or religious life,
the single or married life.

And once I have heard and understood
your call, give me the strength
and the grace to follow it
with generosity and love. Amen.

The Angelus

The angel of the Lord declared to Mary
and she conceived by the Holy Spirit.
Hail Mary....

Behold the handmaid of the Lord,
be it done to me according to your word.
Hail Mary....

And the Word was made Flesh
and dwelled among us.
Hail Mary....

Pray for us, O Holy Mother of God,
That we may be worthy of the promises of Christ.
Let us pray:
Pour forth, we beseech you, O Lord,
your grace into our hearts
that we to whom the incarnation of
Christ your Son was made known by the
message of an angel may,
by his passion and cross,
be brought to the glory of his
resurrection, through Christ Our Lord.
Amen.

Prayer of Saint Francis

Lord, make me an instrument of your peace:
where there is hatred, let me sow love;
where there is injury, pardon;
where there is doubt, faith;
where there is despair, hope;
where there is darkness, light;
where there is sadness, joy.
O Divine Master, grant that I may not
so much seek
to be consoled as to console,
to be understood as to understand,
to be loved as to love.
For it is in giving that we receive,
it is in pardoning that we are pardoned,
and it is in dying that we are born
to eternal life.

The Stations of the Cross
1. Jesus is condemned to die.
2. Jesus takes up his cross.
3. Jesus falls the first time.
4. Jesus meets his mother.
5. Simon helps Jesus carry his cross.
6. Veronica wipes the face of Jesus.
7. Jesus falls the second time.
8. Jesus meets the women of Jerusalem.
9. Jesus falls the third time.
10. Jesus is stripped of his garments.
11. Jesus is nailed to the cross.
12. Jesus dies on the cross.
13. Jesus is taken down from the cross.
14. Jesus is laid in the tomb.

Hail, Holy Queen
Hail, Holy Queen, Mother of Mercy;
hail, our life, our sweetness,
and our hope! To you do we cry,
poor banished children of Eve;
to you do we send up our sighs,
mourning and weeping in this valley of tears.

Turn, then, most gracious advocate,
your eyes of mercy toward us;
and after this our exile, show unto us
the blessed fruit of your womb, Jesus,
O clement, O loving, O sweet Virgin Mary!

The Rosary
A rosary has a cross, followed by one large bead and three small ones. Then there is a circle with five "decades." Each decade consists of one large bead followed by ten smaller beads. Begin the rosary with the sign of the cross. Recite the Apostles' Creed. Then pray one Our Father, three Hail Marys, and one Glory to the Father.

To recite each decade, say one Our Father on the large bead and ten Hail Marys on the ten smaller beads. After each decade, pray the Glory to the Father. As you pray each decade, think of the appropriate joyful, sorrowful, or glorious mystery, or a special event in the life of Jesus and Mary. Pray the Hail, Holy Queen as the last prayer of the rosary.

The Five Joyful Mysteries (by custom, used on Mondays, Thursdays, and the Sundays of Advent)
1. The annunciation
2. The visitation
3. The birth of Jesus
4. The presentation of Jesus in the Temple
5. The finding of Jesus in the Temple

The Five Sorrowful Mysteries
(by custom, used on Tuesdays, Fridays, and the Sundays of Lent)
1. The agony in the garden
2. The scourging at the pillar
3. The crowning with thorns
4. The carrying of the cross
5. The crucifixion and death of Jesus

The Five Glorious Mysteries
(by custom, used on Wednesdays, Saturdays, and the remaining Sundays of the year)
1. The resurrection
2. The ascension
3. The Holy Spirit comes upon the apostles
4. The assumption of Mary into heaven
5. The coronation of Mary in heaven

Prayer of Inner Stillness

Choose a time when you can be alone. Sit in a comfortable position and relax by breathing deeply. Try to shut out all the sights and sounds around you so that you feel the peaceful rhythm of your breathing in and out.

Slowly repeat a short prayer such as "Come, Lord Jesus" or perhaps just the name Jesus.

A Scripture Meditation

1. Pray for inner stillness.
2. Read one of your favorite stories about Jesus.
3. Close your eyes and imagine you are with Jesus.
4. Talk to Jesus about what the reading means to you.

The Storm at Sea

Quiet your mind and body as you breathe deeply.
Pray, "Jesus, be with me."

Listen to God's Word

One day Jesus got into a boat with his disciples. As they were sailing, Jesus fell asleep. Suddenly a strong wind came up, and the boat began to fill with water. They woke Jesus, saying, "Master, master, We are perishing!"

Jesus got up and gave an order to the wind and to the stormy water. They quieted down, and there was great calm.

Based on Luke 8:22–24

Imagine you are in the boat with Jesus. What do you say to the other disciples when you first see the storm? What do you say to Jesus?

What do you say to yourself after Jesus calms the storm?

What are things that can cause storms in your life right now? Imagine Jesus is standing in front of you. Talk to Jesus about how you can become calm.

Decide how you can help others through stormy times.

Pray in these words or your own

Jesus, when a storm comes up in my life, calm my fears.

When I am afraid to do what I know is right, give me courage.

When I am afraid to try something new because I might fail, give me hope.

When I have a big problem that is too big to handle alone, give me trust in you and in those who can help me.

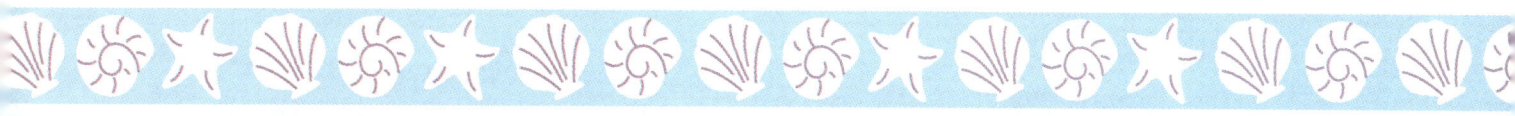

The Ten Commandments

1. I am the Lord, your God: you shall not have strange gods before me.
2. You shall not take the name of the Lord, your God, in vain.
3. Remember to keep holy the Lord's day.
4. Honor your father and your mother.
5. You shall not kill.
6. You shall not commit adultery.
7. You shall not steal.
8. You shall not bear false witness against your neighbor.
9. You shall not covet your neighbor's wife.
10. You shall not covet your neighbor's goods.

The Beatitudes

Blessed are the poor in spirit,
   for theirs is the kingdom of God.

Blessed are they who mourn,
   for they will be comforted.

Blessed are the meek,
   they will inherit the land.

Blessed are they who hunger and thirst for righteousness,
   for they will be satisfied

Blessed are the merciful,
   for they will be shown mercy.

Blessed are the clean of heart,
   for they will see God.

Blessed are the peacemakers,
   for they will be called children of God.

Blessed are they who are persecuted for the sake of righteousness,
   for theirs is the kingdom of heaven.

The Laws of the Church

1. Celebrate Christ's resurrection every Sunday (or Saturday evening) and on holy days of obligation by taking part in Mass and avoiding unnecessary work.
2. Lead a sacramental life. Receive Holy Communion frequently and the sacrament of Penance, or Reconciliation, regularly. We must receive Holy Communion at least once a year at Lent-Easter. We must confess within a year, if we have committed serious, or mortal, sin.
3. Study Catholic teaching throughout life, especially in preparing for the sacraments.
4. Observe the marriage laws of the Catholic Church and give religious training to one's children.
5. Strengthen and support the Church: one's own parish, the worldwide Church, and the Holy Father.
6. Do penance, including not eating meat and fasting from food on certain days.
7. Join in the missionary work of the Church.

Holy Days of Obligation

On these days Catholics must celebrate the Eucharist just as on Sunday.

1. Solemnity of Mary, Mother of God (Jan. 1)
2. Ascension (During the Easter season)
3. Assumption of Mary (August 15)
4. All Saints Day (November 1)
5. Immaculate Conception (December 8)
6. Christmas (December 25)

Corporal and Spiritual Works of Mercy (see page 173)

GLOSSARY

Absolution (page 105)
Absolution is the prayer the priest says asking forgiveness of our sins.

Anointing of the Sick (page 111)
The sacrament of Anointing of the Sick brings God's special blessings to those who are sick, elderly, or dying.

Apostles (page 149)
The apostles were the twelve special helpers chosen by Jesus to lead the early Church.

Ascension (page 33)
The ascension is the event in which Jesus Christ was taken into heaven after the resurrection.

Baptism (page 59)
Baptism is the sacrament of our new life with God and the beginning of our initiation into the Church. Through this sacrament we are freed from sin, become children of God, and are welcomed as members of the Church.

Beatitudes (page 208)
The Beatitudes are ways of living that Jesus gave us so that we can be truly happy.

Bethlehem (page 96)
The town in which Jesus was born.

Blessed Sacrament (page 73)
Another name for the Eucharist. Jesus is really present in the Blessed Sacrament.

Catholic (page 149)
The Church welcomes all people and has the message of God's good news for all people.

Confirmation (page 65)
Confirmation is the sacrament in which we are sealed with the gift of the Holy Spirit and are strengthened to give witness to the good news of Jesus.

Conscience (page 44)
Conscience is the ability we have to decide whether a thought, word, or deed is right or wrong. We form our conscience according to the teachings of the Church.

Consecration (page 77)
The consecration is that part of the Mass in which the bread and wine become Jesus' own Body and Blood through the power of the Holy Spirit and the words and actions of the priest.

Corporal Works of Mercy (page 173)
The Corporal Works of Mercy are ways we care for one another's physical needs.

Disciple (page 15)
A disciple is one who learns from and follows Jesus Christ.

Divine (page 14)

A word that means having the nature of God.

Eucharist (page 71)

The Eucharist is the sacrament of Jesus' Body and Blood. Jesus is really present in the Eucharist. Our gifts of bread and wine become the Body and Blood of Christ at Mass.

Evangelization (page 129)

Evangelization means spreading the good news of Jesus Christ and sharing our faith by our words and actions.

Faith (page 161)

Faith is a virtue that enables us to trust and believe in God, to accept what God has revealed, and to live according to God's loving will.

Fruits of the Holy Spirit (page 67)

The fruits of the Holy Spirit are the good results people can see in us when we use the gifts of the Holy Spirit. They are love, joy, peace, patience, kindness, goodness, faithfulness, humility, and self-control.

Gifts of the Holy Spirit (page 67)

The seven gifts of the Holy Spirit are: wisdom, understanding, right judgment, courage, knowledge, reverence, and wonder and awe. They help us to live and witness to our Catholic faith.

Grace (page 39)

Grace is a sharing in the divine life, in God's very life and love.

Holy Orders (page 123)

Holy Orders is the sacrament that confers the ordained ministry of bishops, priests, and deacons.

Hope (page 167)

Hope is a virtue that enables us to trust that God will be with us in every situation.

Incarnation (page 17)

The incarnation is the mystery of God "becoming flesh," or becoming one of us in Jesus Christ.

Kingdom of Heaven (page 27)

The kingdom of heaven is another way of saying kingdom, or reign, of God in Matthew's gospel.

Laity (page 129)

The laity are single or married people who belong to the Church. Lay people serve the Church in many ways.

Law of Love (page 23)

Love the Lord your God with all your heart, with all your soul, with all your strength, and with all your mind. Love your neighbor as you love yourself.

Liturgical Year (page 82-83)

Advent, Christmas, Lent, the Easter Triduum, Easter, and Ordinary Time make up the seasons, or times, of the liturgical year. Our Church celebrates the liturgical year to help us remember the whole story of the life, death, and resurrection of Jesus Christ.

Liturgy (page 77)
Liturgy is the official public worship of the Church. The Liturgy includes the ways we celebrate the Mass and the other sacraments.

Liturgy of the Eucharist (page 76)
The Liturgy of the Eucharist is one of the two major parts of the Mass. It is made up of the Presentation and Preparation of the Gifts, the Eucharistic Prayer, and Holy Communion.

Liturgy of the Word (page 76)
The Liturgy of the Word is one of the two major parts of the Mass. It is made up of readings from the Old and New Testaments, Responsorial Psalm, Gospel, Homily, Creed, and Prayer of the Faithful.

Love (page 173)
Love is a virtue that enables us to love God, our neighbor, and ourselves.

Marks of the Church (page 148)
The marks of the Church are: one, holy, catholic, and apostolic. These are four great identifying qualities that let people know the kind of community Jesus began and calls us to be.

Mass (page 76)
The Mass is our celebration of the Eucharist. The two major parts of the Mass are the Liturgy of the Word and the Liturgy of the Eucharist.

Matrimony (page 117)
The sacrament of Matrimony is a powerful and effective sign of Christ's presence that joins a man and woman together for life.

Messiah (page 88)
"Messiah" refers to the savior and liberator promised to the people in the Old Testament. Jesus is the Messiah.

Original Sin (page 61)
Original sin is the sinful condition into which all human beings are born. It is the loss of grace passed on from our first parents to all generations.

Passover (page 70)
Passover is a feast in which Jews celebrate God's deliverance of their ancestors from slavery in Egypt.

Penance (page 105)
The penance we receive from the priest in the sacrament of Reconciliation helps to make up for the hurt caused by our sins and helps us to avoid sin in the future. Our penance can be a prayer or good deed.

Pope (page 149)
The pope is the bishop of Rome. He is the successor of Saint Peter and the leader of the whole Catholic Church.

Prayer (page 202)
Prayer is directing one's heart and mind to God. In prayer we talk and listen to God.

Priesthood of the Faithful (page 128)

The priesthood of the faithful is the priesthood of Jesus in which all baptized people share through Baptism and the anointing of the Holy Spirit.

Racism (page 155)

Racism is a sin of prejudice against a person because of race.

Reconciliation (page 104)

Reconciliation is the sacrament in which we are forgiven by God and the Church for our sins.

Reign of God (Kingdom of God) (page 21)

The reign, or kingdom, of God is the saving power of God's life and love in the world.

Sacrament (page 39)

A sacrament is an effective sign through which Jesus Christ shares God's life and love with us. The sacraments cause to happen the very things they stand for. There are seven sacraments.

Sacramental (page 178)

A sacramental is a blessing, an action, or an object that helps us remember God, Jesus, Mary, or the saints.

Sin (page 105)

Sin is freely choosing to do what we know is wrong. When we sin, we disobey God's law on purpose.

Spiritual Works of Mercy (page 173)

The Spiritual Works of Mercy are ways we care for one another's spiritual needs.

Ten Commandments (page 208)

The Ten Commandments are laws given to us by God to help us live as God's people. God gave the Ten Commandments to Moses on Mount Sinai.

Viaticum (page 113)

When Holy Communion is given to a dying person, it is called Viaticum. Viaticum means "food for the journey." Viaticum is often received along with the sacrament of Anointing of the Sick.

Vocation (page 128)

A vocation is our call to live holy lives of service in our Church and in our world.

Worship (page 39)

Worship is praise and thanks to God in signs, words, and actions.

INDEX

Absolution for sins, 105, 107, *209*
Act of Contrition, 105, 107, 202, 205
Act of Faith, 163, 202
Act of Hope, 169, 202
Act of Love, 175, 202
Advent Season, 82–83, **87–92,** 179, 202
Alcohol abuse, 111
Altar, 76, 178
Angelus, 91, 202, 205
Annunciation, 83, 89, 179
Anointing(s), 58, 65, 111, 113, 123
Anointing of the Sick, 38–39, **109–114,** *111,* 199, *209*
   celebrating, 110–111
   living, 111
Apostles, 122, 148–149, 154, 179, 186, 198, 201, *209*
   successors of, 149
Apostles' Creed, 160–161, 179, 202, 204
Aquinas, Thomas (Saint), 73
Ascension of Jesus, 32, *33,* 64, 83, 84, 128, 149, 179, *209*
Ash Wednesday, 82–83, 137, 179
Assumption of Mary, 83, 167, 179
Augustine (Saint), 71

Baptism, 33, 35, 38–39, 47, **57–62,** 59, 154–155, 197, 199, 200, *209*
   celebrating, 58
   living our, 32–33, 58–59, 64, 82, 123, 128, 134, 137, 140, 148, 194
Beatitudes, 198, 201, 208, *209*
Bethlehem, 14, 93, 96, *209*
Bible, 26, 76, 88, 107, 119, 131, 135, 155, 169, 197, 202
Bishop(s), 65, 122–123, 148–149, 151
Blessed Sacrament, 71, 73, *209*
Blessed Trinity, 32, 58, 154, 160, 198
Blessings, 178, 181
Body of Christ
   Church as, 33, 38–39, 51, 58, 64, 71, 77, 79, 148, 199
   Eucharist as, 50, 70–71, 77, 79
Brothers, religious, 129

Cabrini, Frances Xavier (Saint), 180
Catholic, 32, 53, 79, 85, 111, 113, 116, 128, 135, 137, 148–149, 151, 198, 200, 201, 202, *209*
Catholic Church, 76, 104, 122, 148–149, 154–155, 197, 202. *See also* Church
Christians, unity of, in Christ, 50, 51, 94, 148, 154–155
Christian Churches, 148, 154–155
Christmas Season, 82–83, 85, 89, **93–98**
Church, 23, 32–33, 58, 197–202
   as Body of Christ, 33, 38–39, 51, 58, 64, 71, 77, 79, 148, 199, 201
   Jesus' love for, 116
   marks of, **147–152,** 198

   mission of, 15, 20–21, 27, 29, **31–36,** 39, 41, 44, 58–59, 61, 65, 71, 77, 105, 110–111, 117, 122–123, **127–132,** 148–149, 151, 155, 160, 167, 199
   as People of God, 51, 71, 104
   as Sacrament of Jesus, 38, 41
   as teacher, 104, 160, 167, 197, 198
Communal Rite of Reconciliation, 105, 107
Communion of saints, 161, 198, 202
Concluding Rite of Mass, 51, 77
Confession of faith, 151
Confession of sins, 105, 107
Confirmation, 38–39, **63–68,** *65* 199, 200, *209*
   background for, 64
   celebrating, 64–65
   living our, 65, 128
Confirmation name, 64–65
Conscience, 44, 45, 105, 107, 201, *209*
Consecration of the Mass, 77, *209*
Contrition for sins, 105, 107
Corporal Works of Mercy, 173, *209*
Covenant, 70, 77, 116, 119
Creed(s), 14, 76, 149, 160–161, 197
Cross, 27, 71, 82, 140, 178, 184, 198
Crucifix, 179
Crucifixion of Jesus, 27, 140, 179, 185

Deacons, 58, 76–77, 107, 116–117, 122–123, 125, 129
Devil, 134
Diocese, 122
Disciple(s), 14, *15,* 20, 26, 31–33, 39, 44, 50–51, 58, 64, 70–71, 83, 85, 89, 104, 110, 116–117, 122, 128, 131, 148, 149, 154, 159, 160, 167, 173, 184, 185, 197, 198, 199, 200, 201, *209*
Discrimination, working against, 32, 149, 151, 160
Divine, 14, 17, 58, 198, 199, *210*
Divorce, 117, 119
Drug abuse, 111

Easter Candle, 58, 179
Easter Season, 83, 85, 134, **139–144,** 179, 202
Easter Sunday, 44, 82–83, 140, 143, 169
Easter Triduum, 82–83, 140, 143, 202
Easter Vigil, 82, 140
Ecumenism, 155
Elisha, 49
Epistles, 76
Eucharist, 38–39, **49–54, 69–74,** *71,* 199, 200, 201, *210. See also* Mass, rites of
   background for, 50, 70, 82, 140
   dimensions of, 50–51, 70–71, 76–77, 123

   living, 71, 77, 128, 148, 160, 185
   real presence of Jesus in, 50, 71, 73, 77, 200
   special meal and sacrifice, 50, 53, 70
Eucharistic minister, 77
Eucharistic Prayer, 77
Evangelization, 128, *129, 210*
Evening Prayer, 82, 143, 203
Everlasting life, (Eternal) 155, 159, 161, 167, 198
Evil, 103, 157, 175
Examination of conscience, 44–45, 105, 107

Faith, virtue of, **159–164,** *161,* 169, 173, 175, *210*
   as believing, 148, 155, 160–161, 163, 197, 198
   as gift of God, **159–164,** 197
   as living, 58–59, 65, 67, 148, 151, 160–161, 163, 180, 197, 201
   as trusting, 26, 110, 160–161, 163
Family prayers, 17, 23, 29, 35, 41, 47, 53, 61, 67, 73, 79, 85, 91, 97, 113, 119, 125, 131,143, 151, 157, 163, 169, 175, 181
Feast days, 83, 85
Forgiveness, 27, 32–33, **43–48,** 76–77, **103–108,** 199
   of others, 27, 47, 151, 185
   of sins, 27, 44, 77, 103–105, 110, 155, 161, 171, 185
Francis of Assisi (Saint), Prayer of, 29, 205
Fruits of the Holy Spirit, 67, *210*
Fullness of the Holy Spirit, 64

Gifts of the Holy Spirit, 64, 65, 67, 183, *210*
Glory to the Father, 179, 202, 203
God. *See also* Blessed Trinity; Love of God (divine)
   as Creator, 76, 77, 116, 154, 161, 172, 181, 198
   as faithful and loyal, 117, 119
   as forgiving and merciful, 27, 32, 44, 103–105, 107, 111, 200
   as holy, 148
   Father, Son, and Holy Spirit, 58, 128, 154, 161, 166, 169, 198
   One, 148, 154, 160, 198
   presence of, 14–15, 82, 83, 85, 181, 197, 202
   will of, 21, 27, 44, 58, 59, 61, 104, 105, 161, 184
Godparents, 58
Good Friday, 82, 85, 137, 140, 179
Good News, 20–21, 31, 32, 44, 64–65, 76, 82, 89, 91, 104, 122–123, 128–129, 134, 148, 179
Good Shepherd, 8
Gospel(s), 14, 27, 31, 44, 76, 94

†*Italics* refer to definitions

*Bold-faced pages indicate chapters

Grace, 39, 47, 58–59, 77, 97, 103, 111, 116, 128, 157, 198, 199, *210*
Grace before and after Meals, 166, 203

Hail, Holy Queen, 202, 206
Hail Mary, 179, 202, 203
Healing
    Church's mission of, 32–33, 35, 39, 104–105, 110–111, 113, 199
    Jesus' mission of, 20, 27, 110
Health, taking care of, 111
Heaven, 20, 23, 32–33, 69, 110, 128, 159, 161, 167, 198
Holiness, 47, 148, 151, 200
Holy Communion, 51, 71, 73, 77, 113, 117. *See also* Eucharist
Holy Days of Obligation, 44, 79, 208
Holy Family, 94
Holy Orders, 38–39, **121–126**, *123*, 129, 199, 200, *210*. *See also* Bishop(s); Deacon(s); Priest(s)
    background for, 122
    celebrating, 123
Holy Saturday, 82, 140
Holy Spirit, 154, 161, 179, 198
    in Christian life, 32–33, 59, 64–65, 83, 116, 123, 128, 131, 148, 151, 161, 166, 184, 198, 201
    Fruits of, 67
    Fullness of, 67
    as Helper, 32, 58, 83–85, 166, 184, 201
    gifts of, 64–65, 67, 183
    Mary and, 32
    Mass of, 183
    sacraments and, 38–39, 58, 64–65, 71, 77, 105, 110–111, 112, 116, 128, 178, 199
    sign (or seal) of, 64–65, 67, 128
Holy Thursday, 82, 140, 143
Holy water, 142, 178
Holy Week, 82, 140
Homily, 76, 107, 131
Hope, **165–170**, *167*, *210*
    gift from God, 166
    living with, 166–167, 169, 201
    Mary as sign of, 167, 169
    sources of, 166, 169
    virtue of, 160, **165–170**, 173, 175

Immaculate Conception of Mary, 83, 186
Immanuel, 88–89, 91
Incarnation, 17, 198, *210*
Individual Rite of Reconciliation, 105, 107
Introductory Rites of the Mass, 50, 76
Isaiah, 88, 89

James (Saint), 110
Jesus Christ
    as source of hope, 166, 169
    ascension of, 32, 33, 64, 83, 84, 128, 149, 179, 198
    birth of, 14, 82, 94–95, 179, 198
    coming in glory, 82, 89, 91, 198
    death and resurrection of, 14, 27, 31, 44, 50, 58, 61, 70–71, 76, 82–83, 85, 134, **139–144**, 155, 161, 169, 178, 179, 185, 198, 199
    divinity of, 14, 17, 94–95, 155, 161, 198
    forgiveness and healing by, 20, 27, 29, 32, 44, 104, 110
    humanity of, 14, 17, 94–95, 155, 161, 198
    at Last Supper, 50, 64, 70, 77, 82
    naming of, 94
    preaching of Kingdom to all, 20–21, 26, 134, 198
    presentation in Temple, 94, 179
    priesthood of, 58, 59, 123, 128–129
    serving others by, 20, 116–117, 122
    temptation of, 8, 134, 137
Jesus Christ, titles and images of
    Bread of Life, 50–51, 69, 71, 73, 200
    Good Shepherd, 8
    Immanuel, 88–89, 91
    King or ruler, 58–59, 83, 89, 91
    Light of world, 89, 95, 97, 179
    Messiah or Anointed One, 20–21, 31, 82, 89, 91, 198
    Priest, 58–59, 128, 200
    Prophet, 58–59, 123
    Sacrament of God, 38, 41
    Savior, 20, 27, 89, 91, 94, 97, 155, 161, 199
    Son of God, 14, 17, 31, 38–39, 51, 91, 94, 97, 134, 184, 198
    Teacher, 29, 159, 160, 173
Jogues, Isaac (Saint), 63
John (Apostle and Saint), 15, 171, 175
John Paul II (Pope), 165. *See also* Pope
John the Baptist (Saint), 20
Joseph (Saint), 14, 69, 83, 93, 94, 154
Judaism, beliefs of, 154
Justice, 15, 21, 23, 32, 38, 53, 58–59, 88–89, 103, 129, 148, 151, 160, 173, 175

Kingdom of God. *See* Reign of God
Kingdom of heaven, 27, *210*

Laity, 129, *210*
Last judgment, 172–173
Last Supper, 50, 64, 70, 77, 82, 178
Law of Love, 23, 148, 155, 160, 184, 191–196, 201, *210*
Laws of the Church, 79, 201, 208
Laying on of hands, 65, 110–111, 122–123
Lazarus, 14
Lent, Season of, 82–83, 85, **133–138**, 202
Lenten practices, 82, 135, 137
Letters or Epistles, 76
Liturgical year, **81–86**, 202, *210*. *See also specific liturgical season or feast.*
Liturgy, 76–77, *77*, *211*
Liturgy of the Eucharist, 51, 76–77, *211*
Liturgy of the Word, 51, 76, 110, 116, *211*
Love, **171–176**, *173*, 198, *211*. *See also* Law of Love
    gift from God, 172
    of others, 14, 21, 95, 105, 116–117, 135, 148, 172
    virtue of, 160, 169, **171–176**, 201
Love of God (divine), 15, 17, 20–21, 38–39, 65, 94, 95, 104–105, 111, 116–117, 134, 140, 151, 160, 161, 163, 166, 171, 199, 200

Marks of the Church, **147–152**, *211*
Marriage vows or promises, 116–117
Martha, 14, 31
Martyr, 63
Mary, 178, 181, 198
    Assumption of, 83, 167, 179
    devotion to, 83
    feasts of, 83, 186
    Jesus' first disciple, 167
    life of, 14, 32, 83, 85, 89, 93, 94, 154, 167, 179
    sinlessness of, 186
    virginity of, 89, 167, 186
Mary, titles of, 186
    Immaculate Mother, 186
    Mother of the Church, 167
    Mother of God, 83, 89, 186
    Mother of Jesus, 94, 184, 186
    Our Lady of Guadalupe, 83
    Patroness of United States of America, 186
    Queen of heaven, 179
    Sign of Hope, 167, 169
Mary Magdalene, 31
Mass, 50, 58, 73, **75–80**, 200, 202, *211*. *See also* Eucharist
    as memorial, 76
    as prayer of praise, 50, 53
    living the, 76
    ministries at, 65, 71, 76–77, 110, 117, 123, 131
    obligation to take part in, 59, 79
    planning a celebration of, 52, 186
    rites of, 50–51, 76–77
    special meal and sacrifice, 50, 53, 70, 200
Matrimony, 38–39, **115–120**, *117*, 199, *211*
    background for, 116
    celebrating, 116–117
    living, 116–117, 129
    preparing for, 117, 119
Medals, 178, 180, 181
Meditation, 23, 202, 207
Memorare, 203
Messiah, 20–21, 31, 82, 88, 91, *211*
Miracles, 14, 26, 69, 110, 163
Missionary(ies), 63, 129, 149
More, Thomas (Saint), 180
Morning Offering, 203
Mortal sin, 104, 105
Mysteries of our faith, 77, 160
Mysteries of the rosary, 179, 206

*****Bold-faced** pages indicate chapters

215

New Commandment, 32, 198
New life, in Christ, 58, 134, 140, 143, 155, 161, 200, 201
New life of Baptism, 58–59, 61, 134, 140
Newton, John, 103
Nicene Creed, 149, 160, 204
North American Martyrs, 63

Oils, holy, 58, 65, 110–111, 113, 123
Old Testament, 47, 49, 76, 81, 91, 154
Ordained ministers, 122–123, 125. *See also* Holy Orders
    bishops, 65, 122–123, 128–129, 148, 149, 151
    deacons, 58, 76–77, 107, 116–117, 122–123, 125, 129
    priests, 51, 53, 58–59, 76–77, 104–105, 107, 111, 116–117, 121–123, 125, 129
Ordinary Time, 83, 202
Ordination. *See* Holy Orders
Original sin, 58, 61, 186, 198, *211*
Our Father, 20, 23, 77, 107, 117, 179, 202, 203

Palm or Passion Sunday, 82–83, 140, 143
Parable, 8, 47
Parish, 97, 122, 125, 151, 155, 157, 167, 169, 197, 200
Paschal Candle, 179
Paschal Mystery, 140
Passover, 70, 140, *211*
Pastoral ministers, 129
Paul (Saint and Apostle), 33, 38, 50, 79, 148–149, 166, 173, 175
Peace, 15, 21, 23, 27, 32, 38, 53, 58–59, 88–89, 103, 105, 107, 129, 148, 151, 160, 186
Penance for sins, 104–105, 107, *211*
People of God, 47, 51, 58, 71, 83, 104, 154, 160, 201
Pentecost, 32, 35, 64, 83
Pentecost Sunday, 83
Peter (Saint and Apostle), 31, 122, 149, 159, 163, 198
Pope(s), 122, 128, 148–149, *149*, 151, 165, 180, *211*
Prayer, 14, 76–77, 103, 105, 125, 135, 137, 148–149, 151, 155, 160, 167, 173, 178, 179, 181, 197, 201, 202, *211*
    to Holy Spirit, 204
    for inner stillness, 207
    for my vocation, 205
    Prayer celebrations and services
    for Advent, 90
    of Baptism, 60
    for Christmas, 96
    for Easter, 142
    of the Eucharist, 52
    for forgiveness, 46, 106
    to the Holy Spirit, 66, 150, 183
    for hope, 168
    for Lent, 136
    for liturgical year, 84
    for living the Law of Love, 191–196
    for married couples, 118
    Mary Immaculate, 186
    for the sacraments, 40
    for the sick, 112
    Way of the Cross, 184–185
Prayer of the Faithful, 76
Prejudice, **153–158**, 160
Priest(s)
    ministries of, 51, 53, 58, 59, 76–77, 104–105, 107, 111, 116–117, 121–123, 125, 200
    ordination of, 123, 129
    support of, 122–123, 125
Priesthood of the faithful, 123, 128, 211
Prodigal son, 44
Protestant Churches, 154

Racism, *155, 212*. *See also* Discrimination; Prejudice
Real Presence, 38–39, 50, 71, 73, 77, 110, 200
Reconciliation, 27, 38–39, **43–48**, **103–108**, 199, 200, 201, *211*
    background, 38, 47, 104
    celebrating, 38–39, 44–45, 47, 59, 61, 104–105, 107
    living, 27, 105, 160
Redemption, 161 Salvation 76, 149, 186
Reign of God, **19–24**, *21*, 39, 77, 197, 199, *211*
    announcement of, 20–21, 82, 172, 198
    coming of, 166–167
    living for, 21, 23, 26–27, 29, 50–51, 58, 65, 76, 105, 128–129, 131, 151, 160, 166–167, 172
Religions, respect for, 154–155, 157
Religious communities, 129
Resurrection of the dead, 155, 161
Resurrection of Jesus, 31, 44, 50, 58, 61, 70–71, 76, 82–83, 85, 134, **139–144**, 155, 161, 169, 178, 179
Retreat Day, 191–196
Revelation, 160, 161
Rosary, the, 179, 181, 186, 202, 206

Sacrament(s), **37–42**, *39*, 73, 148, 197, 199, 200, 201, *211*. *See also specific sacrament*
    Church as, 38, 77
    as effective signs, 38–39, 104, 110, 113, 199
    Jesus as, 38, 41
    living, 38, 41, 131, 160, 167, 201
    ministers of, 58, 65, 76–77, 104–105, 107, 111, 116–117, 122–123
    seven, 38–39, 41, 199
Sacramentals, **177–182**, *211*
Sacraments of Healing, 39, **43–48**, **103–108**, **109–114**, 199
Sacraments of Initiation, 39, **57–62**, **63–68**, **69–74**, **75–80**, 128, 140, 199
Sacraments of Service, 39, **115–120**, **121–126**, 199
Sacrifice, 50, 70–71, 172, 200
Sacrifice of Jesus, 70–71, 198
Saint(s), 64, 83, 85, 131, 148, 178, 181, 186
Satan, 134
Savior, 20, 27, 88–89, 91, 94, 97, 161, 199
Second Vatican Council, 113, 119
Sermon on the Mount, 29
Sign(s), 38–39, 104
    Christians as, 38, 41, 50
    Jesus as, 38
Sign of the Cross, 65, 105, 107, 179, 203
Simeon, 94
Sin, 21, 27, 44, 47, 71, 77, 82, 94, 97, 104, *105*, 107, 110, 134, 140, 155, 157, 161, 169, 179, 198, 200, *211*. *See also* Forgiveness of sins
Single people, 129
Sisters, religious, 129
Social sin, 104
Sorrow for sins/wrongdoing, 27, 44–45, 104–105, 107, 161
Spiritual Works of Mercy, 173, *212*
Stations of the Cross, 181, 184–185, 206
Statues, 178, 180

Tabernacle, 73
Temptation, 166
Temptation(s) of Jesus, 8, 134, 137
Ten Commandments, 154–155, 184, 201, 208, *212*
Thomas (Apostle), 31
Trinity. *See* Blessed Trinity

Venial sin, 104
Viaticum, 113, *212*
Virgin Mary, 89, 167, 186, 198
Virtue
    theological, 163
Virtue(s), 47, **159–164, 165–170, 171–176**. *See also* Faith; Hope; Love
Visitation, 179
Vocation, 116, 119, 123, 128–129, 131, 203, *212*
    preparing for, 119, 131
Vows, 116–117, 129

Way of the Cross, 184–185, 206
Witness(ing), 63–65, 116
Women
    equality and partnership of, with men, 118
    roles of in Church, 128–129
Word of God, 53, 76, 155, 198
Works of Mercy, 173, 184, 201
Worship, 39, 73, 76, 79, 104, 122, 134, 154–155, 157, 197, 199, 200, *212*

†*Italics* refer to definitions

Answers for Reviews

Lesson 1 (pg. 18): **1.** c **2.** b **3.** a **4.** d
Lesson 2 (pg. 24): **1.** c **2.** b **3.** d **4.** c
Lesson 3 (pg. 30): **1.** c **2.** b **3.** d **4.** a
Lesson 4 (pg. 36): **1.** c **2.** b **3.** b **4.** d
Lesson 5 (pg. 42): **1.** b **2.** c **3.** d **4.** b
Lesson 6 (pg. 48): **1.** forgive sins in His name. **2.** the sacrament of Reconciliation. **3.** when we are sorry. **4.** making an examination of conscience.
Lesson 7 (pg. 54): **1.** c **2.** a **3.** c **4.** b
Unit 1 (pg. 56): **1.** c **2.** d **3.** b **4.** a **5.** c
Lesson 8 (pg. 62): **1.** b **2.** b **3.** d **4.** a
Lesson 9 (pg. 68): **1.** d **2.** a **3.** c **4.** d
Lesson 10 (pg. 74): **1.** d **2.** a **3.** c **4.** b
Lesson 11 (pg. 80): **1.** c **2.** b **3.** a **4.** d
Lesson 12 (pg. 86): **1.** a **2.** d **3.** b **4.** c
Lesson 13 (pg. 92): **1.** Immanuel **2.** Mother of the Savior **3.** light **4.** wise and just
Lesson 14 (pg. 98): **1.** F **2.** T **3.** F **4.** T
Summary 1 (pg. 101-102): **1.** c **2.** a **3.** c **4.** b **5.** d **6.** initiation **7.** healing **8.** service **9.** Holy Spirit **10.** Body and Blood *In 11–20, cross out:* **11.** holy water **12.** our citizenship **13.** holy oil **14.** need help to live **15.** ordinary bread and wine **16.** the Ascension **17.** His ascension into heaven **18.** Christmas **19.** Ash Wednesday **20.** Good Friday
Lesson 15 (pg. 108): **1.** 2, 5, 1, 4, 3 **2.** b **3.** b **4.** c
Lesson 16 (pg. 114): **1.** b **2.** d **3.** a **4.** c
Lesson 17 (pg. 120): **1.** love. **2.** Be true at all times and love one another forever. **3.** His Church. **4.** God's love for the world.
Lesson 18 (pg. 126): **1.** apostles **2.** Bishops **3.** deacons **4.** laying on of hands
Lesson 19 (pg. 132): **1.** F, T, T **2.** vocation **3.** the priesthood of the faithful **4.** evangelization
Lesson 20 (pg. 138): **1.** d **2.** b **3.** a **4.** b
Lesson 21 (pg. 144): **1.** the Mass of the Lord's Supper **2.** and remember the Lord's Passion **3.** and our new life in Christ **4.** Easter Triduum
Unit 3 (pg. 146): **1.** b **2.** c **3.** d **4.** c **5.** b **6.** b **7.** a **8.** the Individual Rite and Communal Rite. **9.** through the sacraments of Reconciliation and Anointing of the Sick
Lesson 22 (pg. 152): **1.** one **2.** holy **3.** catholic **4.** apostolic
Lesson 23 (pg. 158): **1.** F (no circumstance) **2.** F (All Christians) **3.** T **4.** T
Lesson 24 (pg. 164): **1.** b **2.** c **3.** d **4.** c
Lesson 25 (pg. 170): **1.** a **2.** d **3.** b **4.** d
Lesson 26 (pg. 176): **1.** b **2.** d **3.** c **4.** a
Lesson 27 (pg. 182): **1.** Holy water **2.** crucifix **3.** Paschal Candle or Easter Candle **4.** ashes
Summary 2 (pg. 189-190): **1.** b **2.** c **3.** c **4.** a **5.** d **6.** contrition **7.** Sin **8.** lifelong **9.** bishops **10.** priests **11.** pope **12.** Jewish **13.** Trinity **14.** hope **15.** 7, 1, 6, 4, 8, 2, 3, 5

SCRIPTURE REFERENCES

Scripture References in *Coming to God's Life*

Unit 1

John 11:1–44, p. 14
Matthew 8:23–27, p. 14
1 John 4:8, p. 15
Luke 7:18–22, p. 20
Matthew 6:10, p. 21
Luke 7:18–23, p. 22
Matthew 8:5–11, p. 26
Luke 23:34, p. 27
Acts 2:1–13, p. 32
Matthew 20:28, p. 32
John 13:34, p. 32
1 Corinthians 12:26, p. 33
Luke 12:54–56, p. 38
Colossians 1:15, p. 38
John 20:19–23, p. 44
Luke 15:11–24, p. 44
Joel 2:13, p. 46
Luke 15:11–24, p. 46
Psalm 136:1–9, p. 46
Psalm 145:1–13, p. 46
2 Kings 4:1–7, p. 49
1 Corinthians 11:24, p. 50
John 6:35, p. 50
1 Corinthians 10:16–17, p. 50

Unit 2

John 14:16–17, p. 64
Acts 1:7–14, 2:1–13, p. 64
John 6:35, 41, 51, 60–61, p. 69
1 Corinthians 11:23–25, p. 70
Ecclesiastes 3:1, 4, p. 81
Mark 1:15, p. 82
Isaiah 11:2, p. 88
Isaiah 9:1–7, p. 88
Isaiah 61:1–2, p. 89
Luke 1:26–33, p. 89
Isaiah 61:1, 3, p. 90
Matthew 1:18–22, p. 94
Luke 2:21–32, p. 94

Unit 3

James 5:15, p. 110
Numbers 6:24–26, p. 112
Mark 10:44–45, p. 122
Matthew 28:19–20, p. 128
Matthew 4:1–11, p. 134
Mark 1:12–15, p. 136
Mark 11:1–11, p. 134
Luke 24:13–24, p. 142

Unit 4

Ephesians 4:5–6, p. 148
Leviticus 19:1–2, p. 148
Mark 16:15, p. 149
Ephesians 2:20, p. 149
John 6:51–69, p. 159
Romans 8:39, p. 166
1 John 4:7–11, p. 171
Matthew 25:34–36, p. 172
Matthew 25:31–46, p. 173
1 Corinthians 13:13, p. 173
Acts 2:1–11, p. 183
John 20:19–23, p. 183
Mark 14:43–46, p. 184
Luke 23:26–27, p. 184
Luke 23:32–34, p. 185
Luke 23:44–46, p. 185
John 20:11–18, p. 185

Family Pages

Unit 1
John 1:35–39, p. 12
John 14:1–6, p. 18
Matthew 22:34–40, p. 23
Luke 12:32, p. 23
John 5:2-9, p. 24
Matthew 5:1—7:29, p. 29
John 6:66–69, p. 30
John 15:5–8, p. 36
John 7:37–39, p. 42
John 8:4–7, 9–11, p. 48
John 6:10–13, p. 54

Unit 2
John 3:1–6, p. 62
John 16:13–15, p. 68
John 6:35–61, p. 73
John 6:32–35, 37, p. 74
1 Corinthians 10:17, p. 79
John 4:7, 9, 13–14, p. 80
John 17:1, 6, 8, 11, p. 86
John 1:19–20, 23, 29, p. 92
John 1:1–5, 14, p. 98

Unit 3
John 20:19–23, p. 108
John 11:20–26, p. 114
John 2:1–11, p. 119
John 2:1–3, 7–11, p. 120
John 21:15–17, p. 126
John 13:12, 14–17, p. 132
John 21:17, p. 137
John 20:28, p. 137
Luke 22:42, p. 137
Psalm 23:1, p. 137
Psalm 34:1, p. 137
Isaiah 6:3, p. 137
John 18:33, 36–37, p. 138
John 20:11–16, 18, p. 144

Unit 4
John 10:10, 14–16, p. 152
John 9:1–5, p. 158
Matthew 14:22–33, p. 163
Matthew 14:31, p. 163
John 20:25–29, p. 164
John 19:25–27, 30, p. 170
1 Corinthians 13:4–7, p. 175
John 13:33–35, p. 176
Leviticus 19:18, p. 176
John 8:12–14, p. 182

NOTES

NOTES

Acknowledgments

Grateful acknowledgment is due the following for their work on the *Coming to Faith* Program:

Patricia Dobrowski, Project Editor
Karen James, Editor
Program Design, Chattum Design
Production, Monica Bernier

Scripture selections are taken from the *New American Bible* copyright © 1991, 1986, 1970 by the Confraternity of Christian Doctrine, Washington D.C. and are used with permission. All rights reserved.

Excerpts from *Economic Justice for All* Copyright © 1997, 1986 by the United States Catholic Conference, Washington D.C. 20017-1194 are used by permission of the copyright owner. All rights reserved.

Excerpts from the English translation of *Rite of Baptism for Children* © 1969, International Committee on English in the Liturgy, Inc. (ICEL); excerpts from the English translation of *Roman Missal* © 1973, ICEL, excerpts from the English translation of *Rite of Confirmation*, Second Edition, © 1975, ICEL; excerpts from *Pastoral Care of the Sick*; *Rites of Anointing and Viaticum* © 1982, ICEL. All rights reserved. English translation of the Lord's Prayer, and the Kyrie by the International Consultation on English Texts.

The Documents of Vatican II, Abbott-Gallagher edition. Reprinted with permission of American Press, Inc. 106 West 56th Street New York, NY 10019 © 1966. All Rights Reserved.

Excerpts from *Blessed Are You Who Believe* by Carlo Carretto, copyright © 1983 Orbis Books, Maryknoll, NY. Used with permission.

Photo Research

Jim Saylor

Cover Photos

Myrleen Cate: insets.
H. Armstrong Roberts: background and nature insets.

Photo Credits

Diane J. Ali: 12 left, 81 top, 184–185, 179 bottom center.
Animals Animals/Marcia W. Griffin: 57 left.
Art Resource, NY: 38–39; Scala: 82, 159B, 160, 166 left.
Dennis Barnes: 115B, 116.
Myrleen Cate: 7 top, 7 bottom, 7B, 10, 12 center left, 12 center right, 13, 13B–25B, 27, 33, 34, 44, 45, 50, 50–51, 60, 65, 78 bottom, 81 center left, 81 bottom, 105, 109, 109B, 121, 121B–127B, 128, 133 top, 165 bottom, 165A–171A, 174, 147 top right, 147A, B, 147 bottom left, 153, 166 top right, 178–179, 179 bottom right, 181, 191, 192, 194, 207.
CNS/Blimp Photo Company: 148–149; Arturo Mari: 148.
Bill Coleman: 153A, 155 right.
CROSIERS/Gene Plaisted, OSC: 64, 76, 94, 110, 123, 129, 141 center, 177, 179 bottom left, 180, 212.
Kathy Ferguson: 49.
FPG International/Ron Chapple: 61; Color Box: 63.
Christopher Talbot Frank: 57 right.
Nicholas H. Hemmer: 12 bottom.
Profiles West/Allen Russell: 147 left.
Frances M. Roberts: 111 left.
H. Armstrong Roberts: 29, 97, 103, 115B, 117 top, 134–135, 137, 141 top, 141 bottom, 167 top, 167 bottom.
Nancy Sheehan: 58, 66, 77, 78 top, 140, 196.
The Stock Market/Paul Barton: 7 center; Paul Chauncey: 57 top; Peter Beck: 59, 103B, 104, 118, 133 bottom; Bo Zaunders: 79; Jean Miele: 88–89; Anthony Edgeworth: 115, 115A.
Tony Stone Images/Paul Berger: 12 right; Rosemary Weller: 81 center right; Bob Torrez: 111 right; Dale Durfee: 117 bottom; Bill Aron: 154; David H. Endersbee: 165 background; David Olsen: 167 background.
H. Mark Weidman: 153B, 155 left.

Illustrators

Blaine Martin: Cover, Digital Imaging
Wendy Pierson: Cover, Logo Rendering
Skip Baker: 163, 168.
Jim Baldwin: 124, 125.
David Barber: 96.
David Barnett: 8–9, 19B, 20.
Karen Bell: 46, 90, 142.
Teresa Berasi: 161.
Lisa Blackshear: 35.
Robert Burger: 157.
Kevin Butler: 23, 105, 107, 119, 133, 135.
Young Sook Cho: 81B, 82–83.
Gwen Connelly: 57B, 58–59.
Neverne Covington: 26–27.
Daniel DelValle: 11, 53, 131.
Pat Dewitt: 183, 186.
Cathy Diefendorf: 75, 94–95, 156.
Victor Durango: 84.
Bill Farnsworth: 69.
Yvonne Gilbert: 87.
Adam Gordon: 12, 16, 17, 28, 29, 31B, 32, 33, 34, 39, 72, 73, 78, 79, 81, 85, 96, 97, 110, 118, 143, 171, 171B, 173, 179.
Brad Hamann: 41, 174.
John Haysom: 14–15, 69B, 70–71, 172.
Robert Jones: 151.
Ana Jouvin: 177.
Al Leiner: 122–123.
Judy Love: 25, 37, 106, 109, 109A.
Blaine Martin: 136, 162.
Shelley Matheis: 171.
Verlin Miller: 150.
Andrew Muonio: 113.
Cheryl Kirk Noll: 112.
Julie Pace: 184–185.
Julie Peterson: 51.
Wendy Pierson: 148–149.
Rodica Prato: 103.
Alan Reingold: 16, 17.
Dorothy Reinhardt: 75B, 76–77, 116–117.
Frank Riccio: 63, 63B.
Margaret Sanfilippo: 32, 33, 93, 127, 130, 139.
Joanne Scribner: 43.
Bob Shein: 19, 52, 91.
Mark Sparacio: 65, 67, 97, 115.
Tom Sperling: 31, 49, 134–135, 159, 159A.
Nancy Tobin: 175.
Gregg Valley: 22, 94–95.
Dean Wilhite: 128–129.
Jenny Williams: 37B, 40, 72.

T42

Our Catholic Identity

	Page	Use with Chapter
Family Portraits of Jesus	1	1
Migrant Ministry; St. Teresa of Avila	2	2
Servants of the Lord	3	3
Parish Communities	4	4
Important Church Records	5	8
Fruits of the Holy Spirit	6	9
The Gifts of Bread and Wine	7	10
Communion Under Both Kinds	8	11
The Seal of Confession	9	15
Liturgical Colors; Liturgical Time	10	12
Preparing for a Sick Call	11	16
The Ministers of Marriage	12	17
Permanent Deacons; A Daring Priest	13	18
Saints New and Old	14	24
Paschal Candle; Alpha and Omega	15	25

Our Catholic Identity

Family Portraits of Jesus

No one today knows what Jesus really looked like when he walked the earth. But Catholic churches around the world display "family portraits" of him. These works of art help us to understand in a deeper way that Jesus is both human and divine.

What "family portraits" of Jesus do you recall from your parish church? Perhaps you have seen the following:

- the infant Jesus with the Blessed Virgin Mary
- a crucifix
- a statue of Jesus as a boy or as the risen Lord
- stained-glass windows displaying scenes from the gospels
- the fourteen stations of the cross showing how Jesus suffered and died for us.

Make a visit to church on your own. Choose one work of art that tells you about Jesus. Spend a few minutes looking at it prayerfully. Thank Jesus for revealing God's love to you.

A Child Artist

One day a famous artist was traveling in the countryside near Florence, Italy. He saw a shepherd boy drawing a sheep. The boy's "brush" was a pointed stone. His "canvas" was a stone slab. His sheep was so well done that the famous artist took the boy with him as his pupil.

The boy's name was Giotto di Bondone. It was the thirteenth century, and he was about to change Christian art forever. God had given Giotto the gift of drawing biblical scenes that seemed to come to life for people. They made Jesus look as real and familiar as someone in your family.

Giotto's paintings help Catholics to appreciate that Jesus is both human and divine. We can be grateful for the gift of Christian artists whose works deepen our faith by turning our hearts and minds to God.

Learn by heart — Faith Summary

- Jesus Christ is both human and divine.
- Jesus showed us that "God is love" by the things he said and did.
- God works through us and others to show God's love in the world.

Noli me tangere,
School of Giotto, (13th century)

Our Catholic Identity

Kingdom Builders

As people travel around the United States, they often see migrant workers in the fields during harvest time. Migrant workers move from place to place, picking other farmers' crops. They are often paid little and work long hours. Sometimes they are treated unjustly, and their children are forced to move from school to school. The shelters in which they live are frequently poor and rundown.

The Catholic Church is very concerned about the needs of migrant workers and their families. That is why dioceses in which there are migrant workers provide spiritual and social services to help them. There are many priests, religious and lay people involved in this important ministry. This is another example of people in the Church who show us what it means to be kingdom builders.

What are your dreams for the kingdom of God?

Words from a Great Teacher

Over four hundred years ago in Spain, there lived a great kingdom builder. Today we know her as Saint Teresa of Avila. She reminds us that living for God's kingdom involves more than doing activities. She knew from experience how important it is to live a life of prayer.

Teresa's favorite prayer was the Our Father. She said that it was better to pray one Our Father with loving attention than to rush through twenty without thinking. She taught that one way to pray with "loving attention" is to remember that Jesus is always there with us "like a friend in a dark room." Above all, Teresa said, speak to God simply from the heart with love.

Sometime today, pray the Our Father using Saint Teresa's suggestions.

Learn by heart

Faith Summary

- Jesus announced the good news of the kingdom, or reign, of God. The good news is that God loves us and will always love us.
- The reign of God is the saving power of God's life and love in the world.
- Jesus lived his whole life for the reign of God and calls us to do the same.

OUR CATHOLIC IDENTITY

Servants of the Lord

On Holy Thursday, the Church celebrates the Evening Mass of the Lord's Supper. Catholics are often surprised that the gospel reading used at this Mass is not the full account of the Last Supper. In fact, the gospel reading is Saint John's account of Jesus washing the feet of his disciples. Why do you think Jesus did this?

Jesus lived in a dry and dusty country surrounded by deserts. People walked long distances in their sandals. When they came to someone's home, the head of the household would have towels and water brought to them to wash their feet. This was a sign of hospitality.

At the Last Supper, Jesus took this custom and gave it new meaning. Jesus not only provided the water and towels, but he knelt down and personally washed the feet of his disciples. Jesus, the Son of God, was showing himself to be the servant of all. He was serving rather than being served. This is the way he wanted his disciples to live.

Today in many parishes, the ritual of the washing of the feet takes place during the Mass on Holy Thursday. Twelve parishioners come forward, reminding us of the twelve apostles. The priest then kneels before them and washes their feet, drying them with a towel. He does this as a reminder of the beautiful and challenging example Jesus gave to all of his disciples.

How can fifth graders follow the example of Jesus, who became the servant of all?

Learn by heart — Faith Summary

- Jesus invited everyone to live for the reign of God.
- Forgiveness heals the separation from God and from others that sin causes.
- Like Jesus, we try to forgive those who hurt us, no matter how great the hurt.

OUR CATHOLIC IDENTITY

Our Parish Family

Each and every day we carry out the mission of Jesus in our parish. A parish is a community of Catholics who come together under the leadership of a pastor. The pastor is appointed by the bishop of the diocese to care for the needs of the parish family.

We come together each week as a parish to celebrate the Eucharist, the high point of parish life. In the parish we also celebrate the other sacraments, hear the word of God, and come to know the teachings of the Church.

The parish is so important in Catholic life that many Catholics identify themselves simply by the name of their parish: "I'm from Saint Monica's Parish; I'm from Our Lady of Angels' Parish."

Every parish has something special about it. What sets your parish apart as it carries on the mission of Jesus?

Joining A Parish

Every Catholic should belong to a parish. How do we go about becoming a member of a parish? The first thing is to register. We can do this by going to the parish office or rectory and introducing ourselves to the parish staff. The priest or another staff member will ask about our family, our sacramental history (Baptism, Confirmation, First Holy Communion, and so forth), and what needs we may have.

Once we get to know all about our parish family, it will be time to join in the life and work of that parish. We do this by being active in parish activities and organizations.

All the members of the parish should use their gifts and talents for the good of the whole parish community. What talents or gifts can you bring to your parish?

Learn by heart — Faith Summary

- The Holy Spirit helps the Church carry on the mission of Jesus to all people.
- Jesus is the head of the Church, his body, and we are its members.
- Like Jesus, the Church serves people and brings them Jesus' healing and forgiveness.

OUR CATHOLIC IDENTITY

A Record of Baptism

Just as the record of our birth is kept by the city and state, the record of our new birth in Baptism is kept by the Church.

When a person is baptized—either an infant or an adult—the priest or deacon of the parish writes that person's name into a large book called the *baptismal register*. Next to the person's name is written the date of birth, the date of Baptism, the names of the parents and godparents, as well as the name of the priest or deacon who performed the Baptism.

All this information is kept forever in the parish church where the Baptism took place. The baptismal record always stays in the same parish. In this way, the important information of our Baptism will never be lost. We can always call that parish and get a copy of our baptismal record whenever we need to do so.

Other Important Records

The Catholic Church also keeps records of other important information. As time goes on, the information is added to our baptismal record. This happens when we are confirmed, married in the Catholic Church, ordained, or take religious vows. Wherever these events take place in the world, the information is always sent back to the original church of Baptism to be added in the baptismal register.

Where were you baptized? Have you ever seen a copy of your baptismal record? Tell about it.

Learn by heart Faith Summary

- We receive new life at Baptism when we are reborn of water and the Holy Spirit.
- At Baptism we are initiated into, or begin to become members of, the Church, the body of Christ.
- Our Baptism calls us to decide to live for the reign of God.

The Fruits of the Holy Spirit

We know how important the Holy Spirit is in our lives. It is the Holy Spirit who guides the Church. It is by the power of the Holy Spirit that we follow Jesus and celebrate the seven sacraments.

How can we tell whether or not we are responding to the guidance of the Spirit in our lives? The Catholic Church teaches us that the Holy Spirit develops in us certain qualities, or virtues. We call these qualities the twelve fruits of the Holy Spirit. The usual naming of these twelve fruits is as follows: charity, joy, peace, patience, kindness, goodness, generosity, gentleness, faithfulness, modesty, self-control, and chastity.

You may be familiar with most of these qualities. However, two may be new to you: modesty and chastity.

Men and women who are modest have deep respect for the human person. One way they do this is by showing in word and action the dignity the body deserves.

Chastity is another important fruit of the Holy Spirit. People who live the virtue of chastity know how to love unselfishly, responsibly, and faithfully. Chastity calls us to have deep respect for human sexuality—in the ways we act, in what we read, and in what we look at.

Which fruits of the Holy Spirit do you think our world needs most today? Will you pray for them?

Our Catholic Identity

Learn by heart

Faith Summary

- Confirmation is the sacrament in which we are sealed with the Gift of the Holy Spirit and strengthened to give witness to the good news of Jesus Christ.
- In Confirmation the Holy Spirit fills us with the gifts that we need to live our Christian faith.
- We live our Confirmation when we become witnesses to the reign of God in the world.

Special Gifts of Bread and Wine

Whenever we come together to celebrate the Eucharist, we offer the gifts of bread and wine that will become the Body and Blood of Christ.

The Catholic Church knows how important these gifts of bread and wine are. That is why they must be made in a special way.

The wine must be made from grapes, the fruit of the vine. It should be pure and have nothing else added to it.

The bread that we use is very different from the ordinary bread we have in our homes each day. The bread for the Eucharist is called *unleavened bread*. This means that nothing has been added to the bread dough to make it rise before it is baked. That is why the bread is flat. This unleavened bread is made only from wheat. We use this kind of bread because we want to follow the example of Jesus at the Last Supper.

The Church also requires that the bread prepared for the Eucharist be made in such a way that it can be broken into parts, since it will be distributed to the people.

Finally, the bread and wine should be as fresh and well made as possible. After all, the bread and wine will become the Body and Blood of Christ.

When you see the gifts of bread and wine being carried to the altar, remember that they represent you, too. What does it mean for you to offer yourself to God?

Learn by heart — Faith Summary

- The Eucharist is the sacrament of the Body and Blood of Christ.
- Jesus is the Bread of Life. The food that Jesus gives us is his own Body and Blood.
- We respond to the gift of the Eucharist by living for the reign of God.

Communion Under Both Kinds

At the celebration of the Mass, the priest consecrates both bread and wine. These gifts become the Body and Blood of Christ. By the power of the Holy Spirit, Christ is fully and really present both in the Host and in the Precious Blood.

Often when Catholics celebrate the Eucharist, they receive Holy Communion by taking only the Host. At other times, however, we enjoy the privilege of receiving Communion under both kinds, the Host and the Precious Blood from the chalice.

The bishops of the Church have guidelines for us to follow in receiving Holy Communion under both kinds. It is a wonderful privilege as we celebrate the Eucharist together.

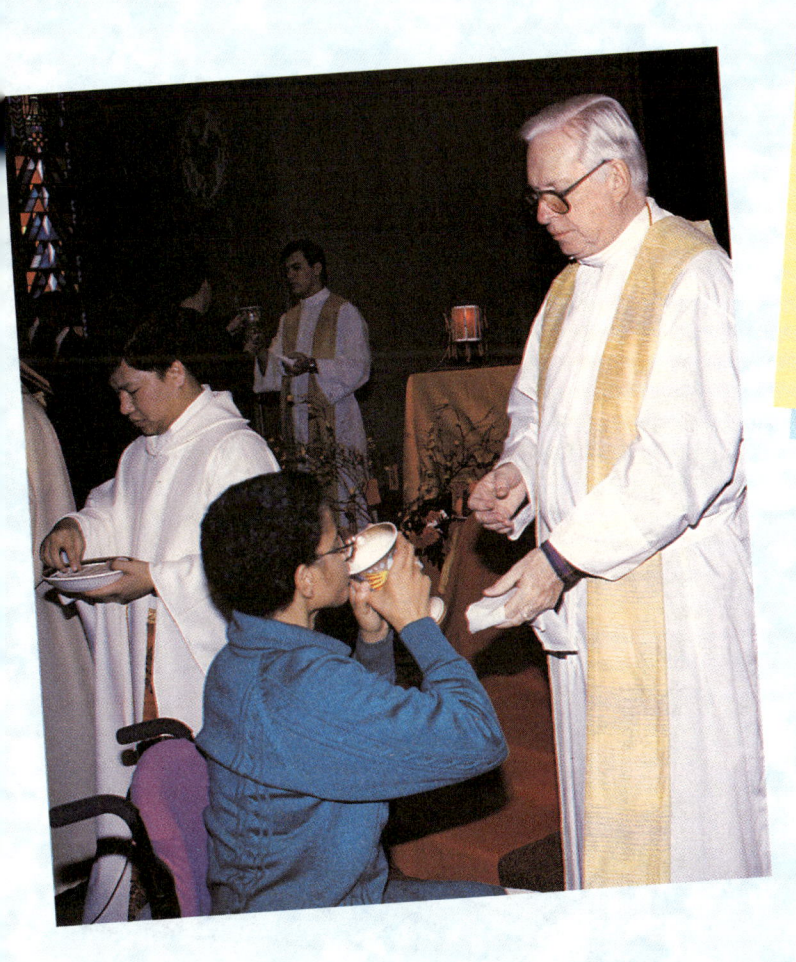

Receiving Communion Reverently

From time to time, we need to remind ourselves of the proper way to receive Holy Communion. When we approach the priest, deacon, or eucharistic minister, we do so reverently. After hearing the words "the body of Christ" or "the blood of Christ," we respond "Amen."

For those receiving the Host in their hands, the proper way is to place one open palm on top of the other. In this way, the Host can be placed on our palm, and we can put the Host into our mouth with the other hand. We never take or grab the Host.

The next time you go to receive Holy Communion, let your reverent example remind others of the importance the Eucharist has in your life.

Learn by heart — Faith Summary

- The two major parts of the Mass are the Liturgy of the Word and the Liturgy of the Eucharist.
- During the Liturgy of the Word, we listen to God's word from the Bible.
- During the Liturgy of the Eucharist, our gifts of bread and wine become the Body and Blood of Christ.

The Seal of Confession

One of the wonderful things for Catholics about the sacrament of Reconciliation is that the confession of our sins is completely private and secret. No one will ever know what we tell the priest during the celebration of this sacrament.

Every priest is bound by a very serious obligation that we call the *seal of confession*. This means that the priest is absolutely forbidden to repeat or discuss what he hears in confession—no matter what!

The reason for this complete secrecy is that the priest, in hearing a confession, acts in the name of God, not in his own name. In fact, the priest's obligation is so total that he may not even talk to us later on about our own confessions unless we give him our permission to do so.

In addition, any person who discovers or overhears in any way what is told in the sacrament of Reconciliation is also bound to complete secrecy. We never need to be afraid to tell anything to the priest in our confession of sins.

OUR CATHOLIC IDENTITY

A Story About the Seal of Confession

In 1393 Saint John Nepomucene was a priest in the royal court of Bohemia. When the king of Bohemia interfered with the running of the Church, Saint John disagreed and tried to stop him. But the king had Saint John tortured and killed.

The people considered Saint John a martyr. According to a popular story, it was said that Saint John Nepomucene had been killed because he refused to tell the king what the queen had said in confession. For this reason, Saint John Nepomucene became known as the patron saint of the seal of confession.

Learn by heart — Faith Summary

- Reconciliation is the sacrament in which we are forgiven by God and the Church for our sins.
- Examination of conscience, contrition, confession, penance, and absolution are important steps in the celebration of Reconciliation.
- In Reconciliation we receive God's help to do his loving will, to avoid sin, and to live as God's people.

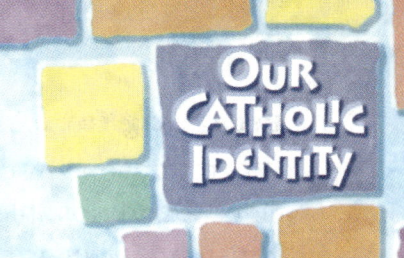

Liturgical Colors

The Catholic Church has many ways to help us pray during the different seasons of the liturgical year. We have different music and different prayers. But we also use different colors to help us enter into each season.

Advent: The colors violet or purple help us to remember that we are preparing for the coming of Christ.

Christmas: To celebrate the joy of Christ's birth, we use the colors white or gold.

Ordinary Time: During the longest season of the year, we use the color green, which reminds us of our hope in God.

Lent: This season of penance and renewal also uses the colors violet or purple.

Easter Triduum: Holy Thursday evening is white; Good Friday is red for Christ's passion; the Easter Vigil and Easter Sunday are white in celebration of the resurrection.

Easter: This season, too, is white or gold as we celebrate our new life in Christ.

Liturgical Year/ Liturgical Day

Our liturgical year does not begin on January 1, as the calendar year does. It begins with the first Sunday of Advent and ends with the feast of Christ the King, the last Sunday in Ordinary Time.

A liturgical day is different, too. Our liturgical day of 24 hours begins in the early evening and continues until the evening of the next day. This is a very ancient way of telling time from the Bible, reminding us of God's presence with us from sunset to sunset. Share with a partner which season is your favorite, and why.

Learn by heart — Faith Summary

- The liturgical seasons of the Church year are Advent, Christmas, Lent, the Easter Triduum, Easter, and Ordinary Time.
- During the liturgical year we also honor and pray to Mary and the other saints.
- The liturgical year reminds us that we always live in the presence of God.

Preparing for a Sick Call

When someone in the family is very sick or elderly, and not able to go out, we ask the parish priest to visit that person. Catholics often call this visit of the priest a *sick call*. The priest comes to pray with the sick person, to bring Holy Communion, and sometimes to celebrate the sacrament of Anointing of the Sick. The whole family can join in the celebration.

This is the way a family can prepare for a sick call.

If possible, a small table covered with a white cloth should be placed near the person who is sick. In this way, the priest can place the holy oil on the table and the *pyx*, or small round container for the Blessed Sacrament. A small crucifix and two blessed candles are often placed on the table, too.

The priest may use holy water to sprinkle and bless the sick person. Then, after the anointing, the priest may wish to remove the holy oil from his fingers. It would be helpful to have cotton, a small piece of lemon, and a small towel on the table for this purpose.

When you ask the priest to visit a sick or elderly person in your family, ask him what preparations he would like you to make for his visit. Sometimes families have special *sick call sets* that have been handed down from generation to generation. How can you help now to prepare for a sick call?

Learn by heart **Faith Summary**

- The sacrament of Anointing of the Sick brings God's special blessings to those who are sick, elderly, or dying.
- Anointing of the Sick is one of the two sacraments of healing.
- We must respect our bodies by caring for them. We must work to eliminate sickness and evil from the world.

Candle Crucifix Candle

Holy Water White Cloth Water Cotton Lemon

The Ministers of Marriage

Tell what you think is wrong with the following statement: "That young couple was married by Father Smith."

Sometimes Catholics are surprised to learn that the bride and groom themselves are the ministers of the sacrament of Matrimony, not the priest. The priest is the official witness of the Church. He offers the prayers, celebrates the nuptial Mass, and blesses the couple. He receives the couple's consent in the name of the Church. He joins with the entire assembly at a wedding in witnessing to a couple's marriage vows.

When Catholics are married, they are required to celebrate their exchange of vows before a priest and two witnesses. This is because marriage is a sacrament. A sacrament belongs to the whole Church, not just to the couple.

Exchanging Rings

Wedding rings are a sign of the love and faithfulness that a married couple pledge to each other. The Church has no rules or regulations concerning the style of a wedding ring. Very often rings are just simple bands.

A long time ago, it was customary for some Catholics to inscribe the inside of the wedding ring, or band, with a prayer or phrase. One favorite prayer was: *In Christ and thee my love shall be.* What words would you put on the inside of a wedding ring to help a young couple remember the meaning of the sacrament of marriage?

Learn by heart — Faith Summary

- The sacrament of Matrimony is a powerful and effective sign of Christ's presence that joins a man and woman together for life.
- Married couples promise to serve each other and the whole Church. Matrimony is a sacrament of service.
- We can prepare now for Matrimony by trying to love others as God loves us.

The Ministry of Deacons

The Church has always held the holy order of deacons in high honor. Men who are ordained priests are first ordained deacons. But many men remain deacons for the rest of their lives. They are called *permanent deacons*. This is their special call, or vocation, in the Catholic Church.

Permanent deacons receive the sacrament of Holy Orders and spend a long time in preparation for it. They may be married, but the marriage must take place before they are ordained. A deacon may not remarry when his wife dies. Once men are ordained by the bishop as permanent deacons, they may never go on to the priesthood. Their ministry is a permanent and special ministry of service to the whole parish community.

BISHOP HEALY

Our Catholic Identity

A Daring Priest

When young James Healy decided to become a priest, he knew he was asking for trouble. He was ordained in 1854. Racism and anti-Catholic prejudice were common.

As the son of an African-American mother and an Irish-American father, James Healy was often the target of racial insults. Even some of his own parishioners in Boston treated him with cruelty. But he loved the priesthood and he would not give it up.

James Healy went on to become the first black bishop of an American diocese in 1875. The people of his diocese in Portland, Maine soon learned to love and honor him as a good shepherd.

We can honor Bishop Healy by following his example of courage and faithfulness to our own vocation.

Learn by heart **Faith Summary**

- Jesus chose the twelve apostles to lead our Church in teaching and worship.

- Bishops, priests, and deacons are ordained in the sacrament of Holy Orders.

- Our ordained ministers lead us in building up the Christian community.

Saints New and Old

The saints whom we honor in the Catholic Church are women and men of all times, races, and cultures. They stand as models of faith in action for us today. Here are several saints who may be new to you.

Between 1839 and 1867, one hundred and three Koreans were martyred for their faith. They were young and old, priests and lay people. Among them was Saint Andrew Kim of Taegu. He was the first native priest of Korea. We celebrate his feast on September 20. On the same day we celebrate another Korean martyr, Saint Paul Chong. Paul was a catechist, a teacher of religion. He, too, gave his life for his faith.

Another saint, Lawrence Ruiz, lived two hundred years before the Korean martyrs. Lawrence was a married man and a Filipino missionary who was martyred in Japan. He was canonized in 1987 and is honored today as the first canonized Filipino saint. His feast day is September 28.

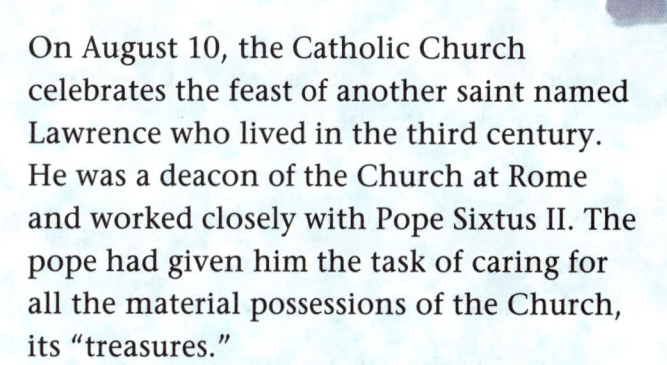

Statue of Saint Lawrence Ruiz, Holy Family Church, N.Y.C.

On August 10, the Catholic Church celebrates the feast of another saint named Lawrence who lived in the third century. He was a deacon of the Church at Rome and worked closely with Pope Sixtus II. The pope had given him the task of caring for all the material possessions of the Church, its "treasures."

It was a time of suffering and persecution for the Church. After the pope had been arrested and killed, Lawrence sold what had been entrusted to him so that he could help the poor and needy. Soon after this, he was arrested and ordered to bring all the Church's treasures to the authorities. Standing before a judge, he gathered the poor and lowly around him and said, "These are the treasures of the Church." The angry judge ordered Lawrence to be killed.

These saints were people of faith. How can you imitate their example today?

Learn by heart — Faith Summary

- The virtues of faith, hope, and love are gifts from God.
- Faith is a virtue that enables us to trust and believe in God, to accept what he has revealed, and to live according to his will.
- The creeds of the Church summarize what we believe.

Christ Our Light

One symbol of hope that is often used in the Catholic Church is the Easter candle. It is also called the paschal candle, since it reminds us of Christ and the paschal mystery—Jesus' life, death, and resurrection.

The Easter candle is blessed on Holy Saturday night during the Service of Light, the first part of the Easter Vigil. In the darkness, the priest blesses a new fire and then prepares the candle.

Very often the priest traces a cross, the numbers of the current year, and the first and last letters of the Greek alphabet on the candle. He says as he does this:

Christ yesterday and today
the beginning and the end
Alpha
and Omega
all time belongs to him
and all the ages
to him be glory and power
through every age for ever. Amen.

Sometimes the priest may insert 5 grains of incense in the candle in the form of a cross. He may say:

By his holy
and glorious wounds
may Christ our Lord
guard us
and keep us. Amen.

Whenever you see the Easter Candle lit in church—at a Baptism or a funeral and all during the Easter season—remember that it is a symbol for Christ our Light. Our hope is in him, who has risen from the dead.

OUR CATHOLIC IDENTITY

Alpha and Omega

The first and last letters of the Greek alphabet—alpha and omega—are used as a symbol of Christ. According to the Book of Revelation in the Bible, Jesus said of himself, "I am the Alpha and the Omega, the first and the last, the beginning and the end" (Revelation 22:13).

Learn by heart — Faith Summary

- Hope is the virtue that enables us to trust that God will be with us in every situation.
- Jesus is our greatest source of hope.
- Mary, the Mother of the Church, is a sign of hope for us.